Atlantic Wars

Atlantic Wars

From the Fifteenth Century to the Age of Revolution

GEOFFREY PLANK

OXFORD
UNIVERSITY PRESS

OXFORD
UNIVERSITY PRESS

Oxford University Press is a department of the University of Oxford. It furthers
the University's objective of excellence in research, scholarship, and education
by publishing worldwide. Oxford is a registered trade mark of Oxford University
Press in the UK and certain other countries.

Published in the United States of America by Oxford University Press
198 Madison Avenue, New York, NY 10016, United States of America.

© Oxford University Press 2020

Library of Congress Cataloging-in-Publication Data
Names: Plank, Geoffrey Gilbert, 1960– author.
Title: Atlantic wars : from the fifteenth century to the Age of Revolution /
Geoffrey Plank.
Description: New York : Oxford University Press, 2020. |
Includes bibliographical references and index.
Identifiers: LCCN 2019054870 (print) | LCCN 2019054871 (ebook) |
ISBN 9780190860455 (hardback) | ISBN 9780190860479 (epub) |
ISBN 9780190860486 (electronic)
Subjects: LCSH: Military history, Modern. | Atlantic Ocean Region—History, Naval. |
Atlantic Ocean Region—History, Military. | War—History.
Classification: LCC D214 .P55 2020 (print) | LCC D214 (ebook) |
DDC 355.009182/10903—dc23
LC record available at https://lccn.loc.gov/2019054870
LC ebook record available at https://lccn.loc.gov/2019054871

3 5 7 9 8 6 4

Printed by Sheridan Books, Inc., United States of America

For Ina

CONTENTS

ACKNOWLEDGMENTS

The evening I first met my wife Ina Zweiniger-Bargielowska we arranged to take a walk the next morning along the Niagara River downstream from the falls. The river was spectacular, churning dramatically, but I was excited by the nineteenth-century British fortifications on the north bank. I started talking almost incessantly, and certainly memorably, about the War of 1812. That was over twenty years ago, and in the intervening years I have continued to fret about the War of 1812, early modern warfare generally, and issues of war and peace. I am obliged not just to Ina, but to everyone who else who has humored, encouraged, and supported me through my career.

I feel particularly indebted to Susan Ferber at Oxford University Press. After I had been thinking about writing this book for a very long time, she made a decisive intervention and convinced me to get to work in earnest in 2014. Since then, every time I have sent her proposals, outlines, plans of action, or drafts she has given them close attention and provided me detailed, cogent advice. I consulted Wayne Lee as I worked out my plan for the book and his advice was invaluable. Christian Koot and the anonymous readers of my manuscript offered important corrections and recommendations. I presented an overview of my project at a conference in 2015 on "The Specter of Peace in Histories of Violence" organized by Michael Goode and John Smolenski and another at the 2017 annual gathering of the British Group of Early American Historians. I received good advice at both sessions, and I am grateful to everyone who took part. During my research and more recently for the final production of this book I have drawn on the resources and staff of art collections, museums, and libraries including the Bayeux Museum, the Beinecke Rare Book and Manuscript Library at Yale University, the Benson Latin American Collection at the University of Texas at Austin, the Bibliothèque nationale de France, the Bodleian Libraries at the University of Oxford, the British Library, the Cambridge University Library, the Germanisches Nationalmuseum in Nuremberg, the John Carter Brown Library, the Library of Congress, the London Metropolitan Archives, the Musei Reali in Turin, the Maritiem Museum in Rotterdam, the Monasterio del Escorial, the Museo de Amèrica in Madrid, the Museo del Prado, the Museum of the City of London, the National Museum of Denmark, the National Museums, Northern Ireland, the Österreichische Nationalbibliothek, the Royal Armouries, the Royal Museums Greenwich, the Rijksmuseum, the Sainsbury Centre for Visual Arts at the University of East Anglia, the Smithsonian Institution, the Staatliche Graphische Sammlung in Munich, the Universitätbibliothek in Heidelberg, the University of East Anglia library, the Uppsala universitetsbibliotek, and the Victoria and Albert Museum. The UEA library's interlending service was indispensable for my work. I also benefitted from research leave from the UEA School of History, and a Publication Award from the UEA Faculty of Arts and Sciences. At UEA Claire Grasby helped me at critical junctures with the financial logistics. Jeremy Toynbee and the staff at Newgen have guided me well through the process of copy-editing and book production. I am grateful to Jon Gregory for the maps. And through it all Ina read every chapter and gave me incisive criticism. I will always be grateful to her.

Atlantic Wars

Europe. Map by Jon Gregory.

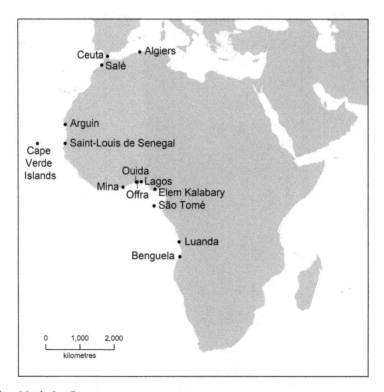

Africa. Map by Jon Gregory.

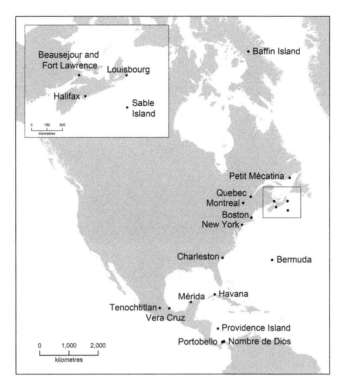

North America. Map by Jon Gregory.

South America. Map by Jon Gregory.

Introduction

Five thousand years ago fishermen on the coast of North America ventured into the Atlantic in large wooden canoes from Labrador, Newfoundland, and present-day Maine to catch cod and swordfish, and hunt for walruses and porpoises. They gathered trophies from their expeditions and made tools from whalebones and swordfish bills. Communities buried their dead with prized possessions including the teeth of sharks and orcas.[1] Then the seafaring declined and eventually it stopped. We do not know why these indigenous Americans withdrew from the deep water. For thousands of years, even as millions of people settled near the Atlantic in Europe, Africa, and the Americas, few ventured far out to sea. Prominent islands including the Azores, Bermuda, the Cape Verde Islands, the Faroe Islands, Iceland, Madeira, Saint Helena, São Tomé, and Principe remained unoccupied. As a consequence, contact between the peoples of the Americas and those of Africa and Europe was delayed. Two thousand years ago, the absence of people on prominent islands distinguished the Atlantic from the Indian Ocean, Polynesia, and the Pacific off Asia. The peculiarity of the Atlantic shaped the early history of European maritime expansion.

By the time European sailing vessels made transatlantic crossings, centuries of maritime conflict on the Baltic, the North Sea, and the Mediterranean had made them potent instruments of war. European colonists and soldiers often struggled when fighting on land in Africa or the Americas, but ships gave them advantages, allowing them to ferry men, weapons, and supplies great distances, and evacuate, retreat, and carry war captives away. Beginning in the eighth century when sailors from Europe began traveling progressively farther out into the ocean, they faced little competition on the deep water from Africans or indigenous Americans. With nearly exclusive control of sailing vessels on the ocean, Europeans and their descendants dominated vast, expanding stretches of water that by the late eighteenth century included most of the Atlantic and also the Pacific off the coast of the Americas at least as far north as California. These waters and the adjacent coastal regions constituted a distinct and increasingly integrated "Atlantic world."

Atlantic Wars. Geoffrey Plank, Oxford University Press (2020). © Oxford University Press.
DOI: 10.1093/oso/9780190860455.001.0001

This book examines the ways warfare shaped human experience around the Atlantic world from the late Middle Ages until the nineteenth century. Wherever colonies were established in the Americas, newly arriving colonial settlers faced armed resistance from indigenous American warriors or fighters from rival colonies and empires. No matter who the colonists were, and no matter what their original motivations may have been for crossing the ocean, their colonies became military projects. Armed conflict affected how and where people lived, who they associated with, how they perceived each other, how they structured their societies, and whether they survived. Military imperatives drove the development of technologies like ships, port facilities, fortresses, and roads that reshaped the landscape on widely separated coasts. Forced migrations made land available for colonial expansion, and the enslavement and transportation of war captives provided labor. Holding people in slavery in the Americas required the deployment of military force.

The pervasive impact of warfare on life around the Atlantic in the early modern period becomes apparent only by examining the oceanic region as a whole. Military technologies and people traveled across the borders of states, colonies, and empires, and beyond the confines of islands and continents. Wars brought diverse people together in an intimate, shared experience. Sailors moved from private vessels to warships, sometimes voluntarily and often through mechanisms of forcible recruitment. As a consequence, during his lifetime a sailor might work and fight under a variety of captains flying different flags. People of indigenous American, African, and European descent fought alongside and against each other at sea and on land. Preparing for war and coping with its consequences involved inclusive communal efforts, drawing in women as well as men, children, and the aged from various parts of the Atlantic world. Some wars, like the Dutch wars against the Spanish in the early seventeenth century, the European imperial wars of the late seventeenth and eighteenth centuries, and the wars of Revolutionary France and the Napoleonic era, directly engaged people in widely scattered regions. Even small-scale, localized conflicts were often shaped by transatlantic influences and had effects far beyond the combat zone. Wars in Africa, for example, had direct consequences for the colonies in the Caribbean and North and South America, where captives were sent for sale.

Scholars have long recognized that the lands surrounding the Atlantic have a distinct, shared history that transcends national or imperial boundaries.[2] There has been an increase in interest in Atlantic history since the 1990s as historians have paid more attention to interactions between Africans, Europeans, and indigenous Americans. Compared to imperial historians, scholars who adopt an Atlantic perspective have a less hierarchical understanding of the relationship between Europe, Africa, and the Americas. They pay less attention to bureaucracy and imperial regulation and instead focus on migration, trade, and the exchange of ideas within a culturally diverse transatlantic environment. While good general surveys of Atlantic history exist, none concentrates on the formative influence of war.[3]

Europeans never dominated land warfare in Africa, the Americas, or the islands of the Atlantic in the way they held the upper hand at sea. On the contrary, European colonists and expeditionary forces were frequently dependent on local allies. New ways of fighting developed as groups learned from each other. A pattern of scattered, isolated conflicts in the sixteenth century evolved into a series of large-scale transatlantic wars in the seventeenth and eighteenth centuries. States and empires became more dominant and widespread reactions against that trend triggered revolutionary struggles in many countries around the Atlantic. In the aftermath of the Age of Revolution, old patterns of cross-cultural alliance fell into disfavor, helping to put an end to the early modern era of Atlantic war.

To elucidate the geographical and chronological dimensions of these developments, this book is organized into three sections. The early chapters explore the origins, extent, and limitations of European and colonial power at sea. The second section examines the technology of land warfare and the alliance networks that shaped the pattern of warfare in regions where Europeans, Africans, and indigenous Americans met. Chapters in this section focus analysis on warfare's influence on expressions of racial animosity, and the pattern of organized violence associated with slavery on both sides of the ocean. The book ends with three chronological chapters tracing the first period of Atlantic war, the transformation of the ocean basin into a single military arena, and the disruption of the early modern pattern of Atlantic warfare during the Age of Revolution. But first we must consider the beginning.

———

In Venice in 1539 an exiled Swedish Catholic priest named Olaus Magnus published a map of Scandinavia and the North Atlantic. Titled *Carta Marina*, it was one of the largest printed maps produced to that date, and by far the most comprehensive chart of the northern reaches of the Atlantic Ocean and the lands surrounding them. The land masses look slightly misshapen and out of scale to modern eyes, but Magnus correctly placed Scotland, the Orkneys, Shetland, the Faroe Islands, Iceland, and Greenland. He included information on ocean currents and appears to have demarcated the boundary separating cold Arctic water from the warmer flows traveling through the Atlantic toward Norway. He decorated his map with images depicting various peculiarities of the people and landscape of the ocean and its shores. Along with several fanciful beasts in the water he included fishermen, hunters, Sami herders harnessing reindeer, a polar

Fig. I.1 Detail from Olaus Magnus, *Carta Marina* (1539). Uppsala universitetsbibliotek.

bear drifting on an ice floe, and driftwood washing up in Greenland. Magnus had never seen most of the places on his map. He learned about them from fishermen, merchants, and sailors he had met in Scandinavia and along the coast of the Baltic, where he had served as diplomat before moving to Italy.[4]

Magnus left the shape and extent of Greenland indistinct and allowed only two parts of the island to intrude over the upper border of his map. He depicted both of those peninsulas as scenes of violence. In a section of Greenland in the upper left-hand corner he showed two men, one much taller than the other, facing off with spears. The small man holds his weapon confidently and appears to be threatening his adversary with an upper thrust. The men are evenly matched. Who are they, and what is the nature of their fight? Do they have a personal quarrel, or are they participants in a war? The men are dressed differently, and the exaggerated physical contrast between them signals that they may have represented distinct populations. In the other part of Greenland Magnus presented a much less ambiguous image of an intercultural clash, as a man dressed in furs wields a bow and arrow and takes aim against a three-masted sailing ship anchored near the shore.

These images deserve attention because there are few records of contact between the people of Greenland and Europeans in the early sixteenth century. It is possible that Magnus drew upon oral reports of incidents from fishermen and other travelers. Alternatively, his images might reflect communal memories from the time of the Norse colonization of Greenland. According to the oldest account we have of this colonization, written in the 1120s, soon after their

Fig. I.2 Detail from Olaus Magnus, *Carta Marina* (1539). Uppsala universitetsbibliotek.

arrival from Iceland in 985 the Norse found "human habitations, both in the eastern and western parts of the country, and fragments of skin boats and stone implements."[5] This brief passage hints at the minimal Norse interaction with the indigenous people of Greenland during the first two hundred years of European settlement on the island. There was very little contact. Initially, the indigenous islanders migrated north away from the Norse, but things changed around 1200 following the arrival of a new population from continental North America, ancestors of the present-day Inuit. The new arrivals established their own settlements near to the Norse and accumulated Norse artifacts, including woolen cloth and large quantities of iron.[6] Whether they acquired these things through trade, scavenging, or raids is not entirely clear. Archaeologists have found little evidence of armed conflict between the Norse and the indigenous people of Greenland, but medieval accounts sometimes refer to violence. Icelandic annals record that in 1379 indigenous warriors "made a hostile attack on the Greenlanders, killed 18 men and captured two boys and made them slaves." In 1420 a traveler in Norway reported that he saw Inuit who had been captured and brought to Scandinavia with their kayaks, which had been displayed in a cathedral. Olaus Magnus recalled seeing a similar display of "small skin vessels fastened to the wall above the west entrance of Oslo Cathedral" in 1505.[7]

Our earliest record providing an Inuit perspective on this early period of European settlement on Greenland dates from the 1760s when an Inuit *angakkuq*, or shaman, gave a Danish missionary an account. According to the *angakkuq*, the Norse had established their settlements before the Inuit arrived from the north. The Inuit wanted to settle among them, but the Norse kept them away and agreed only to trade. Then raiders arrived in three small boats from England to attack a Norse settlement at the mouth of a fjord. The Norse fought back the invaders and seized one of the boats. Surprised by this conflict, the Inuit retreated inland. A year later a whole fleet arrived, intent on plundering Norse farms and seizing cattle. Many Norse settlers died in the ensuing battle, and others fled in ships. Before leaving, the Norse men promised those they left behind that they would return to protect them if the raiders came back. The next year the raiders returned and destroyed the Norse settlement completely. No help arrived from overseas and the Inuit were left to rescue survivors. The Inuit brought Norse women and children away from the coast to live in safety among them.[8]

The *Carta Marina* and the *angakkuq*'s story invite starkly different interpretations of the pattern of violence in medieval Greenland. Neither the map nor the Inuit legend refers to specific, identifiable events. The pictures on the map sprawl across huge territories and are not carefully located in any particular site on Greenland. Instead they are designed to make a general statement, providing illustrations of the purported character and behavior of the island's inhabitants. The *angakkuq*'s story seems to reference time and geography more specifically, but it collapses events that occurred over centuries into a few telling events. In contrast to Magnus's stark images of opposition between rival communities, the *angakkuq* described shifts in relations over time and made distinctions between the local indigenous reactions during various violent episodes. He also drew distinctions between rival European groups and introduced women and children into the scene. Unlike Magnus, the *angakkuq* emphasized opportunities for cross-cultural alliance, mutual assistance, and the blending of cultures.

The contrast between these visions may reflect a difference between European and indigenous perspectives on the pattern of violence in the North Atlantic, but it is important to recognize the diversity of viewpoints in sixteenth-century Europe and eighteenth-century Greenland. By the 1530s, Italians, Portuguese, Spaniards, Basques, and others with experience of the Atlantic recognized the value of forming alliances and the viability of joining forces with armed indigenous American groups. Similarly, in the eighteenth and nineteenth century Inuit storytellers gave competing interpretations of their own past. After the 1760s the legends they told increasingly associated the Norse period with oppositional violence pitting indigenous peoples against the descendants of the Vikings.[9]

Magnus's images belong to a period when Europeans were amazed by the apparent novelty and distinctiveness of the Americas, when many for the first time began to speculate and generalize about the wonders and terrors of the western continents. In the 1760s, by contrast, the Inuit had centuries of experience interacting with Europeans. Danes had established a new colony in Greenland in the 1720s and in the context of colonization the *angakkuq* may have wanted to stress the positive benefits of cooperation.

Both the map and the *angakkuq*'s legend depict Greenland's history with a folkloric, timeless quality and, though Magnus and the *angakkuq* differed greatly in their perspectives, their presentations of early warfare align in important ways. The fighters they portray are men; the *angakkuq* did not suggest that women and children participated actively in the fighting. Both men associated sailing vessels with danger. Drawings on the *Carta Marina* depict perils faced by sailors. Magnus populated the ocean with monsters and drew the remains of shipwrecks along Greenland's coast. In the only intact ship he showed, the lone crew member is targeted by an indigenous warrior. The *angakkuq*, for his part, recalled the violence that could ensue if ships discharged men on land. He described how landing parties arrived without warning, intent only on plunder and destruction. These points of agreement may have reflected nearly universal common experiences, broad general truths about masculine violence, seafaring, and the threat of invasion. But the patterns of communal conflict described by Magnus and the *angakkuq* changed and acquired new meaning on many shores of the Atlantic in the centuries following the colonization of Greenland.

The earliest recorded organized violence between Europeans and indigenous Americans took place in Labrador and on the island of Newfoundland. The Norse came to Newfoundland around the year 1000, when there may have been as many as three distinct indigenous groups living on the island, each with its own material culture. The islanders lived by hunting and fishing. Some moved from permanent settlements to seasonal camps in pursuit of game including waterfowl and other birds, seals, caribou, beavers, and otters. The islanders also fished and foraged for wild raspberries and other plants.[10] The Norse outpost on Newfoundland was smaller than their settlements on Greenland and different in character, numbering between seventy and ninety at its height. Norse men and women overwintered for several years but did not generate much garbage, and the absence of a cemetery indicates that they did not stay for long. When they left, they took most of their valuable possessions with them, including their weapons.[11]

Two Icelandic sagas written in the thirteenth century recall conflict between the Norse who moved to Newfoundland and indigenous Americans. The sagas were written centuries after the events they recall, and like the *angakkuq's* story and the images on the *Carta Marina*, they are best understood as a distillation of collective memories, fears, and fantasies, reimagined and simplified with instructive purposes in mind. The events recounted in the sagas were selected and creatively embellished to highlight themes that mattered to the storytellers and their audiences on Iceland and Greenland.

According to *Eirik the Red's Saga*, soon after an exploratory party from Newfoundland established a camp on the mainland coast of North America, nine boats approached them. A man stood upright in each boat waving a pole. The Norse hoped this was a "sign of peace," but when the men approached, they were startled and frightened by their appearance. The saga describes the indigenous Americans as "short in height with threatening features and tangled hair on their heads. Their eyes were large and their cheeks broad." The boatmen were similarly surprised by the Norse and "stayed awhile marvelling" before proceeding on their way. Months passed before a larger number of men arrived in boats again waving poles, apparently as an invitation to trade. They offered the Norse "dark pelts" and received tiny pieces of red cloth in exchange. They also asked for weapons, but the Norse refused to give them any. The trading session ended when the indigenous American men were surprised and frightened by the arrival of a bull. Three weeks later, a large war party arrived and attacked the Norse "from all sides" with arrows and stones. The Norse ran for shelter under a cliff face, but then a woman among them intervened, chastised them for fleeing, took a sword from a dead Norseman, and charged the archers, slapping the sword against her naked breast. She terrified the indigenous American warriors and they retreated.[12]

The first battle recorded in the *Saga of the Greenlanders* occurred in Labrador. A Norse exploratory party sailing northward along the coast saw three hide-covered boats upside down on a beach. They came ashore to investigate and on closer inspection discovered men sleeping under the hulls, three to a boat. The Norsemen split into separate parties to approach from several angles. They surprised the sleeping men and took eight captives, but one of the men escaped. The Norse killed the men they had seized, and then withdrew to a nearby cape. As they slept on a beach, they left a guard awake to protect them. The guard spied the arrival of a fleet of boats with a large number of archers in them. The Norse hastily built a rough stockade alongside their ship, using the side of the vessel as a wall. They decided to wait out the attack and "fight back as little as possible." The indigenous warriors shot arrows at the Norse and killed one of them, but the rest were protected by their makeshift stockade. After spending some time firing arrows without effect, the warriors pulled back and "fled as rapidly as they could."[13]

The *Saga of the Greenlanders* also recounts conflict near the principal Norse settlement on Newfoundland. The saga suggests that even before the Norse were aware that the island was inhabited, some of the islanders were gathering furs to offer them for trade. When a party of islanders approached the Norse carrying furs, they were frightened by the colonists' livestock. The Norse, for their part, were frightened by the indigenous people and bolted their doors against them. Eventually they enclosed their settlement in a palisade. Even though the two groups were wary and did not share a language, they managed to engage in trade, exchanging bundles of food and furs over the top of the palisade. Then one day during a trading session an indigenous man snuck into the enclosure and tried to steal some weapons. A Norsemen caught and killed him. The death frightened the other islanders in the trading party. They ran off, leaving their furs behind them, and the Norse prepared for battle. The Norsemen lured a group into an open field, released a charging bull against them, and followed up with hand-held weapons. Disoriented and terrified, many of the indigenous Americans were killed.[14]

These stories highlight differences in military technology and tactics. The Norse were familiar with bows and arrows, but they favored close combat with weapons like swords and axes. The sagas emphasize the dilemmas they faced when fighting opponents who fired from a distance and withdrew to avoid casualties. One response was to seek shelter and wait out an attack. Other options included releasing animals against the warriors or taking up swords and axes against them.

The Norse in the sagas seem remarkably ready to inflict violence on indigenous Americans. In an episode recounted in *Eirik the Red's Saga*, a party of Norsemen came upon a bearded man, two women, and two boys. They immediately attacked, sent the adults running, and captured the boys, actions consistent with that of Norse warriors elsewhere.[15] The sagas indicate that the Norse crossed the Atlantic in mixed groups that included people from Iceland and various parts of Europe including Scandinavia, German-speaking central Europe, and Britain. Two Scots, a woman named Hekja and a man named Haki, had earlier been held by the King of Norway as slaves. The Norwegian king assigned them to Eirik the Red who in turn sent them aboard a ship surveying the coast of North America. If the sagas are to be believed, the Scots were among the first Europeans to set foot on the mainland of Labrador.[16] Along with parts of continental Europe, Britain and Ireland supplied the Norse slave trade between the ninth and eleventh centuries. Some British and Irish merchants profited from the sale of captives to the Norse. Norse raiders also captured people in Britain and Ireland and kept them in coastal forts in places like Anglesey and Orkney before taking them to markets in such cities as Bristol and Dublin. Sometimes captive men and women were transferred to urban merchants who sold them for shipment overseas. On other occasions people were sold at market by the same warriors who seized them. Those who were sent abroad were kept in chains while being taken across the Atlantic to Iceland, or across the Mediterranean where they were sold to Muslim traders in Africa and Asia.[17] The slave trade gave the Norse an incentive for fighting, and was a way that war generated profit.

With their distinctive ships, the Norse were able to transport warriors great distances, land men with little notice, and reap profits from kidnapping and plunder.[18] Nonetheless, despite their reputation as fierce raiders, the sagas suggest that the Norse were often on the defensive in North America. Rather than gloating about the superiority of European weaponry, the sagas instead convey insecurity, perhaps implicitly and retrospectively justifying the Norse withdrawal from Newfoundland. The indigenous people described in the sagas were mobile. They came and went unpredictably, and the Norse had difficulty discerning their intentions. The Norse were quick to assume the worst and considered even the physical appearance of indigenous people "threatening." To protect themselves, they kept indigenous Americans at a distance, banned the sale of weapons to them, and encircled their colonial settlements with stockades. The Norse were accomplished sailors, but this skill, the sagas demonstrated, provided them no guarantee of security on land.

According to the *Saga of the Greenlanders*, Bjarni Herjolfsson, the owner and commander of the first Norse ship to reach North America, was the son of an Icelandic farmer who from a young age had "longed to sail abroad." He had first found work on other men's vessels, but after several voyages to distant lands he had won "a good deal of wealth and a good name," and his next step was to purchase a ship. Bjarni was sailing for Greenland when he went off course and saw land to the west. He explored the coast of North America but chose not to beach his vessel or set foot there. Some members of his crew wanted to go on shore, but Bjarni made a pragmatic assessment and said, "this land seems to me to offer nothing of use." He commanded his ship back to Greenland and let others follow up on his discovery.[19] The subsequent struggles of the Norse on Newfoundland suggest that he made the right decision.

After a few years of searching for suitable land for agriculture and resources they could export profitably, the Norse left Newfoundland. Their ships had a limited carrying capacity and they were a long way from the nearest colonial or European markets in Greenland. They may have recognized that they could not support themselves on the coast of North America, but according to the sagas, military considerations influenced their thoughts. Their outpost on Newfoundland was not only costly but dangerous. *Eirik the Red's Saga* describes one group of colonists giving up after a battle with indigenous Americans, as they "realized that despite everything the land had to offer there, they would be under constant threat of attack from its prior inhabitants."[20]

Both sagas contain an anecdote suggesting that the indigenous people of North America chose to reject what the Norse had to offer. In one version of the story a group of indigenous warriors returned to a beach where they had fought the Norse and discovered a dead Norseman with an axe beside him. One man picked up the axe and began to strike a tree. His companions were intrigued by the tool and took turns chopping until one of them struck a stone with the axe and the axe broke. The men decided that the axe was useless if it could not cut stone, so they tossed it away.[21] In the other version of the story, the warriors assessed the axe's power as a weapon. In the midst of a battle, an indigenous American warrior picked up a Norse axe from the ground and struck the man next to him with it, killing him with surprising ease. The leader of the warriors then snatched the axe away and threw it "as far out into the sea as he could."[22]

If this story was intended to depict a general indigenous American response to Norse technology, it may have had a basis in their experiences. The people who lived in Greenland before the Norse arrived apparently retreated from them. The inhabitants of Newfoundland at the start of the eleventh century included ancestors of the Beothuk, who avoided contact with European fishermen and other colonists when they started coming in large numbers in the sixteenth, seventeenth, and eighteenth centuries. But the indigenous American reaction to the arrival of Europeans was far from uniform, with some keen on acquiring things from the colonists.

Similarly, groups of European colonists differed in the ways they responded to indigenous Americans. As they are described in the sagas, the Norse seem to resemble some later Europeans. Their fear of indigenous Americans, their surprise at their appearance, their fumbling efforts to enter trade, and their resort to violence foreshadow the behavior of many European travelers who came to Africa and the Americas in the fifteenth, sixteenth, and seventeenth centuries. But alongside persistent patterns of behavior linking the Norse to subsequent explorers, traders, and colonists, it is important to notice that the Norse on Newfoundland were far more isolated than their successors in the early modern era. They suffered from the limitations of their sailing technology. They also had unusual difficulty communicating with their indigenous American neighbors. They had never established any close association with the islanders and, the sagas suggest, they had difficulty distinguishing between them.

The chapters that follow illuminate how the practice of warfare changed in the centuries following the Norse withdrawal from Newfoundland. Ships became larger, increasing not only their carrying capacities but also their effectiveness as weapons platforms. Ocean-going traffic increased in the North Atlantic, drawing in fishermen, whalers, and merchants from ports across western Europe. Sailing became a very cosmopolitan enterprise as sailors participated in a complex multinational labor market. Sailing men often fought each other and by doing so honed specialized military skills adapted to the oceanic environment. They captured each other, sometimes forcibly recruiting the crews of rival vessels into service on their ships. Violence, captive-taking, and coerced service were typical features of warfare on the ocean long before the Portuguese ventured down the western coast of Africa and the Spanish began their step-by-step progress across the Atlantic from the mid-ocean islands into the Caribbean.

There are important, underappreciated continuities between the period of Norse colonization and later periods of Atlantic history, but the nature of conflict around the ocean changed fundamentally in the fifteenth century. From that time on, nearly everywhere Europeans soldiers, settlers, and traveling merchants encountered indigenous Americans and Africans, they incorporated themselves into African and indigenous American diplomatic, military, and commercial networks. Newcomers and local peoples struggled to understand each other, find common interests, and exploit the opportunities that arose with the expansion of transatlantic commerce. Conflicts arose as a consequence of cultural misunderstandings and differing conceptions of justice and the appropriate use of force, and in many theaters of combat profits could be made by exploiting political instability. African, indigenous American, European, and colonial leaders amassed riches, power, or prestige in the context of war. Many indigenous and colonial communities felt vulnerable in these circumstances and believed that they had to engage in aggressive military action—or, at a minimum, issue dramatic threats—in order to survive. New ways of fighting developed, often involving a combination of hostage-taking, torture, mutilation, and other forms of exemplary punishment, or enslavement and the sale of captives. In Africa and the Americas noncombatant populations were targeted in wars, and captive-taking escalated as belligerents sought to terrorize each other, assert their own dominion, and gain riches through the slave trade. The projection of military power played a central role in the economy of nearly every region of the Atlantic world. Wars altered patterns of family life and directed migration streams carrying millions of people, captive and free, across the Atlantic. Warfare also transformed politics on every continent ringing the ocean. Transatlantic warfare distinguished the era that ended with the Age of Revolution.

PART ONE

WARFARE AT SEA

Ships

Until the fifteenth century, apart from the polar seas, the Atlantic was the world's least navigated ocean. The peoples of the Caribbean traveled and traded extensively amongst themselves, but they did not take their canoes far from the coast beyond the Bahamas and perhaps the southeastern shores of North America.[1] In the far north, successive waves of migrants traveled eastward by sea as far as Greenland.[2] Sometimes ocean currents carried individuals farther. There are intriguing reports from Europe in the Middle Ages of strange-looking men, some dead, some alive, arriving on the shore in kayaks and dug-out canoes.[3] Simply as a function of the distance between landmasses, it was easier to cross the ocean in the north than in the mid-Atlantic, the tropics, or the Southern Hemisphere. Compounding the problem of distance, Africans and Europeans who ventured into the ocean confronted a strong southerly current that could propel explorers down the coast of Africa without any possibility of return. This problem was solved only in the fifteenth century with the discovery of a patch of water west of Africa where opposing currents met. Portuguese sailors found a way to go south down the coast of Africa and return not by retracing their route but instead by sailing westward into the ocean to find the current that would take them home.[4] After this discovery, Europeans began to occupy the islands of the mid-Atlantic. They also started to encounter people in Africa and the Americas who had never before seen European sailing ships.

Those ships were dramatically different from kayaks and canoes. They were larger, more complex and fragile, and more likely to sink when damaged. Therefore, when approaching uncharted coastlines, the Europeans kept a distance from the shore. Seen from afar, their ships made a dramatic impression and helped define the character and identify of the Europeans. An Iroquoian man named Pastedechuoan provided one of the most vivid accounts of that moment of first contact, though he acquired his story second-hand.

Early in the seventeenth century, when he was a small boy, Pastedechouan was taken from his mother's home near the St. Lawrence River and carried to France. In Angers he learned French and the rudiments of Christianity, received

Atlantic Wars. Geoffrey Plank, Oxford University Press (2020). © Oxford University Press.
DOI: 10.1093/oso/9780190860455.001.0001

baptism, and acquired the name Pierre. French Recollect Fathers intended to educate him before returning him to his home country to work as a missionary among the indigenous peoples of Canada. Their plan went awry, however, because during his time in France Pastedechouan lost his native tongue, and when he returned to the St. Lawrence, he struggled to gain readmittance to the community of his birth. After a short marriage, his wife expelled him. The French missionaries disapproved of the way Pastedechouan had tried to reassimilate into indigenous society, and they dismissively declared that he had "become a barbarian like the others." Nonetheless, recognizing that he could still be useful, they took him back into their mission, gave him a suit of French clothes, and employed him as a translator.

This young man had become a foreigner in his own country, and this perspective animated the story he told to illustrate the cultural chasm that originally separated Europeans from indigenous Americans. In 1633 Pastedechouan told the missionaries that "his grandmother used to take pleasure in relating to him the astonishment of the Natives, when they saw for the first time a French ship arrive upon their shores. They thought it was a moving island; they did not know what to say of the great sails which made it go; their astonishment was redoubled in seeing a number of men on deck. . . . as they were unable to understand to what nation our people belonged, they gave them the name which has since always clung to the French, *ouemichtigouchiou*; that is to say, a man who works in wood, or who is in a canoe or vessel of wood. They saw our ships, which were made of wood, their little canoes being made only of bark."[5]

Variations of this story were told and retold across eastern North America for the next several centuries.[6] In the summer of 1672, when the Quaker founder George Fox was traveling through New England, he met a man he identified as an "Indian king" who told him a version of the story in an effort to explain why the indigenous people of New England suffered so much. The man told Fox that "before the English came" a local person had warned the community "that a white people should come in a great thing of the sea." This unnamed person issued a warning that everyone "should be loving" to the white people "and receive them, but if they did hurt or wrong the white people, they would be destroyed." Fox and the "king" agreed that "that Indian was a prophet and prophesied truly," because "this hath been seen and fulfilled." The white people came in their ships, and after the indigenous people wronged them "they never prospered and have been destroyed."[7]

In the late eighteenth century Moravian missionaries working in eastern North America reported in general terms that "The Indians relate, that, before the arrival of the Europeans, some prophets pretended to have received a divine revelation, from which they foretold, that a people would come to them from a country beyond the great ocean, and even pointing out the very day of their arrival. They further relate, that upon seeing a ship arrive on that day, they addressed their countrymen, 'Behold, the gods come to visit us.' Upon their landing, the white people were adored by the Indians, to whom they made presents of knives, hatchets, guns, and other articles."[8]

In 1869, a Mi'kmaq man named Josiah Jeremy told the anthropologist Silas T. Rand that the Mi'kmaq shared a communal memory of the last days before "the coming of the white man." When there were still "no people in this country but Indians," a young woman dreamed that "a small island came floating in towards the land, with tall trees on it and living beings." The next morning, she went to consult "wise men," "magicians and soothsayers," and none of them could tell her what her dream meant. One day later, however, the dream seemed to become a reality, when a French sailing vessel appeared off shore. The Mi'kmaq hunters mistook the men working the sails for bears, and "they all seized their bows, arrows, and spears and rushed down to the shore" in order to shoot them. They stopped in surprise when they saw that the sailors were men. A group of the French climbed into "a very singularly constructed canoe" led by a priest who approached "making signs of friendship" even though, at that time, the two communities had no common language.[9]

All of these stories reflect the vagaries of memory and layers of interpretation accumulated over the generations as the tales were told and retold. When the storytellers conveyed them to missionaries and anthropologists they also imbued them with important messages reflecting what they thought their white visitors should hear. Politics and history affected how the stories were told. The man who spoke to Fox sought to explain why the indigenous people of New England suffered so much after the English arrived. By contrast, Josiah Jeremy, a professed Catholic like most of the Mi'kmaq in the nineteenth century, emphasized French Catholic benevolence and the amicable relations that long existed between the French and the indigenous peoples in and around the colony of Acadia. Nonetheless, Jeremy's story still conveyed his community's sense of wonder and menace on their first sight of a European sailing ship.

History and politics had an even greater impact on African accounts of the first appearance south of the Sahara of European sailing ships. Anyone speaking or writing after the inauguration of the transatlantic slave trade was likely to associate ships with menace, sorrow, and terror.[10] Surprisingly, some of those who were carried against their will across the ocean expressed admiration for the ships themselves and their ability to move over the vast sea. In the eighteenth century a young girl named Belinda was captured in Africa and carried into Boston. Because of her youth, she was allowed to travel across the Atlantic above deck. She did not look away from the suffering of those chained below. Nonetheless, even as she described their ordeal, she expressed fascination with the ocean and the ship that carried her. "Scenes which her imagination never conceived of, a

Fig. 1.1 1888 drawing of a Mi'kmaq petroglyph from Lake Kejimkoojik in Nova Scotia depicting a ship and an adjacent figure. This drawing, like the transcriptions of indigenous American stories about the first arrival of sailing ships, does not simply convey an indigenous perspective. It also reflects the concerns of the transcriber. It is not clear, for example, whether the ship and the adjacent figure on the rock were the work of the same artist or intended to be seen as part of a single composition. It was only in the nineteenth century when the drawings were traced on paper that they were arranged and framed in the evocative way they appear here. Mi'kmaq artists carved images of ships at several places around Lake Kejimkoojik. National Anthropological Archives, Smithsonian Institution.

floating world, the sporting monsters of the deep, and the familiar meeting of billows and clouds, strove, but in vain, to divert her attention from three hundred Africans in chains, suffering the most excruciating torment, and some of them rejoicing that the pangs of death came like a balm to their wounds."[11] Around the same time, another child captured in Africa was lured to the coast by the promise of seeing a ship. The African man who enticed James Albert Ukawsaw Gronniosaw to leave his home promised him that he would see "houses with wings to them" that could "walk upon the water." He told Gronniosaw he would "also see the white folks." Gronniosaw was "highly pleased with the account of this strange place, and was very desirous of going," and so he went.[12]

In some parts of Africa the association between white people and their ships became embedded in language. Just as Pastedechouan's people in North America labeled the French "people in wooden vessels," so Akan-speakers on the Gold Coast of Africa called the Europeans the "lagoon people" because they met them only "at the mouth of the ocean."[13]

The great ships of the early age of exploration were smaller and less heavily armed than the slave ships and warships of subsequent eras. But compared to earlier ocean-going vessels, they were spectacular. They had been designed with intimidation in mind. Many of the features that most impressed onlookers, including the ships' bulk, height, and dark interiors, had been developed with military purposes in mind. In their origins and character, the vessels were instruments of war. European sailing technology developed over several centuries when the Europeans were almost constantly fighting each other and the peoples inhabiting the continent's adjacent shores. As a consequence, nearly every feature of their vessels, from their rudders to their prows, were adapted to facilitate aggression or defense.

———

In 1066 two fleets attacked England. Early in September a fleet from Norway crossed the North Sea, sailed up the Humber, and proceeded upriver before its crew disembarked and marched on York. Later that month another fleet under William of Normandy crossed the English Channel and landed near Hastings.[14] In their equipment and tactics, both groups resembled Vikings. The fighting men on board these fleets did not have any specialized skills in naval combat, nor did the men on the English ships that failed to intercept them. The warriors who manned the vessels were prepared for close combat on the decks of their ships or on shore. They planned to fight as soldiers fought on land and to enter combat on or near the coast. Large-scale engagements rarely occurred far out at sea in the waters off northern Europe in the eleventh century.

Naval warfare in the north changed radically over the next few centuries as a consequence of an increase in communication between northern and southern Europe, and the arrival of oar-propelled galleys, some locally produced, some from the Mediterranean, alongside northern sailing ships. In classical antiquity Mediterranean galleys had had prows below the waterline for ramming and sinking opposing ships. During the Middle Ages the prows had risen and the pattern of combat changed, with more emphasis placed on pulling alongside target vessels, boarding them, and engaging in combat on deck. But even after that transition, naval tactics in the Mediterranean frequently involved efforts to destroy and sink opposing ships on open water, occasionally using elaborate incendiary weapons that threw burning oil onto the vessels and the surface of the sea.[15]

Compared to northern Europe's sailing vessels, galleys were faster over short distances, more maneuverable and therefore better adapted for battles on open

Fig. 1.2 A detail from the Bayeux tapestry depicting William the Conqueror's invasion of England in 1066. The ships resembled Viking vessels. Tapisserie de Bayeux—XIème siècle, avec autorisation spéciale de la Ville de Bayeux.

water. The Portuguese and northern European powers' deployment of significant numbers of galleys in the Atlantic, North Sea, and Baltic triggered a sequence of technological innovations. Galleys had to be adapted to the rougher waters of the north, and sailing ships had to be adjusted vis-à-vis the galleys. The galleys needed higher sides in order to avoid getting swamped in ocean waves, but their reliance on oarsmen always kept them relatively low to the water. The designers of sailing ships recognized that the low profile of galleys was an acute vulnerability and began to reshape their vessels to take advantage of height. They decked over their ships and built high platforms called castles on the bows and sterns. Eventually the castles were incorporated into the intrinsic structure of sailing ships. They erected platforms for archers at the top of their masts, and perhaps most significantly, they fixed their rudders to the sterns of their ships. This adjustment, along with the introduction of new sails, improved maneuverability and made it possible to steer the vessels without relying on oarsmen.[16] Once the oarsmen were dispensed with the ships could grow much higher, making sailing vessels difficult to board and giving men on the ships the advantage of height when firing down on galleys and other rival vessels.

In 1340 an English fleet, with King Edward III on board, sailed eastward along the coast of Flanders and discovered a much larger collection of French warships anchored in the harbor of Sluys, downstream from Bruges. The two forces spent nearly twenty-four hours preparing for battle. Rather than sailing out to meet the English, the French chained their ships together in a defensive posture. The English circled behind them before approaching and then gained the advantage, with archers firing down onto the decks of the French ships immobilized by the chains. The English then boarded the French vessels, and most of the fighting took place on deck. The French started the day with 202 ships and when the fighting ended they had twelve. More than sixteen thousand French soldiers died. The English had taken advantage of the height and maneuverability their new naval technology gave them while the French had prepared for battle in much the same way they might have done in the days of the Vikings.[17]

By the time of the first European voyages into the tropical Atlantic in the fifteenth century, Mediterranean fleets, like their northern counterparts, contained a mixture of galleys and large sailing ships. Galleys had risen to overwhelming prominence during the early Crusades, but by the fourteenth century larger

Fig. 1.3 The Battle of Sluys, 1340, as depicted in Jean Froissart's Chronicles in the fifteenth century. In this engagement the English took advantage of their ships' maneuverability and height. Bibliothèque nationale de France.

sailing ships had arrived in the Mediterranean. With their high sides they seemed
at times almost invulnerable to attack. During the final siege of Constantinople
in 1453, perhaps as many as 150 Ottoman galleys circled around four large
sailing ships but could not take them. The sailors seemed invulnerable, though
they were unable to defend Constantinople.[18]

By the time of Columbus, Mediterranean and northern European sailing
technology had begun to converge, and there was generally a common design
for European sailing ships. Within that broad template, however, the design was
quite flexible, and by the late fifteenth century an array of ship types had been
established, reflecting local building traditions and responding to special navigational challenges and external threats. The three vessels that Columbus took
across the Atlantic in 1492 were relatively small compared to some fifteenth-
century warships. They were not much more than 20 meters long, and they
lacked cannons, a feature that would help shape the design and establish the imposing power of later vessels.[19]

For the designers of sailing ships and galleys alike, the adoption of firearms
was a slow, halting process, marked by a number of technical difficulties. At least
until the fifteenth century most of the gunpowder available in Europe did not
work well in moisture-laden air. After 1400 changes in the process of making
gunpowder made it possible to fire guns on ships. Soon thereafter guns were
brought on board, but initially they were small and designed for wounding or
killing men, not for sinking rival vessels. The idea of using a cannon to sink a
ship required a thoroughgoing reconsideration of naval tactics and significant
changes in the design of both the weapons and the ships. It was difficult to find
a good location to mount the cannon to keep the act of firing from capsizing or
splintering the vessel. Once a suitable location had been found, hulls and decks
had to be redesigned to carry the weight, and sliding gun carriages were developed to lessen the shock of recoil. As early as the 1520s, the Portuguese had
introduced gun decks near the waterline with portals along the sides of their
vessels so that their cannons could be fired broadside. Eventually this design
would be adopted across Europe, but only after sailing ships faced a powerful
challenge from galleys with cannons mounted in their bows.[20]

Though only a few galleys crossed the Atlantic in the early modern period,
they played an important role in the creation of the Atlantic world. Galleys were
the first vessels to mount cannons successfully, and as a consequence they became the most powerful warships in Europe even in northern waters.[21] The
English first encountered galleys with cannons in 1512. An English fleet was
preparing for a skirmish off Brest when French galleys arrived and blasted two
English sailing ships, sinking one immediately and disabling the other. The
event shocked England's naval commanders and initiated a decades-long effort
to mount cannons on sailing ships.[22] The process was difficult, as illustrated by

the misfortune of the *Mary Rose*, King Henry VIII's flagship. The *Mary Rose* first sailed in 1511, but in the 1530s it was extensively rebuilt and given a new hull with portals for cannons. In 1545 the ship sailed out of Portsmouth to meet a French invasion fleet. The winds swirled unexpectedly and the *Mary Rose* tipped. As water poured in through the gun portals, the ship sank, killing all the sailors on board.

The *Mary Rose*, retrofitted to mount cannons, had failed to reconcile three competing trends in ship design, all of which had been spurred by military considerations: 1) the introduction of high decks and looming wall-like hulls to impede boarding; 2) the placement of cannons near the waterline to strike nearby vessels and keep the ship stable when the guns were fired; and 3) the enhancement of maneuverability for skirmishes on open water. Eventually ship designers across Europe found ways to meet all these objectives, though in some places the process took decades. Eventually sailing vessels were fitted with watertight gun ports, and they acquired greater stability when sailing in rough water. In 1587, off the coast of Spain, Francis Drake brought a fleet of large armed sailing ships into the harbor of Cadiz, and a defending force of six galleys failed to deter him. Drake destroyed twenty-four Spanish ships.[23] Responding to this apparent reversal in the relative power of galleys and sailing ships, King Philip II of Spain chose not to include any galleys in the armada he assembled for his planned invasion of England in 1588.[24] As the firepower of sailing ships increased and the threat of attack from galleys receded, a new arms race developed among ship designers.

The gradual transformation of the sailing ship served commercial as well as military purposes. Raising the decks and expanding the hulls made more space available for cargo. Eliminating oarsmen reduced labor costs and made it possible to travel farther without stopping for water and provisions. The gun ports and cannons might appear to have purely military functions, but in the formative period in the development of European sailing technology, combat and trade were almost inextricably linked. In the Mediterranean, city-states like Venice, Genoa, and Pisa fought over shipping lanes and markets.[25] In the Atlantic, North Sea, and Baltic, merchants armed themselves and sometimes sailed in convoys to ward off pirates and privateers.[26] By necessity, merchant vessels were warships. After the retreat of the galleys from northern European waters, maritime commerce and naval operations depended on the same technology and equipment.[27]

Large, armed sailing ships transformed warfare and commerce across Europe. Their impact on local communities from the Middle Ages forward, and their importance in the development of the Atlantic world, can be illustrated in the history of the Basque region on the border of present-day France and Spain. In the eleventh century, taking advantage of changes in naval technology and responding to the expansion of trade between England and Spain, Basque merchants and sailors moved to the Atlantic coast and established ports along the Bay of Biscay. Initially they concentrated on carrying Spanish wool to England, but eventually they diversified and began to exploit the new naval technology in other ways. Basque sailors established fisheries off the shores of France, Britain, and Ireland and then ventured out to Iceland, where they caught cod and eventually began to kill and process whales to supply oil for the English woollen industry. By 1517 Basque fishermen and whalers had reached the coasts of North America. They established seasonal camps in Labrador on the Strait of Belle Isle, less than fifty miles from the site where Norse had briefly settled in the eleventh century.[28]

The Basque experience demonstrates that large sailing ships served a range of purposes, and a variety of factors could influence their design. Basque whaling vessels, for example, were significantly larger than the ships in their fishing fleets. Because of imposing their size, the whaling ships were important military assets. They could have as many as three decks, and by the mid-sixteenth century they carried cannons. They were armed to fire on opposing vessels, and the men on board were equipped for combat on deck. Basque whalers carried firearms, crossbows, pikes, shields, helmets, and body armor. They were armed in anticipation of combat on Atlantic whaling grounds and to defend their vessels and cargo on their risky return to European waters.[29] Whaling ships made the Basques a powerful presence off the coast of Canada.

On several occasions the whalers were mobilized for military purposes. In 1542 when a French expedition under Jean-François Roberval and Jacques Cartier attempted to establish a permanent colony in Canada, the Spanish Navy interrogated Basque fishermen who had been working in the region. A year later Basque whalers took up positions in the Gulf of St. Lawrence to intimidate the French and encourage them to leave. The French would not try to establish another year-round settlement in the region for sixty years. In the 1550s when France and Spain went to war, the Basque whalers were divided, and rival groups took up arms against each other, eventually forcing those aligned with the French to withdraw. Several years later, when one of the dislodged Basque whalers, Johannes de Gaberie, brought his ship back to the coast of Newfoundland, rival Basque whalers attacked, killed several of his men and seized the oil he had collected. In the 1570s when the English began to contemplate the colonization of Newfoundland, they recognized the military significance of the whaling ships and believed that it would be necessary to drive the Basques away. Rather than supporting military action in the waters off North America, the English Parliament chose instead to ban the importation of the Basques' whale oil.[30]

Sailing ships transformed the economy of the Basque country and drew the entire region into a web of international commerce and conflict. The ships physically altered the geography of the region, as thousands of people moved and the coastlines and hinterland were altered to meet the requirements of constructing, outfitting, and maintaining fleets. Deep natural harbors were improved; rivers were dredged; docks and cranes were constructed to service the ships; and large towns grew up beside the ports. Eventually engineers and workmen changed the course of the Nervión River to bring Atlantic commerce into the city of Bilbao.[31] As the coast was altered to serve the ships, so too was the interior landscape. Oak groves were planted specifically for ship construction. In a highly specialized forestry practice unique to the Basque country, proprietors of the woods selected and molded trunks and branches to supply the shapes that were needed in the frames and planking of the hulls.[32]

The Basque response to the problem of timber supply was unusual. Elsewhere trees were more plentiful and Europeans did not have to resort to such specialized forestry. Instead, the pursuit of appropriate timber led shipbuilders to establish elaborate supply networks to acquire wood of appropriate size, strength, and shape. The *Mary Rose* was constructed in Portsmouth, but the ship's beams came from trees as far away as Hampshire and East Anglia.[33] Mast poles presented a special challenge. For masts, the best timbers in Europe came from conifer forests in the hinterland of the Baltic, and English, Dutch, and French shipbuilders went there for supplies. When the English lost access to Baltic timber during the first Anglo-Dutch War, the ramifications were felt across the Atlantic. Northern New England became an alternative source for the English, which spurred the development of New England's nascent shipbuilding industry.[34] Contrary to the warnings of some frantic commentators in the seventeenth century, shipbuilding did not deforest Europe, but it altered the way merchants and governments valued, exploited, and regulated trees.[35]

The most dramatic geographical impact of the development of large sailing vessels stemmed not from the challenge of building them, but from the problem of berthing them. Early modern sailing ships were much more difficult to station than medieval galleys or Viking ships, both of which could be beached.[36] Large sailing ships required good harbors, and therefore they concentrated Europe's major commerce in towns and cities at favored locations. Many of the most successful ports, like Antwerp, Bristol, Hamburg, London, Rouen, and Seville, were located inland at the ends of long narrow estuaries or on the banks of deep rivers some distance from the coast. This provided protection from rough sea as well as sudden naval attack.[37] The requirements of ships directed commercial development in Europe, and with the advent of transatlantic colonization and trade, sailing vessels had similar effects on trade and settlement in Africa, on the islands of the Atlantic and Caribbean, and along the coasts of North and South America.

In the fifteenth century the Portuguese exploration of the western coast of Africa set a pattern.[38] Eager to bring their ships as close as possible to local markets, the Portuguese gravitated toward rivers. They tried to establish posts inland on the banks of the Senegal, Gambia, and Congo rivers, but navigational difficulties, local military resistance, and a dangerous disease environment convinced them to withdraw from most upriver sites. Instead they brought their ships into coastal harbors and encouraged African traders to bring them gold, ivory, and other products, along with prisoners and war captives who they sold as slaves. As a consequence of this pattern of behavior, the draft of ships (the depth of their hulls beneath the waterline) shaped European understandings of Africa's geography. Initially explorers drew a line between accessible coastal and riverine regions and the unknown, presumably dangerous interior, which could only be navigated on foot or by camel, horse, or canoe. Eventually, except around the Portuguese colony of Angola, the entire continent facing the Atlantic became, from a European perspective, one large "interior." Safety could be found only on ships or in the well-fortified castles that slave traders constructed along the coast.[39] Large sailing vessels also defined African perceptions of Europeans. Ships were the basis of European power, but they also restricted its scope and served to reinforce a sense of physical and cultural separation between the inhabitants of the two continents.[40]

European perceptions of American geography were similarly shaped by ships, but they were also affected by the Spanish discovery and conquest of wealthy inland empires in Mesoamerica and the Andes. Prior to the Spanish conquest, those empires had not relied heavily on deep-water harbors or rivers as wide

Fig. 1.4 The castle of São Jorge da Mina, built by the Portuguese on the coast of Africa in the 1470s and subsequently taken by the Dutch. Österreichische Nationalbibliothek/ Wien, Atlas Blaeu, vol. 36:19, fol. 62–63.

and deep as the Spanish ships required. Therefore, the Spanish needed to re-shape the landscape to suit their needs. Before marching on the Aztec Empire, Hernán Cortéz oversaw the construction of a new port city at Vera Cruz. That city survived and prospered, but the Spanish had a much more difficult time establishing ports to service Peru. In 1535, Pedro de Mendoza led thirteen ships into the Rio de la Plata and established the port of Buenos Aires in the vain hope that it could serve as a way station for expeditions traveling hundreds of miles upriver into the Andes. Eventually the Spanish linked Peru to the Atlantic through a shorter but more elaborate route involving transshipment across the Isthmus of Panama.

The early years of Buenos Aires followed an oft-repeated pattern. The tech-nology of ocean-going transportation had brought the Spanish to a place where they could not subsist. Buenos Aires had a shortage of drinkable water, the Spanish did not have reliable trading partners, and the land was barren. Describing the town in its early months, one member of the expedition wrote, "the people had nothing to eat, and were starved with hunger, so that they suffered great pov-erty, and it became so bad that the horses could not go. Yea, finally, there was so much want and misery for hunger's sake, that there were neither rats, nor mice, nor snakes to still the great dreadful hunger and unspeakable poverty, and shoes and leather were resorted to for eating."[41] The Spanish evacuated Buenos Aires in 1542 and would not return for another thirty-eight years. A similar sequence of events occurred repeatedly in North America during the 1530s and 1540s, as French expeditions suffered along the banks of the St. Lawrence River. Dreams of establishing profitable trade routes, the lure of imagined inland riches, and hopes of conquest drew European expeditions up the large rivers of North and South America such as the Oronoco, the Amazon, and the Mississippi, but they would end in disaster.

As in Africa, in North and South America the Europeans' reliance on sailing technology encouraged them to draw imaginary lines across the landscapes they traversed, associating those regions their ships could not easily reach with dis-order and danger.[42] Many of those places had thriving indigenous populations, and most would eventually support prosperous colonial settlements. There was nothing intrinsically deficient or dangerous about the regions beyond the reach of European ships, but explorers feared cutting themselves off from their supply network as they moved farther inland away from the Atlantic, and being vulner-able to hunger, exposure, and attack.

The naval and maritime infrastructure necessary to support colonization took time to develop, and in the early period of exploration and settlement European governments seldom had the resources necessary to support transatlantic expeditions to places far beyond established supply lines. Therefore, in order to succeed each venture had to support itself economically. In the sixteenth and

seventeenth centuries, European merchants and admirals together invested in
harbors, docks, warehouses, forts, and settlements at several strategic points on
the Atlantic coasts of the Americas. In the process they transformed places that
had been obscure, sparsely populated backwaters into centers of commercial and
military power, including Quebec, Boston, Newport, New York, Philadelphia,
Charleston, Vera Cruz, Cartagena, Portobello, Recife, Bahia, Rio de Janeiro, and
Buenos Aires. Virtually all the port cities in the Americas were sited, designed,
and managed in ways that served a combination of military and commercial
interests. The ships that entered the ports similarly played multiple roles as
Europe's navies exploited the military potential and vulnerabilities of fishing,
whaling, and merchant fleets.

The French were the first to send privateers across the Atlantic in large
numbers. In 1523 François I commissioned Jean Ango, a prominent ship out-
fitter in Dieppe, to send ships to raid Spanish shipping. Since the conquest of
Mexico, Spanish ships had been sailing across the ocean laden with extraordinary quantities of treasure. A single prize could easily enrich a ship owner, captain, and crew. When Ango sent privateers into the Atlantic, two of his ships
returned with gold.[43] From that moment on there were many volunteers. First
the privateers cruised southern Spain's Atlantic coastline, but within a few
years some had ventured across the ocean to lie in wait at strategic points such
as the strait between Cuba and Florida. The Spanish responded with dramatic
defensive measures, organizing convoys to carry the gold and silver, requiring
merchants to arm their ships, and imposing a tax to pay for the large warships
that escorted the treasure from America to Spain.

By the end of the sixteenth century the English had replaced the French
as the principal threat to Spanish shipping in the Caribbean. To ward off the
English, Spain's convoys grew larger, and the fleets carrying gold and silver were
merged to increase their firepower. The Spanish also bolstered the defense of
their American ports, even going so far as to call in galleys. Between 1578 and
the 1630s the Spanish crown commandeered more than two thousand men,
many of them enslaved, to row and sail at least twenty galleys across the Atlantic.
The galleys were stationed in Cartagena, Havana and other ports for harbor
defense.[44] Combined, Spain's defensive measures were remarkably successful.
After the convoy system was introduced, the treasure fleet was captured only
once, in 1628.[45]

The European powers differed in their manner of financing, arming and
deploying ships. From the fifteenth century forward, the Portuguese government used its own resources and oversaw the construction of purpose-built
warships to protect its expanding trade network down the coast of Africa into
the Indian Ocean.[46] Portugal's fleet was relatively small. In the sixteenth century,
most other European navies purchased or leased merchant vessels and refitted

them for combat, sometimes fortifying their hulls or adding gun ports.[47] Spain leased merchant vessels for service in its navy.[48] Other countries relied more heavily on privateering as a way to exploit the military potential of commercial fleets. By authorizing private ships to attack and gather plunder, England's Elizabeth I was able to launch a much larger sailing force than her government could afford to build.

In the sixteenth-century Caribbean, England and Spain took contrasting approaches to naval warfare. While the Spanish imposed taxes and expended considerable public sums on its treasure fleet, the English, especially under Elizabeth I, depended on privateers. In the winter of 1585–1586, Francis Drake led an expedition of twenty-two ships and more than two thousand men to the Spanish coast, the Cape Verde Islands, and the Caribbean. At Santo Domingo, Drake and his men captured and destroyed the Spanish galley that had been sent to guard the harbor, burned part of the town, and ransomed the remainder before sailing on to plunder Cartagena. Drake had royal support for this expedition, but most of his vessels and crew were acting on private initiative, intending to profit from plunder. Their success encouraged others to seek fortunes as privateers.[49]

In the late sixteenth century, the Dutch wars of independence against the Spanish Hapsburg Empire changed the pattern of state support for navies across Europe. The Dutch had long been a successful maritime people, with experience in shipbuilding, sailing, and long-distance trade, and they had established elaborate supply networks and markets for their goods from the Baltic Sea to the Mediterranean. The wars for independence began in 1579, but the lengthy, violent struggle that ensued did not impoverish the Dutch. On the contrary, during the conflict they managed to expand their trade. In the 1590s Spanish and Flemish privateers increased their attacks on Dutch shipping, and the United Provinces responded by commissioning warships to accompany their merchant fleet. Organized under the supervision of five separate provincial admiralties, the Dutch navy was eventually deployed for offensive operations, for example attacking the Spanish in the Azores and at trading castles down the coast of Africa.[50] During the twelve years' truce that began in1609, the Dutch continued to maintain their navy because their merchants needed protection from privateers. In 1621 when the truce ended and the Spain launched its last long effort to reconquer the United Provinces, it invested considerable sums in warships, primarily for action on the North Sea.

Spain at this time controlled Portugal and its overseas possessions, and therefore the Dutch confronted both the Spanish and Portuguese in the waters off Europe, in the Caribbean, near the shores of Brazil and Angola, and across the Indian Ocean. The Dutch prevailed in most of their naval encounters because they had more ships, better naval artillery, and well-trained, experienced crews.[51] In many engagements the Dutch were faster and more adept at sailing close to the wind, giving them the ability to choose when to engage in battle. When the time came to exchange fire their gunners were more likely to hit their targets. These advantages stemmed from Dutch public investment in a permanent naval force.[52]

The growing strength of the navy encouraged Dutch commercial development. To facilitate public investment in military forces, the Dutch adopted new methods of tax collection, record-keeping, and government finance. Once the navy had established its power on the North Sea and Baltic, Dutch merchant ships sailing in those waters were able to dispense with the burden of arming heavily for self-defense.[53] For those seeking profit in the more dangerous waters of the Atlantic and Indian Oceans, joint stock companies shielded investors from the full risk of their endeavors, and new banks and maritime insurance made increasing amounts of capital available and secure.[54] By the 1650s the Dutch had not only established the institutional foundations of a modern capitalist economy, but had also developed the political structures and practices historians associate with the "fiscal-military state."[55]

The success of the Dutch demonstrated the advantage of maintaining a permanent navy and posed a challenge to all the other major maritime powers of Europe. Spain strengthened its navy in the first half of the seventeenth century, as did Portugal after it regained its independence in 1640.[56] The English were relatively slow to respond, until the English Commonwealth, concerned for its political survival, built warships and centralized naval administration. Between 1649 and 1651, it nearly doubled the size of its navy, overseeing the construction of twenty warships and seizing or purchasing twenty-five other vessels and refitting them for naval service.[57] By 1660, the English navy had nearly quadrupled in size, expanding to 156 warships.[58] The English and the Dutch would fight three wars between 1652 and 1674, the third of which was part of a larger, longer struggle pitting the United Provinces against Louis XIV's France. During that war the French built their own powerful navy.[59] The Dutch remained formidable, but the English and French emerged as the strongest naval powers on the Atlantic after 1688.

The English Commonwealth's investment in the navy marked the beginning of a long transformation with profound implications for the economy and politics of Britain. Between the 1640s and 1815, the British spent nearly as much on their navy as they did on their ground forces. While the army spent the bulk of its revenue paying and maintaining troops, the navy invested more in dockyards and ships. British military expenditure drove an increase in the cost of government generally, from less than 4 percent of national income in the 1640s to 19 percent by 1815. The British navy became the largest, most expensive, capital-intensive organization in the world.[60]

The expansion of government investment in navies changed the structure of sailing ships. In the first half of the seventeenth century the Dutch developed thoroughly civilian merchant ships, but these vessels could operate safely only in well-patrolled waters, and much of the Atlantic remained dangerous. Indeed, in the Caribbean and off the shores of Africa the early eighteenth century became the golden age of piracy, and privateers cruised American waters long after they had become scarce along European coasts.[61] Therefore for safety most ships crossing the Atlantic continued to carry guns. In the Atlantic world in the first half of the eighteenth century, the most dramatic changes in ship design and construction did not involve merchant ships, slave ships, or fishing or whaling vessels, but specialized warships.

In England Charles II took a personal interest in ship design, appointed shipwrights to his Navy Board, and oversaw the construction of increasingly large, well-armed ships.[62] When the French began to expand their navy in the 1670s they had relatively little experience building such vessels. Therefore, they recruited talent from other countries, including Spain, the United Provinces, and England. The absence of a strong French tradition in this field, and the arrival of a cosmopolitan body of shipwrights employing various design and construction techniques, helped make France a center of innovation. British ship design changed little between the 1690s and the 1740s, whereas in France a strong, creative craft network developed, and prestigious schools were established for the study of fluid mechanics and ship design. By the 1720s French warships were widely recognized as the best in the world. They were faster, more maneuverable, and able to deliver more firepower than their British counterparts. But these warships were also extremely specialized. For commercial purposes, the ships would have been prohibitively expensive, unstable, and cramped.[63] Britain's ship designers received a shock in 1747 when the Royal Navy captured the *Invincible*, a seventy-four-gun French ship that was one and a half times the size of its British counterparts, giving it an array of military advantages.[64] Within a few years Britain was producing similarly large warships.

The specialization of warships, and the enormous sums that the British and the French spent on ships, shipyards, docks, and other infrastructure, made it extremely difficult for any other nation to compete. In the 1770s during the War of Independence, the United States struggled to build warships. The U.S. deployed privateers and launched some vessels commissioned by independent states and the Continental Congress. The new governments erected shore defenses and mined the Delaware River. While they achieved isolated successes against the British, it was obvious to all observers that they would never challenge British supremacy on the open water. The U.S. therefore worked strenuously to secure a French alliance, and in 1781 off Yorktown French naval forces played a decisive role in securing victory.[65] A generation later, during the War of 1812 when

THE INVINCIBLE, FRENCH 74 GUN SHIP, CAPTURED IN 1747.

Fig. 1.5 The French ship *Invincible* following its capture by the British in 1747. Royal Museums Greenwich.

the United States fought the British without the help of a European ally, Britain dominated the ocean.[66]

Surveying Atlantic naval history from the fifteenth century to 1815, it is easy to conclude that European dominance was foreordained and, indeed, that this had been recognized immediately and nearly universally, starting with those fifteenth-century indigenous Americans and Africans who saw sailing ships and thought that they were magic. But on closer examination the story is more complicated, beginning with that moment of first contact. The mere appearance of sailing ships frightened people, but that fear was invariably mixed with curiosity. In 1455 when Aviso Cadamosto sailed to Senegal, he reported that the people on the shore were

> struck with admiration by the construction of our ship, and by her equipment—mast, sails, rigging, and anchors. They were of opinion that the portholes in the bows of ships were really eyes by which the ships saw whither they were going over the sea. They said we must be great wizards, almost the equal of the devil, for men that journey by land have difficulty in knowing the way from place to place, while we

journeyed by sea, and, as they were given to understand, remained out
of sight of land for many days, yet knew which direction to take, a thing
only possible through the power of the devil.[67]

In the Caribbean in 1493 Columbus reported that the islanders had told him
that they "firmly believed that I, with these ships and men, came from the sky."
Rather than associating ships with devils, they thought that Columbus and his
crew were angels, because "all power and good" came from the sky. Columbus
considered this reasonable, "because they have never seen people clothed or
ships of such a kind."[68]

In 1494 Diego Álvarez Chanca, surgeon on Columbus's second fleet,
described the reaction of the inhabitants of Guadeloupe when they first saw
Spanish ships. Initially their response was uniform and simple: "as soon as
they saw the sails, they all ran away." But on the next day, after the ships had
laid anchor, the islanders' caution gave way to curiosity. "Many men and women
walked along the shore next to the water looking at the fleet and marvelling at
something so novel."[69]

The ships were marvelous and powerful, and across the Caribbean over the
next several decades some indigenous men and women continued to run away
from them. Others, however, chose instead to learn how they worked. In 1516,
after Spanish slavers seized a group of islanders from the Bay Islands off the coast
of Honduras and carried them to Havana, the islanders seized control of the ship
and sailed it back to Honduras, covering a distance of more than five hundred
miles.[70] In the early sixteenth century, European sailing vessels were not prohibitively difficult to operate, nor were they—even for the indigenous peoples of the
Americas—impossible to build.

Within two years of the conquest of Mexico, Hernán Cortés oversaw the construction of thirteen sailing ships. He arranged to have iron tools and nails forged
on site, located and collected timber, and watched as the ships were constructed
using indigenous labor on a beach of Lake Texcoco, near the Aztec capital of
Tenochtitlan. Cortés had help from a number of trained Spanish blacksmiths
and at least one shipwright, but his achievement demonstrates that at the time
of the conquest Mexico had the resources, labor supply, and infrastructure necessary to build sixteenth-century sailing ships.[71] Indeed two years earlier, Vasco
Núñez de Balboa had built four sailing ships using indigenous labor in a much
less promising environment, the Isthmus of Panama. In the 1520s and 1530s,
the Spanish built their first Pacific fleet on the beaches of Mexico.[72]

In the early days of colonization in the Americas, European shipwrights had a
monopoly on the knowledge required to build sailing ships, but that monopoly
did not last. The technology of ship construction was not arcane, complex, or
closely guarded enough to keep others out of the industry. In South Carolina,

enslaved men worked as shipwrights and oversaw ship construction.[73] In Brazil the Portuguese promoted shipbuilding, and enslaved men, convict laborers, and others from across the social spectrum became shipwrights.[74] Brazilian ships were prized for their durability and in Bahia in particular, local shipwrights continued to design and build ships into the twentieth century using early modern techniques.[75]

As the Brazilian and New England examples make clear, it was possible in the seventeenth century to open new shipyards in the Americas and produce vessels that could rival their European counterparts. That became steadily more difficult, however, as Europe's ships became more specialized and larger and required increasingly elaborate infrastructure to build. The cumulative effect of capital investment secured European dominance of shipbuilding. But if building powerful ships lay beyond the reach of Africans or indigenous Americans, what kept them from acquiring naval power by seizing ships?

Indeed as early as 1516, one group of indigenous Americans had already commandeered a ship and sailed it across the Gulf of Mexico. Those enslaved people anticipated the actions of other enslaved men and women, mostly from Africa, who launched shipboard revolts and took control of sailing ships. On at least 120 occasions enslaved men and women seized vessels that were carrying them from Africa, steered them to the coast, and swam or paddled back to land. On some occasions the formerly enslaved Africans held white crew members prisoner and forced them to navigate the ship. In other instances, the Africans sailed by themselves. Some sailing ships under African command engaged in naval battles with warships and other slavers lasting for hours, or even days, and sometimes the Africans prevailed.[76]

There are records of many incidents in which Africans and indigenous Americans captured sailing ships, operated them successfully, and deployed them in battle. Among indigenous Americans, Wabanaki warriors operating in the Gulf of Maine, the Bay of Fundy, the Gulf of St. Lawrence, and the nearby Atlantic coast may have been the most successful in their deployment of sailing ships. For nearly two hundred years beginning in the 1580s they seized sailing vessels for their own use, and in wartime deployed them in combat. In 1676 Wabanaki warriors engaged colonial ships in battle, made amphibious attacks, and used a fleet of captured sailing vessels to lay siege to an English fort.[77] Wabanki warriors launched coordinated attacks with multiple ships on one other occasion in the 1720s, but they had nothing like a permanent navy capable of projecting power across the ocean.

The fundamental reason why Africans and indigenous Americans never acquired such naval power was that navies required more than ships. Since the late Middle Ages, Europeans and colonists had invested enormous capital in docks, coastal forts, and port facilities, and established elaborate trade networks to repair and supply their vessels. Any African or indigenous American who violently took command of a sailing ship lacked access to this infrastructure. The commercial and military facilities that enabled sailing around the Atlantic world bolstered and protected European and colonial domination of the sea.

2

Sailors

Early modern sailing ships harnessed wind power with impressive efficiency, but they also relied on human muscle. Men carried barrels of water, fish, wine, gunpowder, shot, and other things onboard, and placed them carefully in the hold. In sixteenth-century Spain even the heavy artillery, which was kept on shore over the winter, had to be hauled by sailors onto the ships.[1] Most of the ships preparing to cross the Atlantic were hand-loaded. The process required physical strength along with coordination and equipment. Men worked together using winches, ropes, and pulleys. They used ropes in similar ways to raise the masts and sails and handle the ship as it crossed the ocean.

One sixteenth-century Spanish commentator invoked Renaissance-era insights into the operation of the human body to describe how sailing ships worked. He compared the ropes to the nervous system and the men who worked them to the soul.[2] The work was both delicate and dangerous, as men needed to maintain their balance on unsteady and slippery decks, grapple with taut ropes carrying loads of hundreds or even thousands of pounds, and maneuver rigging and equipment often swinging in the wind. Sailors had to stay alert to keep themselves safe and avoid wrecking costly equipment or damaging the ship.

Sailors were almost always in short supply, but rather than bidding for their services early modern navies generally paid them poorly. The meager pay reflected the humble background of most sailors and the low place of sailing in the hierarchy of work. Navies enlisted poor and often unfortunate young men. Naval officials feared that bargaining with recruits would compromise the navy's ability to govern men sternly and discipline them if they resisted any orders in the future. When recruiters could not find a sufficient number of sailors willing to sign on freely, they resorted to various forms of coercion. Especially in wartime, force was often necessary because sailors serving on warships received lower pay than they would have working on fishing vessels, whalers, or merchant ships.

Like other inhabitants of the early modern Atlantic world, sailors lived and worked in fragile groups that were multinational, multiracial, and violent, but in other important ways they stood apart from their contemporaries. They

Atlantic Wars. Geoffrey Plank, Oxford University Press (2020). © Oxford University Press.
DOI: 10.1093/oso/9780190860455.001.0001

experienced an unusual level of alienation. Taken far from their original homes to work in all-male environments, they often arrived in foreign ports as strangers. To provide some sailors' perspectives and highlight the variety of their careers, this chapter will examine individuals like Francisco Manuel, a boy who sailed in Spain's West Indies Fleet; the English sailor Edward Barlow; Edward Coxere, an Englishman belonging to the crew of a Dutch privateer; Hans Jonathan, an enslaved man born in the West Indies who served in the Danish navy; Hans Staden, a German who sailed for both the Portuguese and the Spanish; and Nicolás Covoh, an indigenous man from the Yucatán who became a stateless buccaneer. Sailing marked men, stigmatized them, and subjected them to legal restrictions on land and severe codes of discipline at sea.

The sailors' clothing marked them as belonging to a distinct, suspect, and vulnerable category of fighters and workers. They performed strenuous, dangerous work, left home for months at a time, and sometimes never returned. At sea they were subject to constant supervision. They gave up control over their sleep schedules and diet, worked strange hours, and had to be ready around the clock to respond to rough weather and other emergencies. Sailing allowed men to cross national boundaries and move back and forth between commercial and military service. They were able to shift their national allegiances and cross the line separating civilians from the military, but often only at tremendous cost. The sailors' malleability should not be confused with freedom. Prior to the late eighteenth century, when naval culture changed with the rise of an ideology celebrating the ordinary seaman's patriotic service, sailors suffered social degradation and legal liability on every shore of the ocean.

Sailors came from the lowest ranks of European and colonial society. In the 1570s, Juan Escalante de Mendoza asserted that the bulk of the sailors in Spain's West Indies fleet had been "poor men and the sons of poor fathers."[3] Detailed studies of recruitment into the Dutch navy in the seventeenth and eighteenth centuries lead to a similar conclusion. Dutch sailors came from impoverished regions and poor urban districts, and not all of them were Dutch.[4] Poor young men traveled long distances looking for work before reaching port cities like Lisbon, Seville, Amsterdam, and London. In France, naval recruiters grew accustomed to enlisting half-naked and hungry men who had sold their clothes to pay for the cost of traveling to the recruiting sites. The recruiters offered them stale sea-biscuit from the stores of returning ships in a sometimes-futile effort to bring them back to health.[5] In France and elsewhere, naval recruits were often young. Some had been driven from their homes by parents who were no longer able or willing to support them. Others were orphans.

Navies across Europe recruited poor boys, but even among the impoverished there were some who would not contemplate becoming a sailor. In the 1781 Admiral Jan Hendrick Van Kinsbergen asked the leaders of Amsterdam's Jewish

Fig. 2.1 The durable, practical apparel worn by seventeenth-century mariners identified men as sailors and provided little indication of a man's specific national origins. Museum of the City of London.

community to give a dispensation allowing Jewish boys to work on the Sabbath, skip prayers, and eat non-Kosher food so that they could join the navy. The Jewish leaders refused. Although Jews made up 10 percent of Amsterdam's population, and some of them were poor, virtually none of them enlisted for naval service.[6]

When Francisco Manuel arrived in Seville in the 1580s he was "a lost boy, who could not say who his father nor his mother was, nor where he came from."[7] He became a ship's page at the age of seven, and over the next several years he was "loaned" from one ship captain to another, acquiring skills and experience along the way. Eventually he became a pilot, a position of significant responsibility, guiding the ship.[8] As Manuel's career suggests, some sailors could rise through the ranks if they had talent, applied themselves, and endured. But often sailors' careers were short, which resulted in a young average age for many warship crews. Most early modern warships carried large numbers of young people with little experience in sailing. In Spain's sixteenth-century West Indies fleet, boys entered service as children and in their early years they took orders and instruction from nearly every adult on the ship. In 1759 when the French warship

La Glorieux took to sea, one-third of the crew were boys and young men who had never sailed before.[9]

A pervasive hierarchical order prevailed on warships to facilitate teamwork and allow men to develop and disseminate skills. Inexperienced sailors could be a danger to themselves and others. Within days of joining the crew of the English ship *Naseby* in 1659, Edward Barlow was assigned to a team of forty or fifty men at the capstan, the large spool that drew up the anchor cable. Looking back on that moment years later, he acknowledged, "I did not know where I did good and where I did not in that kind of work." For the capstan to operate four large beams had to be inserted into a vertical cylinder. The men divided into groups to push the beams and make the spool rotate. Barlow did not know where or how to join in and when one of the officers asked him to move he stumbled. Just at that moment the beams swung quickly and one hit him in the head. Barlow fell through an open grating, and "my head going down foremost struck against one of the spar shores in the hold." His skull was fractured.[10] In 1701 Barnaby Slush argued that a "ship of war" was "too big and unmanageable a machine to be under the conduct and government of boys and novices." The work was beyond them even in calm waters. The trouble increased "in high running seas and turbulent weather, when their hearts within are apt to sink long before the vessel."[11] Young sailors needed guidance and time to acquire courage and skill.

They also had to acculturate to a distinctive way of life. Though ships varied in size, in the sixteenth century a typical Spanish warship had a crew of sixty-nine.[12] Larger vessels required more men. By the 1740s and 1750s, the largest French and British ships carried more than four hundred sailors.[13] The crews were substantial because sailing required effort at every hour of the day and night. The men had to work in shifts. In Spanish ships, boys turned over an hourglass every half hour and loudly prayed with each turning. Officers in various parts of the ship answered with their own recitations, which signaled that they had heard the boy and knew the time. Eight of these litanies indicated that four hours had passed and a work shift had ended.[14] On British ships in the eighteenth century an officer kept a similar hourglass. He rang a bell at the end of each half-hour interval, and after eight chimes the shifts, or "watches," would change. At the start of each watch a new team of men climbed onto the deck to work the sails for four hours, giving the previous team a rest.[15]

These carefully managed watches were part of an elaborate system to direct and coordinate labor. Large warships were hierarchically ordered, with authority flowing from the captain to his lieutenants and tiers of other officers. Each officer supervised the men assigned to him, distributing rewards and punishment according to their performance and sometimes almost on a whim. The captain presided over the entire workforce, wielding an authority that sometimes seemed "well-nigh unlimited."[16]

Fig. 2.2 Christoph Weiditz, *Trachtenbuch* (c. 1530). Sailor pulling a rope. Hs 22474
© Germanisches Nationalmuseum.

Captains differed in the ways they exercised power. In December 1754, when
Augustus Hervey's steward arrived late and delayed his ship's departure from
Gibraltar, Hervey punched him but quickly regretted doing so. "I hit my knuckle
against his teeth and cut the tendon, so that my hand swelled very much and was
very painful a long time."[17] More commonly, captains administered punishment
with sticks or whips and ordered other men to administer the beatings. There
was a customary taboo against striking a sailor on the face, and some captains
were reprimanded or even sanctioned for beating men excessively.[18] Most
captains recognized that the best way to maintain order was to appear orderly
themselves in the way they oversaw discipline. During a six-month deployment
off the coast of the Shetland Islands in 1760, Dutch Captain Andries De Bruijn
punished only 7 of the 125 men under his command. He ordered a few sailors

placed in irons. He ordered one violent man to walk through the ship in hand-cuffs, and after discovering additional evidence against that man, he convened a council of war which sentenced him to be ducked from the yardarm, whipped, and abandoned on shore.[19]

Even before he expelled that man from his ship, De Bruijn had sought to dis-tance him from the rest of the crew. The punishments he sanctioned served as a warning to the others but at the same time singled out the disobedient sailor "as a rogue." In every navy, commanders were on guard to protect their authority, and one of their worst fears was mass rebellion. When discussing sailors among themselves, they often voiced their fears of them. In the eighteenth century one French officer complained that the "seafaring people" of his country were "nat-urally dissolute, insubordinate, and always treated with too much gentleness."[20] Despite that officer's sentiments, mutinies were rare on large naval warships be-fore the revolutionary era, and if they did occur it was likely to be close to land.[21]

In 1758 the Marquis de Duquesne, an admiral in the French navy, faced in-subordination throughout his fleet. He ordered at least four men put to death but could not get his sailors to work. They stayed in port because they had not been paid.[22] Similarly, one of the rare mutinies in the Dutch navy occurred in port in 1779, again in a dispute over pay.[23] Insurrection at sea was feasible on small vessels and private ships, but mass mutiny was less likely on large warships in the open ocean because the prospect of fighting on deck terrified not just the officers but also the sailors. Seizing control of a large vessel would always be difficult, and the challenge of restoring order and sailing under a new chain of command was daunting. Men knew that they had to work together to manage a ship. The requirements of survival provided a powerful incentive to cooperate and main-tain discipline on the ocean. Disorder threatened everyone and for that reason sailors watched each other closely, gave direction to each other, and corrected each other's poor performance.

While at sea, a sailor had no respite from the company of other men. On Spanish warships in the sixteenth century, sailors were not officially allocated any particular place to sleep. Men competed to claim space on deck for their bed-ding, erecting small fences that sometimes made it difficult to walk from one side of the ship to the other. Officers issued orders to clear paths across the deck and keep the floor around each cannon free from mattresses, blankets, and bodies.[24] Crossing the Atlantic on a French warship in 1734, Father Luc François Nau was assigned to sleep below deck near the cannons. He complained, "We could not get into our berths without banging our heads and shins twenty times. . . . The rolling of the ship threw down our berths and hopelessly entangled them. Once, I was pitched onto a poor Canadian officer whom I unintentionally caught as if I had been a rat trap. It was a quarter of an hour before I could extricate myself. Meanwhile the officer was smothering and had scarcely any breath to swear at me."[25] British warships in the middle of the eighteenth century had a more systematic way of allocating sleeping space. Most of the sailors were granted a space 14 inches wide in which to sling a hammock, and the spaces were distributed in a way that assured that every other space would be vacant during each nighttime watch, so that every man had, in effect, a 28-inch-wide column of air for his hammock.[26]

There were very few women on warships. Before sailing from Seville, one Spanish commander received orders that if he discovered any woman on the ships in his fleet, "whoever brought her on board should be punished as you see fit, and she should be put ashore at the first land arrived at that is populated by Christians."[27] Some women disguised themselves as men to work at sea, and on rare occasions naval officers hired women without disguise to serve. Hannah Giles worked as a nurse on a British hospital ship in 1749. A sailor on the warship *Amazon* went by the name of William Prothero but turned out to be an eighteen-year-old woman and the lover of another sailor. Other women may have boarded illicitly and never appeared on the manifest. They would have come on board under cover, hidden among sailors complicit in their subterfuge, and paid the victualler off-the-books for their food. British naval officers sometimes openly brought their wives, mistresses, or prostitutes onboard, but ordinary sailors had to be more discreet.[28] It is unlikely that there were many female stowaways. Provisioning a ship for months at sea was a challenge, and captains were protective of their stores.

Europe's naval powers developed elaborate bureaucracies to provide their sailors with the necessities of life.[29] In the eighteenth century the British admiralty produced an annual plan, in outline form, for feeding tens of thousands of men.[30] The Dutch, by contrast, empowered ship captains to supply their own crews, giving them an allowance according to the number of men under their command and holding the officers liable if their provisions spoiled or ran short. Under this system Captain Eland du Bois purchased provisions with the assistance of his wife Maria, who arranged for the delivery of much of the food, while her cousin, a brewer, supplied beer for the sailors.[31] Operating within local, familiar networks was one way to assure quality control. The French navy adopted another strategy. To protect their sailors from the risks associated with rotten meat, French naval intendants oversaw the collection and slaughtering of animals at designated arsenals, with the carcasses salted and packed on site.[32] Among all the European navies, the British in the eighteenth century offered the most varied diet. In addition to salted meat, British warships carried large numbers of live poultry and livestock.[33] The standard ration for a sailor in the British navy included bread and beer every day along with some combination of beef, pork, peas, oatmeal, butter, and cheese.[34] But British crews still sometimes suffered from malnutrition. In one notorious episode off the Pacific coast of Mexico in the 1740s, more than a thousand sailors died of scurvy.[35]

Officers suffered misfortunes and discomforts along with their crews, but navies seldom had difficulty recruiting officers. For a young man with the right social connections, there were good incentives for taking such a post. The initial pay may have been low, but officers had opportunities for advancement. In the Spanish, Dutch, and British navies they could receive profitable contracts and earn generous prize money. They had patronage power and stood in line for overseas administrative posts.[36] Clerks and pursers had similar ways to make money on warships, and surgeons were paid according to the number of patients they saw, making their work potentially lucrative.[37] Other shipboard workers with special skills, including coopers, sailmakers, and carpenters, could bargain with naval recruiters for better pay.[38] But common seamen individually never had much bargaining power.

Why, then, did anyone choose to become a sailor? In 1648 Edward Coxere did so to escape the nagging of his parents. They had always thought of him as a promising boy. They had sent him away from his home in Dover to spend a year in rural France learning the language. Coxere had returned home fluent in French, and he impressed a merchant who came to his house to interview him. As he recalled later, "care was taken to put me to a trade" and it was decided that he would go to the Netherlands to train as a wine cooper. Coxere went to Zeeland but did not like it, and within a week he was on a ship back to England. His friends and family were surprised and disappointed when he returned. Facing their disapproval, and unhappy with the work they had found for him, he resorted to sailing as an alternative. As he put it, "I not settling my mind to a trade, my lot fell to the sea." He signed on as an apprentice with the captain of a private ship and hated his first voyage. "To harden me to the sea the master would run after me with a rope's end, more to scare me than to hurt me, as since I perceived. The master's mate would run after the master, as if he would hold him. Though they did it in jest, I took it in earnest." That first voyage lasted seven weeks. When the ship returned Coxere quit and went back to his parents' house, but soon "the old tiresome tone was sounded in my ears again: 'What trade now?'" Unable to find another option, he agreed to become an officer's servant on a warship called the *Saint George*, on which his brother was already working.[39]

Coxere's service on the *Saint George* was brief. Shortly after the ship sailed from Portsmouth one of its gunpowder stores exploded and fire spread through the decks. Coxere climbed down the stern onto a crowded boat and was rowed to safety. His brother also survived, but many other sailors drowned or were burned. Finding himself again unemployed, Coxere chose to work next on a merchant vessel, serving as a cabin boy for an Irish captain operating out of

Amsterdam. Their first trip took them to Spain, where the voyage abruptly became a military mission. Coxere's master contracted with the Spanish authorities
to lead a fleet of troop carriers ferrying soldiers up the coast of the Bay of Biscay
to fight the French. For the next five months they sailed off the shore attacking
French ships and taking their cargos. Much to the consternation of the Spanish
soldiers, they never landed. Instead the ship seized so much sugar, fish, wine,
cloth, marmalade, and money that at the end of the season the captain retired.
Coxere was once again out of work. He signed up to serve on a Dutch fishing
vessel plying the waters off the coast of Africa, and this job, like his previous
one, became military. His skipper acquired a letter of marque authorizing him
to raid English ships. Perilously for Coxere, they sailed into the English Channel
where they were surprised by an English ship and surrendered. Coxere had to
conceal his origins to avoid prosecution for fighting against England. Luckily for
him, after years of working alongside Flemish-speaking men he had acquired an
accent. "No man took me to be an Englishman, so that I scaped being carried
away." He wanted to see his mother and father, and so on the road to Dover he
continued to disguise himself and pass as a Dutchman to avoid impressment
into Oliver Cromwell's navy.[40]

Many young men like Coxere became sailors only after trying other ways to
support themselves. Boys poorer than he was took intermittent jobs as porters or
dockworkers before accepting work at sea. Some boys became sailors reluctantly,
while others sought advancement and adventure. Whatever their motivations
and no matter how long their initial term of service, they knew that enlisting on
a ship entailed a greater loss of freedom than other lines of work. Sailors went
where their captains carried them, and on shore they were often vulnerable to
forced military recruitment.

As Coxere knew from hard experience, sailors on merchant vessels, whalers,
and fishing ships performed many of the same tasks and endured many of the
same hardships as their counterparts in the navy. They had to travel for months at
a time, sleep in cramped quarters, eat heavily preserved food, maintain watches
through the night, perform heavy work, and prepare themselves for combat.
Privateers and pirates attacked merchant ships, fishing vessels, and whalers
at sea, and private vessels responded by arming themselves for defense, especially in wartime. This was a constant feature of sailing on the Atlantic well into
the nineteenth century.[41] In 1762 a Quaker minister named John Churchman
went to Philadelphia looking for a ship to carry him to the Caribbean, but as
a pacifist, he did not want to sail on any ship that "carried arms for defence."
When Churchman arrived, there were five merchant vessels on the waterfront
preparing to sail for the Caribbean, but he would not board any of them because they all had cannons.[42] The men who worked on those ships included
some who knew how to operate heavy artillery. Sailors also routinely armed

The IDLE 'PRENTICE turn'd away, and sent to Sea.

Proverbs Chap. X. Ve.1.
A foolish son is the heaviness
of his Mother.

Fig. 2.3 "The Idle 'Prentice Turned Away and Sent to Sea," plate 3 of William Hogarth's "Industry and Idleness" series, shows a desperate young man with few options cajoled into becoming a sailor. Under the picture is a verse from Proverbs: "A foolish son is the heaviness of his mother." © Victoria and Albert Museum, London.

themselves personally in preparation for fighting on deck. This was especially true on slaving ships.

Under these circumstances, private fleets unavoidably recruited, hired, and trained a potential labor force for navies. Recognizing the military value of private vessels and their crews, European monarchs promoted the expansion of commercial sailing.[43] In 1563, Queen Elizabeth's government encouraged the eating of fish on Wednesdays as a way to expand the fishery and thereby make more sailors available for military service.[44] In the seventeenth and eighteenth centuries, governments continued to value merchant fleets as a training ground for mariners, even though, as warships became larger and more specialized, it was increasingly necessary to retrain the sailors they recruited from private ships.[45] But there was a simple, common problem with relying on the fishery, the slave trade, whaling, or other commerce as a source for recruits for the naval service. Consistently, almost everywhere, navies paid sailors less than private shipmasters did.

The wages offered for work on private ships increased in wartime, and for sailors willing to take a chance, privateering provided another potentially lucrative option.[46] The masters of privateering vessels did not always pay wages, but if they successfully took prizes they paid sailors much more than any navy did, especially in the Caribbean where crew members could earn as much as six times what they would have received in wages on a naval vessel.[47] Dutch and British navy ships sometimes augmented their sailors' wages with prize money, but their prize-distribution systems were heavily skewed toward officers, leaving common sailors with as little as a quarter of the proceeds to share among themselves.[48] Low pay and poor shares reflected the status of sailors on warships. In 1665 the Dutch naval administrator John de Witt insisted that the sailors' wages should be fixed according to an "iron law." If the naval officers wavered from this principle and bargained with sailors, they would end up operating only at the discretion of riff-raff.[49]

Unwilling to pay competitive wages, naval recruiters frequently resorted to compulsion and found ways to force sailors to work on warships. In wartime Spanish commanders issued levies requiring the merchant ships sailing with them in convoy to hand over members of their crews. This custom often resulted in long disputes over who was required to pay the sailors brought over to the warships.[50] The Dutch had no statutes authorizing the seizure of individual sailors, but on occasion Dutch naval authorities selectively closed ports to keep merchant ships, fishing vessels, and whalers from leaving the harbors. Deprived of their livelihoods, men enlisted in the navy. Another variation of this strategy involved negotiating with shipmasters to recruit men for the warships. In one episode in 1659, Dutch whalers hired and surrendered 1,200 men.[51] The French were more systematic. Beginning in 1689, France maintained a register of able-bodied sailors and petty officers between the ages of sixteen and sixty, and everyone on the list was subject to conscription. British policy was governed by a combination of statute and custom. Parliamentary acts authorized the forcible enlistment of any "able-bodied men" without work or the means to support themselves. This was a broad remit, but following a centuries-old tradition, the recruiters' instructions stipulated that they should seize only "seamen, seafaring men and persons whose occupations or callings are to work in vessels and boats upon rivers."[52] To gather such men, the Royal Navy appointed special officers for each coastal district. These men hired gangs of lieutenants and deputies who patrolled the streets, inns and taverns looking for sailors. They could identify them by their clothing. Those who refused to join the navy were vulnerable to arrest. Operating in this way over a four-month period in 1755, Captain Patrick Baird took 410 men from the streets of the single town of King's Lynn.[53]

Britain's Royal Navy also seized sailors from vessels at sea. In the eighteenth century the navy stationed warships along the approach routes to Britain's ports. In wartime they stopped as many as one-fifth of the returning merchant vessels, and one-third of the slave ships, to take men from their crews.[54] Slave ships were targeted with special rigor because they had surplus crew members after the enslaved had disembarked, and the sailors on such ships often acquired transferable skills that were useful in the navy, patrolling ships, intimidating and punishing captives, and sometimes fighting them on deck.

Sailors resented forcible recruitment. In 1668 Barlow was taken from a merchant vessel just off the coast at Dover and conscripted into service on a warship. To prevent him from escaping he was kept at sea. "I was not suffered to go ashore in any place in a half a year afterward, which was my great grief."[55] During the Seven Years' War Admiral Edward Boscawen worried that the men who had been forced to serve under him were in a poor mental state for combat. "The dread of going to the West Indies, as well as the regret of being pressed, hangs heavy on many."[56] Faced with such despondency, naval officers sometimes took drastic measures to prevent men from deserting.

Impressment made many people unhappy. Merchants, whalers, and fishermen opposed the work of press gangs. In towns across the British Empire government officials sought local legal exemption from impressment, and sometimes brought charges against members of the recruiting gangs. In some places, crowds gathered to fight the press gangs. In Boston, Massachusetts in 1747, crowds fought in the streets for three days against gangs sent by the Royal Navy.[57] In Liverpool in 1759, a crowd formed on short notice to defend the crew of a Greenland whaling ship resisting impressment. Women "exclaiming against the press-gangs" shielded the men after the recruiters opened fire, and one woman was "shot through the legs by a brace of balls."[58] The gang seized seventeen whalers, but with the help of the local crowd others escaped.[59]

Alongside piracy, privateering, the slave trade, and the general violence of Atlantic whaling and fishing, the practice of impressment blurred any distinction that might have existed between formal military service and private employment. Through forcible recruitment, sailors moved frequently between commercial vessels and state-owned warships. Impressment also had the effect of internationalizing the crews of vessels. Coxere made himself Dutch to avoid the press gang. Commenting on this kind of behavior in 1668, Barlow observed that the threat of impressment made "many poor men so unwilling to sail in His Majesty's ships" that they "abandon their country, finding better entertainment in another."[60] Some sailors chose to leave their home countries, but many others, through a variety of mechanisms, were forced to do so.

Africans began serving on Portuguese ships as early as the 1430s.[61] Portuguese sailors captured men from the coast of Africa and made them serve as local guides. They took some of these men to Lisbon for technical training before returning them to sea as pilots. Though these men had been kidnapped into service and did not choose their careers, piloting gave them authority and some freedom within the confines of the sailing ship. Pilots were valued because the

Fig. 2.4 "Manning the Navy," a print published in 1798 to protest impressment. London Metropolitan Archives, City of London.

ship's survival could depend on them. On dangerous coastlines pilots had to be trusted, and to perform their assigned function they had to command. In the sixteenth century several Portuguese men of African descent served as pilots, and not just for Portugal. In the 1570s, Manuel Luis, a native of Portugal described as "black in colour with a large body," piloted a Spanish galleon in the Caribbean.[62]

There were also large numbers of Africans serving among the ordinary crew members of Spanish and Portuguese ships. Many of these men became sailors working on slaving vessels. In the early seventeenth century Jesuit missionary Alonso de Sandoval boarded slave ships arriving on the coast of South America at Cartagena, looking for Africans who might help him proselytize. He reported that he never failed to find among the apprentice mariners men from Africa who could translate for him. On one ship arriving from the region of Guinea-Bissau Sandoval had an African sailor ask the assembled captives "if they wanted to be like whites."[63] African apprentice mariners were never quite "like whites," but if they served on slaving ships they could acquire special status. They were valued not only for their knowledge of geography but also their language skills and familiarity with diverse cultures. They moved across the Atlantic in both directions and facilitated transactions on the coast of Africa and in American ports. With these benefits in mind, in 1721 the British Royal African Company directed all their ship captains to include on their crews "two or three Negroes between 16 and 20 years of age."[64]

In the 1690s, the French navy recruited enslaved men from San Domingue to help sail their warships in the Caribbean, and in every Atlantic empire, enslaved men worked on privateers.[65] Bermuda took the practice to an extreme. Some Bermudan ships in the eighteenth century were manned almost entirely by men held in slavery. In 1782 a privateer called the *Regulator* sailed from Bermuda with seventy-five men on board, seventy of whom were enslaved. After the *Regulator* was captured by a US ship and taken to Massachusetts, those men were all offered freedom. They declined, declaring that they would prefer to return to their lives as mariners in Bermuda even if that meant that they had to remain in slavery. It is difficult to determine their reasons for making that decision. Some may have simply been satisfied with their lives, but it is equally likely that they feared leaving the community they knew to start a disorienting new life in North America where they still might have faced mistreatment.

Within the context of the Atlantic, the *Regulator's* crew was unusual not just because so many crew members were enslaved, but also because they all haled from the same isolated community and had generally known one another from childhood. Sailing more typically brought strangers together. In 1600, only 51 percent of the crews of Zeeland's men of war came from the United Provinces. Nearly 15 percent of the men came from England and Scotland, and more than 16 percent came from German-speaking countries and the coasts of the Baltic.[66] The number of foreign-born sailors on Dutch vessels fluctuated, but in 1709, 45 percent of the men sailing in Zeeland's men of war were foreign, and between 1720 and 1733 the crews of warships sailing out of Amsterdam were only 50 percent Dutch.[67]

In some navies there were dramatic examples of crew members from different countries turning against each other. In 1565 off the coast of Florida, the Spanish warship *San Pelayo* experienced a rare shipboard mutiny, with national animosities at its root. A coalition of French, Flemish, and eastern Mediterranean sailors rose in arms and took over the ship. They outnumbered the Spanish in the crew, but they were divided among themselves and soon demonstrated the difficulty of executing a mutiny successfully. After a period of violent disagreement, they resolved to sail back across the Atlantic to France, but they could not navigate effectively and sank near the shore of Denmark. In response to such episodes, the Spanish crown beginning in 1568 issued regulations limiting the number of foreigners who could serve on its ships in the West Indies, but the regulations were difficult to enforce. Recruiters, ship captains, and sailors often lied about the national origins of new recruits, and it was often difficult to determine nationality in the early modern era. The French sailors who took part in the shipboard revolt on the *San Pelayo* had gained the trust of their Spanish officers by claiming to be Catalan.[68]

Most of the time, the imperatives of shipboard life, with sailors living together in close quarters and working in teams, encouraged men to adapt, learn new languages, and get along, but if sailing promoted any sense of solidarity or kinship between the men of different nations within the confines of a ship, those good feelings often broke down after the men returned to shore. Sailors often had difficulty navigating the discriminatory challenges they encountered on land, particularly men of indigenous American or African descent.

In 1745 Anthony Gaviallo worked on a Spanish galley guarding the harbor of Havana.[69] There were more than a hundred men on board, most of them rowers. In April the ship was surrounded and captured by a fleet of privateers operating out of New York and New England. The privateers released most of the men, but after identifying Gaviallo as "an Indian man," they carried him off along with eighteen other men they described as "Indians Molattos & Negroes" for sale in the mainland British colonies. Ten of the men were sent to Rhode Island and immediately sold into slavery. Gaviallo and eight others were brought to New York where the Admiralty Court offered to release them if they could present "proof of their being free men." Gaviallo managed to produce such proof, but four of his fellow crew members failed to satisfy the court and were sold at auction. A few years earlier nineteen sailors captured from Spanish vessels had been brought to New York, identified as "Negroes and mulattoes," and sold into slavery. Despite protesting that they were innocent and "freemen in their own country," five of the men had been charged, tried, and hanged for taking part in a conspiracy to burn the city.[70] Most of Gaviallo's crewmates fared better. Upon hearing of their plight, Spanish officials in Havana sent documents to New York certifying that the men were free. Most of them were eventually released from slavery, but at least one of them had died before the letters arrived in New York.

In most parts of the Atlantic world, at least until the Revolutionary era, sailors of African descent routinely risked enslavement on land, not just after their ships surrendered but even when they returned to their home ports victorious. In 1762, to his own surprise, Olaudah Equiano was sent back into slavery after his successful wartime service in the British navy.[71] Hans Jonathan had a similar experience in Denmark in the early nineteenth century. Jonathan enlisted for service on a Danish warship in 1801, just days before a hostile British fleet approached Copenhagen and attacked. Like many others who joined the navy at that moment, he had mixed motivations. One person who knew him said simply, "He wanted to go to war."[72] But Jonathan also wanted freedom and believed that by enlisting he was taking a decisive step away from the woman who held him as a slave. After taking part in the defense of his city, he and another enslaved sailor sued for freedom. Their captain supported their claim and went so far as to secure a positive intervention from the Crown Prince of Denmark, but the courts eventually sided with Jonathan's purported owners. The sailor was arrested, handcuffed, and brought to jail where he waited for months for the outcome of the trial. The court ruled that he remained a slave and authorized his owner to send him to the West Indies for sale, but before she could do so he escaped, left Denmark, and eventually sailed to Iceland.[73] Well into the nineteenth century there were many islands, coves, and ports around the Atlantic where men could evade detection or capture.

In the eighteenth century, deserters from the French navy could be punished with lifelong service as rowers in galleys, while in the Dutch and British navies deserters could hang.[74] Those punishments were rarely inflicted, however, because sailors who absconded were difficult to find and the threat of lifelong bondage or execution had the counterproductive effect of keeping men from returning to their ships. A more effective tactic was to withhold their pay. In 1666 Barlow waited impatiently while naval commissioners boarded his ship to distribute money. Like the rest of the crew he was owed for eighteen months' service, but the commissioners gave them only half of what was due, "paying us nine months' pay and keeping nine more in hand for fear of our running away from the ship."[75] In the eighteenth century the British navy adopted a policy of never paying sailors in foreign ports. For that reason, men who saw action off Havana in October 1748 were left unpaid until June 1749. Others waited much longer. Crews who served at Cartagena in 1741 were still petitioning for compensation in 1750.[76]

Poorly paid, frequently cheated, and vulnerable, sailors often stayed together between periods at sea. They congregated in dense urban neighborhoods with cheap accommodation. In Seville they crowded into boarding houses called *coralles*, large enough for a hundred sailors at a time along with their family members, if they had any. There were dozens of coralles in Seville, most of them near the docks.[77] In eighteenth-century Boston, mariners similarly stayed near the waterfront. They came and went and could not as a group be classed as permanent residents, but at any given time they could be 10 percent of the city's population.[78] Sailors came from many countries and spoke different languages. Their ability to disappear into dockside districts frustrated naval commanders. For sailors in sixteenth-century Spain, serving in the West Indies fleet was the cheapest way to travel to the colonies. Sailors routinely deserted as soon as their ships reached the Americas, though this violated immigration restrictions and the terms of their enlistments.[79]

With many of them already living beyond the reach of the law, sailors frequently attracted predators. Thieves roamed waterside districts, along with loan sharks, gamblers, prostitutes, and others coaxing men to give up money.[80]

Immersed in this environment, sailors themselves often committed crimes. Some supplemented their income by trafficking in merchandise. Carrying small parcels around the Atlantic was not intrinsically illegal, but in ports and along some coasts communities of traffickers hid from customs officials and tax collectors, as small-scale commerce integrated sailors into an array of networks including smugglers and others operating at the margins of legitimate commerce.[81] Some sailors formed violent criminal gangs. In the sixteenth-century Caribbean, thieving gangs of officers and sailors terrorized parts of Cuba and coastal Mexico. They committed several rapes and targeted women of African and indigenous American descent.[82] In eighteenth-century London, sailor gangs were distinguished by their clothing, but it was difficult for anyone to identify them individually, so they were rarely apprehended, tried, or punished for their crimes.[83] These circumstances gave sailors a bad reputation. In 1539 Friar Antonio de Guevara observed, "The sea is the cloak of sinners and the refuge of malefactors."[84] Slightly more sympathetic observers suggested that sailors lived double lives. The sailor could be trustworthy, cooperative and disciplined at sea, but "when he gets in port he pays it off with a vengeance, for knowing his time to be but short he crowds much in a little room, and lives as fast as possible."[85] Sailors' memoirs support the notion that they led double lives, but writers often emphasized that sailing carried them away from their original, ordered homes, rejecting the idea that they were naturally riotous on land and that shipboard life gave them needed discipline.

Describing his first departure sailing down the Thames on a warship, Barlow commented poetically, "Here hath the husband parted with the wife, the children from the loving parent, and one friend from another, which have never enjoyed the sight of one another again, some ending their days in one foreign land and some in another, and some by war and some in peace, and some by one sudden means and some by another."[86] Six years after writing these words, Barlow married. Not only was his marriage difficult because of the demands of his life at sea, but also because he married his wife after raping her. Lodging in London between voyages, Barlow noticed one of the servants in the house where he was staying, a woman named Mary Symons, in bed. According to his journal he "got on in to her bed and surprising her once being quite unknown to her and much against her will for indeed she was asleep but being gotten in to the bed I could not easily be persuaded out again." Barlow sailed away, but when he next returned to England, she sent him a letter asking to see him. At their meeting, "she told me that she was with child of me and weeping most pitifully and saying she was undone and did not know where to go or where to turn herself if I denied to marry her." Barlow was surprised. In his journal he wrote, "I take God to witness I did not enter her body although I did attempt something in that nature, but it seemed she had conceived by what I had done." He agreed that they should marry even though several of his "acquaintances and friends" told him he should not accept a wife so poor. Three days after the wedding he sailed off on an eight-month voyage to Jamaica. His new wife Mary Barlow moved in with her father in Gloucestershire.[87]

Much of the drama in Coxere's life centered on his efforts to return to his mother and father and, after he married, his struggle to stay in contact with his wife and son. Sailors' wives did not always endure the violence that Mary Symons experienced, but even in the absence of attack they often suffered from their husbands' transience and long absences. An advertisement published in the *Pennsylvania Gazette* in 1768 vaguely hints at marital alienation. In the ad, John Ross disowned his wife and absolved himself of marital responsibility. He cited "her conduct during my absence the last two voyages beyond sea" and declared that she had "forfeited all my future connection with, or regard for her."[88] Compared to Mary Barlow, Ross's wife may have been less encumbered. The ad does not mention any children.

Some men went to sea to escape conventional family life and were happy to live almost exclusively in the company of men. Only one-quarter of the sailors in the eighteenth-century British navy were married.[89] Outside of religious orders, no other work separated men so radically from women. As one writer in the eighteenth century observed, the sailor had "the least occasion of any man living" for a wife, "for he has everything made and dressed to his hand, and he that cannot be his own laundress is no sailor."[90] Sailors also sometimes had sex with each other, though this was against naval regulations. The British navy punished sodomy with death. In 1761, less than a month after he enlisted in the British navy, a boy named Thomas Finley was hanged for engaging in homosexual sex.[91] Sailors' shipboard sex is difficult to study, let alone quantify, because the only evidence that survives emerges from a community wracked by violence, where men were subject to severe and quickly administered punishment and everyone had to be careful what they said.[92]

The peculiar circumstances of the sailors' lives encouraged many men to conceal many features of their lives, and not just with regard to sex. Coercive pressures and widespread suspicion led sailing men to hide their origins and reinvent themselves, obscuring their own histories and character. Sailors were widely distrusted.[93] Anyone who crossed borders, shifted allegiances, and lingered in contested territories was likely to face scrutiny, and sailors were subjected to particular skepticism because they traveled farther than others, and there was often only poor communication between the places they went. Often no one knew for certain where they had been.

In his autobiography, published in 1557, German sailor Hans Staden wrote that he had left his home ten years earlier, traveling first to Holland before proceeding to Portugal.[94] He left home because he wanted to sail to the other side of the world, but when he arrived in Lisbon the India fleet had already departed. Unable to sail to Asia, and unable to speak Portuguese, he found a German-speaking innkeeper who helped him enlist as a gunner on a ship bound for Brazil. Sailing under a Portuguese flag, the ship was licensed to attack other European ships off the Atlantic coast of Africa and French vessels trading in American waters. Staden saw action against a Spanish merchant vessel on the coast of Africa. His ship seized a pirate vessel in the Atlantic near the Azores and exchanged fire with a French vessel in the waters off Brazil. After landing Staden fought alongside Portuguese colonists and enslaved African warriors in a battle against indigenous Brazilians. By the time his ship returned to Lisbon he had de-cided to go to Spain and sail from there to the Spanish American colonies. After making his way to Seville on board an English ship, he enlisted on a Spanish warship bound for the Rio de la Plata. In 1549 he crossed the Atlantic again, this time in a convoy of three warships. Buffeted by storms, the ships were separated and struggled to reunite. After reaching South America one of the ships sank in a harbor, and another was wrecked. Staden found himself stranded on the coast of Brazil without any prospect of returning to Spain. In 1554, along with some other surviving crew members including at least one man from France, he made his way to the Portuguese colonial settlement at São Vicente where he enlisted as a soldier for Portugal. Staden's Portuguese commanders sent him with three other men to garrison a blockhouse on an island near the coast of Brazil. None of the other men were Portuguese. They survived by hunting and foraging as well as trading with local Tupinikin people for food. After four years on the coast Staden had mastered the Tupi-Guarani language.

One day, according to Staden's autobiography, Tupinamba warriors ambushed him on the mainland. They brought him to their camp and told him that their gods had directed them to capture and execute a Portuguese. Upon hearing this, Staden pled for his life. He was German and had never been Portuguese, he contended, and the people of his homeland were allied with the French, who were the Tupinambas' principal European trading partners. To test him the warriors introduced him to a Frenchman, but when the man spoke French Staden could not understand him. When asked about this, Staden told his captors, "I have been so long out of my country that I have forgotten my lan-guage."[95] According to Staden's description of this encounter, he was thinking fast and talking strategically, omitting distracting details and seeking to convey a simple, exculpatory message. The answer he gave his interrogators, that he had lost the language of the country of his birth, spoke to a sense of alienation shared by many sailors around the Atlantic world.

A few weeks later Staden was ransomed. He made his way to Germany where he was "examined and questioned on all points concerning his shipwreck and imprisonment."[96] He had lived with Tupinamba warriors for four months, and he had to explain how he had survived among them when others they had captured were killed. Once again he had to defend himself. To prove his innocence and distance himself from the warriors, in his autobiography Staden suggested that he had always been extraordinarily calm and clever, and he described the Tupinamba as negatively as he could. He reported that they had threatened not just to kill him but to eat him, and he described their cannibalism in exquisite detail. Staden's account of cannibalism fascinated European readers in the sixteenth century, and it is important for historians because of its was influence, but many scholars warn that Staden was a practiced storyteller and he may have been lying, or at least embellishing his narrative, to protect himself.[97]

The less well-known story of Nicolás Covoh raises similar interpretive issues. Covoh was Mayan and, according to testimony he gave to a Spanish colonial court, he was born in the center of the Yucatán peninsula. As a young man he moved to the coast of the Gulf of Mexico where he supported himself, his wife, and his daughter by fishing. He shared a small boat with another Mayan man named Francisco Can. In 1661 he and Can were forced onboard a French sailing ship. The Frenchmen seized their boat and carried the two fishermen to Tortuga where, according to Covoh's testimony, they were put to work. Covoh and Can fished for French masters. They met buccaneers on Tortuga who taught them to use firearms, and in 1666 they boarded a sailing ship and participated in a large-scale raid on the South American mainland. Upon their return to the island they were freed from their masters. Covoh made no attempt to return to his family in Yucatán, but instead continued to sail with buccaneers. In 1668 he was captured and brought to trial in Nicaragua.

Covoh's testimony provides insight into the lives of buccaneers and indigenous sailors in the seventeenth-century Caribbean, but his story also raises difficult questions. Did he try to craft his testimony to win over his interrogators in Nicaragua?[98] Covoh told the court that he left his original family behind in Yucatán, and eventually acquired an African woman on Tortuga as a slave. His claims concerning her require particular caution. His intentions toward her are unclear. He reported that he lived in a small house with her along with Can, a third indigenous American man, and several other enslaved people. Covoh said that he began to worry that the African woman was vulnerable to attack, and so he moved her out of the house for her own safety.[99] Tortuga was unusual in many ways in the 1660s, but the sexual dynamics that apparently worried Covoh were common across the Caribbean. When Covoh took the woman to his house, is it plausible that he was unaware of the threats she would face? Covoh presented himself as an innocent, and his aim in providing this testimony was to absolve himself from blame. Recounting his experiences over the previous seven years, he pleaded for leniency by insisting that he had been repeatedly coerced and fooled, and lost control of his life.

This was a common complaint among sailors in the early modern Atlantic world. They risked a seemingly endless array of apparently random misfortunes. Their ships had to pass through darkness and fog, negotiate winds, currents, tides, and waves, and evade shallows and rocks. Even merchant and fishing vessels were vulnerable to attack. Sailors risked injury from shot, blades, or shrapnel, and also from swinging booms, entangling ropes, trips, and falls. In the sixteenth century, the Spanish West Indies fleet kept a record of the scars on the faces, hands, and bodies of its sailors for identification purposes. One register listed two thousand men, half of whom had been wounded. The rate of injury among eighteenth-century sailors in the waters off North America may have been higher.[100] Additionally, sailors were at the mercy of provisioners. No one on board a ship had any choice but to eat what was supplied, and sailors frequently died of thirst, starvation, or disease. In 1746 thousands of French sailors died after falling sick or going hungry when their provisions began to spoil midway through a transatlantic voyage. The captain of the *Castor*, one of the ships in that fleet, was desperate to provide for his ailing crew of 188 men and began attacking, boarding, plundering, and sometimes sinking fishing vessels and other small ships off Newfoundland just to seize their water, biscuit, fish, and cattle.[101] When typhus struck a French fleet in 1757, more than ten thousand sailors fell ill. Most of them were discharged to recover or die on their own, but more than a thousand died while still in French service.[102] During that same year, according to British admiralty records, very few sailors in the Royal Navy were killed in combat or died from combat-related wounds, but 130 drowned, 169 died in sick quarters, 1,425 died in hospitals, and 776 were listed simply as having "died on board ship."[103]

Faced with such uncertain and potentially bleak prospects, sailors often concluded that mysterious forces controlled their lives. As a group they were seldom reputed to be religious, but their rituals, memoirs, letters, and behavior in times of crisis suggest that many of them believed that angels, saints, the God of the Bible, and perhaps other gods determined their fates. In 1586 the Inquisitor General of Mexico made a list of prayers spoken by sailors which he thought should be banned. The prayers were fervent and specific, but from the perspective of the inquisitor they failed to express sufficient fidelity and obedience to the Church. One prayer was directed to Saint Clare and asked "That she be pleased to give us clear skies night and day and bring us good weather and keep us from bad shoals, and bad fleets, and bad company, and that she be pleased to bring us safely to a good harbor. Our Father, Ave Maria." Another read, "Saint Nicholas, be pleased to guard our keel, our tiller, our bridge, and the rigging that extends beyond the rail and inside the ship."[104] There was nothing unusual or deviant about pleading for help from a divine power, but in contrast to the sanctioned prayers spoken by imperial promoters and government officials, the sailors' prayers operated on an intimate scale and did not subordinate the immediate concerns of sailing men to the higher causes championed by their captains, the Spanish Empire, or God.[105] The sailors made no assumptions about God's ultimate purpose in directing events, nor did they express any certainty about the long-term future.

Life on the water may have affected the sailors' perception of God's role in human affairs, leading them to question whether he was methodical, consistent, or purposeful in dispensing his favors.[106] The ocean does not run simply in one direction, nor does the course of events for those who sail. Along with chaos at sea, many sailors experienced disorder on land. Family catastrophes put boys on the road, and chance encounters with naval recruiters brought them onto warships. Given the pervasive violence of life on the Atlantic, young sailors knew that they risked warfare when they boarded a ship. The whims of private ship captains could lead them into combat. The crews of most of the ships that went to war on the Atlantic included some men who had enlisted

Fig. 2.5 The Mataro ship model, c.1470. Votive ship models like this were donated to churches across Europe as prayers for the protection of particular ships and their crews. Maritiem Museum, Rotterdam.

to fight and others who had been carried on board by force or arrived as a result of personal misfortune or happenstance. A large portion of the crew had
no prior interest in the outcome of the struggle their captain was engaged in.
Before going aboard, they had had no reason to pick a side in the battles they
were now expected to fight.

3

Combat at Sea

In 1609, two canoes, one manned by armed warriors and the other by paddlers and Munsee traders, approached Henry Hudson's ship the *Halve Maen* off the coast of North America. The traders gestured to indicate that they wanted to barter for knives. Hudson's men were suspicious. They allowed only two un-armed Munsee men on board their ship and then took them hostage. The men remaining in the canoes paddled away, but they returned later that day with two new men to take the place of the original captives. The men on the *Halve Maen* agreed to the exchange, but after it was accomplished one of the new hostages jumped overboard. The crew held onto their remaining hostage until they were satisfied that the Munsee party would leave them alone.[1]

Three weeks later, upriver, the men of the *Halve Maen* were less cautious and invited several people on deck. Londoner Robert Juet, a member of the crew, recorded what happened.

> The people of the Mountaynes came aboord us, wondering at our ship and weapons. We bought some skinnes of them for Trifles. This after-noon, one Canoe kept hanging under our sterne with one man in it which we could not keepe from thence, who got up by our Rudder to the Cabin window, and stole out my Pillow, and two shirts, and two Bandoleeres. Our Master's Mate shot at him, and strooke him in the brest, and killed him. Whereupon all the rest fled away, some in their Canoes, and so leapt out of them into the water. We manned our Boat, and got our things againe. Then one of them that swamme got hold of our Boat, thinking to overthrow it. But our Cooke took a Sword, and cut off one of his hands, and he was drowned.[2]

Juet and the other men of the *Halve Maen* had learned a lesson, that the coasts of North America were dangerous. The Munsee men had learned something equally important. Ships capable of crossing the ocean were difficult to board. In some times and places, for example off the coast of West Africa in the fifteenth

Atlantic Wars. Geoffrey Plank, Oxford University Press (2020). © Oxford University Press.
DOI: 10.1093/oso/9780190860455.001.0001

century, warriors in canoes firing arrows and throwing javelins were capable of
driving sailing vessels away.[3] But paddling to a ship, climbing onto the deck in
the face of hostile fire, subduing the crew, and taking control of the vessel was
a formidable challenge. There are few accounts from anywhere in the Atlantic
world of warriors using canoes to seize sailing ships.[4]

In 1657 off the Canary Islands, Thomas Lurting, an officer on a ship called
the *Bristol*, took part in a large-scale, coordinated attack on a Spanish fleet which
had just crossed the ocean with treasure from the Caribbean. During the battle
he left the *Bristol* and tried to board a Spanish galleon he saw anchored near a
castle. He knew that boarding a sailing vessel from a smaller craft was difficult.
He thought the Spanish ship had been left unmanned.

> I took the Long-Boat to go on Board a Galeon, that lay on Shoar near to
> another Castle, supposing that the Men were not on Board; but there
> were some, and they lay close on Board, until we came two or three
> Ships length of them, and then they rose up and fir'd several Guns at us;
> but being so near the Ship, all their Shot went over us. . . . Then on our
> return towards our Ship, they from several Castles and Breast-works,
> fired briskly at us with great and small Shot, which came very near us;
> notwithstanding we all got safe on Board our own Ship.

The most effective way to board a sailing ship was from a vessel of comparable
size. The French privateers who attacked Spanish vessels in the Caribbean in the
1520s and 1530s ran directly to the side of the targeted ship, leaped or crossed
over on ropes or bridges, and engaged the Spanish in combat on deck.[5] A manual
for naval warfare published in Mexico in 1587 advised captains to bombard a
targeted ship before firing grappling hooks and chains. Men would then haul the
chains tight to pull the ships together, and combat would proceed on deck. In
anticipation of battle, the attacking warship's crew would be armed with knives,
swords, and pistols. Half the men would serve as the boarding party, while the
remainder stayed behind to defend their own ship.[6]

Warships in the seventeenth century were designed and equipped to impede
boarding. The ships carried netting to entangle any men who tried to scale their
sides. Raised decks, fore and aft, served as platforms for firing down on attackers.[7]
Many ships used grating for sections of the deck, allowing the defending crew
to hide but still see the attackers above.[8] The ship's architecture and equipment
gave the defenders some advantages, but for both sides, fighting on shipboard
was likely to be chaotic and costly. Men slashed and shot at each other at close
range and sometimes used incendiary weapons to set fire to the deck and other
wooden structures. Few sailors could swim, so any attempt to escape overboard
was risky.

One way to comprehend the naval history of the early modern era is to recognize the hazards of boarding and trace the efforts of naval planners and officers to find other means of combat. Beginning in the early sixteenth century, after guns were first mounted on the decks of sailing ships, there was a perceptible, steady progression toward an era when talented ship captains could evade hostile fire and direct the destruction of opposing vessels from a distance with impunity.[9] While this chapter will recount that progress, there is more to the story of naval warfare than that. Ships left unmanned and unguarded could always be commandeered, and ships under sail could be seized from the inside by people already on board including crew members, captives, and guests. Even though boarding for combat began to decline in the sixteenth century, seamen continued to fight on deck to defend their ships. A great deal was at stake in those battles. Mutinies and shipboard rebellions among the enslaved challenged the authority and interests of ship captains and the empires they served, the developing norms of naval combat, and the pretense of imperial order across the Atlantic world.

———

One obvious way to destroy a wooden ship is to set it on fire. The Great Armada the Spanish sent to attack England in 1588 carried thousands of clay pots packed with gunpowder which were designed to be lit by a fuse and then launched onto the deck of an opposing vessel. The firepots could be thrown by hand, tied to a rope and hurled, or sent airborne with a sling.[10] Another common way to set a ship aflame was to sacrifice a ship of one's own, set it on fire, and release it to drift toward the opposing fleet. In 1688 Wabanaki warriors constructed a specially designed floating "Firework," or raft, "about Eighteen or Twenty foot square." They "fill'd it up with Combustible matter, which they Fired; and then they set it in the way, for the *Tide* now to Flote it up" toward a fleet of New England ships.[11] Their effort failed because a contrary wind blew up, keeping the "firework" from the ships until the waves extinguished the flames. Fireships worked more reliably when they were manned. From the 1630s forward, the French navy loaded fireships with incendiary material and employed specially skilled crews to sail the vessels close to their targets. The crew members would then set fire to their own vessel, leap off, and attempt a hasty retreat by boat.[12] This tactic was adopted by several European navies. Fireship crews also sometimes boarded targeted ships to set them on fire. In 1657, after his adventure in the longboat, Lurting sailed in a small vessel he called a "pinnace" with the intention of setting fire to three Spanish ships. His ship "fir'd a Gun, and in the smoak thereof we got on Board the Galleon, receiving no harm (the *Spaniards* having left them), and I instantly set one of them on Fire, which burnt the other two Galleons."[13]

Lurting and his crew were fortunate. Admiral Edward Vernon's instructions for British fireship crews in the Caribbean in 1740 provide a sense of the challenges such men faced. Vernon warned the men they would be punished if they neglected their duty, and he promised them extra compensation if they performed well. He told them to be alert for opportunities. If they saw a Spanish ship with damaged rigging, they were to close in on it quickly to set it on fire. He also called on them to intervene if they saw a British ship "overbourne by a superior force of the enemy's." In those situations, they were to navigate up and "burn such ships of the enemy's as press hardest upon them." Vernon indicated that he would have liked to direct the fireships' actions with flag signals, but he knew "it can't be expected, you should be able to discern such signals through the cloud of smoke we may be in." Therefore, the crews had to act on their own initiative. He separately ordered the captains of other ships to rescue the fireship crews from the conflagrations they started by pulling them from the water.[14]

Given that fireships and other incendiary devices were always risky to deploy, from the sixteenth century on, naval planners preferred to rely on artillery shot to damage, disable, or sink ships by force of impact. In 1588, Pedro Coco

Fig. 3.1 Incendiary grenade, or firepot, found in the wreck of the *Trinidad Valencera*, a ship of the 1588 Spanish Armada. National Museums, Northern Ireland.

Calderón witnessed the seemingly relentless bombardment of the flagship *San Martin* in the English Channel.

> The enemy attacked our flagship with a great fusillade from seven in the morning, which lasted for more than nine hours, and on the starboard side fired so many shot that more than two hundred struck the sails and the flank of the hull, killing and wounding many men; and they caused the loss of three great guns, knocking them from their carriages so that they could no longer serve, and they tore through much of the rigging, and from the shot which pierced the waterline, the galleon was taking in so much sea that two divers could hardly mend the leaks, working at it with tow and lead plates and working both pumps all day and night.[15]

One strike was seldom enough to disable or sink a ship. The English failed to sink the *San Martin*, due to technological challenges that would preoccupy naval architects for years to come. In the seventeenth century, shipyards across Europe produced specialized warships that grew progressively larger, more stable, and sturdier, to provide platforms for more cannons and to make the hulls strong enough to withstand repeated bombardment.

The widespread adoption of heavy artillery affected the experience of combat. When ships fought with cannons, crews risked personal injury and death from shot and shrapnel. They additionally faced the danger of damage to the vessel. To cover their own flight and disable their opponents, ship captains often ordered their men to fire when their side of the ship was rolling upward, to aim for their adversaries' rigging; but if they were confident of their own superior strength they were likely to target the opposing ships' hulls at the waterline.[16] Damage to the rigging could leave a ship drifting, but if the hull was breached the entire crew could drown. With the rise of heavy artillery, self-preservation became a team effort involving dozens of men with specialized tasks. The fate of every fighter individually depended on the fortunes of the ship.

In August 1759, off the coast of Portugal, Olaudah Equiano served on the British flagship *Namur* at the Battle of Lagos. "My station during the engagement was on the middle-deck," he later wrote, "where I was quartered with another boy, to bring powder to the aftermost gun." Equiano "had to go through nearly the whole length of the ship" to get the powder. "I expected therefore every minute to be my last; especially when I saw our men fall so thick about me; but, wishing to guard as much against the dangers as possible, at first I thought it would be safest not to go for the powder till the Frenchmen had fired their broadside, and then, while they were charging, I could go and come with the powder; but immediately afterward I thought this caution was fruitless."[17]

Both Equiano and Lurting thanked God for allowing them to survive naval combat, and in that regard they both believed that their destinies were beyond their control. But Equiano, in contrast to Lurting, thought his fate was inescapably tied to that of his ship. For a brief instant, he thought about timing his actions to minimize the personal risk he was facing, but he quickly realized that there was no point in running, no point in even ducking when the French opened fire. No matter what he did, he remained exposed to shrapnel, and if God had willed it he would have burned and drowned along with everyone else on the *Namur*.

Artillery battles between ships were completely different from skirmishes involving fireships or battles on deck where seamen struggled face-to-face against their adversaries. By contrast, when ships ran against each other to inflict damage, or fired cannons at each other, opponents were separated by their hulls and the water. Equiano knew that he was fighting the French, but he did not mention any individual Frenchmen in his account of the Battle of Lagos.

In November 1759 off the coast of France, William Spavens was a crewman below deck on the British ship *Vengeance* at the Battle of Quiberon Bay. His account of the action is almost devoid of human actors other than ship captains. He describes the ships moving at their captains' directions, maneuvering, opening fire, securing triumph, or foundering.

> At fifteen past two o'clock in the afternoon, Sir John Bentley in the *Warspight* of 74 guns, being come alongside the *Formidable* of 80 guns, (their Rear Admiral's ship) the engagement commenced. . . . When the *Warspight* had exchanged a few broadsides, she shot a-head, and gave place to the *Revenge,* and she to the *Dorsetshire,* &c, each ranging alongside the next ship in the enemy's rear. . . . The *Superb* being fighting her lee guns, was taken in a squall, filled, and went down. A little after, the *Thesee* also sunk alongside the *Magnanimie,* and the *Formidable* struck to the *Resolution,* which caused great confusion in the enemy's fleet. . . .

In Spavens's description of the battle, sailors appeared only after the fighting ended, as if they emerged out of the gun smoke and sea spray. Spavens writes that on the *Formidable,* "most of her officers, and a great part of her crew, both seamen and mariners" were killed. "Our boat took up four of the men belonging to the *Thesee*; the rest, together with all or most of the *Superb*'s crew, amounting to about 1,650, perished. The ships going down in about fifteen fathoms of water, only their mast heads were to be seen; and we could perceive several of their dead men in the tops, and hanging amongst the shrouds and rigging."[18]

It was not just the physical distance between ships, or alienation between warring parties, that led sailors to view naval battles as struggles between vessels rather than men. Success in such engagements required extraordinary teamwork and the suppression of ego. Sailors had to concentrate on their assigned tasks to survive. We will never know fully what happened below deck on the ships that sank at Quiberon Bay. Summarizing the action, one French officer suggested that the French had displayed great courage, but also disobedience, ignorance, confusion, and ineptitude. Watching the French ships from a distance, a British chaplain came to similar conclusions. The British would have been in trouble, he wrote, "if the enemy had preserved any degree of composure, or fired with any sort of direction, but their confusion was so great, that of many hundreds of shot, I do not believe that more than thirty or forty struck the ship."[19]

Equiano's account of the Battle of Lagos highlights both the effort involved in maintaining focus and the risks entire ships faced if sailors failed to attend to their specific tasks. During the battle he struggled against distraction as he saw men around him "dashed to pieces, and launched into eternity." When he saw his master wounded he wanted to go by his side, "but though I was much alarmed for him and wished to assist him I dared not leave my post." Equiano continued carrying powder to his cannon, but when he unloaded the cartridge boxes he discovered that he and his mate had an additional, unexpected task to perform to avoid "blowing up the ship." The boxes were rotten and spilled gunpowder onto the deck. Despite the danger this presented, Equiano kept supplying the cannon, and the gunner kept firing. They frantically doused the spilled powder with water to prevent an explosion.[20]

If they were following orders, everyone on board a warship during a battle stayed focused on assigned tasks. This was particularly true for low-ranking sailors like Equiano who were charged with servicing cannon, but increasingly in the seventeenth and eighteenth centuries even ship commanders believed that they should operate in an orderly, almost mechanical fashion as part of a fleet.

In 1639 the Spanish assembled a large armada designed for action off the coast of the Netherlands. They were overt about their intentions and seemed to invite the Dutch to engage them in a large-scale battle. Accepting the challenge, a Dutch fleet confronted the Spanish off the eastern coast of England. Initially the Spanish had more ships than the Dutch, but the captains of the Dutch ships were more effective in coordinating their actions. Boasting about the operation afterward, the Dutch commander Maarten Harpertszoon Tromp recited a speech that he claimed to have given to his captains at a council before the battle commenced.

> The other ships which you see sailing about in disorder merely increase the numbers of the Enemy and not his force; and since they only serve to increase their confusion, the more of them that you find the surer you will be of victory. Withal I say that if with the eleven ships which we have here, we wish to give battle to the seventy which we see before

us, it will appear rash, but if we of these eleven, can make one single
ship, then those who form such an unwieldly monster, if they attack us,
they will be the rash ones; for who in his senses would try to attack an
unbreakable rock defended by the five hundred cannon which we have
amongst us?[21]

Tromp is credited with promoting the "line ahead," the tactic of aligning the
ships in a fleet stern-to-bow, so that all of the ships' broadside guns face in the
same two directions. In the abstract, this approach to naval warfare brought
discipline to a new level. As Tromp described it, even the ships' commanders
surrendered their autonomy. The entire fleet became, in effect, "one single ship"
with devastating firepower.

Prior to this innovation, ship captains who intended to bombard opposing
vessels usually tried to strike fast and escape. They sailed into action firing from
the bow, moved past broadside to allow the cannons on one side of their ship to
fire, and then pivoted to bring the cannons in the stern and the remaining side
of the ship into action. Once they had accomplished this maneuver, they pulled
away to a safe distance for reloading.[22] Ships operated autonomously, or if they
coordinated their actions it was simply by following the leader. Attacking ships
entered the skirmish in turns.

Naval tactics changed after 1639, but in practice the line ahead was neither
as simple to execute nor as decisive as Tromp suggested. Problems on board any
ship, a breakdown of discipline, or a mishap like Equiano's spilled powder, could
disable or destroy a vessel and break the line. Navigational challenges, such as
coping with shifting winds, currents, and unknown shallows, made keeping in
line difficult.[23] Communication presented a formidable challenge. It was not always possible for admirals to deliver detailed battle instructions in person, as
Tromp did to at least some of his ship captains. Indeed, even at the Battle of the
Downs, Tromp's original forces were reinforced by scores of additional Dutch
vessels whose captains had not heard of his plan and did not hold to his line.
Their initiative and success, operating outside the line, helped secure the Dutch
victory.[24] To facilitate coordination between ships, the French navy pioneered
elaborate signaling systems, with various colored and patterned flags delivering
different commands depending on the masts they flew from. But high seas, bad
weather, and smoke impeded visibility, and in some large-scale battles the ships
spread out toward the horizon beyond sight of each other. Furthermore, even
if flag signals could be relayed to all the ships in a fleet, by the time the captains
received their instructions the circumstances of the battle might have changed.
Commenting on these problems in 1799, Horatio Nelson suggested that rather
than complying with detailed orders ship captains should ask themselves, "What
would my superiors direct, did they know what is passing under my nose?"[25]

The communication problem was just one of many challenges naval commanders faced fighting on immense, unpredictable bodies of water. Navigation could be difficult on any sea, but the expanse of the Atlantic, with its oceanic winds and currents, heightened the challenge. As early as 1503, in

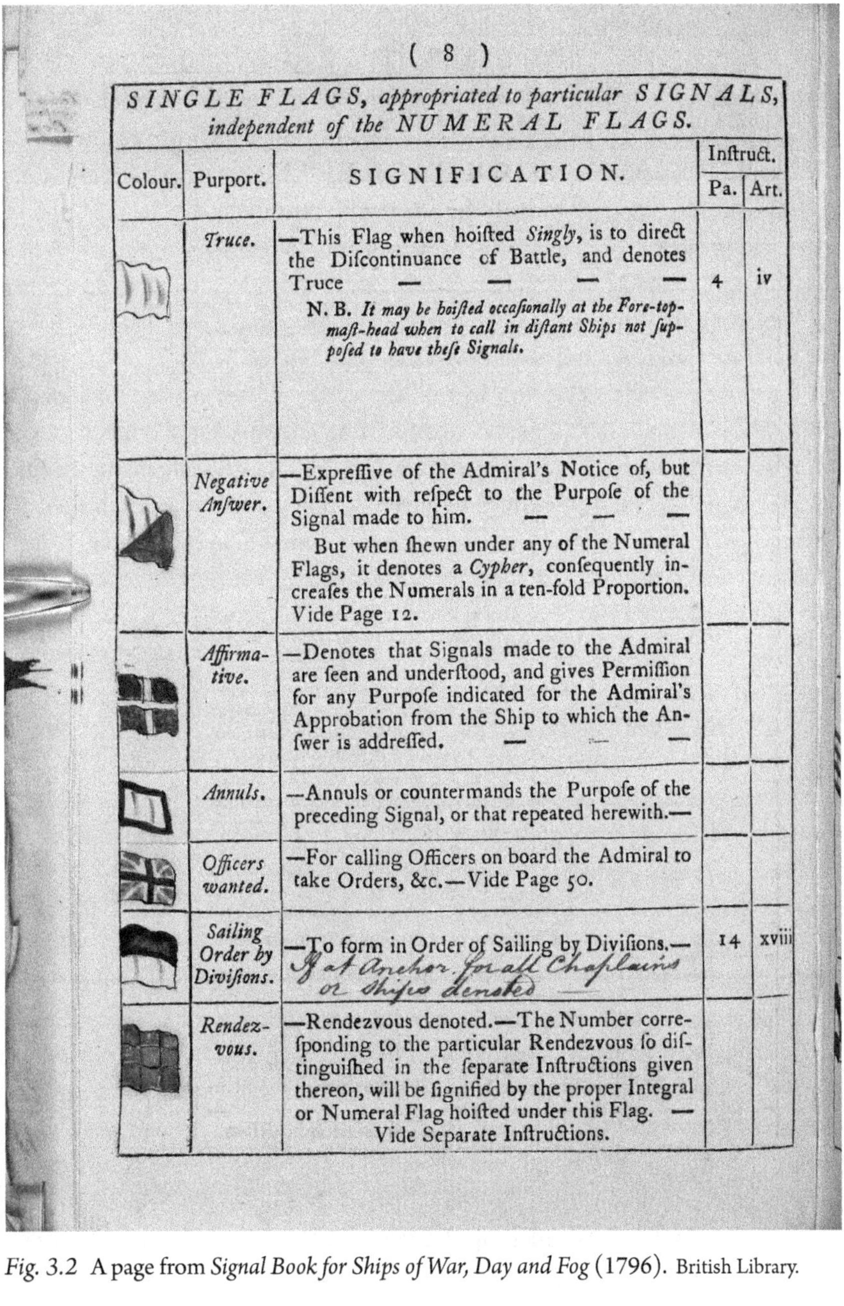

(8)

SINGLE FLAGS, appropriated to particular SIGNALS, independent of the NUMERAL FLAGS.				
Colour.	Purport.	SIGNIFICATION.	Inftruct. Pa.	Art.
	Truce.	—This Flag when hoifted *Singly*, is to direct the Difcontinuance of Battle, and denotes Truce — — — — N. B. *It may be hoifted occafionally at the Fore-top-maft-head when to call in diftant Ships not fuppofed to have thefe Signals.*	4	iv
	Negative Anfwer.	—Expreffive of the Admiral's Notice of, but Diffent with refpect to the Purpofe of the Signal made to him. — — — But when fhewn under any of the Numeral Flags, it denotes a *Cypher*, confequently increafes the Numerals in a ten-fold Proportion. Vide Page 12.		
	Affirma-tive.	—Denotes that Signals made to the Admiral are feen and underftood, and gives Permiffion for any Purpofe indicated for the Admiral's Approbation from the Ship to which the Anfwer is addreffed. — — —		
	Annuls.	—Annuls or countermands the Purpofe of the preceding Signal, or that repeated herewith.—		
	Officers wanted.	—For calling Officers on board the Admiral to take Orders, &c.—Vide Page 50.		
	Sailing Order by Divifions.	—To form in Order of Sailing by Divifions.— *If at Anchor for all Chaplains or Ships denoted*	14	xviii
	Rendez-vous.	—Rendezvous denoted.—The Number correfponding to the particular Rendezvous fo diftinguifhed in the feparate Inftructions given thereon, will be fignified by the proper Integral or Numeral Flag hoifted under this Flag. — Vide Separate Inftructions.		

Fig. 3.2 A page from *Signal Book for Ships of War, Day and Fog* (1796). British Library.

recognition of the importance and difficulty of navigating the Atlantic, the Spanish crown established the *Casa de la Contratación* in Seville to regulate trade with the West Indies. Among its many functions, the *Casa* authorized and distributed sea charts that pulled together observations and navigational advice from dozens of pilots who had crossed the ocean. Some of these charts were huge, as wide as two meters, and provided compass directions for crossing hundreds of miles of sea. Other, smaller charts conveyed more localized, detailed knowledge. The charts were state secrets. Spanish pilots took an oath not to show their charts to foreigners, but in the meantime rival royal courts developed their own charts, and as the sixteenth century progressed the various kingdoms of Europe competed to recruit men with navigational skills and knowledge.[26] The race to perfect and control navigation continued through the eighteenth century and included Britain's celebrated program to establish a reliable gauge of longitude.[27] Throughout the early modern period, ship captains had difficulty pinpointing their own positions, but even when they managed do so with reasonable accuracy they had no reliable way to locate rival ships and fleets beyond the horizon.

Ships could evade detection in the immensity of the ocean. This was a problem for commanders seeking confrontation and presented opportunities for those who might have been outgunned in a large-scale fight. In the summer of 1778, Pierre Andre de Suffren, a captain in the French fleet in Boston Harbor, offered unsolicited advice to Admiral Charles Hector, comte d'Estaing. Suffren observed that given the relative strength of the British navy off the coast of New England, the French had "little hope for successful high-profile ventures at sea." But Suffren went on to suggest that it would be a shame if they wasted the summer. "The only way our naval forces could be put to good use would be to prepare a detachment of ships to attack Newfoundland. There would still be time to destroy their fishing trade, capture several vessels and, especially, take many prisoners."[28] Suffren recognized the value of slipping away over the horizon to launch surprise attacks. Like all the other captains of his era, he also knew that some ships were easy to find because they congregated predictably in special waters, such as those fishing off Newfoundland.

Naval battles generally occurred in places where ships could be easily found. Warships lurked in well-established sea lanes, around ports, and in rivers. In the 1620s Dutch privateers concentrated on the Brazilian coast and the shipping channels off the coast of West Africa. In 1627, Piet Heyn oversaw the capture of thirty-eight Portuguese ships off Brazil.[29] Small-scale attacks and large-scale battles tended to occur in heavily traveled places. Usually this was near the coast, and sometimes it was upriver. In 1667, toward the end of the Second Anglo-Dutch War, a Dutch fleet sailed up the River Medway near the mouth of the Thames. Finding the English fleet at anchor and poorly guarded, the Dutch deployed fireships to burn several of the largest English vessels. They also boarded and seized the flagship *Royal Charles*.[30] England's greatest naval defeat in the war thus took place on a river in Kent.

Ships on the open sea were more likely to escape. When a confrontation seemed imminent, each ship captain assessed his chances, and if he sensed his own weakness he might try to sail away. The ensuing chases could last for days. Chases tested the endurance and skill of the crews as well as the maneuverability and speed of the vessels. To lighten their crafts for the sake of speed, crews sometimes jettisoned water and other supplies, making chases across the ocean fatal, even without a shot fired.

Deception sometimes worked as an alternative to escape. It was difficult to identify ships at a distance, and when crews were too far apart to shout to each other or exchange papers, they generally relied on flags. According to standard practice, a ship's flag was a sign of its captain's authority and flew only when he was on board. It was meant to indicate that he represented his sovereign, that he held jurisdiction over his ship and crew, and that they all enjoyed the protection of the law.[31] But especially in war zones where ships frequently changed hands, a vessel might easily carry more than one flag. In 1746 Captain Augustus Hervey saw a ship he tentatively identified as a French privateer, and he judged it was

Fig. 3.3 Willem Schellinks, *Burning of the English Fleet near Chatham*, depicting the Dutch raid on the English fleet in the Medway, June 1667. Rijksmuseum, Amsterdam.

"best to decoy him." He recorded later, "I hoisted a Dutch jack, and he answered me with a Danish one; I then spread a French ensign and pennant." After he had thus falsely identified his ship as French, Hervey flew a flag signaling distress, the other ship approached, "and as soon as ever I had him under my guns I spread my English colours." After a brief exchange of fire, the other ship surrendered. Harvey confirmed the identity of his opponent only after the battle had ended. He had indeed taken a French privateer.[32]

In the face of intimidating power, surrender was always an option, but it carried its own risks. In 1480, eleven Spanish ships lay anchored off the coast of West Africa draped in white cloth in a futile effort to impede the contagion afflicting the crew. Early one morning four Portuguese ships discovered them, and as one Spanish witness remarked, "There was no need for a battle. Without a doubt four of the Portuguese vessels were able to overcome easily eleven of ours." It would have been a battle of the fit "against the sick, the armed against the defenceless, the lively against the dispirited." After the Spanish surrendered, the Portuguese took command of their vessels and sailed them up the coast to a village where they hoped to trade for gold and captives. To display their power to the Africans, they paraded the Spanish before the country's king. Three days later they divided the prisoners, placing the Basques on "two of the least service-able caravels," supplying them with "a small amount of provisions," and advising them to make their own way back to Europe. They then took the remainder of the prisoners to Grand Canary Island and confined them (according to the Spanish) "in gloomy dungeons." The prisoners suffered hunger and "daily threats of death."[33]

The fortunes of prisoners taken at sea varied depending on the needs, capacities, and whims of the victorious commanders. In 1580 when Francis Drake sailed the *Golden Hind* northward up the Atlantic coast of Africa, he seized several Spanish and Portuguese vessels. He impressed some of the crews into service on his own ship but allowed others to sail away. The *Golden Hind* was full, his own crew was overstretched, and he had no way to keep them. Drake retained his most valuable prisoner, a pilot familiar with the shipping lanes along the African coast.[34]

In the seventeenth and eighteenth centuries, a widespread perception that mariners were scarce and valuable made prisoner exchanges diffi-cult. The French navy sought cartels with the British for the exchange of naval prisoners, but British policymakers balked for fear of restaffing their opponent's fleets.[35] In the absence of exchange agreements, many French sailors who surrendered to the British were never released. During the Seven Years War the British admiralty processed 64,373 French prisoners, 8,499 of whom died in Britain. According to historian James Pritchard, it is likely that as many French sailors perished in British prisons as died in service on France's ships.[36]

The exchange of prisoners in wartime was an "ancient custom" among Europeans.[37] Both at land and at sea, implicit codes of military honor, engrained ethical norms, and the fear of mass reprisal encouraged military commanders to spare their prisoners, keep them, and negotiate for their conditional release. But naval warfare differed from warfare on land because no one drew a sharp distinction between belligerents and noncombatants at sea and the crew of any ship, whether involved in hostilities or not, could be subject to impressment. In the eighteenth century, fishermen in the English Channel complained that they had fewer rights than sailors on warships. In times of war fishermen could be seized, held against their wills, and forced into indefinite terms of military service on naval vessels.[38]

Different groups of mariners received contrasting treatment as prisoners. After a ship surrendered, the victorious commander sorted through the crew members of the captured ship to determine on a case-by-case basis whether they deserved to be included in any possible prisoner exchange. In the late seventeenth and early eighteenth centuries, the French were unlikely to be lenient toward any French Protestants found serving on British naval vessels. The British similarly sought to punish any British or Irish Jacobites they captured on French warships.[39] African sailors were in jeopardy if their ships surrendered to the French or the British in the eighteenth century, since both navies sold naval prisoners of African descent into slavery.[40]

As on land, the fate of prisoners taken at sea depended on their status, or more specifically their captor's assessment of whether they should enjoy the customary protections that were assumed to govern European warfare. But their fate also depended on the authority of their captors. In the autumn of 1682, forty men set out from Santiago de Cuba in a ship carrying sugar, tobacco, and marmalade. They sailed southward across the Caribbean with the aim of selling the produce in Cartagena. They knew they were crossing dangerous waters. Their ship was armed with twelve cannons, and the men carried pistols and swords to defend themselves in case of attack. Before they reached the coast of South America they saw three fishing ships in the distance. One of the largest, flying an English flag, approached them and opened fire. Another, flying a Dutch flag, arrived half an hour later and joined the attack. The third fishing ship flew a French flag, and when it approached, the Cubans opened fire and shattered its rigging. But ultimately the Cuban ship was overwhelmed. The Dutch ship came alongside, and its armed crew boarded. Shortly thereafter, the English ship also closed in and its crew came on board. There may or may not have been fighting on deck. The account of this incident is vague on that question, but at least two of the Cuban sailors were killed, and seven were wounded, perhaps by cannon

fire and shrapnel. The survivors surrendered. The boarding parties took command of the Cuban vessel and sailed it, with their prisoners on board, to a small
harbor on the South American mainland, where the Cubans watched while their
captors turned on each other. First the commanders of the three fishing vessels
argued, and then their crews. More than one hundred men in total joined the
dispute and took sides. They were arguing over the allocation of the captured
ship and its cargo, but their controversy had consequences for the prisoners,
since it would determine who their masters would be.[41]

There is no reason to think that any of the scores of fishermen and sailors who
joined in this squabble intended to make an ideological statement. Nonetheless,
their participation in the argument over the disposition of the Cuban ship, the
distribution of its cargo, and the allocation of new crew assignments on four
vessels demonstrated the fragility of imperial power at sea. European and colonial governments relied on privateers, but the practice continuously created
conflicts of interest, as investors, captains, and sailors sought to profit from military service. The vastness of the Atlantic and its adjoining seas and coastlines
made rigorous enforcement impossible, allowing captains and sailors to take action on their own, and redefine their contractual obligations, military duties, and
political allegiances. Most systems of military discipline maintain a distinction
between combatants and noncombatants, but in early modern naval warfare the
line separating the two was blurred and would remain so as long as fishermen
and other mariners were available for impressment into military service, and
merchantmen and fishing vessels continued to venture into battle as privateers.

For similar reasons, it was perpetually difficult to distinguish privateers
from pirates. Among the commanders of the three fishing vessels that attacked
the Cuban ship, only two had commissions for privateering. The third, according to the laws of most of the European empires, was either operating
as a subordinate officer to the other two, or working independently without
sanction or authority, as a pirate. The third captain refused to accept subordination, but in this case it hardly mattered. The three commanders had many
common interests and had been able to cooperate well at sea. They eventually reached a compromise agreeing to divide their spoils and drop off their
prisoners at the South American port of Riohacha. This was almost certainly
good news for the captives, who would be able to find work and return to
Cuba if they desired.

A few pirates, especially in the late seventeenth and early eighteenth centuries,
embraced their status as outlaws, for example by displaying pirate flags and issuing lurid threats to intimidate targeted vessels. But many others exploited the
legal ambiguities surrounding piracy. Legally, the distinction between pirates
and privateers hinged on the interpretation of vaguely worded commissions and
implicit lines of authority. Some pirates forged documents they believed they

would need, studied the law, and prepared arguments in case they might have to insist in court that they were really privateers.[42] There were some, however, who by virtue of their language, culture, and appearance, would never be able to convince anyone that they had a license from an imperial or colonial government.

In August 1725, Samuel Doty, a fisherman from Plymouth, Massachusetts, sailed his 25-ton sloop the *Tryal* into the Atlantic, heading for the shoals around Sable Island. Though he knew it would be dangerous, he stopped for water along the way on the coast of Nova Scotia. There had been fighting in and around the colony intermittently over the previous five years. Mi'kmaq warriors had taken up arms against Britain's colonial administration, and many local Acadians, descendants of French colonists, supported the Mi'kmaq emotionally and logistically. Doty was familiar with Nova Scotia and spoke both English and French, and his crew included indigenous Americans as well as colonial New Englanders. As he approached the coast, he recognized an old acquaintance, an Acadian man named Jean-Baptiste Jedre, dit Laverdure. He waved at Laverdure and invited him to come on board the *Tryal*. Laverdure accepted the invitation. He gathered four others, including a Mi'kmaq man named James Mews, two other Mi'kmaq men, and Laverdure's thirteen-year-old son, and together they paddled a canoe out to the ship. When they arrived, Doty asked them if they had any news, and Laverdure responded that there was "peace between the English and the Indians."[43] Doty cheered and invited Laverdure into his cabin for a drink.

Boarding parties seeking to take vessels intact faced a dilemma respecting the application of violence. To succeed, they needed to intimidate the crew, impose order, and claim possession of their prize.[44] They knew this would require an impressive show of force, but they did not want to sink the ship or damage it severely. The goal was to forcibly assert control of the vessel while minimizing the risk of sending valuable plunder and potential captives to the bottom of the sea. One common tactic was to cultivate the targeted crew's trust and place them in a vulnerable position, then announce abruptly that they were under attack and demand their surrender. Sometimes trust could be established simply by raising a flag signaling alliance or shared allegiance. Sometimes boarding parties gained admission by offering to trade. In Doty's case, the attackers feigned friendship. Not only did Laverdure and his companions greet Doty warmly, they invited him on shore to visit Laverdure's mother. Doty agreed, and when he went to see the woman, whom he identified as "Mrs. Giddery," he believed that he was making a social visit, but Laverdure's Mi'kmaq associates said that by the time Doty had entered Madame Guédry's house, he was already a captive.

The rest of crew of the *Tryal* faced similar confusion. Nearly all of them went on shore for water, and when they landed they were met by Mi'kmaq and Acadians who shouted, "now the English and Indians were all one brothers."[45] But when the fishermen turned back toward the sea they saw a party of Mi'kmaq

warriors paddling toward their ship. One man stood up in his canoe, fired a
musket, and cried out in English, "Now English men, call for quarter."[46] Phillip
Sachimus, an indigenous American sailor working for Doty, was the only crew
member on board when the Mi'kmaq warriors pulled up to the ship. The
boarding party climbed onto the deck and formed a circle. They talked among
themselves, and then one of them ran toward Sachimus and slashed at him
with a knife. Laverdure's son, among the boarding party, aimed a musket at
Sachimus, who was so terrified that he could not recall in detail what happened
next. The men gathered some of the ship's rope and tied Sachimus up. Then
they summoned Doty and the remaining members of his crew back to the ship.
Madame Guédry and her son Alexander accompanied Doty on his return. By
the time they arrived, Laverdure and many more Mi'kmaq men had come on
board, along with at least one Mi'kmaq woman and two of her children. Doty
reported that the men shoved him and dragged him across the deck, threatening
to kill him and any of the crew members who remained on shore. One of the
Mi'kmaq men "attempted to strike him with his hatchet" before another man
intervened to prevent the attack.[47] Other crew members were treated similarly.
The men who boarded the Tryal were careful not to injure anyone, but they also
tried to keep Doty and his crew in nearly constant terror. Eventually the entire
crew of the fishing ship complied with the demands of their captors.

Laverdure and Mews steered the Tryal away from the coast, but they had
many tasks to fulfill, so they ordered Doty and two other members of the original crew to take turns at the helm. They treated the men roughly. John Roberts
reported that during the night Laverdure woke him, called him a "son of a bitch,"
rolled him out of his hammock, and told him to steer.[48] At another moment
Mews told Roberts to bring him bread, and after Roberts brought a bag full of
biscuit, Mews "beat him around the cabin, calling him Son of a Bitch, etc."[49]
On any commandeered vessel there was likely to be tension over the preservation and allocation of water and provisions. If the Tryal had not been short of
fresh water, Doty and his crew would never have come close to Nova Scotia. But
their attackers had less to fear from such shortages since they were operating
near their homes. Doty's crew watched anxiously as Laverdure, Mews, and the
others ostentatiously consumed the ship's provisions, burning candles all night,
eating bread, butter, cheese, pork, and sugar, drinking rum and other liquor, and
smoking the fishermen's tobacco.

In stark contrast to the eighteenth-century trend in large-scale naval combat,
battles on deck were intimate. They often began with misplaced trust and
generated a furious sense of betrayal. Attackers relied on visceral terror as they
sought to intimidate their adversaries into submission. If a crew resisted, the
battle would be fought in tight quarters with weapons at close range. Men sought
refuge in dark corners, in the cabin and below deck. They grappled in darkness

and fired blindly into closed spaces. They wielded muskets, knives, axes, and clubs. In an age when large-scale naval warfare was becoming increasingly formulaic, mechanized, and anonymous, the intimate character of combat on deck contributed to the vehemence of the official reaction to incidents like the attack on the *Tryal*. There was also a widespread perception that attacks of this kind challenged European and colonial domination of the sea. After the boarding party took control of the *Tryal* it became a scene of imperial power reversed, with Mi'kmaq issuing orders and berating the English, taking full occupation of the cabin and all its amenities, and settling in comfortably, in family groups including women and children. From the colonial perspective, this was a profoundly unsettling sequence of events.

It was never clear in this case who commanded the boarding party. Laverdure, a French-speaking colonist, played an important role by gaining Doty's trust and drawing him away from the ship. After the Mi'kmaq boarding party seized control, Laverdure called himself the "skipper," took the British flag from the mast, tied it around his waist, and tucked a pistol into it. Meanwhile James Mews, the most prominent of the Mi'kmaq, took Doty's hat, placed it on his own head, and called himself the "captain." Both men gave orders to the captive crew and invited their relatives on board.

Laverdure's mother, Madame Guédry, spent several hours in the cabin of the *Tryal* eating, drinking, and smoking with the boarding party. Her account of the event indicates the complex power relations between Laverdure and his Mi'kmaq associates. She told her son that she "did not ask the Indians on board the reason why they took the sloop from the English in time of peace, because she understood some time before, they designed to take what English vessels they could, notwithstanding the peace, by way of reprisals."[50] The Mi'kmaq men who took possession of the ship wanted to hold Doty and the other fishermen hostage as in retaliation for two local Mi'kmaq warriors who were being held by New Englanders.

If this was indeed the attackers' original plan, they probably intended to bring the ship ashore in a secluded location and send a message to colonial authorities in Nova Scotia and Massachusetts demanding a prisoner exchange. But before they could enact that plan Laverdure and Mews saw another ship in the distance, and they worried that it was "English." They were having enough trouble commanding the *Tryal*. Facing attack from another ship, they were outgunned and outnumbered. Surrender was not an attractive option, because if they fell into British custody at sea they were certain to be taken to Boston for trial. They tried to maintain bravado and appear terrifying and accommodating at once. They announced to Doty that they would seize the other ship, "kill all the English Men on board," restore the *Tryal* to Doty and his crew, and sail off in their new prize.[51] Laverdure and Mews may originally have had limited objectives, but the danger

Fig. 3.4 "Captain Worsley," a pirate, depicted in *The History and Lives of all the most Notorious Pirates and their Crews* (London, 1727), 112. The axe and cutlass were common weapons for combat on deck. Library of Congress.

of their situation briefly turned them into committed outlaws, broadcasting their intention to continue raiding from ship to ship.

The distant ship turned out to be French. The Mi'kmaq maintained good relations with the French, and so the battle they feared never occurred. But soon thereafter, Doty and the other fishermen reassessed their situation, banded together and fought to regain control of the *Tryal*. They wrestled with the boarding party one man at a time. Getting hold of muskets, they fired into the cabin and provoked three men to jump overboard. The *Tryal* was miles from shore, so the men may well have drowned. Toward the end of the fight, in a last effort to avoid capture, Laverdure's son grabbed a long spike that the fishermen had used to hoist fish into the hold and tried to stab Nathaniel Sprague with it. He tore Sprague's shirt, but missed his flesh. Along with his father, grandmother, and uncle, and the Mi'kmaq men, women, and children who had boarded the vessel, the boy was confined in the hold. Doty eventually released most of his captives, but he took five, including Laverdure and his son, to Boston where they were tried, convicted, and hanged.

In the decade leading up to this incident, there was a concerted, transatlantic, international effort to eradicate piracy across the Atlantic. In Europe and the colonies, French, Dutch, Spanish, Portuguese, and British courts tried pirates and sentenced more than four hundred to hang.[52] But they could not eradicate the problem. Piracy continued in part because there were profits to be made from attacking ships, but plunder was not the only motivation for commandeering vessels.[53] Sailors rose in rebellion against their own forcible recruitment, harsh shipboard discipline, and low pay. In rising against their captains, they faced many of the same tactical challenges that the men who took the *Tryal* did, and they adopted similar solutions. They relied on ambush, issued lurid threats, and fought using axes, knives, small arms, and whatever tools were at hand. Successful mutineers risked capture and prosecution as outlaws. Therefore, like the boarding party that captured the *Tryal*, once mutineers were in possession of a ship, they often had little choice but to keep fighting other vessels. Their circumstances made them pirates.[54]

On-board attacks could threaten any ship sailing the Atlantic, but of all the captains and crews on the ocean, the men working on slaving vessels were the most vulnerable to and apprehensive of combat on deck. Jean Barbot, the master of a slaving vessel, reported, "we keep all our small arms in a readiness, with sentinels constantly at the door and avenues to it; being thus ready to disappoint any attempts our slaves might make on a sudden." Barbot's crews also meticulously disarmed their captives. "We use to visit them daily, narrowly searching every corner between decks, to see whether they have not found means, to gather any pieces of iron, or wood, or knives, about the ship, notwithstanding the great care we take not to leave any tools or nails, or other things in the way."[55] The masters of slaving vessels hired extra crew to confine and constantly guard the enslaved men and women they carried. As a result, the crews of slaving ships were generally 50 percent larger than those of other vessels of similar size.[56] Barriers sealed off sections of the deck, and chains held the captive men to the walls in the darkness below. The crews of slaving vessels often allowed captive women on deck and brought them into the cabins, which gave the enslaved opportunities to rise up. Ottobah Cugoano, carried as a slave from the coast of Africa in 1770, recalled that soon after he and the other captives had left the coast, "a plan was concerted amongst us, that we might burn and blow up the ship, and to perish altogether in the flames." According to the plan, "It was the women and the boys who were to burn the ship, with the approbation and groans of the rest." The plan faltered after one of the women, who was sleeping with a sailor, warned him before the fire could be set.[57] While sometimes enslaved women and children took action on their own in shipboard uprisings, more often they exploited their ability to manipulate their captors, roam the deck, find and conceal keys, and plan ambushes. Usually men did most of the fighting.[58]

In 1721, off the coast of present-day Ghana, three hundred captives were brought on board the *Ferrer's Galley*, a ship from London on its first slaving voyage. Most of the captives were men who knew each other well because they had recently fought together as a unit, unsuccessfully trying to defend their village against a raid. The ship's Captain Messervy was new to the slave trade. Hoping to maintain good relations with these men, he served them meals on deck. Ten days after the *Ferrer's Galley* left the coast for Jamaica, Messervy was on the forecastle among the captive men, watching as they ate boiled rice from little tubs. Then several of the men seized him and began striking him in the head with their tubs until, it was reported later, they had "beat out his brains." This was the start of a coordinated attack. The noisy assault on the captain served as a signal. Another group of men ran to the forecastle and then, in formation, charged in the direction of the stern, toward the crew on the raised quarterdeck.

In anticipation of events like this, slave ships were equipped with barricades sealing off the quarterdeck.[59] The barricade gave the crew shelter, but it was also pierced with holes for weapons in defense. The defenders thrust pikes through these holes at their attackers, and they fired muskets at the men. In this case the crew may have hoped to kill the leaders of the uprising and intimidate the others into submission. But the African men continued to rush the barricade, and the outnumbered crew had to resort to riskier, costlier fire. They loaded cannons with "partridge-shot," swiveled them until they pointed over the deck, and fired generally in the direction of the attacking men. In the end, eighty of the ship's three hundred captives were killed. Some had been pierced, some shot, and some drowned after leaping into the ocean.[60]

Many reports of shipboard uprisings like this exist. The accounts generally emphasize the long or impossible odds captives faced and suggest that their struggles were futile. The men, women, and children confined in slaving vessels almost always outnumbered the ship's crew, but they were unarmed, while the crew members were formidably equipped to fight them. When the ships were still close to the coast of Africa, a considerable number of captives escaped and

Fig. 3.5 A 1794 depiction of an uprising on board a slave ship, with the crew behind the barricade on the raised quarterdeck, firing toward the bow at the captives. From C. B. Wadstrom, *An Essay on Colonization, Particularly Applied to the Western Coast of Africa* (London, 1794). British Library.

managed to swim to shore. Captives also sometimes had allies on the coast who could support them militarily by firing at the crew from land.[61] But on the high seas, shipboard battles were desperate, if not suicidal. The women who plotted to burn the ship carrying Cugoano had no plausible way to achieve anything other than punishing their captors and ensuring their own deaths.

Through the seventeenth and eighteenth centuries, an increasingly powerful European and colonial ideology celebrated large-scale naval battles pitting ships against each other at a distance. In schematic, idealized accounts of naval war, the sea was an uninhabited battlefield. There was no permanent population of noncombatants at sea, and when ships fired at each other, the men of the opposing forces never saw each other's faces until the fight was over. The crews discharged their weapons in response to flags. Every ship functioned as a unit and sailed in a fleet operating in formation under commanders responsible to the governments of Europe, the European colonies, and after 1776, the colonies' successor states. This depersonalized vision of naval warfare reflected important technological, tactical, and ideological trends, but it failed to encompass the full range of combat at sea.

Across the Atlantic world well into the nineteenth century, battles raged frequently on the decks of ships. Huge sums of money were spent and many lives were lost defending vessels from internal violence. These shipboard battles challenged governmental authority. They had the potential to weaken Europe's naval supremacy and the stranglehold that the Europeans and their descendants held over maritime commerce. The scale of the threat varied by region. Captives who fought for their own release from slaving ships were most likely to succeed and survive near the African coast. The Wabanaki mariners who sailed the rocky inlets of Maine, New Brunswick, and Nova Scotia were familiar with the local shallows, currents, and landmarks, and their knowledge gave them an advantage over most of those who pursued them. Pirates in general had favored waters, and they thrived in places where navigation was difficult. It helped too to have supporters on the coast. Some shipboard captives off the coast of Africa received aid from the mainland. The Wabanaki sailors had help from Acadian, Mi'kmaq, and other Algonkian communities onshore. Many pirates found refuge in Cornwall, where people profited from smuggling. But the battles waged on shipboard were never sufficiently coordinated or extensive to imperil the commercial and military foundations of European and colonial power in the Atlantic world. The ships' dependence on port facilities limited the impact of piracy, mutiny, and other shipboard rebellions. Throughout the Atlantic world, any group illicitly seizing a sailing vessel was likely to have difficulty keeping the ship on the water for long. Pirates could sometimes resort to subterfuge to service their vessels, but indigenous American warriors and self-liberated African captives had nowhere to go to receive the services and equipment necessary to keep a ship afloat.

4

Ships and Military Power on Land

As weapons platforms, ships were capable of bringing dozens, or in fleets hundreds, of pieces of heavy artillery close to shore to bombard coastal fortifications, towns, and camps. Ships served as troop carriers, and with the aid of landing craft fleets could send thousands of soldiers suddenly into a zone of combat or allow them to unexpectedly land to initiate an invasion or siege. They carried reinforcements and supplies over long distances to sustain fighting forces and beleaguered colonial populations. They were also vehicles for shifting population, making it possible to remove conquered garrisons and the townspeople who supported them. Ships could be deployed to evacuate large swaths of conquered territory, transforming the cultural character of an island or an entire section of a continent.

In all these ways, ships were powerful, but they were limited in the areas they could operate effectively. As their firepower and carrying capacity increased, ships grew heavier and required deeper water for safe passage. Successful naval operations close to shore required constant attention to the depth of channels and other factors, including tides and shifts in the underwater topography. These navigational challenges could be accentuated by defensive measures taken by people on shore, including fortifications constructed on high lands overlooking deep channels leading to protected bays. If military commanders succeeded in landing men on shore, they often had difficulty communicating and coordinating with them. Large expeditionary forces frequently outnumbered the local population in the places where they landed, an imbalance that could create vexing logistical difficulties. Landing parties needed food, water, and other supplies, and even if the invaders were willing to antagonize the people of the region they invaded, their needs often outstripped the resources available in the vicinity. They needed a constant flow of new provisions and armaments. Often in large-scale operations, the arrival of thousands of soldiers disrupted local economies and led to food shortages, famines, and epidemics. Ships were the essential tools of European imperial expansion across the Atlantic, but throughout

Atlantic Wars. Geoffrey Plank, Oxford University Press (2020). © Oxford University Press.
DOI: 10.1093/oso/9780190860455.001.0001

the early modern period, European and colonial military leaders learned repeatedly through hard experience that naval supremacy did not guarantee conquest.

In 1580 the king of Portugal died, and Philip II of Spain claimed the Portuguese crown. A large Spanish army invaded Portugal to secure Philip's claim. At the same time, far from the mainland, on the Atlantic island of Terceira in the Azores, islanders held out against Spanish authority and vowed allegiance to Don Antonio, the Portuguese claimant to the throne. In 1581 forces loyal to Philip occupied and fortified another island in the Azores, São Miguel, and for the next two years the islands were a battleground. France intervened in support of Antonio, as did several powerful English privateers. Hundreds of warships and thousands of men came to join the fight. An English visitor on Terceira in 1581 reported that fifteen forts were under construction.[1] In 1582 the French brought Antonio to the islands, along with a fleet of sixty ships and seven thousand men. The Spanish responded by sending dozens of warships, twelve galleys, and sixteen thousand soldiers and sailors. This was France's largest overseas expedition in the sixteenth century, and securing the Azores became a huge investment for Spain.[2]

The Azores attracted military investment because they were important economically and strategically. Heavily armed Spanish fleets carrying gold and silver from Mexico and Peru regularly stopped at the islands for water and other provisions before proceeding to Seville. Fishing vessels, slaving ships, merchants carrying various goods across the Atlantic, pirates, and privateers came to the Azores. Court officials and imperial promoters in England and France imagined that capturing the islands would weaken Spain and eventually help break Spain's grip on the Netherlands, Portugal, and Portugal's colonies. The leaders of the French expedition in 1582 believed that after seizing the Azores their next project could be the conquest of the Cape Verde Islands, followed by Brazil.[3] They were conducting an experiment to determine whether such schemes were viable. In military terms, the French and their Spanish opponents were testing the limits of large-scale, long-distance amphibious warfare.

It went badly for the French. Soon after their fleet arrived and anchored off the island of São Miguel, the commanders with "captains of the land and sea forces" boarded boats and explored the coastline. Their initial assessment was that they had come to the wrong place. "They found that they were so near the fort, which commanded them, and was furnished with many good pieces of artillery, that it was impossible, without very evident loss, to go and fight under the fort." The officers returned to their ships "to consider some other method." Eventually they chose to land elsewhere on the island, but the landing was "very troublesome, the sea being high, so that the greater part of the boats which took the men were smashed and lost on the rocks of the coast." The men who survived had to fight Spanish soldiers as soon as they climbed on land. Eventually the Spanish retired to the safety of their fort, leaving the French who had been "knocked about and had got wet in the landing," leaderless and seeking shelter among the islanders.[4]

Recognizing the challenges faced by the landing party, the commanders of the fleet brought Antonio in a launch close to the shore, so that he might coordinate the action, inspire the islanders and give courage to the soldiers from the safety of the water. Eventually Antonio came on shore, but he could not salvage the operation. For several days the landing party fought Spanish exploratory parties outside the fortress walls, but they did not have the artillery necessary to bombard the fort, nor did they have the water or provisions they would need to undertake a long siege. Furthermore, they feared alienating the islanders. Near São Miguel's main settlement, Antonio and his officers posted guards "to keep the soldiers in hand and check the pillage and any injury to the inhabitants." As a consequence, the men "suffered much in regard to victuals."[5] Upon hearing that Spanish reinforcements were arriving in a large fleet, the French abandoned the island, withdrew to their ships, and prepared for naval combat. At sea, the Spanish took advantage of tricky winds to outmaneuver, board, and sink several French ships, and kill the French naval commander. Most of the French escaped to Terceira, but they brought disease with them which spread across the island.

In 1583 another Spanish fleet arrived with over a hundred ships and twelve thousand men to attack the depleted French forces on Terceira. In contrast to the French a year earlier, the Spanish brought specialized landing craft, "flat bottomed barks," to take their soldiers ashore, and with overwhelming force they seized control of the island.[6] Philip II was thrilled by this turn of events. In 1585 he decorated the walls of his palace at El Escorial with detailed murals depicting the battles in the Azores. The victory bolstered Spanish confidence and may have led them to underestimate the difficulty they would face in their attempt to invade England.[7] It is clear in retrospect that rather than demonstrating the facility of amphibious operations, the battles in the Azores in the early 1580s revealed the challenges military leaders faced when they tried to use sea power to impose their will on land.

Whether the intention is to land troops, deliver supplies, or carry large numbers of people away, the first step in any amphibious operation is to bring ships close to shore. Weather could pose a challenge, particularly if the ships approaching the shore faced an opposing fleet, like the Spanish did off England in 1588. But many coasts were difficult to navigate even in fine weather and in the absence of hostile forces. As Jean Barbot discovered off the coast of west Africa, hidden natural hazards could be deadly.

In 1699 Barbot took a ship called the *Albion* to the Niger Delta to buy war captives as slaves. With a carrying capacity of 300 tons and mounting twenty-four cannons, it was large for its day, and the officers of the *Albion* were wary of approaching the shore. The ship's hull, at its lowest point, was fourteen and a half

Fig. 4.1 Niccolò Granello, "Disembarkation of the Spanish tercios in the Terceiras islands," Fresco in El Escorial. © Patrimonio Nacional.

feet below the surface of the water. Initially the sailors dropped anchor fourteen miles out at sea, "thinking it impossible to find a proper channel to carry so tall a ship in." The crew kept their distance and sent a longboat up the Bonny River to trade. While they waited on shipboard for the longboat's return, they dispatched a pilot in a small boat to make soundings of the water around them and perhaps discover a navigable channel, but the weather was treacherous and the pilot struggled all day and into the evening to get back to the ship, "the wind and sea being so high."[8] The next morning, straining in those winds, one of the *Albion's* anchor cables snapped.

Three days later, still waiting for the longboat, the men on the *Albion* saw a large canoe approaching. Canoes had little difficulty navigating the surf. As the canoe came near, the sailors recognized the longboat captain on board with nine rowers, a delegation from Bonny, and three African pilots. The pilots brought written testimonials with them from several English ship captains who vouched for their knowledge, skill, and experience directing ships into the river mouth.

The longboat captain warned Barbot of the difficulty of the passage. He had managed to get his boat to the river but had grounded on the sand banks on his way back and had been forced to return to Bonny. While there, he had hired the canoe. He had also learned that there might be rich rewards awaiting them if they could bring the *Albion* up the river. In Bonny he had met an English ship captain who had just purchased five hundred men and women as slaves. The slaver told him "as soon as the Blacks could see our ship at sea, they immediately went up the river to buy slaves." If the *Albion* could make it up the river, they would be able to buy hundreds. On hearing this, and receiving further assurances from the pilots, Barbot and his officers agreed to bring in their ship "if possible."[9] They decided to try the next morning.

The day dawned brightly, and eager to set off in fair weather, the officers ordered the sailors to raise the first of the ship's two anchors, but the men could not pull it off the ocean floor. All hands were ordered to the capstan to draw up and spool the anchor cable, but it snapped. Barbot speculated that that anchor had been "deep stuck in mud" or "among rocky stones." Losing it was a problem, but the difficulty was compounded in the afternoon when the men tried to lift the second anchor and its cable broke. Now the *Albion* was free but unable to moor in the open water. "To save our ship, as well as our persons if possible," the men resolved to sail immediately for the river mouth. Twice their soundings indicated they were in fifteen feet of water. The stern of the ship repeatedly scraped against the sand. Once the "stroke was very violent," and everyone on board expected to be wrecked, but the ship survived, skimmed into deeper water, and sailed up the river. The men spent hours positioning the ship within the deepest channels of the river and sent a boat out to borrow an anchor from an English ship moored on the bank. Working by moonlight they found a place in the river where even a small anchor would hold them. Once they were safe, Barbot asked the pilots why the voyage had been so difficult. He scolded them and said they had been "of no use in our distress." But the pilots had local knowledge, and they defended themselves, saying that the river's channels had changed since the last time they made the journey. "They never were sensible of so shallow water at the bar."[10] The *Albion* spent nearly six weeks at its mooring. Barbot and his crew purchased captives not just in Bonny, but in other towns they reached in smaller craft. They bought 583 people "of all ages and sexes . . . all very fresh and sound, very few exceeding forty years of age." They also purchased "yams, goats, fowls, wood and water, and some cows and calves" as provisions for their voyage across the Atlantic.[11] In anticipation of their departure Barbot sent a pilot out in a small craft to trace the route taken by another slave ship. That ship reached deep water without a scrape, and the *Albion* followed the same series of channels into the ocean.

Shallow water, hidden rocks, and shifting sands made many shores around the Atlantic inaccessible. The interplay of tides and currents, erosion and shifting accumulations of silt, sand and rocks created hazards even in deep harbors with protection from wind. Ship captains generally steered away from shallow waters and visible rocks without considering attacking the coasts behind. But even when gaps appeared in the natural defenses and colonial settlements with docks and ships signaled the possibility of a navigable channel, cautious sailors stayed away if they were unfamiliar with the local seascape. In 1672 when a Dutch fleet under the command of Cornelius Evertsen approached the French colony of Cayenne on the Caribbean coast of South America, he dispatched pilots and scouts to find a landing site. The main harbor lay behind a rocky, narrow straight, and Evertsen did not dare take his warships directly to the docks. His reconnaissance party found a nearby beach that might have been approachable at high tide, but the ships would have had to retreat within two hours of the landing, leaving the soldiers on shore to fend for themselves. Evertsen chose to move on and search for more vulnerable settlements.[12]

In the 1590s and early seventeenth century, following the failure of Spain's attempted invasion of England and the successful revolt in the Netherlands, the Dutch became Europe's most accomplished practitioners of amphibious warfare. In 1596, operating under English command, Dutch forces arrived from the sea and participated in sacking the Spanish port of Cadiz.[13] By the 1620s, the Dutch were attacking Spanish and Portuguese forts around the Atlantic including Salvador in Brazil, San Juan de Puerto Rico, and São Jorge da Mina and Luanda on the coast of Africa.[14] Sheltered, deep-water harbors like these attracted investment in the form of dredging, docks, and fortification. In well-guarded harbors the defenses might include a fort built to withstand sieges and other batteries on nearby islands or headlands overlooking the water. Cannons in these positions were more potent than artillery on ships. They were protected by earth and stone walls, they were fixed in place and easier to aim effectively, and they had a height advantage.

After decades of experience, the Dutch developed effective tactics for raiding and seizing fortified harbors. They exploited surprise, destroyed merchant ships at anchor, deployed large numbers of soldiers in small boats, and laid siege to harbor fortifications.[15] Nonetheless, often even the Dutch had difficulty. Their most successful and consequential amphibious landing in the Americas in the seventeenth century, at Pernambuco in 1628, nearly had to be jettisoned after they sank a double line of Portuguese ships chained together. The defenders of the harbor had intended to set those ships on fire to ward off the Dutch, but when the ships sank, they became an even more effective defense, serving in effect as a reef to keep the Dutch away from the coast. The operation against Pernambuco was salvaged only after another Dutch fleet arrived and found a place to land troops south of the harbor. Two thousand men came ashore and proceeded overland to encircle the Portuguese.[16]

Every imperial power on the Atlantic spent large sums on coastal forts, but an effective defense against amphibious attack also required the deployment of other military technologies that were less sophisticated and relatively cheap. In the eighteenth century the French fort at Louisbourg was regarded as one of the

Fig. 4.2 George Isham Parkyns, "View of Halifax from Georges Island." Watercolor, 1801. Halifax, Nova Scotia had typical eighteenth-century harbor defenses. British Library.

most formidable outposts on the coast of North America, but when a British fleet arrived in 1758, both the attackers and the defenders recognized that the fate of the fort would be decided on the nearby beaches where British soldiers in small craft intended to land. In anticipation of combat the French piled logs and fallen trees on nearly every beach within a few miles of their fort. They stationed men at each site to fire on the British soldiers as they waded through these obstacles. The British succeeded at Louisbourg only after a contingent of their soldiers in small boats found an inlet that the French had considered inaccessible and therefore left undefended. Approximately 150 British men clambered ashore, climbed over a hill, and took some Frenchmen defending another beach by surprise. They sent those French soldiers running and cleared a landing site for thousands.

Though the first-arriving soldiers played a decisive part in the capture of Louisbourg, sailors also had a critical role in the operation. They brought soldiers and landing craft to the zone of combat, warehoused the necessary equipment, and helped ferry it ashore. It took nearly a month to supply the besieging forces at Louisbourg with the cannons and ordnance they needed to take the fort. The sailors also prevented the French from receiving their own supplies. British ships stationed in the surrounding waters blocked ocean-going commerce and prevented the French from receiving any reinforcement by sea.[17]

The difficulties that large ships confronted when they approached the coast shaped the pattern of military action across the Atlantic world, helping prevent

Europeans and colonists from simply using their dominance of the deep ocean to take control of islands and coastal lands. Natural hazards did not affect all vessels equally. Canoeists could navigate coasts in the Americas and Africa where large ships could not go. Shallows also favored the masters of small ships. In 1668 French buccaneer François L'Olonnais led a fleet of ten ships of various sizes, the largest mounting sixteen guns, to the northern coast of South America to sack the Spanish colonial town of Maracaibo. In order to reach the city, the ships had to pass through a brackish tidal estuary. The best channel into the lagoon was narrow and partially blocked by sand banks, which forced ships to sail near a fort.[18] L'Olonnais anchored away from the strait and sent men in small boats to land some distance from the entrance into the estuary. The cannons on the Spanish fort pointed out to sea, so the landing party approached from behind. They came "without any other arms than swords and pistols."[19] The soldiers in the Spanish garrison fought them off for several hours, but eventually fled the fort. According to one account, the men of the garrison ran toward Maracaibo shouting, "the pirates will presently be here with two thousand men or more," but the sacking of Maracaibo had to be delayed.[20]

The next day, with the Spanish fort disabled, L'Olonnais led his ships through the strait, but the estuary bottom was scattered with sand banks "no more than six, seven, or eight feet in depth."[21] These shallows were "very dangerous, especially to mariners unacquainted with them."[22] L'Olonnais ordered the fleet to pause and wait for high tide. In the meantime, many of the inhabitants of Maracaibo and the surrounding villages gathered their most valuable possessions, loaded them into boats and canoes, and paddled across the estuary to landing places beyond the sailing ships' reach. Most of the townspeople, including "wives, children and families," saved themselves and their belongings from capture.[23]

Once it was safe for the ships to come near enough to the shore, the attackers boarded canoes they had bought as landing craft. They plundered Maracaibo and another nearby town, ranged through the surrounding countryside taking prisoners and seizing money, livestock, and goods, and demanding ransoms. They never intended to conquer and permanently occupy Maracaibo. They did not have the manpower, weaponry, or supplies for that kind of operation. They took over six hundred prisoners for ransom, mostly people who had been held as slaves in and around Maracaibo, but after four weeks their provisions began to run low. The raiders had exhausted most of the food they had found. Their prisoners were starving and beginning to die, and so they judged that it was time to depart. L'Olonnais and his men had enriched themselves at the expense of the Spanish and they had also learned some lessons. For their next raiding venture, against the coast of Nicaragua, they deployed ships of various sizes, most of them small, and they took care to supply their fleet with large numbers of canoes.[24]

The Caribbean offered the masters of small ships many ways to maneuver. With its complex geography and wide variety of islands, the waters were difficult to patrol. In the seventeenth century especially this left stretches of coastline vulnerable to small-scale raids. The natural features of the sea and surrounding landscape also helped protect the various peoples of the Caribbean from naval blockade. Dutch writers in the eighteenth century suggested that the Caribbean islands belonged to two trade networks. The "large circuit" tied the islanders to Africa and Europe, while the "small circuit" linked the islands to each other and the mainland colonies of North and South America.[25] The size difference referred to the ships as well as the distance they traveled. The vessels passing from island to island were typically single-masted craft with fewer than eight crew members.[26]

Following the adoption of intensive plantation agriculture and the arrival of tens of thousands of enslaved workers, small islands around the Caribbean lost the ability to feed themselves, and so many planters on these islands became conscious of their vulnerability to blockade.[27] But the multiplicity of islands, the complexity of the geography, and the ability of small ships to find shelter and evade capture made starving plantations difficult. During the War of the Austrian Succession and Seven Years' War, the British navy attempted to blockade French-ruled islands and territories around the Caribbean, but hundreds of small ships evaded the patrols. They carried enough food to maintain the islanders in times of difficulty, and they shipped enough sugar, coffee, captives, and money to keep the plantation economies operating.[28]

Colonial settlers and garrisons on islands and coastal sites could protect themselves from blockade and attack if they had allies, trading partners, and multiple sources of supply. But mainland coastal outposts could be vulnerable if they had only one outlet to the sea and lacked support from the surrounding local population. These dynamics could empower indigenous people. The two Dutch assaults against the Portuguese fort of São Jorge da Mina on the coast of West Africa illustrate the power local people could wield during amphibious operations.

In 1625 a Dutch fleet of fifteen ships carrying 1,200 soldiers and sailors attempted to seize São Jorge da Mina. They had intelligence suggesting that the fort was vulnerable. The garrison numbered only fifty-six men, and several of them were sick. The Dutch had allies at Terra Poquena, a town fifteen kilometers from the fort. They landed one thousand men there without facing local resistance. They also received guidance and some assistance from local Sabu warriors. The Dutch soldiers left Terra Poquena in the morning for the day-long march to São Jorge da Mina. They arrived outside the fort at dusk and had time to set up their camp before local warriors allied to the Portuguese charged and attacked. The Dutch were startled and overwhelmed. They managed to fire one volley from their muskets before they were set upon with machetes. More than four hundred were killed. Several Sabu warriors died with the Dutch, but others switched sides. After the landing party was routed, the commanders of the fleet tried to use their shipboard cannons to bombard and intimidate the local population and destroy the castle, but their guns inflicted little damage. The Portuguese cannons on land had the benefit of height and superior accuracy.[29]

The Dutch withdrew from the attack in 1625, but over the next twelve years the balance of power shifted. Between 1625 and 1637 the Dutch West India Company sent eighty ships to the region while only five caravels arrived from Portugal with supplies. Dutch traders recruited partners and allies along the coast, while the Portuguese had little to offer by way of trade and became increasingly isolated. In 1637 Dutch commanders secured support from the Kingdoms of Sabu and Komenda, and a thousand local warriors agreed to join in another attack on São Jorge da Mina. One thousand Dutch soldiers also took part. The Portuguese still had allies among the people living near the fort, but they were outnumbered. While warriors and soldiers battled in the village near the fort, a Dutch contingent hauled a large gun to the top of a nearby hill. Facing heavy artillery on land and at sea, the Portuguese surrendered.[30]

In a different colonial context, the Dutch reconquest of New York in 1673 similarly illustrates the influence of local populations on naval sieges. After its campaign in the Caribbean, the Dutch fleet under the command of Cornelius Evertsen conducted raids along the coast of North America before arriving at New York. Though the fleet had pulled back from Cayenne, it became more aggressive as the campaign progressed, attacking ships and taking prizes. The Dutch commanders sent a landing party to occupy the island of St. Eustatius briefly, but their aim was not conquest. The Dutch faced a formidable challenge fighting the French and English simultaneously, and the commanders' instructions directed them only to "capture and ruin everything possible" in the French and English colonies.[31] They decided to take and hold New York only after they heard that the Dutch colonists there "complained bitterly about the hard rule of the English."[32] The English had conquered New York from the Dutch only nine years earlier. Expecting a friendly reception, Evertsen and another officer sent a letter addressed to the "good citizens of the city" asking them "kindly" to "persuade the Governor to turn over the fort and city to us forthwith."[33]

The townspeople did not rise up against the English, but they notably failed to respond when their English governor tried to call out the militia to defend against the Dutch attack, and someone in the city disabled English cannons outside the fort. Twenty-one Dutch ships carrying three thousand men sailed into the bay and approached New York Harbor. Their opponents on land may have numbered a hundred. The Dutch faced no armed resistance from the water. When they landed six hundred soldiers to encircle the fort, hundreds of city dwellers greeted them cheering, and marched with them down Broadway. The Dutch ships opened fire, and seeing the soldiers approaching with their supporters, the garrison raised a white flag over the fort. The bombardment continued for a short while in spite of this because no one on the ships could see the flag of surrender through the smoke.[34]

It was easier for navies to seize coastal forts if they had support from local populations, but late in the Seven Years' War, beginning with the conquest of Louisbourg in 1758, and proceeding over the next few years with the capture of Quebec, Guadeloupe, Martinique and Havana, Britain's Royal Navy undertook several successful amphibious operations without the aid of anyone living in the immediate vicinity. The Royal Navy's victories in European waters and its control of strategic straits in Europe prevented the French from challenging it at sea.[35] But even in the places where British naval power seemed strongest, amphibious operations were costly and difficult. In the spring of 1759, French ships were able to evade an attempted British blockade and get supplies to Quebec.[36] Later that spring and summer the British had much more difficulty navigating the river, and proceeded cautiously, meticulously preparing charts for each stretch of the journey.[37]

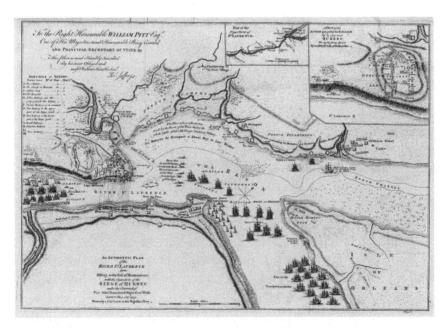

Fig. 4.3 Captain James Cook charted the St. Lawrence River in 1759 to facilitate the amphibious British operation against Quebec. This map of the action, published in 1760, is based on his charts. Courtesy of the John Carter Brown Library.

When the British arrived to lay siege to Quebec, they were outnumbered by the defending French troops. In an effort to weaken the French, the British bombarded and raided farms and villages along the riverbank for dozens of miles and virtually destroyed the city of Quebec, but as autumn approached, they did not enjoy an obvious advantage over their adversaries. They had to act quickly to complete their operations before the river iced over and trapped their ships. The British victory was not a foregone conclusion. Most historians discussing the fall of Quebec in 1759 have concentrated on the commanders' peculiar tactical choices on the day of battle: James Wolfe's decision to march his soldiers up the cliff from the river to the field outside the fort, and Louis Joseph de Montcalm's response, sending soldiers out of the fort to engage the British on level ground in battle.[38]

While amphibious operations along the St. Lawrence were difficult, the British navy faced even greater challenges in the Caribbean. In 1759 British forces failed to take Martinique from the French. They subsequently took Guadeloupe only after months of fighting and thousands of deaths.[39] Bringing large numbers of unseasoned men to the tropics exposed them to contagion, and more men died of disease than wounds. According to Captain Richard Gardiner, men were dying in large numbers even before the British arrived at Martinique. "The troops, unaccustomed to the climate, suffered greatly from fevers, from the flux, the scurvy from the use of salt provisions, and from an accidental evil, the small pox which broke out amongst the transports."[40] In 1762 Britain made additional conquests in the Caribbean including Havana. The British forces attacking Havana suffered a death rate of nearly 50 percent.[41]

Military commanders launching seaborne raids, sieges or invasions relied on shipboard cannon to sink, disable or deter opposing ships, to bombard forts and other coastal defenses, to demoralize local populations, and to protect landing parties by firing at the soldiers and warriors who opposed them, but the most important military function of ships was to transport soldiers, settlers, and supplies. At a pivotal moment in the first Anglo-Powhatan war, in 1610, the English nearly abandoned Virginia.[42] Governor Thomas Gates arrived in Jamestown in late May and found houses empty, looted, and partially disassembled for firewood. The Powhatan had been laying siege since the previous October. The colonists were unwilling to venture beyond the boundaries of their settlement for fear of attack and were starving. More than half of them had already died. After quickly surveying the landscape, Gates saw that they might have to evacuate. He gathered the townspeople and made a speech. He offered them a share of the provisions he brought on his ships and told them he would study whether the colony was sustainable, but if the colonists could not feed themselves, "he would make ready and transport them all into their native country." On hearing this, according to one observer, the people of Jamestown gave a "shout of joy."[43]

They felt ready to go. Gates spent the next two weeks making an inventory of the colony's food resources, surveying the fields and sending men out into the Chesapeake Bay to see how many fish they could catch. After this investigation it was agreed "by a general approbation, that to preserve and save all from starving there could be no readier course thought on then to abandon the country."[44] But it would not be easy to sail away.

Even the weakened and diminished population of Jamestown was too large to take directly across the Atlantic in the vessels that Gates had on hand. Gates calculated that they had insufficient food to sustain all the people of Jamestown through a transatlantic journey. The colonists would have to find new provisions in the middle of the ocean, so he resolved to take the colonists to the fishing grounds off Newfoundland where they might split up and join fishing crews. It was a desperate plan, but it seemed better than any alternative. Gates was the last to leave Jamestown on June 7, 1610. When the governor left the docks and looked back, there was "no one giving farewell."[45]

Famously, the fleet evacuating Jamestown met resupply ships within hours of their departure. They turned around and Virginia survived. The evacuation and subsequent restoration of Jamestown serves as a reminder of the importance of ships as vehicles for bringing people across the ocean and supplying them. This turn of events altered the military fortunes of the Powhatan Confederacy and the future of English colonization in North America.

The Portuguese townspeople of Salvador da Bahia had a similar experience in 1624 and 1625. In the spring of 1624, in a bold amphibious operation, a Dutch force of three thousand men conquered, looted, and occupied Bahia.[46] Some Portuguese colonists fled to organize armed resistance in the countryside and kept the Dutch confined to the city. When the news of the fall of Bahia reached Madrid, the Spanish and Portuguese assembled a fleet of fifty-six ships to carry more than twelve thousand soldiers across the ocean to take it back. The ships sailed from different ports in Europe and Africa and gathered at Cape Verde before proceeding to Brazil. The fleet carried soldiers from Flanders, Naples, Portugal, and Spain. Many of the Portuguese had been pulled from the garrisons of African trading posts. They arrived at Bahia in April 1625. After a month of fighting the Dutch surrendered.[47] Many Portuguese colonists may have celebrated this event as a liberation, but Bahia soon confronted the almost inevitable problems that arose in the early modern era following a sudden arrival of thousands of soldiers. The new arrivals from Portugal camped outside the city while the Spanish soldiers occupied and ransacked the town. Moving large numbers of soldiers across the ocean was expensive, logistically difficult, and often politically explosive. The events in Bahia following the Dutch surrender helped poison Spanish–Portuguese relations not just in Brazil but in Europe as well. The Spanish and Portuguese would never cooperate militarily on this scale in the Americas again. Significantly, no European power would send so many soldiers across the ocean for another century.[48]

Large armies disrupt the pattern of local life wherever they go, straining food resources and altering power dynamics. This is true whether they arrive by sea or land, but these effects are often more severe following a seaborne invasion. In the early modern era, ships could deposit men by the thousands on unfamiliar terrain, and some communities never recovered from the impact of a single large-scale landing. On June 2, 1755, thirty-four ships carrying more than two thousand soldiers from New England and Britain arrived at a small British outpost near the eastern end of the Bay of Fundy called Fort Lawrence. Protected by the small British garrison and its cannons, the newly arriving soldiers disembarked without facing armed opposition, but the landing was still extremely challenging. The ships and landing craft were crowded together in the harbor and contended with the largest tides in the world.[49] With guidance from New England sailors who knew the region and its difficulties, they managed to get on shore. Their arrival changed the region permanently. Within days the newcomers had marched to Beauséjour, the site of a French fort a few miles away. They vastly outnumbered the French garrison in that fort, even counting the volunteers the French had recruited from the local colonial population, the Acadians. The siege of Beauséjour began on June 12, and the French surrendered on the sixteenth. Then the British began preparing to remove the Acadian population.

According to British estimates in 1755, there were eight thousand Acadians living along the shores of the Bay of Fundy. The governor and council of Nova Scotia offered several justifications for expelling them, but their argument for taking action quickly was pragmatic. They wanted to exploit a momentary military advantage. The ships and the men they had brought to the Bay of Fundy could not be kept there indefinitely, and "on the removal of the fleet & troops, the province will be in no condition to drive them [the Acadians] out of their possessions."[50] The removal of the Acadians was a logistically complex amphibious operation. Soldiers were ordered to block roads and destroy villages along possible overland escape routes. At sea the Acadians' "shallops, boats, canoes, or vessels of any kind" were ordered seized or destroyed.[51] Adult male colonists and older boys were captured and detained in forts and camps, while their mothers, sisters, wives, and daughters were ordered to tend cattle, harvest crops, and make provisions for their onward journey. Most of the ships that had carried the soldiers and their supplies to Fort Lawrence left the region to carry cannons and supplies to Boston and New York. Other ships were sent from Halifax to the Bay of Fundy to carry away the colonial population. Each of the vessels was expected to transport at least a hundred people, and the largest could take nearly four hundred.[52] In mid-September the first Acadians were ordered onto transport ships, and the last ships sailed from the vicinity of Beauséjour on October 13. In total the ships carried more than six thousand Acadians from the Bay of Fundy to the British colonies farther south along the coast of North America, from Massachusetts to Georgia. Some of the ships ran low on provisions before they could disembark the people in their holds. It took more than a month to reach the southern destinations, and it was mid-December before some of the Acadians sent to Georgia were released from their ship. They were starved, and many were ill.[53]

The Acadians were hardly the first colonial group to be targeted for removal or destruction. Since the sixteenth century, the firepower and carrying capacity of ships had led imperial leaders in a variety of contexts to believe that they could deploy fleets to halt, redirect, or reverse the process of colonization. In 1560, the newly arriving Portuguese governor of Brazil, Mem de Sá, resolved to destroy a five-year-old French post on a small island in Guanabara Bay. The French colony's population fluctuated, but at its peak it may have approached a thousand. Most of the inhabitants were indigenous people: Tupinamba allies and trading partners of the French, captives held as slaves by the French, and women and children living with the soldiers and colonists. Mem de Sá sent twelve ships to surround the island. The ships spent three weeks bombarding the fort before the soldiers on board could land. After two days of difficult fighting they completed the conquest.[54] Ships functioned in this operation as troop carriers as well as instruments of destruction. They were not deployed to evacuate or resettle the island. The French and indigenous Brazilians who survived the bombardment and siege escaped by canoe and raft. Once the fort was abandoned, the Portuguese blew it up. They would not return for four years.[55]

In 1614 and 1615, when fleets of Spanish and Portuguese vessels besieged a new French colony on the northern coast of Brazil, at Maranhão, the action resembled the earlier Portuguese attack against the French in Guanabara Bay, except that the resolution of the conflict required the use of ships as vehicles for evacuation. In 1613 eight ships carrying three hundred fighting men arrived to attack the French at Maranhão. The Spanish and Portuguese disembarked a short distance from the French fortifications. The French had indigenous allies, and after a short, fierce battle with the landing party, they retreated from their settlement. Out of reach of the landing party, the French sent emissaries to negotiate a cease-fire. The French and Portuguese negotiators agreed to send a joint delegation to Spain and France to resolve their dispute. The two French colonists and two Portuguese Brazilians sent as diplomats failed to reach a compromise. A second Iberian fleet arrived at Maranhão in 1615 and found the French colonists "distressed and short of supplies from France."[56] The attacking ships blocked the harbor and demanded that the colonists abandon the region permanently. To encourage and facilitate the colonists' departure, the Iberians offered to transport them to France, and they agreed.[57]

When the Spanish destroyed the English and French colonies on Nevis and St. Kitts in 1629, they used their ships to carry English and French islanders away. Four Spanish galleons arrived off Nevis and engaged in a chaotic but ultimately successful naval battle against ships near the port. After one of the Spanish ships grounded near the shore within range of the cannons of a small English fort, the captain of another Spanish ship resolved to land soldiers to fight on the island. Surprised and outnumbered, the English fled from the coast, but Nevis was not like Maranhão. There was no rich hinterland to escape to, and no indigenous community large or prosperous enough to take in refugees. The English faced isolation and starvation in the woods, and so they returned to surrender to the Spanish, who loaded them onto their ships. The Spanish dismantled the fort and burned all the English houses and warehouses before sailing away with the colonists in their holds to attack nearby St. Kitts.

Though Spain had claimed St. Kitts since the time of Columbus, the island was the site of two rival colonial settlements, English on the north of the island and French on the south. When the Spanish arrived with overwhelming force in 1629, both the French and the English surrendered. The colonists of St. Kitts were boarded onto the Spanish ships to join their counterparts from Nevis. At the end of these operations the Spanish held more than two thousand captives below deck. They transported most of them to Europe in the vessels they had seized off Nevis. They kept six hundred as hostages and only released them after they promised not to return to the islands. Many immediately broke their promises and returned to re-establish their colonies on Nevis and St. Kitts.[58]

The Caribbean was the scene of several mass evacuations in the seventeenth century. In 1631 a Spanish fleet carrying more than a thousand men expelled the Dutch from St. Martin. Under the terms of the capitulation agreement, the Spanish agreed to carry the Dutch islanders to Holland.[59] In 1641, another Spanish fleet of similar size conquered and evacuated the English from Providence Island, destroying a colony that had lasted more than ten years. The transportation the Spanish offered to the Providence Islanders was less generous than what they had provided the Dutch leaving St. Martin. The Spanish carried 350 English colonists to Cadiz and expected them to pay their own way from there to England or New England.[60] In 1672 an English amphibious assault on Tobago resulted in the deportation of all the Dutch colonists there to Curaçao and Barbados.[61]

Long before the expulsion of the Acadians in 1755, there had been similar operations in the northern reaches of the Atlantic. In the sixteenth century armed groups of whalers and fishermen repeatedly wrecked one another's seasonal settlements and coastal camps. The violence continued after colonists began

Fig. 4.4 Félix Castello, "Recapture of St. Kitts, 1629" (1634). Museo del Prado.

to settle year-round along the coast of Newfoundland. As populations rose more effort was required to dislodge rival groups, and as the entangled histories of Newfoundland and Louisbourg demonstrated, ship-board evacuations were often reversible. In 1696, French forces attacked English settlements on Newfoundland and forcibly transported nearly five hundred colonists to England and France.[62] Following the restoration of peace between France and England in 1697, hundreds of English fishermen and their families returned.[63] The French and the English shared Newfoundland until the second decade of the eighteenth century, when most of the French fishermen left to help establish Louisbourg. After New Englanders seized Louisbourg in 1745 they shipped more than two thousand French soldiers and civilians to France.[64] Many of the people they evacuated from Louisbourg returned in 1749, and when the French at Louisbourg surrendered again to the British in 1758, there was an even larger evacuation: approximately ten thousand soldiers and civilians from Isle Royale (present-day Cape Breton Island) and more than three thousand colonists from Isle St.-Jean (Prince Edward Island). All of these evacuees were slated to be carried across the ocean, but they did not all complete the voyage. Two transports leaving Prince Edward Island sank, killing everyone on board, and in total approximately 1,600 people died from drowning or disease.[65]

The large-scale deportations from Cape Breton Island and Prince Edward Island strained the logistical capabilities of the British army and navy, but they effectively transformed those islands. As colonial populations grew, orchestrated episodes of mass migration became increasingly difficult to manage. The population of French Canada was at least seventy thousand when the colony was conquered by the British in 1759 and 1760. This exceeded the carrying capacity of any imaginable deportation fleet. Holding Canada without expelling the French colonial population presented a special challenge and triggered a wide-ranging reconsideration of British imperial policy.[66]

The evacuation of colonial populations was always a selective process, and the sorting of people in these operations reveals a great deal about the role of ships in configuring power relations across the Atlantic world. When the Spanish seized Providence Island in 1641, they captured 731 people including 350 English colonists and 381 other islanders held as slaves. While the English colonists were offered transportation to Spain, the enslaved men, women, and children were carried to Cartagena and Portobello to be sold.[67] Similarly, in 1691 when English forces attacked French plantations on St. Kitts, Marie-Galante, Saint Barthélemy, and Guadeloupe, the English captured "eighteen hundred men, besides women and children and Negroes." They carried the French colonists to Hispaniola, but set the enslaved people apart to be "divided as plunder."[68]

There was a similar pattern regarding indigenous people, who were rarely if ever transported alongside colonists. In Maranhão in 1615, the Spanish and Portuguese never contemplated evacuating indigenous people. In other places where indigenous Americans could be surrounded, captured, and taken to ships, they were likely to be sent to places where they could be controlled, maintained, and exploited. Though the practice provoked controversy in all the European empires, indigenous American people were frequently captured, transported in ships overseas, and sold as slaves.

In 1645 during the Anglo-Powhattan war, colonists in Virginia shipped many indigenous American prisoners "over eleven years of age" to the West Indies "to prevent their returning to and strengthening their respective tribes."[69] In 1675 during King Philip's War, Plymouth colony sent 178 prisoners to Spain where they were sold as slaves.[70] Later, New Englanders shipped other indigenous American captives to the West Indies. They sent so many to Barbados that in 1676 that island's assembly passed a law "to prohibit the bringing of Indian slaves from New England to this island."[71] The assemblymen warned that as a result of the influx of indigenous American war captives, "greater mischief may happen to this island than from any Negroes."[72] The Barbados statute targeted the "masters" and "commanders" of sailing ships, and threatened them with the confiscation of their vessels if they brought in any more indigenous American prisoners from New England.[73]

The moral and pragmatic arguments over the sale of indigenous war captives grew louder in the English colonies following King Philip's War. Nonetheless, the practice continued for several decades. In Charleston, South Carolina, English colonial officials and slave traders paid indigenous warriors for war captives who were subsequently sold abroad as slaves. The Carolina economy relied on slave labor, but the colonists preferred to purchase Africans and send indigenous American captives away. Historian Alan Gallay has estimated that before 1715 the number of indigenous American captives the colony sent overseas exceeded the number of enslaved people the colonists brought in from the Caribbean and Africa.[74] Some indigenous Americans targeted for capture and sale in South Carolina voluntarily sought exile overseas to avoid enslavement. In 1711 a Cuban ship captain named Luis Perdomo carried 270 indigenous men, women, and children from Florida to Havana. These exiles were fleeing Yamasee warriors who intended to sell them in Charleston. Perdomo reported that he left behind hundreds of other indigenous people, perhaps as many as two thousand, who had wanted to sail to Cuba to escape the South Carolina slave market. He said he would have brought more of them to safety and freedom "had he had the vessels."[75]

Perdomo believed that his ships offered some indigenous people in Florida a way to escape danger. The families he assisted, and others who pleaded for his help, hoped that by crossing the water they could place a barrier between themselves and their attackers. Ironically, the Virginians and New Englanders who sent war captives to the Caribbean professed a similar aim, to put a distance between themselves and their adversaries and use the ocean for protection. Refugees who crossed the Atlantic to escape religious persecution in Europe thought about the vastness of the sea in a similar way, as did European imperial officials who sent rebels and other convicts to the Americas as bound laborers. The ocean could separate antagonists, but in most cases, rather than diminishing conflict, crossing the ocean or shipping people overseas only transformed the perception of warfare by moving violence beyond the horizon. The African military leaders who took captives and sold them into the transatlantic slave trade had many of the same incentives that motivated the Virginians and New Englanders who sent indigenous Americans to the Caribbean. The slave trade was a business, and large fortunes could be made marketing and exploiting captives, but in the early modern era shipping captives away was also an increasingly pervasive feature of warfare.

Expeditions like Barbot's 1699 voyage up the Bonny River had an enormous cumulative effect. The largest mass migration in the early modern Atlantic was the transatlantic slave trade. Between 1500 and 1760, approximately two million Dutch, English, French, Portuguese, and Spanish migrants came to the Americas, but during that same period Dutch, English, French, Portuguese, and Spanish ships carried more than twice as many Africans—4,380,000—across the Atlantic as slaves.[76] Between 1500 and 1760, slave ships crossed the ocean on more than thirteen thousand occasions and on average each voyage carried three hundred people against their will. According to our best estimates, 36 percent of the captives were women and girls, and 14 percent overall were children. These voyages resembled other amphibious military operations. As Barbot's experience suggests, large ships sometimes struggled to get near the coast, and often by necessity people were transferred from canoes and other small vessels onto ships. Provisioning the captives was a constant challenge, and the longer the voyage the more difficult it was to keep them fed. Disease threatened everyone on board, especially on longer trips.[77] Between 1500 and 1760, the average mortality rate for captives crossing the ocean was 17 percent.[78] Nonetheless, despite these circumstances and the frequency of uprisings and combat on deck, the transatlantic slave trade was not normally viewed among Europeans or colonists as a military operation. The slave ships seldom formed carefully coordinated fleets and rarely followed detailed orders. Though European and colonial

Fig. 4.5 The ruins of Valongo Wharf in Rio de Janeiro, where hundreds of thousands of enslaved Africans disembarked after crossing the Atlantic. Shutterstock.

governments encouraged the trade, slave traders generally worked spontaneously and opportunistically, hurrying to places where captives were available
and taking them wherever they might profitably be sold.

Slave ships dominate histories of the slave trade because of the existence of
detailed records of the activities of traders who operated along Africa's coast
and the markets in the American colonies where they sold people. Records on
the process of enslavement, by comparison, are relatively sparse and anecdotal
because slave ships seldom participated in the process of capturing people and
there were no bookkeepers recording the violent process that brought millions
of Africans into bondage.

Understanding the military dimensions of the slave trade requires taking into
account the African fighting forces responsible for enslaving people on land as
well as the transatlantic trade as an amphibious operation. British slave trader
William Snelgrave recounted an incident in which West African sellers sold
captives at reduced prices in their haste to see them shipped away. According to
Snelgrave the "conquerors" were "glad to get something for them at that instant,
since if a ship had not been in the road, they would have been obliged to kill most
of the men-captives, for their own security."[79] Though they did not control the
ships that would carry their captives, these men recognized the military value
of transportation across the ocean. Like military leaders in other parts of the
Atlantic world, they sought to consolidate power by shipping their rivals away.

PART TWO

WARFARE ON LAND

The Technology of Warfare on Land

In 1634 hundreds of Tarairiu men, women, and children came to the coastal fort at Reis Magos in Brazil to greet soldiers under the direction of the Dutch West India Company who had driven the Portuguese from the coast. The Tarairiu and the newcomers from the Netherlands held ceremonies together, and as part of the festivities Tarairiu warriors and West India Company soldiers tried to impress each other with military displays. Dutch artillerymen fired cannons from the walls of the fortress, and Tarairiu bowmen responded by shooting arrows in an hour-long demonstration of their proficiency.[1] There were similar performances at various places around the Atlantic world in the sixteenth and seventeenth centuries as people with distinctive military technologies met and showed off the efficacy of their arms. The martial displays at Reis Magos were friendly, but on many other occasions the demonstrations were lethal.

In 1609 in eastern North America, on the shore of a large lake he named for himself, Frenchman Samuel de Champlain introduced a body of Haudenosaunee warriors to firearms. He was traveling with indigenous American allies and would have been helpless without them, but his account of his encounter with the Haudenosaunee effectively proclaims his belief in European supremacy. "When I saw them making a move to fire [arrows] at us, I rested my musket against my cheek, and aimed directly at one of the three chiefs." Champlain had four balls in his musket. His first shot killed two of the men immediately. The third man was wounded and died later. According to Champlain, "The Iroquois [Haudenosaunee] were greatly astonished that two men had been so quickly killed, although they were equipped with armor woven from cotton thread, and with wood which was proof against their arrows." After one of Champlain's French companions opened fire, the warriors "lost courage, and took to flight, abandoning their camp and fort."[2] The noise of exploding gunpowder, the speed of shots fired by muskets, and the severity of the wounds they inflicted startled and disoriented the warriors.

Guns were intimidating on first impression, but other weapons could be equally unnerving. In the 1440s when Portuguese expeditions were just

Atlantic Wars. Geoffrey Plank, Oxford University Press (2020). © Oxford University Press.
DOI: 10.1093/oso/9780190860455.001.0001

beginning to venture south of Cape Verde, the westernmost point in Africa, a party of twenty-two Portuguese soldiers in two boats left their sailing ship and rowed up a wide river. With the tide rising behind them they paddled toward a village but before they could reach it, they were met by twelve canoes carrying several dozen warriors with large bows and arrows. One canoe slipped around to reach the bank of the river, allowing its group of warriors to oppose the Portuguese from land. These men began shooting arrows while those in the remaining canoes paddled toward the Portuguese from behind. After the warriors in the canoes began launching arrows, the Portuguese turned their boats around. Surrounded, outnumbered, and facing a frightening barrage, they rowed desperately against the tide toward their ship, but by the time they reached it all twenty-two men had been struck. The arrows had been tipped with poison. Four of the Portuguese men died before reaching the sailing vessel, and in the next several hours, sixteen more would perish, along with two of the seven men who had stayed behind on the sailing ship and had also been struck by poisoned arrows. Two of the wounded men survived, but they spent twenty days recovering. The remaining five were disoriented, shaken, and terrified. According to the chronicler of these events, they left the site of the battle "weeping and sorrowing." They moved "in fear of the hateful enemies they knew to be near them, from whose deadly wounds so many and such brave men had died in a very brief space."[3]

Most historians of military technology in the early modern era emphasize the influence of gunpowder, which arrived in the Mediterranean and Europe from China in the thirteenth and fourteenth centuries and spread from there to large parts of Africa and the Americas in the fifteenth and sixteenth centuries. Within Europe, scholars have suggested that the introduction of gunpowder triggered a military revolution that changed not only the continent's fighting forces, but also Europe's financial systems and governmental bureaucracies.[4] In Africa, historians have claimed that the distribution of firearms stirred a "gun-slave cycle," arguing that Africans sold slaves to Europeans to acquire guns, and as a consequence guns became necessary for defense as well as raiding. Over time, rivals launched attacks with increasing frequency to acquire slaves with the aim of selling them to Europeans to acquire guns.[5] Historians of the indigenous peoples of the Americas have also emphasized the transformative impact of firearms alongside the introduction of other significant technologies like metal blades and horses.[6] But in Europe, Africa, and the Americas, the changes attributed to gunpowder occurred gradually, sometimes over centuries, and during the period of transition, in every society, a huge array of economic, demographic, and cultural forces drove change. Even within the field of military technology, gunpowder was only one of several early modern innovations. In some parts of the Americas the introduction of horses from Spain drastically changed warfare.

On land, most military technology changed hands easily. Trading weapons often served the interests of the European empires both in economic and military terms. And there were some indigenous technologies that Europeans and colonists never mastered. African and indigenous American warriors had distinctive weapons and support systems of their own. Indigenous craftsmanship continued through the early modern period as warriors found ways to exploit and respond to changes in their social and physical environments. The development of new regional military technologies, combined with the logistical difficulty of bringing European ways of fighting to other continents, impeded the extension of European power. Nothing the European empires brought to other continents gave them dominance on land in the way that ocean-going ships provided them supremacy at sea. The discussion that follows focuses on a few key military technologies: gunpowder, armor, fortification, poisoned arrows, dogs, horses, and canoes.

In Europe, one of the earliest effects of the adoption of gunpowder was an increase in the cost of fortifications. The continent's old medieval walls were vulnerable to heavy shot. With gunpowder, cannons could lob balls over them, or smash their thinner, higher sections to send masonry down. The weakness of medieval walls was demonstrated repeatedly in various military sieges in Europe in the fifteenth century. Chronicles of the Spanish conquest of Granada describe their impact. At the siege of Ronda, for example,

> The bombardment was so heavy and so constant that the Moors on watch could hear each other only with great difficulty . . . nor did they know which sector most needed support, for in one place the cannon knocked down the wall and in another wrecked the houses and, if they tried to repair the damage . . . they could not, for the unending hail of fire from smaller weapons killed anybody on the walls.[7]

There may have been other ways to respond to the challenge of gunpowder and heavy artillery, but the civic and military leaders of Europe chose to redesign their fortifications.[8] Abandoning their old practice of building walls high to ward off scaling ladders, they began to build forts low with thick walls backed by earth to withstand cannon shot and create secure platforms for defensive artillery. Ditches around the forts trapped attackers. Bastions protruded into the ditches, and the walls of the new forts were angled to provide gunners sweeping sight-lines and lines of fire "so there may be no shelter about the place where the enemy might lodge himself, but what may be discovered by those within, not only from the front, but from the sides, and even from behind, if it be possible."[9] This new architecture was designed to keep attackers at a distance. To defend themselves, garrisons were equipped with an array of specialized guns appropriate for firing at different ranges, including small firearms for shooting into the surrounding ditch and cannons, which by the seventeenth century could fire more than a mile.

Early modern artillery fortresses were expensive to build, man, and equip, but the expense was deemed worthwhile because these forts were more resilient than medieval castles, and they were difficult to take by surprise or storm. In most instances, the only effective way to capture an artillery fortress was through a protracted siege. An attacking army would dig trenches around the fort beyond the reach of its longest-range guns, and then gradually move forward, digging continuously and constricting the circle. Executing a siege in this manner routinely required at least twenty thousand men, and the process took months. Sieges spoiled the landscape and strained the logistical capacities of attackers and defenders alike.[10]

While heavy artillery changed the nature of siege warfare in Europe, hand-held firearms slowly transformed the operation of the continent's armies in the field. That process took time because armorers and soldiers struggled with the technical challenge of finding an efficient way to load and ignite explosive powder to propel shot from the end of a portable narrow tube.[11] There were also problems with accuracy. Well into the sixteenth century, crossbows had some tactical advantages over firearms because arrows could be launched more rapidly and hit their targets more precisely. European soldiers also continued to wield pikes. In 1571, the Hapsburg army in the Netherlands had more than twice as many pikemen as musketeers.[12] By the eighteenth century, most European infantry carried firearms, but that did not mean the end of close combat. At the Battle of Prestonpans in 1745, Jacobite Scottish Highlanders used broadswords with devastating effect. Like other experienced, well-trained soldiers in eighteenth-century Europe, the Highlanders were proficient with firearms, but they still carried swords, and their guns were tipped with bayonets so that they could double as thrusting weapons.[13]

Close combat continued, but by the eighteenth century the transformative effect of gunpowder was visible on every European battlefield. At the start of the seventeenth century soldiers wore metal body armor and helmets, but with the proliferation of firearms the use of body armor declined. In 1600, after years of theoretical debate, experimentation, and practice drills, the Dutch army deployed artillerymen in ranks so that each line could come forward in sequence, fire, and provide cover for the other ranks behind them, giving the men in the back time to reload and prepare for their turns. In a battle on a Flemish beach in the summer of 1600, the Dutch used volley fire in this way to kill four thousand Spanish and Italian horsemen and infantry at close range. After this demonstration of the effectiveness of infantry volley fire, the practice spread. As early as 1605 the Ottoman army was deploying the tactic against Hungarians.

Descriptions of infantry volley fire began appearing in field manuals, and soon it was common across Europe.[14]

The costs associated with building, equipping, and manning artillery fortresses, besieging them, and deploying infantry with firearms gave an advantage to European states that were able to raise and spend money efficiently. The expense grew steadily through the early modern period as a result of competition between centralized states and an increase in the size of Europe's armies. Between 1500 and 1700 several of the most powerful European armies became ten times larger.[15] Before 1500, the French fielded between 30,000 and 60,000 men in wartime, but in the 1690s France deployed 400,000 soldiers.[16] Gunpowder comprehensively transformed European warfare.

Gunpowder's influence in other regions varied. In January 1591, Ahmad Al-Mansur, the Sultan of Morocco, ordered five thousand fighting men armed with muskets and a few light cannons to cross the Sahara and attack the forces of the Songhay Empire in central West Africa. The Sultan's army included men from Spain and Portugal as well as North Africa. Some rode on horses, and

Fig. 5.1 Workshop of Jacob de Gheyn II, ca. 1600. Soldier loading a musket. The cumbersome and time-consuming task of loading a musket left unprotected soldiers vulnerable. Rijksmuseum, Amsterdam.

some traveled on foot. By the time the expedition reached the Niger River two months later, two thousand of the men had died, and the survivors were exhausted, hungry, and ill. On March 12 they met their opponents, more than ten thousand Songhay horsemen, and perhaps as many as thirty thousand warriors on foot. The Songhay foot-soldiers were mostly armed with javelins, but among them was a corps of skilled and resilient archers.[17] Though outnumbered, the northerners prevailed. Their victory that day demonstrated the potency of firearms, but the circumstances were peculiar. The Songhay had attacked in a line with their horsemen on the sides. Deploying what must have been a common tactic, their infantry drove thousands of cattle toward the Moroccan forces, not anticipating what would happen next. When the Moroccan guns fired, the cattle reared and retreated, stampeding back through the Songhay army. Divided and scattered, the Songhay continued to fight for a time, but they could not regroup.

Guns had been fired in West Africa before, but never so effectively. The Songhay Empire, already weakened by internal divisions, collapsed. Firearms allowed the Moroccans to defeat the Songhay in 1591, but events over subsequent years and decades demonstrated the limitations of their usefulness in West Africa. With their small numbers and limited armament, the Moroccans were able to occupy only a small part of the former Songhay Empire. Communications were difficult. Cut off from Moroccan authority, the invaders eventually split into small, armed, virtually independent groups, known locally as the "shooters." For more than a hundred years, the descendants of the Moroccan army maintained a local monopoly on firearms, but their arsenals were small because it was expensive to bring guns across the Sahara. In the meantime, their neighbors learned to respond more effectively to gunfire. Massed cavalrymen, no longer startled by the noise of gunfire, were able to prevail in pitched battles. With only small numbers, the shooters used their firearms more effectively in small-scale raids.[18]

Larger numbers of firearms arrived on the coast of West Africa as items of exchange in the transatlantic slave trade. The volume of gun imports grew after the mid-seventeenth century when the English entered the trade and as less expensive, more effective muskets became available.[19] By the 1730s European merchants were bringing approximately 180,000 firearms a year into Africa. Later in the century Britain alone would send more than 300,000 guns to African slave traders every year.[20] Armed with these weapons, some African kingdoms fielded large armies of infantry, expanded their territories, introduced new tax regimes, and built fortifications roughly similar to those being constructed around the same time in Europe. In 1728, the West African king of Dahomey was reported to have "deep ditches around his entire country, as well as walls and batteries" mounted with cannons. A visitor to Dahomey's royal compound in 1772 passed through mud-brick walls that were nearly a mile long, twenty feet high, and interrupted by blockhouses.[21] Dahomey and other West African states fielded thousands of infantrymen with muskets, massing the soldiers in opposition to cavalry or dispersing them systematically in small units to attack their opponents from several angles at once.[22]

Dahomey's walls were a monument to the power of the kingdom and a reminder of the challenges of fighting wars following the introduction of gunpowder, but in other parts of West Africa such constructions were unnecessary. The city of Benin, for example, already had effective defenses, built before the arrival of European traders and firearms. Benin was enclosed within ditches and wide earthworks that withstood shot.[23] Smaller communities with fewer resources built similar fortifications around their villages.[24] The defenses often incorporated sections of swamp and dense forest that hindered the advance of troops.[25] In some parts of West Africa intrinsic features of the landscape rendered firearms almost useless. In heavily forested or marshy regions, it was difficult to deploy men systematically and coordinate fire. In places where men could not cover each other by operating in disciplined groups they were often left exposed and unprotected, struggling with the common disadvantages of firearms, their unreliability, slow rate of fire, and inaccuracy. Some African people did not value firearms highly. European slave traders frequenting the coast of Guinea-Bissau, for example, discovered that iron spear-points, knives, swords, and arrows were in greater demand than guns.[26]

Like large parts of Africa, much of South America was covered by terrain poorly suited for firearms. John Mawe visited the Minas Gerais region of eastern Brazil in 1808 and 1809, and he reported that the indigenous people there "had a great dread of firearms and betake themselves to flight whenever they hear them." Mawe lamented that "these weapons are by no means so general among the settlers as they ought to be," but he went on to observe that "the few they have are of indifferent make, and frequently altogether useless." Exaggerating slightly, he reported that on the rare occasions when soldiers entered the region and confronted indigenous fighters, "no combat takes place" because the local warriors "run away as speedily as possible." Rather than fighting back with firearms or otherwise engaging in large-scale battles, the warriors of the Minas Gerais relied on stealth. They would "render themselves invisible by tying branches and young trees about them, and fix their bows imperceptibly, so that, when a poor negro or white happens to pass near them, they seldom miss their aim." Mawe also reported that the warriors dug "pit-falls, in which they place pointed stakes, and cover them with twigs and leaves" to trap their adversaries.[27] Tactics like these impeded colonization in some parts of the Minas Gerais well into the nineteenth century.

In some other parts of the Americas, firearms spread rapidly. Spanish conquistadors distributed weapons to their allies almost everywhere they went, and rival sources of firearms soon became available as a result of divisions between Spanish leaders, desertions, and internal rebellions. In the sixteenth century, only a few years after their entry into the region south of the Biobío River in central Chile, the Spanish faced resistance from Araucanian warriors carrying firearms. Spanish deserters provided the warriors with guns, and over the next several decades the Araucanians augmented their arsenals through battlefield seizures and raids. Before the end of the century they were producing their own gunpowder from local seams of volcanic sulphur, saltpeter, and charcoal.[28] During the seventeenth century firearms became even more widely available as rival European powers increasingly competed for allies and trade. In the 1640s most Mohawk warriors carried guns, and many of their indigenous allies and adversaries were similarly equipped.[29] By the end of the seventeenth century, indigenous Americans from the Gulf of Mexico to the southern fringe of the Arctic had armed themselves with guns.

As warriors adopted these weapons, they developed their own distinctive tactics. The Araucanians initially avoided pitched battles with the Spanish. They chose instead to take soldiers by surprise on mountain passes and along other narrow corridors. Guns were useful in these ambushes, but the warriors also relied on other military tools, including some they had developed specifically in response to the Spanish. They hung snares to pull Spanish riders from their horses, and dug trenches floored with spikes to impale those who fell in. They also continued to use bows and arrows, slings, lances, spears, and clubs.[30]

The wide diffusion of firearms encouraged experimentation. In North America it was rare for indigenous warriors to seek out or engage in large-scale battles. More commonly they would wait in ambush, forming a loose semicircle, and attack by surprise. An eruption of gunfire would startle their opponents at the start of an assault. To heighten panic, warriors would scream before closing in with tomahawks and other weapons that bludgeoned and cut.[31] This tactic worked best against small parties, but it could be used against entire villages, and a prolonged campaign of ambushes could deplete large armies.[32]

In the Americas as in Europe, one of the most common, dramatic, and visible effects of the introduction of gunpowder weapons was the widespread abandonment of body armor. For centuries, Iroquoian warriors had covered themselves elaborately before entering combat. They wore wooden helmets and covered their chests, thighs, and arms with wood, woven reeds, and leather.[33] This clothing offered almost no protection from bullets, and in the seventeenth century warriors across eastern North America began to fight in "thin, light dress, generally consisting of nothing more than a shirt, stockings and mogasins, and sometimes almost naked."[34]

After the arrival of Europeans, epidemic disease struck urban centers in the Americas, and towns and cities were abandoned in many regions. The decline of urban life in places like the Amazon basin reduced the need for fortification.[35]

Elsewhere, for example among the Haudenosaunee, towns became fewer and more scattered, but retained their defensive architecture. In places where villagers continued to shelter behind stockades, designs changed as warriors responded to the challenge of defending their villages against people with firearms. In the 1640s the Huron and Haudenosaunee began building square or rectangular forts, sometimes with bastions and sometimes with towers at the corners.[36] In 1713, Tuscaroras built a stockade with roofed, protruding bastions. They also dug underground bunkers inside the enclosure.[37] The Hurons redesigned their forts with advice from the French, and the Tuscaroras similarly drew on colonial models in their military constructions, but neither group simply adopted European designs. As they reshaped and strengthened their stockades and other defenses, the Huron, Tuscaroras, and other eastern North American groups used and adapted designs and building methods that had evolved locally over centuries as well as responding to the arrival of new kinds of weapons.

Many hand-held weapons, or the raw materials necessary to produce them, were traded and shipped across the Atlantic in the early modern era. In the St. Lawrence region, indigenous warriors adopted metal arrowheads, axes, knives, and swords as early as the 1620s, only a few years after the French arrived at Quebec.[38] In some parts of Africa, slave traders discovered that the demand for iron for hand-held weapons outstripped the demand for guns, a pattern that persisted through the eighteenth century.[39] The transatlantic trade in fully assembled weapons and militarily useful metals had a destructive impact, as European and colonial merchants made fortunes and acquired leverage over their trading partners by offering them guns, other finished weapons, and metals. People in Africa and the Americas sold them furs, ivory, gold, or captives to gain short-term military advantages. When merchants competed for customers, rival indigenous powers often competed militarily, and so warfare encouraged transatlantic commerce, and trade with Europe encouraged war. There were exceptions to this pattern. West Africa retained its own iron industry even though it suffered from European competition.[40] In parts of Mexico after the Spanish conquest, some craftsmen still produced obsidian projectile points.[41] And some communities in Africa and the Americas retained their poisoned arrows.

In 1572, when Francis Drake raided the Spanish port of Nombre de Dios on the isthmus of Panama, his men carried muskets, bows and arrows, burning lances, and pikes. The defenders deployed a similar array of weapons, and both sides improvised with fire, spears, arrows, and blades. Nearly blinded and panicked under a torrent of English arrows, some of the Spanish resorted to holding their muskets by the barrel and using them as clubs.[42] During this raid and in many other American battles in the sixteenth century, the weapons that most terrified the Spanish were arrows. After Drake and his men had withdrawn to a nearby island the Spanish governor sent a messenger to him to plead, according to English reports of the event, that "because many of their men were wounded with our arrows," they needed to learn whether the arrows were "poisoned or not." Fearing that they were, the Spanish asked, "how their wounds might best be cured?"[43] On the islands and coasts surrounding the Caribbean, many indigenous warriors used arrows with poison that was generally lethal, but caused the wounded to suffer slow and painful deaths.[44] According to a chronicler writing in the 1550s, Caribbean warriors tipped their arrows with "the juice of a certain herb, and whoever is wounded by one of these is certain to die biting himself like a mad dog."[45] Drake did not approve of poisoned arrows, and though he received support from indigenous allies, he proudly told the messenger "it was never his manner" to use them.[46]

Poisoned arrows were feared in North and South America and on both sides of the Atlantic. In 1654, native peoples fleeing a war zone on the banks of Lake Erie told the French in Montreal that the Erie or "Cat Nation," a mixed community of Algonkian and Iroquoian refugees, had assembled two thousand men "well skilled in war, although they have no firearms." The Erie warriors, it was said, "fight like Frenchmen, bravely sustaining the first discharge of the Iroquois, who are armed with our [French] muskets, and then falling upon them with a hailstorm of poisoned arrows, which they discharge eight or ten times before a musket can be reloaded."[47]

The poisoned arrow's effectiveness depended in part on the poisoner retaining and concealing detailed knowledge of the formula and its potential antidotes. To dramatize this point, a warrior in Gambia in 1731 showed an English visitor "a vast number of arrows, which were daubed over with a black mixture said to be such rank poison that if the arrow did but draw blood it would be mortal, unless the person who made the mixture had a mind to cure it, in whose power it only was to do."[48] The poisoner's reliance on secrecy helps explain why poisoned arrows were exclusively local products. The precise formulas used were never disseminated widely. Furthermore, it was assumed that the poisons were dangerous to make. In 1599, after decades of military service in and around the Spanish colony of New Granada, Captain Bernardo de Vargas Machuca, drawing on hearsay and expressing his own fear, reported that the indigenous people of South America allowed only "the very oldest women" to make poison for arrows. He claimed that the process involved boiling a variety of venoms together in a single pot. The women would tend the fire, stir the mixture, and invariably die from inhaling the vapor. For Vargas Machuca, the apparent barbarity of this production method reinforced his deep-seated cultural aversion to poison. For centuries Europeans had associated poisons generally, and poisoned arrows in particular, with deceit and dishonor, and for all these reasons, poisoned arrows, unlike guns, would never become items of long-distance commerce.[49]

Fearing ambushes and combat at close range facing not just firearms but also arrows, slings, clubs, and hatchets, colonial soldiers in the Americas kept wearing metal armor even after that kind of protection had begun to decline in Europe.[50] They also revitalized and revised another fading European tactic in deploying dogs. As vigilant sentries and as trackers, dogs could serve colonial armies in ways no human could. Vargas Machuca recommended using dogs to foil surprise attacks. "Dogs," he wrote, "reveal an ambush from a great distance, for they smell it."[51]

The dog's tracking ability was augmented by its power to intimidate. Many indigenous American groups had dogs of their own, but before the arrival of the Europeans their dogs had been smaller, less fierce by reputation, and quieter. The indigenous people of Mexico remembered their first encounter with Spanish dogs in frightening terms. Sixteenth-century storytellers reported that the dogs who arrived with the conquistadors were "very large."

> They had ears folded over; great dragging jowls. They had fiery eyes—blazing eyes; they had yellow eyes. They had thin flanks—flanks with ribs showing. They had gaunt stomachs. They were very tall. They were nervous; they went about panting, with tongues hanging. They were spotted like ocelots; they were varicoloured.

According to local legend, when Moctezuma heard about the Spaniards' dogs he was terrified.[52]

Vargas Machuca suggested that all one had to do to overcome a lone indigenous warrior was "loose the dog; later it finds the Indian without the soldier going with it, and there it is until the people arrive, having the Indian cowered."[53] Dogs could perform military service simply by making warriors "cower," but they could also bite and kill. As early as 1494, Columbus set a pack of dogs against his indigenous opponents on Hispaniola.[54] In 1622, following the Powhattan strike against Virginia, Edward Waterhouse argued that the colonists could score an easy retaliatory victory by "pursuing and chasing them with our horses and bloodhounds to draw after them, and mastiffs to tear them."[55] Later in the seventeenth century, other English colonists cited Virginia's example to justify sending dogs against indigenous Americans.[56]

Dogs may have given some European forces a military edge in the early stages of conquest and colonization in the Americas, but that advantage gradually declined in the seventeenth century because dogs were prone to escape and in effect switch sides, breeding without any regard to pedigree. Furthermore, in the vicinity of some English colonies, indigenous American groups purchased European and colonial dogs. In the 1670s colonists on Long Island complained that the Shinnecocks kept "great dogs," and "do

Fig. 5.2 Thedore de Bry, "The dogs of Vasco Nunez de Balboa (1475–1571) attacking the Indians." British Library.

nourish and bring up kennels of them."[57] By the late seventeenth century when Algonkian warriors fought New Englanders in an extended sequence of wars, the adversaries fielded roughly equivalent canine sentries and packs. Soldiers and warriors traveled with dogs and targeted them in the initial phase of attacks.[58] In 1675, before she was captured in Massachusetts during King Philip's War, Mary Rowlandson believed that she was safe behind the protection of her town garrison's "six stout dogs." If any warrior came to her door, she thought, the dogs were "ready to fly upon him and tear him down."[59] But the dogs failed to respond on the night when Rowlandson was taken, and she never learned what happened to them. Major Benjamin Church's expedition up the Bay of Fundy in 1696 may provide a clue. Church traveled with indigenous American warriors, and on one occasion he left them while they raided a coastal settlement of French-speaking colonists. When Church returned, he saw the colonists' dogs, along with their livestock, "lying dead about their houses, chopped and hacked with hatchets."[60]

Methods of using animals in warfare, like other forms of military technology, changed as they spread across the Atlantic world. The history of mastiffs, bloodhounds, and other dogs in the Americas illustrates the cascading, unpredictable effects of colonial contact. Animals were not only traded, stolen, or seized in raids, they also often simply ran away. And with animals the interplay of human cultural influences was complicated by a set of biological imperatives involving food, reproduction, and the maintenance of health. Animals evolved in response to the challenges presented them, and in some cases, they literally changed shape. This is what happened after indigenous American dogs bred with European mastiffs.

Soldiers and warriors across the Atlantic world relied on countless animals in warfare. In various places they rode or drove camels, mules, donkeys, oxen, and cattle. These and other animals, some domesticated, some not, assisted human communities as sentries. Dogs played several different roles in warfare. Horses, similarly, had many functions. Like the deployment of dogs in the Americas, the spread of horses on both sides of the Atlantic reveals an interplay of cultural, biological, and environmental adaptations.

In 1456 before sailing down the coast of Africa, Alvise Cadamosto acquired some "Spanish horses" which he had heard were "in great demand in the country of the Blacks." South of the Senegal River he met the leader of a province of the Wolof kingdom who was interested in trade. The African leader had come to the shore on horseback accompanied by a guard of 150 infantry and fifteen cavalrymen. Cadamosto gave him the Spanish horses, along with riding equipment and some other items, in exchange for a promise of a hundred captives Cadamosto could take as slaves. The Jolof leader agreed to these terms and immediately delivered Cadamosto a twelve-year-old girl, as Cadamosto put it, "for the service of my chamber." Cadamosto sent the girl onto his ship before setting off with the Africans to tour the province.[61]

Cadamosto believed that horses would be valuable items of exchange in the slave trade, but over the next several centuries they would not play as prominent a role as he had imagined. During his travels he discovered several reasons why. Horses were bulky, expensive to transport by ship, and difficult to feed and keep healthy. Horses were valuable in parts of West Africa, but the local merchants and leaders had no desperate need for expensive imports, and at least as far as horses were concerned, they never became dependent on European trade. Portuguese and other European merchants would continue to sell horses in West Africa, but these imports did not alter the regional military culture. They only added to the local breeding stock. West Africa had horses of its own.

Originally domesticated in Asia, horses arrived in West Africa by several routes. The antiquity and variety of West Africa's horse breeds is indicated by the wide number of unrelated words for "horse" in different West African languages.[62] The region's original horses may have been brought westward from Egypt and Nubia. Others arrived later from the north across the Sahara. There

Fig. 5.3 A man with elaborate headgear, a sword and a shield, riding a horse. A bronze statuette from sixteenth-century Benin. British Museum.

were dramatic regional variations in the breeds and the ways they were ridden. In the early modern period, some West Africans used saddles while others abraded the backs of their horses and rode on the scar tissue.[63] Small horses were valued more for their speed and agility than for their strength. Men riding small horses usually carried javelins, charged quickly up to a certain distance, and then launched their weapons. They also carried knives and if they were attacked at close range, the warriors were ready to defend themselves but rode off quickly. The introduction of large horses from across the Sahara, along with saddles and stirrups, made it possible to use the animals in different ways. Warriors on large horses fought each other with thrusting spears and charged against infantry with slashing swords, swinging low and relying on the cutting edge of the blade. Africans never adopted the European technique of tucking the spear under the arm and relying on the power of the horse to give force to the spear thrust. Men in Africa used their own strength to hold and thrust the spear. To defend themselves against opposing cavalry they began wearing armor, often combining padded cloth with chain mail. Only a large horse could carry the weight of a rider in that kind of armor.[64]

Large horses were continuously in demand in parts of West Africa. Traders brought them across the Sahara and bred them south of the desert.[65] Some West African armies rose to power on the backs of such horses. In the 1720s it was said that the kingdom of Oyo in central Nigeria fielded "a great army of horse, consisting of many thousands, (for they never use infantry)." During their campaigns against Dahomey, the Oyo horses were initially startled and disorganized by gunfire, but eventually they overran much of the kingdom, forcing Dahomey's army to retreat into wooded terrain. Unable to pursue their military adversaries into the forest, the Oyo raided the countryside. The Dahomey army stayed in the woods as Oyo cavalry laid waste to much of the kingdom. But all was not lost, because horses had their own limitations. Dahomey's soldiers "patiently endured these calamities" because they knew that the Oyo "would be obliged to retire in a little time, on account of the rainy season that was approaching, and for want of forage."[66]

The contest between Oyo and Dahomey illustrates both the military usefulness of horses, and some of the environmental constraints that limited their use. Cavalry charges require open terrain. It is difficult to run horses quickly through forest, and they need pasture or fodder, which limits them both seasonally and geographically. But in Africa the most important constraint was disease. The farther south one traveled in West Africa, the more difficult it was to maintain horses. In many places the prevalence of trypanosomiasis, a disease carried by the tsetse fly, made keeping horses impossible.[67]

Disease was less of a limiting factor in the deployment of horses in Europe, but other environmental problems restricted them. Swamps, wide rivers, and steep or rocky terrain challenged horses. To overcome such difficulties, Europe's military leaders prioritized making territory accessible. In the seventeenth century, state-sponsored boards of military engineers expanded their remits beyond the design and construction of forts and began mapping the landscapes of Europe to identify potential invasion routes and recommend infrastructure to facilitate mobilization and defense. On the advice of the British Board of Ordnance and with soldiers performing much of the manual labor, between 1726 and 1737 General George Wade oversaw the construction of 40 bridges and 259 miles of road in the Scottish Highlands. These roads and bridges were designed to facilitate troop movements, ease communication between forts, and make the Highlands more accessible.[68] Not just in Scotland but across Europe, state investments in mapping and roads followed almost inexorably from the introduction of gunpowder weapons, the new technology of fortification, and the expansion of the continent's armies. These developments changed the military significance of the horse.

In Europe as in Africa, men on horseback still conducted raids, fought alongside infantry, skirmished on the edge of battlefields, and charged opposing armies in the closing phases of engagements.[69] But these were tactical choices that a commander might decline. A large army could fight without cavalry. It could not travel or survive without draft horses. In 1562 the Duke of Anjou's army required more than 1,000 horses to haul twenty heavy guns with their powder and ammunition.[70] In 1646 during the Thirty Years War, two Bavarian regiments had more horses than men.[71] In seventeenth-century France, armies with 60,000 soldiers could easily have 40,000 horses, 20,000 cavalry mounts and 20,000 animals for haulage. The draft horses pulled more than guns and ammunition. Their carts contained tents, cooking equipment, fuel, and food, and not just human food. Horses hauled their own fodder, and it was heavy and bulky. As much of 40 percent of the horses' cargo load was their own food. The seasonal availability of fodder dictated the calendar of combat. Armies withdrew in the winter and returned only when the grass returned. Even at the height of summer the supply of fodder constrained the army's options. Soldiers and their horses needed to move intermittently to find fresh grass and grain.[72] The Europeans' dependence on horses for warfare helps explain much of the difficulty they faced in bringing their way of fighting to the Americas.

When Hernando de Soto took his army of 600 to Florida in 1539, he brought 220 horses with him.[73] In the early stages of his long campaign the horses were useful militarily. Spanish chroniclers record that when de Soto commanded an attack against the palisaded town of Mabila, his horsemen rode in a line with lances forward, spearing warriors and driving them behind their stockades. Later that day the cavalrymen fought alongside infantry as they burned the town. When de Soto realized that his forces had prevailed, he rode through Mabila shouting prayers of thanksgiving and lancing warriors along the way. The inhabitants had unwittingly prepared the ground for the Spanish horsemen. They had burned all the houses and vegetation around their stockades to create a firing zone in anticipation of attack. Without experience with horses, they did not know that they had cleared a field for cavalry, and when the horsemen arrived, the villagers did not know how to resist the charge.[74] De Soto's horses performed well during the attack on Mabila, but overall the expedition proved difficult for them. Many died in battle or were killed quietly by indigenous Americans. Others drowned crossing rivers or were made lame after marching for years, eventually without horseshoes, through fields and forests. When the survivors reached the Mississippi in July 1543 there were fifty horses remaining, and most of them were useless for haulage or warfare. The Spanish slaughtered all but twenty-two of them, and in an ironic demonstration of the animals' diminished value for transportation, they lashed canoes together in pairs and led the remaining horses onto the crafts sideways so that their front hooves were in one canoe and their rear in the other. But then the canoes came under attack, and weary of defending their horses, the Spanish butchered the last of them. Four or five escaped.[75]

Seeking to avoid de Soto's fate, European and colonial military leaders across the Americas built roads to facilitate horse travel. In eighteenth-century Brazil, gangs of enslaved laborers overseen by soldiers cut roads through the forest to allow the movement of troops and equipment. Military men often joined in the toil, sometimes working day and night to keep the roads open and extend the routes.[76] In North America in 1757, at a pivotal moment in the Seven Years' War, General John Forbes designed a road from eastern Pennsylvania across the Appalachian Mountains. He ordered the construction of forts and blockhouses at forty-mile intervals along the route so that horses and men would not have to carry excessive supplies. He also placed garrisons at these outposts to help guard troop movements and supply trains. Mobilizing thousands of soldiers and laborers, he spent most of the year building this road. In November he arrived at his destination, Fort Duquesne. The road had allowed him to bring a large, well-equipped, and provisioned army across the mountains. Facing overwhelming force and abandoned by its indigenous allies, the French garrison retreated.[77]

While armies toiled to reengineer some American landscapes to make horse transportation viable, in other parts of the Americas there was no need to change the landscape at all. Spanish colonists brought horses to New Mexico in the seventeenth century, and the Pueblo revolt against colonial rule in 1680 dispersed those animals beyond the colony's borders.[78] Pueblo traders sold horses to neighboring people and other horses escaped. The American Plains were well suited for them. Horses released from New Mexico (and elsewhere) bred and spread without human supervision, and by the early nineteenth century there were approximately two million wild horses on the southern Great Plains. There were also hundreds of thousands in human possession, including many held by indigenous tribes.[79] Several indigenous American groups acquired horses and firearms in the eighteenth century, and they developed a new method of combat, firing guns from horseback at a distance.[80] A few, like the Comanches on the southern plains, and the Sioux in the north, rose to dominate vast territories.[81]

By tracing the triumphs and struggles of horses in the warzones of the Atlantic world, it is easy to discern geographical patterns, highlighting the military importance of terrain, disease environment, climate, and vegetation. These environmental factors, and others, constrained combatants in the early modern era, forcing soldiers and warriors to adjust their ways of fighting, not just their choice of weapons, but also their methods of transportation and haulage. In places inaccessible to horses, the best alternative was often the canoe.

Canoes were formidable instruments of war across much of the Atlantic world. In contrast to horse-drawn carts or ocean-going ships, they were ideal for amphibious warfare. In and around the Caribbean, warriors in canoes could land almost anywhere.[82] The canoe's capabilities could make everyone in a region vulnerable and helped create a climate of constant, low-level anxiety similar to the widespread fear that the Vikings instilled by fighting from beachable craft in medieval Europe. For more than two centuries after the first Spanish expedition to the Caribbean, Europeans and colonists remained unsure where Carib warriors came from or how many they were.[83] The mystery surrounding the Caribs contributed to their fierce reputation. Widely depicted in almost demonic terms, Caribs were considered the most frightening warriors in the world.[84]

In the Caribbean, Africa, and the Americas, warriors sometimes landed their canoes and hid them before proceeding to attack their opponents on foot, but the vessels could also serve as platforms for firing at opponents from a distance. Men fought from canoes using bows and arrows, spears, and handheld firearms. Some war canoes on the coast of Africa mounted guns.[85] Canoes could also have large carrying capacities, and they covered distances with little friction or expended energy compared to other transportation methods.

Fig. 5.4 A 1628 woodcut by Matthaeus Merian depicting the Powhatan attack on Virginia. Most accounts of the engagement suggest that the warriors walked up to the colonial settlements in an apparently friendly manner before turning on the colonists. There are no eyewitness accounts of canoe landings. Nonetheless, Merian's image conveys a strong sense of the terror they could invoke. Courtesy of the John Carter Brown Library.

Like horses, dogs, knives, swords, and firearms, canoes could easily change hands. Indigenous Americans offered canoes to colonists and taught them how to use and build them. Only a few years after the first English settlers arrived at the Plymouth colony, one of them, Thomas Weston, was not only making his own canoes but building some for indigenous Americans.[86] Canoes varied greatly in their design and construction, but the simplest ones were fairly easy to make. In New Granada, Machuca declared that canoes were "of great service in many undertakings," and he recommended that soldiers make their own dugouts.[87] Drawing perhaps on African experience as well as observations of other canoeists in the Caribbean, men and women escaping slavery in the Danish West Indies made canoes to take to the mainland or neighboring islands. This was perceived to be such a threat to social order that in the early eighteenth century the privy council of St. Thomas ordered the felling of every tree on the island suitable for canoe construction.[88]

With the right materials, tools, and time, it was not difficult to build a canoe, but deploying them in large numbers for military purposes required intricate planning and coordination. This was revealed dramatically in the summer of 1709 with the failure of an British-led effort to attack Canada from the south. A regiment raised in Connecticut was responsible for logistics. In July the soldiers assembled in Albany, New York. Gathering on the banks of the Hudson, men loaded canoes with provisions, guns, powder, and ammunition. They paddled the canoes upstream, approximately ten miles, until the river became too shallow, and then they unloaded and packed their cargo onto horse-drawn wagons. The horses pulled the wagons down eighteen miles of road before the canoes were put back into the water, and then reloaded for another stage of paddling. Eighteen miles farther upstream the regiment reached another carrying place, where the canoes were taken out of the river again. The canoes were unloaded, and horses were employed carrying the packs and canoes overland to the next stretch of navigable river. This process was repeated several times. Even with the canoes in the water, transportation was difficult. In some stretches of river men waded "up to their armpits to drag the canoes along."[89] But the horses were the first to balk.

As one participant in the expedition put it, "the horses are tired and can go no longer."[90] They were "serviceable in the beginning in carrying provisions over the great and little carrying places," but they grew "feeble by the hard work and violent hot weather" and were "not well fed."[91] In an effort to keep the horses alive and healthy, the men began to offer them grain from the supplies that were meant to feed the soldiers. Other supplies were dropped along the way, soaked, or stolen. As the soldier put it, "By these several carriages and shiftings from canoes to wagons, and from wagons to canoes and so forward from canoe to canoe it may easily be conjectured what loss there is."[92] The regiment had recruited fifteen indigenous Americans from Long Island to oversee "managing the canoes," but even with their assistance the effort descended into chaos.[93] The soldiers deserted. "Our people quit their canoes and came home ragged and torn and some half-starved."[94]

In inland regions, canoes were restricted to particular routes. This favored travelers familiar with the river's rocks, trees, bends, currents, landing places, and stretches where navigation was impossible. But the predictability of the route left canoe convoys vulnerable to ambush. In the seventeenth century the Haudenosaunee exerted influence over a region stretching several hundred miles from the Hudson River Valley north beyond Lake Ontario and west beyond the Ohio. Haudenosaunee military power derived in part from the warriors' ability to surprise and overwhelm their opponents on rivers and strategic riverbanks.[95]

As they were in the Americas, canoes were widely available for sale in Africa. In the 1670s and 1680s, Jean Barbot identified seven towns on or near the southern coast of West Africa where Europeans could buy canoes.[96] But without extensive local knowledge and social capital, Europeans would have had difficulty using the vessels militarily. On the Niger Delta, Barbot saw canoes carved from a single tree, seventy feet long and seven or eight feet wide. He reported that men "commonly hang at the head of the canoe two shields, and on the sides some bundles of javelins, in a readiness to repulse any attempt that may be made on them in their voyages along the rivers." The canoes had benches, a retractable awning, and a hearth for cooking. Eighteen "hands" could handle one, but in preparation for combat the canoes could carry "seventy or eighty men, with all necessary provisions to subsist them, being generally yams, bananas, chickens, hogs, goats or sheep, palm-wine and palm oil."[97] As Barbot's description suggests, maintaining a war canoe involved much more than simply taking care of the physical object. The vessels lay at the center of elaborate social networks including merchants, armorers, provisioners, and warriors.

From the Niger Delta across the North American Great Plains, the forests of Brazil, the Sahara, the Caribbean islands, the Hudson River Valley, the foothills of the Andes, and the large battlefields of Europe, the diversity of landscapes around the Atlantic assured that no single military technology would work effectively everywhere. This circumstance impeded, or at least slowed and complicated, the imposition of European authority overseas. The geographical limits constraining different ways of fighting assured that the Atlantic world's peoples would continue to meet in dynamic zones of conflict, collaboration, innovation, and violence. Rather than dictating terms to indigenous peoples, colonists and imperial leaders had little choice but to seek alliances.

Warriors

In 1493, within a year of the first appearance of Spanish ships in the Caribbean, violent clashes erupted between the arriving soldiers and indigenous warriors, beginning on Hispaniola. The fighting on that island continued intermittently for the next thirty years, and according to many commentators the events on Hispaniola established a pattern for the American mainland. The most influential early chronicler of the Spanish conquest was Bartolomé de las Casas, who asserted that Hispaniola experienced "the wholesale slaughter of its people and the devastation and depopulation of the land."[1] According to Las Casas, Columbus and his crew initially received a warm welcome, but their relations with the local people deteriorated quickly. Spanish soldiers seized food supplies, kidnapped and raped women, and engaged in acts of sadistic violence that escalated into massacres. They made slaves of the surviving islanders, prevented them from caring for their children, and either left them to starve or worked them to death. Writing in 1542, Las Casas declared that the Spanish committed the same atrocities in colonial ventures in other parts of the Caribbean and on mainland North and South America. "The pattern established at the outset has remained unchanged to this day, and the Spaniards still do nothing save tear the natives to shreds, murder them and inflict upon them untold misery, suffering and distress, tormenting, harrying and persecuting them mercilessly."[2]

Las Casas is justly credited with raising European awareness of the human cost of colonization, but his account of early colonial warfare was inaccurately simple. To highlight the brutality of the Spanish conquest, he emphasized the islanders' peaceful nature, and he drew a stark contrast as if the battle lines had simply set European newcomers against indigenous people. He described the islanders as naïve, militarily weak, and relatively unaggressive, even though warfare had long been endemic on Hispaniola and preparation for combat had been a pervasive, imperative feature of life on the island for centuries before the Spaniards arrived. The Spanish knew this, because they fought alongside local allies in Hispaniola. They exploited indigenous military recruitment networks not only to gather, supply, and deploy warriors, but also to commandeer laborers. Remnants of the

Atlantic Wars. Geoffrey Plank, Oxford University Press (2020). © Oxford University Press.
DOI: 10.1093/oso/9780190860455.001.0001

islanders' old power structures and military traditions survived and were incorporated into the Spanish administration on Hispaniola, at least until the Spanish
began importing large numbers of enslaved laborers from Africa.

This chapter briefly examines the cross-cultural experience of conflict on
Hispaniola in the decades after the arrival of Columbus before discussing the
Atlantic world more broadly. Across Africa, the Americas, and Europe, nearly
every community designated a select number of individuals to fight in war.
Raising, training, supplying, and deploying the fighters engaged the efforts of
nearly everyone else. Warfare bound communities together, giving a band, village,
tribe, or nation in a common cause. But the shared experience of conflict also
crossed vast social divides, bringing together people with different allegiances
and customs. To survive and prosper in the early modern era, communities
around the Atlantic had to maintain a difficult balance between fighting wars
and maintaining subsistence. Their solutions to this challenge varied greatly, but
their commonalties are often more striking than their differences.

Warriors and soldiers who met each other in battle engaged in intimate
communication and faced death together. Europeans, Africans, and indigenous Americans often fought side-by-side as allies or within integrated military
units, and even when they confronted each other as antagonists they were constantly alert to the possibility of compromise or surrender. Warfare also brought
noncombatants together. The work of military preparedness involved so many
people that in some communities it shaped social relations from cradle to grave.
This was true in Africa, Europe, and the Americas, and when the inhabitants of
different continents met, the challenge of fielding forces became a shared experience on a transatlantic scale. Communities separated by the ocean worked together within complex, shifting, multiethnic alliances. Societies opposing each
other also, ironically, worked simultaneously on common tasks. When distant,
antagonistic groups engaged in warfare they had no intention of cooperating,
but before any battle could occur large numbers of people within each community labored to provide, equip, and maintain the combatants.

The lives of people across the Atlantic world changed together as the pattern of warfare changed. One of the most important trends in the early modern
period was the deployment of fighters over greater distances and for longer
periods of time. In most places, the social distance between combatants and
noncombatants increased, as forces grew larger and operated more independently from local power structures. Long-term, long-distance deployment altered
the meaning of military service and strained the logistical capacities of small
villages and transatlantic empires alike.

When Christopher Columbus landed on the shore of Hispaniola in 1492,
the island became the focus of Spain's first colonization efforts in the Western
Hemisphere. Columbus left a small contingent of soldiers behind on the island

when he returned to Spain. The admiral came back with a much larger fleet in 1493. Michele da Cuneo accompanied him and according to his reports, upon their return they encountered a dismal sight. Da Cuneo reported, "we landed and found all of our men dead and still lying here and there on the ground, without eyes."[3] Columbus realized, too late, that he had left the soldiers virtually defenseless, and after this incident he knew that he could proceed with colonization only with local military support.

The people of Hispaniola had a well-established system for mobilizing military forces. The island was divided into chiefdoms led by men called caciques, who based their authority on kinship ties. The caciques kept groups of men around them ready to take up arms, and when they felt it necessary to summon more, they could call up most of the men within their chiefdoms.[4] During his visit to Hispaniola, da Cuneo observed that there were few old men and that women seemed to do much of the work.[5] Both of these features of life on the island reflected the impact of endemic warfare. The islanders' marriage practices, kinship networks, and political structure accommodated high wartime casualty rates and the consequent shortage of adult men. In some regions of Hispaniola, these social arrangements allowed female-dominated communities to uphold their traditional way of life for decades, even after most of the men had been summoned away by the Spanish or died from violence, abuse, and disease.[6]

After 1493, Spain's military commanders sought advice from caciques. Their military operations were therefore often steered by communal rivalries on the island, as Spanish commanders literally took directions from their allies. Even after the Spanish had asserted their domination over Hispaniola, they relied on caciques to gather tribute and requisition laborers. The caciques summoned and deployed male laborers for the Spanish in the same way that they had previously commanded their men to fight. Laborers were pulled from their villages for six months at a time.[7]

Disease decimated the population, adding to the toll exacted by combat and excessive labor demands. More men died than women because the Spanish required men to work in their gold mines and farms. Some indigenous villages survived for decades, but eventually the Spanish colonists' demand for labor and tribute impeded the islanders' ability to grow food.[8] As early as 1517 a group of friars wrote to Madrid complaining that Hispaniola was depopulated. The land was fertile but there was no one to cultivate it. They warned that without a subsidized influx of settlers Hispaniola would have to be abandoned.[9] As an interim measure the Spanish coordinated the consolidation of indigenous villages, with soldiers forcibly transporting people to form larger, economically viable units. Some islanders resisted militarily, and as late as the 1530s there were small-scale attacks on the Spanish near the coastal colonial settlement of Puerto Real. After that, the islanders were no longer able to field an effective military force.[10]

Nonetheless, contrary to what Las Casas suggested, the indigenous people of Hispaniola were not wholly exterminated, nor did they abruptly end their resistance to Spanish power. After their military capacity dissolved it is likely that the islanders' remaining acts of resistance were isolated and uncoordinated, like the struggles of a Carib captive acquired by da Cuneo in 1493. She slashed at him with her nails and "raised unheard of cries" when he raped her.[11] She fought alone.

Warfare is an intrinsically communal endeavor.[12] Societies that engage in war must select certain individuals for combat, and then prepare, equip and sustain them, and coordinate their actions. The various societies ringing the Atlantic differed in the ways they selected individuals for combat. Some allowed women to assume leadership roles, for example. The Kingdom of Dahomey fielded female warriors, but the overwhelming pattern was to deploy boys and men. In some communities, boys were prepared for military service from a very young age and fighting was perceived, at least for males, to be a stage in every man's life. Other groups specialized, either by making military training and service a mark of elite status, or by fielding permanent armies of unfortunates and slaves. There were important contrasts in the age profile of fighting forces, but generally children were excluded from combat roles. There was also a wide disparity in the ways communities fed and supplied their fighters in the field. In some regions, entire villages were dismantled and relocated to follow warriors in their campaigns. At the other extreme, in many places fighters were sent out unsupplied in the expectation that they would feed themselves by foraging, barter, and plunder.

As Las Casas indicated, there were several lasting precedents set by the Spanish conquest of Hispaniola. The exploitation of local alliance networks, the betrayal of former allies, the adoption of exploitative forced labor regimes, the decline in the local population, and the fateful resort to imported slave labor foreshadowed events across the Americas. Disease followed colonization nearly everywhere. Near newly founded colonies, epidemics attacked populations already weakened by warfare, dispossession, environmental distress, poverty, and exploitation. Nonetheless, while it is important to recognize the parallels between events on Hispaniola and subsequent developments on the mainland of North and South America, the distinctions are also important. Elsewhere in the Americas indigenous populations regrouped and found new ways to assert themselves militarily and diplomatically.

Everywhere, the challenge of fielding, maintaining, and controlling fighting forces required complex social arrangements. Each community's response to this challenge reflected its power structure, wealth, and method of allocating economic resources. Historians, ethnographers, and anthropologists have observed a close connection between patterns of subsistence, social organization, and ways of deploying men for combat. Archaeologists have argued that many egalitarian societies engage in warfare frequently, with small groups of warriors operating on their own initiative. Warriors from such societies may occasionally band together to engage in large-scale battles, but more typically they perform ambushes and raids. Chiefdoms, by contrast, structure their forces hierarchically, make more elaborate preparations for war, and send fighting men out with orders from members of a military elite.[13]

During the long process of European conquest and colonization in North and South America, some indigenous communities managed to survive without fighting or preparing for military action. Though their ancestors had fought against the Swedes and Dutch, the emergent Delaware nation defined itself during its formative period in the late seventeenth and early eighteenth centuries as a peaceable people occupying a special position within an alliance network including the six nations of the Haudenosaunee and several colonies of the English Empire.[14] Even more resolutely, the Wampanoag of Martha's Vineyard renounced warfare in the seventeenth century and though they suffered at various times, they established a community without fighting that survives today.[15] Throughout the Americas indigenous peoples responded in their own ways to the challenges posed by the arrival of Europeans and Africans. Nonetheless, in most instances, the cohesion, strength, and endurance of indigenous American societies depended on their ability to maintain fighting forces.

One ancient formulation suggests that military hierarchy and discipline are marks of civilization, and some historians have argued that the professionalization of military service is an integral component of modernization. Writing in the 1970s, French historian André Corvisier drew a distinction between soldiers and fighters. According to Corvisier, soldiers pursue a vocation and are paid for their work. They live in barracks or camps and have officers who supervise them continuously, maintain discipline, and keep them from returning to their families. Corvisier claimed that the world has had disciplined, professional soldiers only in modern times. He insisted that the knights and peasants who fought Europe's battles in the Middle Ages were mere "fighters" rather than soldiers.[16]

Like a great deal of scholarly military history, Corvisier's scheme contains a continental bias. Comprehending early modern history on an Atlantic scale requires taking into account the variety of ways in which different societies selected, ordered, equipped, and supplied men and women for engagement in combat. Adopting a more inclusive perspective highlights the distinguishing features of all military service and draws a line between warfare and the struggles of fighters like the woman who tried to resist Michel da Cuneo without preparation or social support. There were men and women like her in nearly every theater of conflict.

In most places, children are taught about warfare from a very young age. The purpose of this education was seldom to prepare everyone for battle. On the contrary, more often the acculturation process involved identifying the criteria that distinguished the warrior from everyone else. The lessons may have come from family members, spiritual leaders, mentors, or playmates, but regardless of the child-rearing practices prevalent in any given village, region, or city, children had to learn rudimentary rules about the application of physical force. This is essential for social cohesion and it made warfare possible.

Though societies surrounding the Atlantic differed greatly in their ways of selecting, acculturating, and training fighters, virtually all of them maintained a military culture distinguishing warfare from other acts of violence and designating certain individuals to fight. Though the categories they used varied greatly, certain patterns recurred throughout Africa, the Americas, and Europe. For example, in general it was men, rather than boys, girls, or women, who were selected to fight in war.

Among the Aztecs in the sixteenth century, some boys were dedicated to warfare, at least symbolically, from birth. They were given small shields and swords when they were four days old, and these items, along with their umbilical cords, were buried in symbolic battlefields pointing in the direction of anticipated adversaries.[17] At the age of twenty days, boys were taken to a ceremony at the schools where they would later be trained as soldiers, and as they grew older their appearance reflected their dedication to military service. When ten years old they began to grow a tuft of hair at the back of their heads which they would not be able to cut until they had entered combat and successfully seized a captive. At fifteen they entered their formal military training, first at school and then as apprentices following warriors into action.[18]

When certain kinds of military service are associated with elite status, particular implements of warfare such as horses or swords can become markers identifying a person's place within a social hierarchy. Possessions and skills may continue to mark out elite status even after their military utility declines. In late medieval and early modern Europe, for example, swords became fashionable items for male members of the gentry and aristocracy, worn even by those who had no intention of entering battle. But the swords remained weapons, and they continued to carry important symbolic significance, distinguishing the gentry from commoners, men from women, and men from boys.

During the sixteenth century in his advice manual *The Schoolmaster* Roger Ascham recommended an array of mock-military activities for the sons of gentlemen and nobles, including "play at all weapons, to shoot fair in bow or surely in gun."[19] As Ascham suggested, play in early modern England could blur the distinction between fun and military training even after the introduction of gunpowder. A seventeenth-century toy matchlock recently fished out of the

Fig. 6.1 The sixteenth-century *Codex Mendoza* depicted Aztec rituals performed for four-day-old boys in which they were given male "insignias" in the form of implements useful for adult life including arrows and a shield. MS. Arch. Selden. A.1, fol. 57r. The Bodleian Libraries, University of Oxford.

Thames contained a fully effective firing mechanism.[20] Of course playing with toys did not fully prepare a boy for military action, and only a fraction of the boys who engaged in war-themed play grew up to become soldiers. But even if a boy had no ambition to join the military, his toys and games implicitly taught him to associate military action with maturity, privilege, and masculinity.

Gender structured military culture everywhere in the Atlantic world. The Aztecs who gave shields, bows and arrows to newborn boys held a parallel ceremony for girls. Female babies received equipment for spinning and weaving.[21] Among the Caribs on the northern coast of South America, when war chiefs assembled to plan and prepare for attacks, they conducted rituals that involved women and young men in starkly contrasting roles. The men drank a special beer prepared with the blood and organs of tigers, snakes, and human beings, and they performed dances that helped prepare them for battle. The women watched

Fig. 6.2 Seventeenth-century toy matchlock discovered in the Thames. Royal Armouries.

the dances and urged the warriors on, to strengthen their resolve. The ceremonies invoked spirits and formed an important part of Carib communal life.[22]

Nearly everywhere, combat was associated with manhood, but in Europe and Africa, societies under pressure armed others. In times of crisis kingdoms in the Bight of Benin sent children and women to fight alongside better-trained men.[23] In 1728 King Agaja of Dahomey, facing invasion, recruited significant numbers of women into his army. His initial purpose was to make his forces appear larger, but eventually women in Dahomey assumed important combat roles. One observer saw forty women with muskets helping guard the royal palace and ninety women under arms in a company returning from the field. By 1781, the kingdom's army included eight hundred armed women.[24] Dahomey was exceptional.

In the early seventeenth century, when much of central Africa descended into war, a group called the Imbangala sustained itself through continuous fighting. The Imbangala erected temporary forts that they used as bases for plundering, terrorizing, dispersing, capturing, or killing the surrounding population. They replenished their manpower by seizing and assimilating adolescent boys, and incorporating them into their fighting forces.[25] This recruitment strategy, using intimidation and force to remove boys from their villages and cultures, was not sustained in the long run. By the mid seventeenth century some of the Imbangala had established their own kingdoms and drew recruits from among the people they governed.[26]

In his survey of global warfare since ancient times, John Keegan placed all the world's combatants into six categories: self-styled elite warriors, mercenary fighters, regular troops, slaves, conscripts, and militia. Keegan acknowledged, however, that his categories blurred into one another. Since they fought for pay, regular soldiers resembled mercenaries, and it is sometimes difficult to distinguish conscripts from the enslaved.[27] Few complex societies rely on only one method of mobilization. For example, in the Calusa kingdom in southern Florida in the sixteenth century, the king maintained a subsidized, permanent body of warriors, but he could also call on villages to augment his forces with irregulars. A general summons could raise large numbers of troops. When Ponce de Leon came to the coast in 1513 he faced eighty canoes of warriors firing arrows.[28]

Many West African states relied on levies, summoning men to serve at times of crisis. According to one account from the 1670s, drummers were dispatched in the night to call the local men into service. In this manner an army could be assembled in fifteen days.[29] Kings and captains in towns maintained permanent personal guards, some of whom were enslaved. These forces were augmented by militia.[30] Additionally, merchants maintained their own armies, and there were mercenary captains who hired units out to supplement other local forces.[31] In the eighteenth century Dahomey established permanent, tax-supported units with uniforms, flags, and firearms. These uniformed troops were said to number three thousand and were supported by ten thousand other fighters including boys summoned from villages. Villages gave up the boys at a young age to be raised in the army away from their families and turned into soldiers.[32]

Like their counterparts in Africa and the Americas, Europe's land forces in the early modern era included a mix of mercenaries, militiamen, professional soldiers, volunteers, and conscripts. There was a trend, however, toward centralization, and regular professional soldiers came to dominate Europe's largest armies. But even as armies professionalized they often exploited and reinforced traditional methods of mobilization. Across Europe, army recruiters worked within local power structures.[33] Defending this practice, one commentator asked rhetorically, "is it credible that a peasant will so readily enlist with a Serjeant or Drummer he never saw before, as with the brother or son of his landlord under whom he has all his life lived?"[34] Using community leaders as recruiters made enlisting men easier, and it also, at least in theory, strengthened the cohesion of the corps. Thus, Europe's armies contained units dominated by soldiers from the same region, clan or name.[35]

In times of prosperity recruiters paid high bounties to the men they enlisted, but in hard times they saw no need to pay anything in advance. In Marseilles in 1707 several members of the opera's orchestra enlisted in the French army "because they were dying of hunger."[36] Though men frequently enlisted in groups as these musicians did, at the other extreme individuals opted for military service when they were desperately alone. In 1632, an English law clerk named Thomas Raymond traveled to The Hague in the vain hope of finding employment at court, and after his scheme collapsed military service became his next option. As he described his situation, "I had in this brave place a very unbrave life," and so "from the court to the camp I went." Raymond enlisted as a pikeman in a mercenary company and saw action within a year.[37]

Training has a profound effect on the structure of armed forces. Some fighting methods, on horseback, for example, or using swords and javelins, require extensive training. Such training cannot be accomplished at short notice, and this militates in favor of maintaining permanent specialized troops. Reflecting this dynamic, some West African armies included distinct classes of warriors. Elite fighting men wielded swords, while common soldiers and the enslaved fought with javelins or bows and arrows.[38] Bows and arrows were nearly ubiquitous, and they were usually the weapons of the irregulars. In West Africa and elsewhere, conscripts were generally not well trained since they were summoned only intermittently and with little advance warning. They brought their weapons with them, but may have known how to use them only for hunting.[39] Many weapons can be used both for hunting and combat, but it is seldom easy to transfer hunting skills to the battlefield.

Wars are not like hunts because animals do not arm themselves and fire back. In comparison to hunters, warriors need to protect themselves and respond effectively to their adversaries' defensive measures. Their projectile weapons often need greater penetrating power in order to pierce armor. Thus, firing in battle forcefully requires distinctive skill. Furthermore, warriors need a different kind of attentiveness to anticipate return fire and protect themselves against the efforts of their opponents.[40] Pikes and spears are often depicted as "democratic" weapons because, it seems, they are inexpensive to produce and almost anyone can use them.[41] To be sure, holding a pike is not difficult, but fighting with a pike is more challenging, requiring protecting oneself while holding the pike. Similar defensive skill sets were needed to throw spears, launch arrows, or use firearms. In almost all military contexts individual survival and the viability of the fighting force required a combination of dexterity, agility, discipline, coordination, quick communication, and group cohesion.

For these practical reasons, military leaders around the Atlantic world used various forms of dance to train fighters and prepare them for battle. In 1751, in the northern Appalachian Mountains, Presbyterian missionary John Brainerd watched Haudenosaunee warriors dance in a circle around a fire, responding to the rhythm of a rattle and a drum. The warriors "jumped round with great swiftness as one man, or as though they had been framed together." They tightly coordinated their actions as they adjusted their posture and movements, sometimes running erect, "sometimes half bent, and sometimes seeming to let, or rest themselves on the strength of their knees, but still going round in the same order." The men made the aggressive purpose of the exercise clear by chanting and contorting their faces. As Brainerd described them they were "making a most hideous noise, and seeming to try to look as fierce and furious as they could."[42]

Twelve years earlier and a few hundred miles away, men and women escaping from slavery in Georgia had used dance in a similar fashion, to prepare themselves physically for combat. During the Stono Rebellion a small core of rebels marched south toward Spanish Florida, attracting recruits along the way. According to one contemporary account, the rebels "increased every minute by new Negroes coming to them, so that they were above sixty, some say a hundred, on which they halted in a field, and set to dancing, singing and beating drums."[43] Some observers thought that this had been a mistake, and that the rebels had begun celebrating prematurely, but as historian John Thornton has suggested, it is more likely that they were drawing on African military traditions and dancing as a way to get ready for further action.[44]

The European corollary to these dances was drill, a ritual of coordinated body movement that became increasingly formalized and elaborate through the early modern period. In his influential *Treatise on Military Discipline* in 1727, British drillmaster Humphrey Bland recommended teaching soldiers to glance and step precisely in unison. "When they face to the right, the men should do it on their left heels, and when they face to the left, they should do it on their right heels. . . . All who are in motion, must lift up and set down their right feet together, and do the same with their left." Eighteenth-century military drill obviously resembled dance, and the resemblance made Bland defensive. The "common objection" to drill, he admitted, was "that it looks too much like dancing, and makes the men appear with too stiff an air." He conceded that raw recruits might struggle awkwardly with drill, "but a little time and practice will bring the men to perform it in so easy and genteel a manner that the objection will vanish." After learning to drill men will "walk with a bolder air, giving them a freer use of their limbs, and a notion of time" that could serve them well in combat.[45]

Proficiency in dance and drill could completely alter the manner in which a man used his body. These exercises also provided context for teaching specific skills related to particular weapons. Around the Atlantic world men danced with swords, or bows and arrows, or spears and shields, and they drilled with swords, pikes, firearms, and grenades.[46] The dances and drills had to be adapted to meet the requirements of the weapons, and the practice of drill changed as battlefield technology changed. In the seventeenth century European drillmasters placed a premium on minutely coordinated action and hoped to condition men to respond automatically to orders. In the words of one historian, "soldiers were trained to execute commands literally, without reflecting upon or attempting to understand their purpose."[47]

No one ever succeeded in training up a perfectly regimented army of automatons. In the eighteenth century many voices questioned both the feasibility and the advisability of the program. Nonetheless, the ambitions of those seventeenth-century drillmasters are instructive because they illustrate

Maniere dont les PRÊTRES CARIBES souflent le Courage.

Fig. 6.3 Bernard Picart, eighteenth-century. A war dance in present-day
Venezuela. Courtesy of the John Carter Brown Library.

an essential lesson about military training, one that applied to all the societies
ringing the Atlantic in the eighteenth century. Training instilled discipline and
conditioned men to coordinate their actions. Sometimes coordination was
achieved in an egalitarian fashion, but more often it required deference and
obedience.

Describing battles, and seeking to generalize and identify what they always have in common, Keegan emphasized "human" factors: "men struggling
to reconcile their instinct for self-preservation, their sense of honour and the
achievement of some aim over which other men are ready to kill them."[48] Within
Keegan's formula there are clues to the variety of ways fighting forces maintain

order at moments of violent crisis. In the midst of battle some warriors may have internalized a set of military values prioritizing virtues such as bravery, service, and honor. Additionally, or alternatively, they may share a commitment to their military objective so strongly that they are willing to risk their lives to achieve it. But the "instinct for self-preservation" may override these concerns. Infantry battles in central Africa in the sixteenth century frequently ended when the fighters on one side turned and ran for their lives. This could trigger chaos as warriors who had been fighting alongside each other scuffled to get out of each other's way. Sometimes well-trained and equipped warriors kept to the rear of the action to intimidate those ahead of them, or perhaps to cover the warriors' flight. Those who fled scattered back to their villages, and if too many escaped it could be difficult, if not impossible, for the army to reform.[49] A fighter who deserts assumes great personal risk. Keegan emphasizes that on a day of battle some warriors may have little choice but to obey orders and fight, because disobeying and fleeing would be more dangerous.

To coordinate their actions, fighters need to find a way to proceed with a common plan. Sometimes this can be achieved simply through mutual agreement, but more often the process entails placing pliable members of the unit under the direction of leaders. In the 1820s, according to one witness, Comanche chiefs assembled in council to hear testimony from "old men," who were "admitted to provide the lessons they have learned in their long experience." The "whole matter" was "discussed with sagacity and prudence, and the advantages and disadvantages of each course of action carefully weighed." If the council approved military action, they first agreed among themselves what their "rallying points" were before identifying "the strategy and tactics to be used against the enemy in all foreseeable circumstances."[50]

The council's directions were flexible. Especially after the introduction of horses and firearms in North America, many indigenous American societies adopted military tactics relying on surprise, spontaneity, and improvisation. For the system to work the warriors needed to share an understanding of their objectives. Most indigenous American nations also placed great stress on military virtue, and their fighters displayed a measure of self-control in the face of death that amazed European and colonial observers. Those indigenous American men who were unable to face death bravely suffered ostracism. In 1750 New Englander William Douglass, who otherwise had little good to say about indigenous Americans, conceded that their warriors generally had "great fortitude of mind." He claimed that "without any appearance of fear or concern, they suffer any torture and death."[51] New Yorker Cadwallader Colden described Haudenosaunee warriors in similar terms and concluded that they were braver than the ancient Romans.[52] European and colonial observers were astonished to see such discipline, because they associated honor with social class and had far lower expectations for their own common soldiers. Indigenous American societies were more egalitarian, but some hierarchies still operated in their manner of fighting wars.

Traditionally, indigenous American warriors would seek help from spirits before entering combat, and to secure this spiritual support they engaged in a wide variety of rituals. Some fasted and swore off sex. Some danced for days at a time. While warriors prepared themselves for fighting, war chiefs or councils read omens to discern whether spirits would aid them in their cause.[53] Customs like these regulated indigenous warfare across much of North and South America. Carib war chiefs claimed shamanistic power and used divination to discern the movements of their enemies. The war chiefs were revered. After they died their bones were preserved, dyed red, and displayed in communal halls.[54]

The hierarchical structure of fighting forces reflected general patterns of stratification in society. Some African kings appointed their relatives to positions of command, while in other parts of Africa military offices were hereditary.[55] In Britain offices were sold at high prices. Ordinary Britons could not afford to purchase positions of command, or to dress and equip themselves, or to entertain others in the ways expected of high officers.[56] In Europe powerful military offices were held almost exclusively by the high born and wealthy.

The social chasm that separated European officers from the soldiers under their command was visible in the architecture of army camps. Thomas Raymond served under a colonel who traveled with a maid, a cook, a groom, and two other servants. The colonel had a kitchen tent and a servant's tent, one tent for his own quarters and another for meals, meetings, assemblies, worship services, and entertainment.[57] Raymond, by contrast, was not even given a bed. He built a sleeping platform out of parts of an old tent stuffed with straw on a lattice of tree branches and twigs, but when the army moved he had to leave this makeshift piece of furniture behind. Thereafter he sought comfort and shelter wherever he could find it, but on one rainy night he slept directly on the ground wrapped in a cloth that became increasingly soggy.[58]

To keep men in place and obedient under such conditions, European armies depended on the threat and imposition of severe physical punishments. The general consensus across Europe was that ordinary soldiers were desperate men who had been coerced into service or otherwise joined because they had no choice. Without a continuing threat of force, they could not be relied upon for service.[59] To keep men obedient, French military law in the seventeenth century prescribed whipping, branding, nose- and ear-cropping, the cutting off of hands, and a variety of quick or painful deaths by firing squad, hanging or fire.[60] Whipping was the most common punishment in European armies. In the eighteenth century a man caught trying to desert from the British army might receive a thousand lashes for his attempted flight.

The severity of the military code shocked new recruits and others unfamiliar with it. During the Seven Years' War, New Englander David Perry was sent to serve alongside British soldiers in Nova Scotia, and he saw three men tied up to be whipped for what he considered "trifling offenses." "By the time they had received three hundred lashes, the flesh appeared to be entirely whipped from their shoulders, and they hung as mute and motionless as though they had been long since deprived of life." Looking back on this experience sixty years later Perry interpreted it as a display of a peculiarly British form of cruelty, and suggested that his reaction against it, and the displeasure of the other New England recruits, anticipated the unrest of the Revolutionary war.[61] There was some truth in this assessment, but the New Englanders' clannish resentment of British authority reflected a dynamic common in virtually all large military forces in the early modern Atlantic world. Large forces were composites, made up of smaller units that had been recruited separately. If the men who made up those units felt any emotional loyalty at all, it was much more likely to be to their small unit rather than to the army as a whole.

Military culture by its very nature sets warriors apart from others. Nonetheless, in the early modern period most fighters retained strong links to their original families and neighbors. They often fought in units composed of people they had known since childhood. In many places, noncombatants, including family members and other people from the fighters' villages, towns, and regions, traveled with them on campaigns and provided logistical support. Equipping, feeding, and rewarding soldiers and warriors consumed resources and energy, and whenever fighters traveled, the people they left behind had to compensate and adjust to their absence. In many areas ringing the Atlantic, the stress of living without the fighters became more extreme in the seventeenth and eighteenth centuries because military units were deployed across greater distances for longer periods of time. Especially in the aftermath of large-scale wars, new challenges arose when the long-absent soldiers and warriors returned to their homes.

Any group, nation, or empire wishing to pose a credible military threat must have the capacity to move fighters, supply them, maintain them, and keep them healthy. The difficulties inherent in meeting these challenges vary according to the size of the force deployed, the technology used for travel, the distance the force has to cover, the intended duration of the campaign, the climate and resources of the surrounding landscape, and the nature of the fighters' relations with the local population. A relatively small, simple operation on hospitable terrain requires less logistical infrastructure than a longer, larger-scale, complex attack. On the northern coast of South America, Carib war chiefs oversaw provisioning for the warriors they led into battle. The warriors' wives and other women cooked manioc for the men to carry in war canoes. The canoes also carried smoked meat, and the men supplemented their diet by fishing as they traveled. When they stayed in allied villages, those villagers fed them, and sometimes they did so willingly, though there was always a fine line between hospitality and plunder. The challenge of feeding warriors placed a limit on the Caribs' ability to deploy men over long distances or for extended periods.[62]

In many West African states conscripts brought their own weapons with them and supplied the army with horses, camels, and provisions. In effect, they paid for their own deployment. Because the men had to arm and supply themselves, conscript armies were not generally well equipped.[63] In regions where militia forces predominated, militiamen similarly brought their own weapons with them and were expected to carry at least eight days' worth of provisions when summoned for service.[64] After their provisions ran out they had various options. Sometimes they deserted, sometimes they foraged, and sometimes they bought food from the inhabitants of the regions they passed through. Anticipating that long campaigns would exhaust the soldiers' supplies, central African armies often carried additional provisions, employing the warriors' wives and some conscripts to transport food and equipment.[65] The Kingdom of Kongo relied on conscripts who were expected to respond to a call-up with weapons and fifteen days' worth of supplies.[66]

In North America, indigenous warriors commonly supported themselves by hunting and foraging. Indeed, in eastern North America the close association between warfare and hunting shaped the landscape. Villages and confederacies kept buffer zones between them, depopulated regions where game flourished and hunters risked attack. The intensity of the fighting in buffer zones varied in response to political circumstances, but the geographical pattern persisted: these hunting grounds were war zones. Even if hunters entered a buffer zone primarily in the pursuit of game, they prepared themselves for combat. Similarly, if warriors entered the buffer zone to attack a military opponent, during their campaign they would live off the land, hunting and fishing for subsistence.[67]

The further indigenous American warriors ranged, however, the less likely they were to confine their hostilities to buffer zones, and outside those areas warriors were more likely to depend on the resources of settled communities through hospitality, trade, tribute, or plunder. In the early modern period many indigenous American warrior bands began to travel greater distances in response to an array of new dynamics including resource depletion, forced migration, the development of elaborate exchange networks for captives, long-distance trade networks for furs and other goods, and the introduction of horses. Among livestock keepers and horse-riding peoples such as the Navajo and Comanche, raiding became a central component of warrior culture.[68] Among others including the various inhabitants of the Ohio River Valley, warriors relied on agricultural produce to support themselves in times of conflict. In the 1790s during their conquest of Ohio, the US military took advantage of this by indiscriminately burning the local indigenous peoples' corn. On one day in September 1790, General Josiah Harmer reported that his men had burned twenty thousand bushels of corn across a wide area along with "vegetables in abundance." Harmer believed that this destruction of crops had delivered a crushing blow to his opponents.[69]

In almost every militarily active society around the Atlantic, the logistics of fielding forces changed during the early modern era. In Africa the consolidation of political power and experimentation among rival states encouraged innovation, as did the intensification of conflict. Some West African rulers maintained permanent armies and compensated the soldiers with shares of plunder, an arrangement that encouraged and perpetuated war.[70] During the Kongolese civil wars in the late seventeenth century, entire populations including noncombatants were moved to support military operations. Houses were temporary, and the people did not maintain private property. This facilitated moving whole villages, including conscripts and their extended families, to provide material support to troops.[71] Similarly, in regions of West Africa in the eighteenth century, villages were dismantled and reassembled so that villagers could provide logistical support to soldiers on campaign in exchange for protection.[72] In the 1770s a West African ruler named Farakaba broke with common practice and paid his troops, making them directly dependent on him for their sustenance and compensation. He deployed a reliant and powerful army, and some other regional rulers subsequently followed his example.[73]

In 1530, when the Spanish conquistador Nuño de Guzman left Mexico City on a military campaign, he commanded 150 Spanish cavalrymen, a similar number of Spanish infantry and, according to his estimate, between seven thousand and eight thousand indigenous Americans. The indigenous participants in the expedition were known to the Spanish as "indios amigos" and they included porters, laborers, and cooks as well as warriors. One Spanish observer reported that every soldier was assigned "an Indian woman to cook food," and that ten thousand indigenous men were employed "to carry the packs of the Christians."[74]

In Europe the challenge of campaigning was compounded by the increasing size of military forces. By the 1630s during the Thirty Years' War, armies with over a hundred thousand fighting men faced each other. The commanders struggled to transport their forces and keep them armed, quartered and fed. Tens of thousands of traders, laborers, and servants, including thousands of women and children, followed the armies to provide logistical support.[75]

In 1633 the men in Raymond's unit were paid at regular intervals, but their ability to purchase provisions depended on the vagaries of the local market and each soldier's ability to manage his financial affairs. One of Raymond's fellow soldiers regularly ran out of funds two or three days before payday. Unable to eat, the man tied a bone above his bed and smelled it at intervals in an effort to stave off hunger. Raymond remembered him "calling earnestly" for payday to come: "Pay day, O pay day, O sweete pay day, come away, make hast . . . O I see pay day. Courage. Twil be here I am sure to morrowe morneing."[76] This poor soldier suffered loudly but in patience. Others in Raymond's camp resorted to violence. On one occasion, two men discovered a barn filled with straw. Raymond watched as one of the men stood guard over the barn while the other tried to sell batches of straw individually to soldiers. Their scheme collapsed after others came and attacked the building from the rear, ripping the barn down and inadvertently making the straw free for the taking. Raymond thought this episode illustrated "the devastation that an army brings into a countrie," but he also noted that the worst plunderers were not the soldiers themselves but their self-appointed, unofficial suppliers. Exaggerating for effect, he asserted that "the hangers on of the army doe most of the mischeife."[77]

When European armies marched in the first half of the seventeenth century, they were commonly followed by thousands of service-providers including porters, sutlers, laundresses, and mechanics. These servants and traders may have sometimes outnumbered the soldiers and offered services that were indispensable for military operations. Some members of this "camp community" had familial or contractual ties to individual officers and soldiers in the army. Others were free agents who followed the soldiers spontaneously, viewing large armies as a lucrative opportunity. The men and women in the support train competed with each other for customers and supplies, and they were often operating in environments of severe scarcity and devastation. Property rights were ill defined in the vicinity of army camps and battlefields. Servants, sutlers, traders, soldiers, officers, their families, and local populations could become desperate and inured to violence.[78]

To alleviate some of these problems, in the late seventeenth and eighteenth centuries, European armies increasingly sought to supply soldiers directly and supervise the commercial markets surrounding their bases and encampments. The reforms applied both to armies on the march and to stationary units garrisoned in towns and forts. Large forts such as the British outpost at Gibraltar became experimental sites for military reform. Commanders at such outposts wielded enormous social and economic power, negotiating with local traders, making bulk purchases, and authorizing sellers to trade with officers and soldiers. The fort at Gibraltar became the center of a closely regulated market town.[79] European forts like the one at Gibraltar became models for others on the coast of Africa and the Americas, though the cost of transportation and supply kept those outposts smaller. Nonetheless, in places such as Halifax, Nova Scotia, Havana, and Louisbourg, European army bases became complex, tightly regulated, lucrative markets.

Fig. 6.4 Virgilius Solis, sixteenth century. A boy and woman traveling in an army baggage train. Rijksmuseum, Amsterdam.

On a rocky island off the coast of North America, far from their ancestral homes in France, the professional soldiers at Louisbourg formed a self-contained community. Records from 1752 indicate that only 5 percent of the approximately one thousand troops were married. If any of the soldiers married a woman from the nearby fishing settlements he was expelled from the garrison.[80] The men relied on each other for support. They ate, slept, and drank together. Common soldiers took orders from their officers, were paid by their officers and purchased food from them, often falling into debilitating debt. Arguments erupted in the fortress canteens. The local priest complained that the eating halls were "schools of Satan, places where there are only blasphemies, imprecations, loathful words, speeches filled with obscenity."[81] Some of the men hated this social environment, but others grew attached to it.

Before the mid-seventeenth century, European soldiers had frequently brought their wives with them on campaigns, or established temporary partnerships with women for the duration of a conflict. The support trains that followed armies in Europe provided additional female company, with cooks, laundresses, prostitutes, nurses, and others marching alongside the soldiers. The centralization and increasing professionalization of logistical support after the 1650s led to a dramatic decline in the female presence.[82] Long-distance deployments, especially across the Atlantic, isolated fighting men further. While some soldiers established roots in far-flung camps, it was a challenge to convince men to enlist for service far from home. In 1775 one British commentator worried that military recruiters would find men "mighty shy of enlisting, when, in answer to the very first question which they put, to wit, Where the Regiment is? they shall be told they must sail many thousand miles before they can join it, and know that when they do so, they must be exposed to climates in which their ideas increase in horror in proportion to the distance."[83]

Serving far from home, in a distant or mobile camp, entailed emotional adjustments. This was true all across the Atlantic world. After the introduction of gunpowder weapons to Africa's "Gold Coast," the region's armies became larger and were more reliant on conscripts. Pulling men away from their fields caused subsistence problems, and on several occasions military campaigns were abandoned because the men deserted and went home to plant and tend crops.[84] In societies where women did most of the agricultural labor, the pattern of desertion was less seasonally predictable. Indeed, some historians and archaeologists have suggested that among Iroquoian peoples, increasing agricultural productivity spurred men to leave their villages to hunt and fight and prove their value since women performed most of the agricultural work.[85] This view is disputed, however, and even for Haudenosaunee men long-term deployment far from home was difficult. In the early eighteenth century the British discovered this when they attempted to station Haudenosaunee warriors permanently in Nova Scotia. After a year, the men abandoned their post and walked overland hundreds of miles to their old homes.[86] Similar dynamics affected other groups of indigenous American warriors. In 1758 at Fort Duquesne on the banks of the Ohio River, the French suffered defeat after hundreds of allied indigenous warriors marched west to return to their families in the Great Lakes region.[87]

For anyone joining a military force, deployment represents a break with the past. All fighters leave behind a former life, sometimes tentatively and temporarily, but often permanently. There is a sense of departure embedded intrinsically into military experience, and in the early modern Atlantic world this was felt particularly acutely by the enslaved. The history of slavery in the Americas is punctuated by rare but unusually violent large-scale uprisings. Many of those who took part had prior military experience in Africa or the colonies, but for all the fighters, taking up arms was a big risk. These were fierce and uncompromising fights. Those who took up arms against their masters had no intention of returning to them, and in any event that option would rarely have been available because their old masters, anxious to maintain uncontested authority, seldom showed leniency to those perceived as rebels. Women fought alongside men in several of these wars, and for most who fought to put slavery behind them, the decision to take up arms constituted a stark, irreversible renunciation of their formal lives.[88]

Military service sometimes offered a way out of slavery, and this was true not only for rebels, but also for the larger number of men who took up arms for their masters or their masters' empires. The Spanish employed enslaved men in their wars of conquest in the Americas from Columbus's time on. During the initial conquest of the Aztec Empire, most of these men worked as servants or auxiliaries, but as the sixteenth century progressed, an increasing number of enslaved men assumed combat roles. Sebastian Toral came to America in the 1530s and fought under Spanish commanders in the wars against the Maya. He remained enslaved during his military service, but was rewarded with freedom, established his own home, and raised a family in Mérida, the town the Spanish constructed on formerly Mayan-ruled land on the coast of the Yucatán. Toral's life was a series of dislocations, and military service was one more separation following his crossing of the Atlantic as a slave. By the time he had settled down in Mérida he had left his original home far behind. Unable to return, through fighting he found an opportunity to pursue a new life.[89]

Nearly all the European empires in the Americas armed and deployed enslaved men. The practice was controversial because weaponry gave the men intrinsic power, and the positions of trust they assumed through military service often seemed incompatible with their servile legal status. For the sake of ideological and legal consistency, to maintain the fighters' loyalty, and to provide an incentive for good service, most enslaved soldiers were offered freedom at the time of their enlistment or after their service had ended. Masters, however, frequently resisted this practice. Juan Valiente was celebrated as a military hero during the Spanish conquest of Chile, and after the fighting ended he was rewarded with an estate near Santiago. Nonetheless, he still had to ward off a legal challenge from his former master who wanted him to return to his life as a slave.[90]

While military service took many enslaved men far from the places where they had lived in bound servitude, other people held in slavery took up arms to defend their masters' plantations. In the 1640s and 1650s, when Portuguese planters in Brazil rose against Dutch rule, men and women held as slaves on Portuguese plantations armed themselves and assumed defensive positions in front of their workshops and cabins and fought against the Dutch. A few years earlier the leaders of the Portuguese uprising had declared that anyone held in slavery "who does his duty in defense of divine liberty will be freed and paid for all that he may do."[91] Without testimony from the fighters themselves there is no way to know for certain why they defended the plantations. They may have thought of those places as their permanent homes and expected to stay there after the fighting ended. But even if they thought that way, it is likely that they believed military service would change their lives. Fighting was promoted as a way to freedom.

Though he was a poor black servant and not quite a slave, Joseph Johnson Green had never experienced anything like freedom until he joined George Washington's continental army at the age of eighteen. He came from a small town near Plymouth, Massachusetts. His mother was an Irish widow, and his father was, in Green's words, "a negro servant to the Hon. Timothy Edson Esq." Green's mother had hired him out as an apprentice at the age of five, and he remained bound to the same master until he entered the army. Others in similar circumstances may have looked back at their enlistment as a moment of liberation, but Green claimed to remember it only with regret. On several occasions during his service to Edson he had engaged in petty theft, but his misbehavior escalated in the army. He became "addicted to drunkenness, the keeping of bad company, and a correspondence . . . with lewd women." Shortly after his enlistment, Green stole fifteen shillings, a dozen biscuits, a pillowcase filled with sugar, and a bottle of rum from a pub. Later he was caught trying to steal the

Fig. 6.5 Matheus van den Broeck's 1651 depiction of enslaved Brazilians fighting off a Dutch attack. Courtesy of the John Carter Brown Library.

silver buckles off two shoes and was punished with a hundred lashes. In October 1781, when his unit was at West Point and short of food, Green joined with two companions to steal cheese, butter, and chocolate from the stall of a private food-seller who was provisioning the army. Green was caught and whipped a second time, again with a hundred lashes.

After receiving his discharge, Green married. He had two children but did not settle into civilian life easily. He continued thieving. By his own account he committed major crimes several times a year, and in the summer of 1786, he was sentenced to hang for burglary. Awaiting execution, he wistfully remembered that his mother had warned him never to enter the army. He asked a fellow prisoner to write a poem for him, which was published after he was hanged. The poem began,

> Let all the people on the globe,
> Be on their guard, and see
> That they do shun the vicious road
> That's trodden been by me.[92]

Green's commentary on the long-term effects of military service reflected preoccupations that were peculiarly strong in the eighteenth century. The increase in the size of military forces contributed to a widespread perception on both sides of the Atlantic that veterans returning from wars were a threat. Some commentators like Green judged former soldiers morally responsible for their misbehavior. Others associated demobilization with social crisis and systemic dysfunction. Military service acclimatized men and women to bad behavior, jobs were scarce in the immediate aftermath of wars, and no society in the early modern Atlantic world had the economic capacity to reintegrate thousands of former soldiers into civilian life smoothly. A few months after Britain demobilized on a large scale in 1748, one writer complained that "our disbanded soldiers and seamen are starving, or robbing in the streets for want of bread."[93] The sense of crisis surrounding the end of Britain's war with France in 1748 helped inspire an array of legal and social reforms in the fields of policing as well as poor relief.[94] In the United States after the end of the Revolutionary War, veterans of the Continental Army demanded back pay and pensions, but the army was generally unpopular and the soldiers' agitation for financial support met resistance. The ensuing controversy exacerbated the new nation's political unrest and continued to divide Americans for decades.[95]

In contrast to Europeans and colonists, some indigenous American groups conducted cleansing rituals to mark a warrior's return from combat. Men lived in isolation for a set number of days, fasted, and joined chanting women in visits to their village leaders.[96] As long as these customs were respected, they helped warriors navigate the transition back to a more peaceful life. Embedded within these rituals was sense of rhythm, taking men back and forth between the conditions of war and peace. But in eastern North America in the late eighteenth and early nineteenth centuries many groups faced a more traumatic kind of demobilization as they grappled with irreversible defeats. In the wake of the American Revolution the Seneca faced disease, displacement, game depletion, and political changes that devalued warrior traditions. They confronted a series of crises with particularly troubling consequences for men. The Seneca were increasingly dependent on agriculture for subsistence, but many men resisted assuming the traditionally female role of tending crops. Some fell into alcoholism and random violence. Lives were ruined and some villages destroyed, but eventually the Seneca rebuilt, and by the nineteenth century their crisis had become the occasion for cultural revival.

Handsome Lake, the prophet who led the revival in its formative years, had been "much engaged in war prior to and during the American Revolution."[97] In 1765 he had fought against Cherokee and Choctaw warriors, and in the next decade he campaigned alongside British troops and loyalist Americans during the Revolutionary War. Another warrior remembered Handsome Lake at a moment of triumph in 1780 when the two of them, with six other warriors, entered the house of a family of New Yorkers who had fled, leaving their breakfast on the table. The warriors "helped themselves—didn't wait to sit down. . . . snatched & devour'd what they wanted to satisfy the cravings of hunger—the first food they had tasted for two days."[98] Handsome Lake distinguished himself as a warrior, but after the fighting ended he eventually lost direction and his life collapsed. Recalling his worst moment, he remembered running drunk, armed, and naked with other men through his village, ready to attack anyone.[99] A few days after that incident he fell ill, and lapsing in and out of consciousness he had the first of a series of visions that would establish the Seneca's Longhouse Religion.

The pain attendant to demobilization can have the effect of perpetuating warfare, because when societies instill military values in boys at a young age and grant wealth, power, and status to fighters and military leaders, peace may be associated with the loss of opportunity and prestige for some men. Under these circumstances, some may pursue warfare for its own sake. We should be cautious, however, before claiming that any culture is intrinsically warlike. Societies are commonly depicted in this way by outsiders as a slur, with the implication that they are incapable of autonomous change. This is what happened Europeans began to write and rewrite the history of Dahomey.

Dahomey, originally a small state overshadowed by more powerful neighbors, burst into European consciousness in the 1720s after it expanded militarily under the leadership of King Agaja. Dahomey challenged and eventually overthrew the rulers of Ouidah, one of the most important slave-trading markets in West

Africa. An Englishman named Bulfinch Lamb was held captive in Dahomey during Agaja's rise to prominence. According to Lamb, Agaja had two palaces, each with perimeter walls "about a mile and an half round." The walls were lined with the skulls of men he had killed in battle, "as thick as they can lie on the walls one by another."[100] Lamb was eventually released and came to England carrying a letter to George I that Agaja had dictated to him. In the letter Agaja boasted, "My grandfather was no warrior, and only enlarged his kingdom by conquering one kingdom, my father nine, but my brother fought seventy-nine battles, in which he subdued several petty kingdoms. But myself have fought two hundred and nine battles, in which I have subdued many great kings and kingdoms, some of which are continually revolting and keep me employed."[101]

Agaja fascinated different groups of English writers for various reasons. In 1734 William Snelgrave depicted him as a cannibal and suggested that he was much like other African leaders. Other English writers viewed the king as a champion of order in Africa whose conquests promised to end the vicious cycle of petty raiding and slave-trading.[102] As the eighteenth century progressed and the English debate over slavery intensified, this second interpretation of Agaja's significance became entwined within a larger debate over the relationship between African warfare and the slave trade. In 1744 William Smith reported that he had met Africans west of Dahomey who "account it their greatest unhappiness that they were ever visited by Europeans. They say, that we Christians introduced the traffic of slaves, and that before our coming they lived in peace; but, say they, it is observable, that where-ever Christianity comes, there come with it a sword, a gun, powder and ball. And indeed thus far they say right, for the Christians are continuously at war one with another."[103] In the 1750s and 1760s, Quaker abolitionist Anthony Benezet relied on statements such as these to argue that the European empires' demand for slaves provoked and sustained warfare in Africa, and that in the absence of the slave trade the continent would have been peaceful. Eventually Agaja became a hero to Europe's abolitionists. They remembered him as a leader who had tried to free his people from the cycle of violence that the slave traders had inspired and perpetuated. European defenders of slavery, by contrast, argued that African culture was intrinsically violent, and indeed that the slave trade rescued men, women, and children from the misery of living in a zone of continuous warfare.[104]

Neither of these interpretations can withstand close historical scrutiny. The transatlantic slave trade did not introduce warfare to Africa. On the other hand, it is clear that the pattern of warfare changed after European merchants arrived along the coast. Agaja did little to suppress the slave trade, but he innovated in important ways by centralizing authority, establishing tax-supported military units, giving his soldiers uniforms, and arming women. In the lands he governed some old military traditions were put aside, a sign of the fragility of local custom.

There were similar developments across the Atlantic world in the early modern era. Few military cultures remained intact for very long. Ways of war changed. They were seldom passed down unaltered from father to son across multiple generations. It was always quite possible, indeed a common occurrence, for warrior traditions to end.

In the absence of warfare young adult males generally have lower mortality rates than other population groups, but wars reverse this pattern. The effect depends, of course, on the intensity and duration of conflict, but estimates from the seventeenth, eighteenth, and early nineteenth centuries in Sweden, Spain, and France suggest that in wartime between 10 percent and 30 percent of all adult males died as soldiers.[105] Aggregate statistics on a continental scale are not available for the early modern era, but records from specific campaigns suggest that European battles usually wounded or killed between 7 percent and 25 percent of the soldiers involved, with the losing side suffering the higher losses.[106] Soldiers also died from malnutrition and disease. Spoiled food, poor sanitation, dirty water, and infestations of vermin encouraged contagion. There were few if any typhus epidemics in Europe during the Middle Ages, but in the sixteenth century the disease spread quickly through overcrowded army camps.[107] Until the mid-seventeenth century the bubonic plague menaced European armies, and later in that century smallpox increased in virulence, killing thousands of soldiers. The threats the soldiers faced were cumulative. Hunger made them more susceptible to disease and less effective in combat. Ill soldiers became hungry and weak, and the wounded were vulnerable to disease and malnutrition. There is no way statistically to disentangle the mortal effects of these dangers, but throughout the early modern era in Europe, more soldiers died in camp than in battle.

In Sweden and Finland between 1620 and 1719, 30 percent of all adult men died as soldiers.[108] Death rates like this will skew the age profile and sex ratio of a population and have demographic consequences. Usually, however, communities can compensate for the loss of mature males. Widows remarry, and men who might have otherwise remained single are more likely in wartime to find partners. In parts of the Atlantic world husbands took multiple wives and, as wartime casualty numbers increased, so did the number of women sharing a man. A French traveler in the Illinois country in the late seventeenth century reported that women outnumbered men there by a ratio of four to one.[109] In the 1680s when Robert de La Salle passed through that country he was startled by the number of men he met with three or more wives.[110] Portuguese records suggest that in eighteenth-century Angola women outnumbered men by approximately two to one. In Angola the demographic impact of warfare was exacerbated by the slave trade and its demand for male captives. There, as in the Illinois country, polygamy was a logical response. Plural marriages allowed communities to continue even after losing large numbers of men.[111]

Large population groups can survive the loss of a significant proportion of their young adult men, but that demographic pattern does little to ameliorate the traumatic impact of adult male deaths on families or small bands and villages. The ability of societies on a large scale to absorb losses stands in contrast to the pain and difficulty faced by communities on a local level. This pattern helps explain the different ways wars were fought in various parts of the early modern Atlantic world. Anthropologists who categorize communities and political units by their size and complexity generally associate small groups with a particular kind of armed conflict. Families, villages, bands, and small tribes are more likely to count deaths one at a time and fight to avenge a single killing. Often, they will continue to fight until their opponents have suffered an equal loss. Their adversaries, of course, will see the conflict from their own perspective, and therefore a feud will often perpetuate itself, with every death seen as an injury demanding redress.[112] Approaches to warfare that highlight the cost of each death generally include ritual actions designed to accentuate pain and sanction retributive justice. In several indigenous American societies, family members were encouraged to mourn publicly and call for vengeance. War captives were tortured dramatically. Some captives were spared and adopted into the mourning family, some were enslaved, and others killed. Scalps became trophies and prized gifts.

In the sixteenth century the arrival of armed European colonists with their distinctive ideologies and practices, epidemics, dislocations, and depopulation disrupted indigenous American ways of war. In many places deaths came so frequently and in such great numbers that the old manner of responding to death could no longer be maintained. By the end of the seventeenth century some groups—the Haudenosaunee most famously—sought to put aside feuding because the cost was too high.[113] But old practices designed to accentuate suffering continued, and indeed proliferated, among colonists and indigenous Americans alike. Rituals that had once been used to emphasize the impact of individual deaths were deployed in campaigns to exact communal retribution against large populations and instill widespread terror. This trend reflected changes in the practice of land warfare affecting much of the Atlantic world.

7

Horror

In 1455 a young Venetian merchant named Alvise Cadamosto took part in a three-ship expedition commissioned by Prince Henry "the Navigator" of Portugal to explore the far western coast of Africa.[1] Cadamosto's account of his voyage provides one of the earliest detailed European descriptions of the region south of the Senegal River. The landscape was strange to him and so were its inhabitants. He believed that he had entered a place resembling "another world."[2] According to Cadamosto, the people living immediately south of the river "almost all constantly go naked, except for a goatskin fashioned in the form of drawers, with which they hide their shame." Their chiefs were "continually at war."[3] When they met in battle, warriors thrust horn-tipped lances at each other, threw barbed iron darts and fought with curved iron swords. Cadamosto emphasized how different these clashes were from battles fought in Europe. There was little or no cavalry and no long-distance artillery. The warriors fought at close quarters with no armor other than shields made from animal skin. This was war unlike any that Cadamosto had witnessed or heard of, and he described it with amazement.

> Their combats are very fatal; since their bodies are unprotected, many are slain. They are very courageous and brutal, for in danger they prefer to be killed rather than to seize the opportunity of fleeing. They are not terrified at seeing their companions fall, as though, being accustomed to this, they are not grieved by it; and they have no fear whatever of death.[4]

The wondrous feature of this kind of warfare was not that the men risked death or injury. In Europe cavalry charges and projectile weapons could kill men instantly, cut, maim, or decapitate them. Europeans also engaged in close combat, but as Cadamosto described it, war in this part of Africa required a different kind of courage. The action was unrelenting and intimate. There was no time for grieving, and no mercy for anyone who showed fear.

Atlantic Wars. Geoffrey Plank, Oxford University Press (2020). © Oxford University Press.
DOI: 10.1093/oso/9780190860455.001.0001

European, African, and indigenous American observers often responded in terror when they encountered unfamiliar people, weapons, and ways of fighting. In 1522, when the bishop of Santo Domingo, Alessandro Geraldini, described Carib warriors, he suggested that they exhibited nearly superhuman agility, steadiness, and focus.

> Carrying many arrows in their left hands, and constantly rising high with leaps from side to side to avoid being killed by our men's artillery and arrows, they go into battle with their bodies naked and painted with various colours; once they have shot their arrows, they run with incredible speed to nearby woods, of which there is great abundance on all sides, and when least expected, they return to attack their enemies with incredible force with new arrows and poison.[5]

Like Cadamosto in Africa, Geraldini emphasized how different the Caribbean style of fighting was from anything seen in Europe. He could not imagine that any European could have the strength, skill, stamina, or fortitude to fight the way that Caribs did. Among early travelers like Cadamosto and Geraldini, a dawning sense of European incompetence led to exaggerated assessments of the indigenous warriors' physical prowess, courage, and ruthlessness.

In the 1550s French shoemaker Jean de Léry traveled to Brazil in the company of French Protestant missionaries. After a few months in South America he joined "four thousand of our savages in a battle that took place on the seashore."[6] The engagement pitted indigenous Brazilian forces against each other. According to Léry, when the adversaries met,

> as soon as they were within two or three hundred feet of each other, they saluted each other with great volleys of arrows, and you would have seen an infinity of them soar through the air as thick as flies. If some were hit, as several were, they tore the arrows out of their bodies with marvellous courage, breaking them and like mad dogs biting the pieces; all wounded as they were, they would not be kept from returning to the combat. It must be noted here that these Americans are so relentless in their wars that as long as they can move arms and legs, they fight on unceasingly, neither retreating nor turning their backs. When they finally met in hand-to-hand combat, it was with their wooden swords and clubs, charging each other with great two-handed blows; whoever hit the head of his enemy not only knocked him to the ground but struck him dead, as our butchers fell oxen.[7]

Though Léry claimed to be recounting first-hand experience, he also relayed rumors and apprehensions that had been circulating among Europeans for decades. African and indigenous American warriors had frightening reputations. As stories of their abilities spread they became more elaborate in the retelling.

With their ships and port facilities, Europeans and colonists had access to capital-intensive technologies that were beyond the reach or aspirations of most Africans or indigenous Americans, but European military technology operated effectively only in a restricted geographical range. In both Africa and the Americas, it was widely assumed that indigenous warriors could fight easily in landscapes that were impenetrable to Europeans. They did not attribute the indigenous warriors' effectiveness simply to their superior local knowledge. Instead they spread stories suggesting that African and indigenous American men had unusual physical capabilities and tolerances. Sometimes it was said that they could leap more nimbly or crouch more silently than Europeans, that they could go longer without food or water, or more easily withstand heat or cold. Or, as Léry described them, they could shrug off excruciating pain. The warriors' insensitivity to pain, in turn, made them less concerned about the suffering of others.

Some Africans and Americans found strength in these stereotypes. Terrifying warriors were valuable as allies and dangerous to cross. Sometimes just by encouraging rumors, but on other occasions by performing ritualized acts of violence, warriors could enhance their fearsome reputations. For their part, facing frightening opposition in areas they sought to govern but could not control, colonial officials relied on indigenous allies to take advantage of their reputedly terrifying skills. They also improvised in the ways they fought the indigenous peoples who opposed them.

A common feature of warfare is that opponents will often emulate each other and increasingly resemble each other the longer a conflict persists. This dynamic has been observed in many contexts around the world. War is intrinsically competitive, and if one adversary deploys an effective weapon or tactic it makes sense for the other to negate the advantage by adopting the same way of fighting. Outrage and the desire for revenge can have a similar effect. Communities will respond to a sense of injury by demanding retribution, and the logic of proportionality often leads them to respond to any perceived atrocity in kind.[8] The early modern Atlantic world was peculiar, however. Despite the widespread borrowing and diffusion of weapons and tactics, and despite military alliances linking diverse populations of soldiers and warriors, the homogenizing effects were offset in many arenas of conflict by the persistence of taboos, ideological inflexibility, communal terror and disgust, and nearly intractable misunderstandings.

All wars can be confusing, frightening, and dispiriting, but the disorienting impact of combat around the Atlantic in the early modern era was unique. The spread of infectious diseases resulted in millions of deaths in the Americas, and in Africa the cumulative toll of the transatlantic slave trade removed and killed people on a similar scale. In the midst of these traumas, several military practices had the effect of accentuating violence and suffering and intensifying the perception of cultural and racial difference. When Europeans, Africans, and indigenous Americans began to engage with each other they did not share a common, effective way of interpreting each other's actions, and in the fifteenth and sixteenth centuries the warring peoples of Africa, the Americas, and Europe had distinctive methods for sending messages through violence. On each continent, with regional variations, elaborate rituals and codes of conduct defined the terms of acceptable behavior, authorizing or forbidding torture, sexual violence, execution, dismemberment, the display of body parts, the killing of noncombatants, and other demonstrative acts associated with warfare. In the confusion of the early violent encounters, myths arose that helped define and divide the peoples of the Atlantic world, promoting stereotypes and steering policies and patterns of behavior. To get a sense of the special horrors of war around the Atlantic, it is instructive to begin with widespread fears of cannibalism.

A few weeks after crossing the Senegal River, Cadamosto sailed up the Gambia River. Four miles from the coast he and his shipmates were surrounded by Mandinka warriors in canoes. Cadamosto estimated that they faced 17 canoes and approximately 150 warriors. The Mandinka were surprised at the sight of the sailing ship. "Checking their course and lifting up their oars, the men lay gazing as upon a marvel."[9] For a moment, the Mandinka and the Europeans stared at each other. "They made no movement to us, nor we to them." But when the other two ships arrived the warriors began to "shoot off their arrows," and the gunners on the ships opened fire. The guns briefly halted the action. According to Cadamosto, the warriors "stood in astonishment" watching the artillery shot, but as soon as the barrage paused they resumed their attack. The Portuguese crossbows similarly fascinated the Mandinka but failed to deter them.[10] Eventually, after a "stiff fight," the ships pulled together, with the smallest of the three vessels protected by the hulls of the larger ships. In effect, they presented the warriors with high walls and reduced the utility of their arrows, and so the Mandinka withdrew.

Cadamosto was amazed by the apparent fearlessness of the warriors at the start of this engagement. He was mystified by their readiness to risk their lives in battle. After the fighting ended, with the aid of an interpreter, he shouted a question to some Mandinka men in a canoe a few hundred yards from his ship. Why had they attacked?

They replied that they had had news of our coming and of our trade with the Negroes of Senega, who, if they sought our friendship, could not but be bad men, for they firmly believed that we Christians ate human flesh, and that we only bought negroes to eat them; that for their part they did not want our friendship on any terms, but sought to slaughter us all.[11]

Cadamosto's report from the Gambia in 1450s is the oldest surviving record of the rumor that Europeans ate African captives, a story that would widely circulate and persist for centuries.[12]

In 1734, when Francis Moore traveled up the Gambia accompanied by Job Ben Solomon, a man who had been held as a slave for two years in Maryland, he reported that the people they met were surprised. Meeting Ben Solomon took away "a great deal" of their "horror" at the thought of being held in "slavery amongst the English," because up until that time they had "generally imagined that all who were sold for slaves were generally either eaten or murdered, since none ever returned."[13] In 1797 Mungo Park met a group of men and women in transit to the Gambia River where they were to be taken downstream and sold to European traders. According to Park, "they viewed me at first with looks of horror, and repeatedly asked if my countrymen were cannibals. They were very desirous to know what became of the slaves after they had crossed the salt water. I told them that they were to be employed in cultivating the land, but they would not believe me."[14]

The story spread far beyond the Gambia River. In the 1670s and 1680s, slave trader Jean Barbot observed that many people in the kingdoms of Oyo and Benin were "positively prepossessed of the opinion, that we transport them into our country, in order to kill and eat them."[15] In his general advice to fellow slave traders in 1734, William Snelgrave recommended providing new captives with reassurance. "When we purchase grown people," he wrote, "I acquaint them by the interpreter . . . what they are bought for, that they may be easy in their minds (for these people are generally under terrible apprehensions upon their being bought by white men, many being afraid that we design to eat them)."[16] Later in the eighteenth century the Jamaican assembly banned the practice of inviting crowds of purchasers onto arriving slave ships because, it was said, "such crowds of people went on board and began so disgraceful a scramble as to terrify the poor ignorant Africans with the notion that they were seized by a herd of cannibals, and speedily to be devoured."[17]

There was logic behind the theory that cannibalism drove the slave trade. The story could explain how hundreds, thousands, and ultimately millions of captives disappeared without leaving any physical remains. The idea gained authority through repetition, and some people claiming knowledge of the workings of the slave trade promoted the fear of cannibalism for their own ends. Snelgrave thought that slave traders should reassure the people they held, but other European merchants thought it could be useful, on occasion, to keep their captives afraid.[18] More commonly, Africans promoted the story as a warning against the danger of enslavement. To make them wary, parents warned their children that they would be eaten if they were captured. Recalling the moment when, at the age of thirteen, he first saw white men, Ottobah Cugoano reported that it "made me afraid that they would eat me, according to our notion as children in the inland parts of the country."[19]

This cannibal myth had important implications for the operations of the slave trade. As Cadamosto witnessed, the fear it generated sometimes motivated warriors to take up arms and resist capture. Among those who were seized, the dread of cannibalism increased the motive to escape. Park indicated that the "deeply rooted idea, that the whites purchase Negroes for the purpose of eating them, or selling them to others that may be devoured hereafter, naturally makes the slaves contemplate a journey toward the coast with great terror." As a consequence, their guards had to "keep them constantly in irons and watch them very closely to prevent their escape. They are commonly secured by putting the right leg of one and the left leg of another into the same pair of fetters. By supporting the fetters with a string, they can walk, though very slowly."[20] Along the Gambia River, and in other regions of Africa, the fear of cannibalism increased the cost and danger of capturing and transporting women and men, intensified their physical suffering, and made the experience of enslavement more humiliating and degrading. According to Barbot, captives expecting to be eaten sometimes starved themselves to make themselves less appealing as food, and some fearful captives died of starvation.[21]

Europeans commenting on these beliefs tended to dismiss them as fantastical and ridiculous. In the eighteenth century, the slaves' apparent credulity seemed to confirm the stereotype of "poor ignorant Africans."[22] But many of the European writers who discussed African captives' fears in this way harbored their own beliefs about cannibalism outside of Europe. Even as they dismissed the Africans' theories, they found support within those stories for their own belief that cannibalism was widespread in Africa and the Americas. Barbot argued that the Africans' readiness to believe that they would be eaten on the other side of the Atlantic provided evidence that they "used to eat human flesh in their own country."[23] In 1702 Dutch slave trader Jan Snoek advanced a similar argument, suggesting that those "who imagine, that we buy them and carry them off only in order to eat them" must have been drawing on experience. Such a "jealousy," he wrote, "would not probably enter their thoughts if they did not certainly know that there were man-eaters in the world." Snoek felt certain that some Africans were cannibals, and to support this assertion he cited not only the African captives' fears but also the "undoubted truth" that there were "men-eaters" in other parts of the world, especially Brazil.[24]

There are well-documented instances of cannibalism in early modern Africa. In seventeenth-century central Africa the Imbangala performed dramatic rituals centered on human sacrifice and the consumption of body parts.[25] Some indigenous American groups performed similar rituals, and there are reports of aggressive cannibalism in early modern Europe.[26] In Lyon during the St. Bartholomew's Day Massacre in 1572, a mob allegedly roasted and shared the heart of a Protestant.[27] None of these examples suggest that cannibalism was widespread in Africa, the Americas, or Europe, nor do they support any suggestion that people routinely ate others for nourishment, which was the fear that most terrified Africans captured for the slave trade and Europeans venturing into Africa and the Americas.

Within a month of his arrival in the Caribbean, Columbus was convinced that somewhere in the islands there lived one-eyed men with dog-like snouts who ate humans.[28] The Caribs did not fit this physical description, but Columbus and his crewmates eventually identified them as cannibals. The stories they traded about them gradually developed into an elaborate myth. Geraldini believed the stories, and in 1522, in the same letter in which he described the Caribs' acrobatic abilities, he described their feasts.

> The Caribs . . . took the bodies of those they had captured in war and, if they were plump, they roasted them hanging from large trees on poles, or boiled them in large pots made of clay, first cutting off their heads and discarding them; if they were too thin, they stuffed them with various rich foods, which we do with fowls which we are saving for a feast day. Something must be said about the captive children: the pitiless men make them all eunuchs immediately, and after they have fattened them up, they gather them on a holiday of their country and make them sit in the middle of a circle, the wretched group of humans fattened for food.[29]

In contrast to the rituals surrounding cannibalism that honored the dead, cannibalism for nourishment, as imagined by the fearful people of the Atlantic world, was intrinsically associated with animality. According to Geraldini, the victims were treated like fowl. Andrew Battell, an Englishman in the service of the Portuguese, described the Imbangala as "the greatest cannibals and men-eaters that be in the world, for they feed chiefly on men's flesh [notwithstanding of their] having all the cattle of that country."[30] Cannibals like these were terrifying and dehumanizing, and they often secured a powerful hold on the imagination. Snoek believed that such men existed, and he described their power succinctly when he recounted his experience trading for ivory along one stretch of the African coast. Men boarded his ship to sell him ivory, and according to Snoek,

"Their teeth with which they eat human flesh, when they can come at it, were as sharp as awls; wherefore I should not advise any to set foot on land here, who is not fond of being buried in their bellies."[31] Snoek kept his distance.

Some people accused of cannibalism recognized that the accusation increased their power to intimidate and exploited their reputations to enhance their fearsomeness. In North America, the Abenaki warrior who took custody of New Englander Elizabeth Hanson in 1725 sought leverage over her by exploiting his reputation as a cannibal. He told Hanson that her baby would be "killed and eaten." On more than one occasion he asked her to find a stick that could serve as a skewer, and each time she found one he directed her to strip her baby naked so that he could "feel its arms, legs and thighs." Invariably he would declare that the child was "not yet fat enough" for slaughter. Hanson was skeptical of this performance. She doubted he was "in earnest" and suspected that he was behaving in this way "with a view to afflict and aggravate me."[32]

Even unfounded fears can have important geopolitical and military consequences. Soldiers and warriors can gain an advantage by frightening their adversaries. Snoek's dread of cannibalism, for example, kept him off the coast. But notably, nothing in Snoek's description of his encounter with the ivory traders suggests that they knew he thought they were cannibals. He gives no indication that they wanted to frighten him. They never threatened to eat him, but when they opened their mouths he was afraid of their teeth. The men's front teeth had been modified, a widespread practice in western and central Africa. Filing teeth was a rite of passage in some communities and served as a signal of group identity.[33] It had nothing to do with cannibalism, at least not until men like Snoek imagined that there was a link.

As the example of cannibalism illustrates, some of the greatest terrors generated by warfare in the Atlantic world stemmed from misapprehensions. Men, women, and children facing the actual threat of violent raids and enslavement compounded their fears by misreading their opponents' intentions. Frightened people shared their fears, rumors spread, and legends founded on fantasy developed. These legends helped define and cement stereotypes. The mid-seventeenth century Quakers came to North America hoping to discover a spiritual affinity with the people they called the continent's "heathen," but even they believed that the indigenous people of North America were "men-eaters."[34] After Quakers settled among the Lenape and other Algonkian peoples in New Jersey and Pennsylvania, they recognized that those people did not eat human flesh, but many Quakers nevertheless remained scared of other indigenous Americans and assumed that the people of Florida, for example, routinely ate stranded travelers who stepped onto their coast.[35]

Venturing into Africa and the Americas, European travelers feared being eaten. They also dreaded becoming cannibals themselves or allying too closely with people who ate human flesh. This fear helps explain the vehemence of their condemnations of the practice as well as their fascination with it. Cannibalism came to represent "the precise opposite of Christian society." Writers associated the practice with "the greatest crimes of humanity," and when describing it they often let their lurid imaginations run wild.[36]

Even as cannibalism served as a marker distinguishing the "civilized" from the savage, accusations of cannibalism somewhat paradoxically helped insinuate Europeans and colonists into indigenous alliance networks, encouraging them to take sides with some American groups against others. In the Caribbean, Geraldini distinguished the Caribs from other islanders who cooperated with the Spanish imperial project. He claimed that Spain's allies were "unwarlike" and "lived righteously and honourably with a marvellous fairness to all."[37] In other imperial contexts such morally simple dichotomies were difficult to maintain. In the seventeenth century, French soldiers and settlers in the Caribbean fought alongside Carib warriors even as some French writers circulated stories of Carib cannibalism.[38] Similarly, the French in Canada published elaborate stories describing their own allies as cannibals.[39] In Brazil, the French also maintained

Fig. 7.1 André Thevet, "Portrait of a Cannibal King," Woodcut, 1575, based on French reports from Brazil. Courtesy of the John Carter Brown Library.

alliances with peoples they believed were cannibals. Léry described cannibalism among the allies of the French, but he did not condemn those people as strongly as he did other indigenous Brazilians who he claimed ate human flesh raw, without ceremony, "like dogs and wolves."[40]

None of the Europeans who wrote about American cannibalism can be easily trusted. Though it was widely rumored and feared, cannibalism was utterly unfamiliar to most Europeans, Africans, and indigenous Americans. Reports on the practice were inevitably affected by shared anxieties and fantastic myths. Other terrifying wartime practices were more commonly witnessed and reliably documented. The torture of prisoners, the dismemberment of corpses, the display of body parts, and attacks on noncombatants stoked rage and helped alienate people from one another, but in those cases, it was often the manner and context of the performances rather than the violent acts themselves that drew controversy.

In the early seventeenth century the Algonkian peoples living on the New England shores of Long Island Sound valued heads, hands, and other body parts taken from their adversaries. As trophies they served as potent gifts. Indigenous leaders exchanged body parts to ratify and secure alliances. During the Pequot War in the early 1630s, some colonists understood the meaning of these gifts at least in general terms. They received heads from their indigenous allies solemnly, accepting them as a "pledge" of fidelity and "testimony of their love and service."[41] But the colonists seldom reciprocated by giving body parts away. Instead they collected the heads and found ways to display them. On the Connecticut River the commander of Fort Saybrook "set all their heads on the fort," and his collection grew steadily.[42] As one colonist noted, heads "came almost daily."[43] The Narraganset and Mohegan allies of the colonists found themselves participating in a head-gathering enterprise that was expanding in scale and becoming increasingly anonymous. The activity's meaning had changed.

A variety of warring peoples across the Atlantic world removed heads from defeated people and placed them on display. Aztec cities were decorated with human skulls exhibited in rows. The Spanish reported seeing tens of thousands of skulls hung together in this way, and archaeologists have uncovered collections of skulls with large holes on each side, apparently for rods.[44] In Ireland in the 1570s, Humphrey Gilbert ordered his men in the evening to collect the heads of those they had killed during the day. Gilbert lined the path to his tent with them.[45] On his way to see the king of Dahomey in 1727, William Snelgrave passed "two large stages, on which were heaped a great number of dead men's heads, that afforded no pleasing sight or smell." Snelgrave's guide told him that the heads had belonged to four thousand war captives who had been ceremonially killed three weeks earlier.[46] All of these displays served as demonstrations of power. The heads were evidence of battlefield success and represented a continuing assertion of control over human remains. Putting heads on display denied families and opposing nations the ability to dispose of their dead as they would wish. Some of the implications of the display of heads were common across cultures, and sometimes the gesture seemed easy to interpret as men moved from one part of the Atlantic world to another, but divergent meanings were attached to the practice.

In Europe most of the heads on exhibition were those of criminals, and the sight was frightening in part because the dead had been deprived Christian burials. When Gilbert chose to put heads on display at his military camp, he morally condemned his adversaries. He intended not only to intimidate, but also to humiliate and dismiss them. The Aztecs understood decapitation differently. They dressed their captives elaborately before killing them and performed ceremonies before and after the execution. Important captives had their hearts removed as a spiritual offering before their heads went on display. The ceremony was undoubtedly frightening, but it was not designed to demean the captive.[47] Decapitation also had meanings in Dahomey that made little sense to most European observers. When Snelgrave described seeing heads "heaped" and rotting, he suggested that they were treated disrespectfully, almost like garbage. But the kings of Dahomey valued those heads. One ethnographer has suggested that

Fig. 7.2 Juan de Tovar, sixteenth-century. An Aztec skull rack. Courtesy of the John Carter Brown Library.

they were "one of the treasures" of the kingdom "equal to the greatest riches."[48] In Dahomey, only kings could possess heads. In other west African societies individual soldiers took the heads of men they captured or killed. A soldier with these trophies was "careful to put them in his home in a prominent place to make his bravery known to his posterity."[49] By contrast, most Europeans and colonists had little interest in the long-term preservation of the bodies or heads of their dead opponents. During its war against the Wulstukwiuk and Mi'kmaq east of the St. Croix River in 1696, the government of Massachusetts offered ranger companies bounties for the scalps of the indigenous American men they killed,

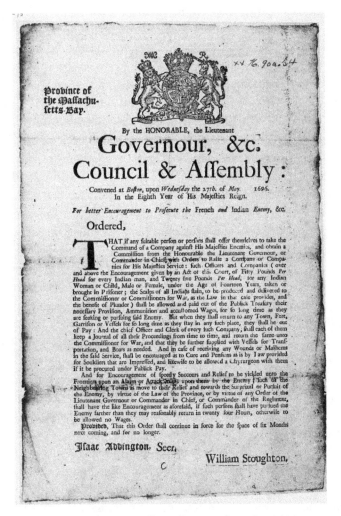

Fig. 7.3 Massachusetts proclamation offering bounties for scalps, 1696. Library of Congress.

and smaller prizes for any women and children "taken."[50] For New Englanders, a scalp no longer had any lasting significance except as evidence of a killing.

The Massachusetts prize money was available to ranger companies that included both colonial and indigenous American fighters. The European taboo against taking body parts as trophies was not nearly as powerful a restraint as the one against cannibalism. Portuguese commanders defending their fort at São Jorge da Mina in 1625 and 1637 paid African warriors for the heads of Dutch West India Company soldiers.[51] In the mid-eighteenth century in eastern North America, French military officers paid indigenous American warriors for British scalps.[52] On rare occasions colonists and soldiers from rival empires scalped each other, though usually this happened in the context of accusations of treason or other criminal activity.[53] Despite the colonists' participation in the taking of scalps, they continued to associate the practice with savagery.

Anthropologists have suggested that small, nomadic, family-based bands generally avoid violent conflict, while village-based groups are likely to engage in feuding, and regional powers such as chiefdoms and states tend to approach warfare more impersonally, with less specific regard to the individuals killed.[54] Theories like this can be difficult to apply, especially in the early modern Atlantic world where social categories were mixed as result of disease and political upheaval. Chiefly societies dissolved and scattered, new chiefdoms arose, empires invaded, and complex leagues and alliances were formed. Wars often involved networks of allies and adversaries with different understandings of the importance and purpose of violence. Still, it is useful to focus on the distinguishing features of the feud as a set of markers separating one kind of warfare from another. Feuding operated according to a distinct logic that distinguished it from large-scale warfare between states.

In the sixteenth and seventeenth centuries many indigenous societies in North America pursued feuds. They responded to homicide as a communal injury and sought redress against the offending group. European commentators expressed surprise at the absence of indigenous mechanisms for identifying, apprehending, and (in their view) adequately punishing individual criminals. As French missionary Gabriel Sagard observed, within some indigenous groups wrong-doers could make amends simply "by means of a present."[55] Europeans and colonists were equally astonished that some indigenous communities punished members of an offending group without any regard for whether the person suffering punishment was personally responsible for the original offence. Actions that indigenous people interpreted as promoting justice, including the careful, deliberate torture of war captives, mutilation and the display of body parts, appeared unjustified to European observers who frequently condemned indigenous Americans for their seemingly indiscriminate cruelty. Paradoxically, a common European response was to exact retribution on a communal scale, punishing whole societies without regard to proportionality.

In the bloodiest engagement of the Pequot War, colonial soldiers supported by Mohegan and Narragansett allies set fire to the Pequot village at Mystic and killed those who tried to escape. Hundreds of Pequot men, women, and children were killed, a large number of them burned. According to one colonial officer, at the end of the fighting "our Indians came to us, and much rejoiced at our victories, and greatly admired the manner of the English men's fight, but cried 'mach it, mach it,' that is, it is naught, it is naught, because it is too furious, and slays too many men."[56] They would have preferred to take prisoners and decide their fates individually.[57] The burning of the Mystic village revealed stark contrasts between colonial and indigenous American expectations for warfare.[58] The massacre also occurred during a time of intense and influential controversy in Europe and the colonies over the proper conduct of war.[59] New England's military and political leaders were conscious of the issues at stake, and after the destruction of the village they debated whether their use of force had been excessive. One participant cited Biblical precedents to justify the indiscriminate slaughter of non-Christian people.[60]

Arguing against critics who blamed Massachusetts for the violence, Deputy Governor John Winthrop invoked tactical considerations, the Pequot's refusal to surrender, and the risk of future attacks from them. To highlight the justice of the colonists' cause and the severe danger the Pequots posed, he cited their treatment of one prisoner, a man named John Tilley. Winthrop complained that Tilley was completely innocent but Pequot warriors had nonetheless tortured and dismembered him.

> About the middle of this month, John Tilley, master of a bark, coming down Connecticut River, went on shore in a canoe, three miles above the fort, to kill fowl, and having shot off his piece, many Indians arose out of the covert and took him, and killed one other who was in the canoe. This Tilley was a very stout man, and of great understanding. They cut off his hands, and sent them before, and after cut off his feet. He lived three days after his hands were cut off, and themselves confessed that he was a stout man, because he cried not in his torture.[61]

The torture of captives was common among many indigenous peoples in North America.[62] Specific practices and expectations varied, but as Winthrop suggested with respect to Tilley, captives who persevered bravely often received their captors' respect. Along with the exchange of treasured trophy heads, torture contributed to a military culture that promoted the application of violence in measured ways and focused on individual victims as group members without concern for that person's particular guilt. For their part, Europeans and colonists associated torture, like the display of heads, with criminal prosecution.

Violent judicial interrogations in Europe and the Americas could last for weeks. In criminal cases the men assigned with tormenting the accused were usually the ones who would perform the execution.[63] Judicial torture was conducted intimately in cells, but the subsequent application of the death penalty was a public performance. In parts of Europe and the colonies, convicts were burned alive in front of audiences, hanged, decapitated, or disemboweled and pulled apart by the limbs with the aid of horses.

The display of heads, judicial torture, and public execution declined in Europe in the seventeenth and eighteenth centuries as part of a general movement

Fig. 7.4 A type of torture rack used in Europe during interrogations to extract information and confessions from prisoners. *Constitutio criminalis Theresiana* (Vienna, 1769), p. 24, Figure 3. British Library.

against public displays of aggression.[64] But there was a complication in the timing of this development, with important consequences for the future of the Atlantic world. The dismemberment, torture, and killing of prisoners fell into disfavor in European military practice long before they were banned in the context of legal proceedings.

In the early seventeenth century, citing classical authorities but also responding to the horrific violence of the Thirty Years' War, Dutch philosopher Hugo Grotius argued against the display of bodies during military campaigns and claimed that anyone who "hinders" the burial of the enemy dead "gives an affront to nature" and "is an enemy to piety."[65] Grotius made similar pronouncements about other military practices and was one of a growing number of commentators arguing for a code of conduct for war.[66] In 1631 William Gouge articulated the views of an increasingly powerful European consensus when he gave this advice to soldiers: "Show that thou delightest not in blood. Shed no more than of necessity." Gouge added, "Slay not such as cannot hurt thee," and "Put not those whom thou flayest to exquisite torments." The fighting men of Europe did not always follow such ethical guidance, and Gouge significantly acknowledged that there were exceptions to the precepts he listed, including what he called "requiting like for like."[67] Precepts like these did not always restrain the soldiers representing the European empires in the Americas. Often they served instead to stoke a sense of righteous outrage and fortify the Europeans and colonists in their determination to answer violence in kind.

In 1758, preparing for a campaign against the Mi'kmaq on Cape Breton Island, British General Charles Lawrence told his soldiers that their opponents were the "only brutes and cowards in the creation" willing to "scalp and mangle the poor sick soldiers and defenceless women." Since the Mi'kmaq behaved in a deplorable manner it was appropriate for his men to "entertain them in their own way." According to Lawrence, the Mi'kmaq's campaigns were "not war but murder."[68]

Nine years earlier Nova Scotia's governor, Edward Cornwallis, had made similar arguments to justify paying soldiers for the scalps of Mi'kmaq men and bounties for women and children taken captive. The orders Cornwallis issued, like the 1696 Massachusetts bounty offer, left it unclear whether payment would be available for the scalps of women and children. In 1724 a similarly ambiguous proclamation in Massachusetts led not only to the enslavement but also to the killing of women and children in present-day Maine, and in 1744 the Governor of Massachusetts had offered bounties for the scalps of Mi'kmaq women and children "killed in fight."[69] Cornwallis argued that his 1749 policy followed "the custom of America." He labeled Mi'kmaq attacks against colonists "murders," and he and his council were adamant that their own campaign against the

Mi'kmaq should not be classified as "war." The Mi'kmaq, they said, "ought to be treated as so many banditti ruffians, or rebels to his Majesty's government."[70]

When seeking to distinguish their violent campaigns from conventional warfare, Lawrence and Cornwallis wrestled with a paradox that had troubled colonial and European military leaders throughout the Americas almost since the time of Columbus. If indigenous warriors were "brutes and cowards," "banditti ruffians," and "murderers," and the imperial authorities responded by following their "custom" and treating them "in their own way," did it not follow that the representatives of the empires were knowingly committing the very same acts that they condemned as crimes? The obvious answer to this question was yes unless there was a special justification for the imperial forces' actions. One ostensible solution to this conundrum lay in the charge of rebellion that Cornwallis levelled against the Mi'kmaq.

In order to justify the targeting of men, women, and children, it was not enough for men like Cornwallis to cite extreme provocation, because if imperial forces were drawn into a relentless cycle of unrestrained violence, their claim that they represented a legitimate, formal legal order would collapse. For this reason, whenever imperial forces retaliated against the alleged outrages of indigenous forces by responding in kind, they had to insist that they were adopting extraordinary, temporary measures and laying the groundwork for the eventual introduction of a more orderly, formal system of administering justice. Cornwallis believed that the men who took scalps from the Mi'kmaq were representatives of order, and he claimed the indigenous warriors who opposed them were "rebels." Rebels like these, Cornwallis suggested, collectively promoted perpetual violence and chaos.

Representatives of nearly every European empire in the Americas punished indigenous people for failing to respect imperial authority and behave in accordance with European norms. The starkest and most extravagant expression of this stance was the *Requirimento*, a document produced in 1512 that the leaders of Spanish expeditionary forces were supposed to read to the inhabitants whenever they reached lands the Spanish had not entered before. The document, written in Spanish, argued for the authority of the Pope and explained that he had granted the king and queen of Spain dominion over the Americas. Everyone hearing these words, regardless of whether they understood them or consented, was expected to obey Spanish authority. The text ended with a warning that if they disobeyed they would be treated as rebels and punished severely.[71]

In 1545 eight Franciscan friars were appointed to introduce the indigenous peoples of the Yucatán to Christianity. Over the next seventeen years they were joined by as many as thirty others, but the task they faced was daunting. They were supposed to minister to hundreds of thousands of souls. In 1562 the Franciscans discovered that many Mayan communities across the Yucatán continued to perform their own traditional ceremonies. Refusing to admit failure, the missionaries responded by ordering the seizure of Mayans in groups of twenty. According to one witness,

> when the Indians confessed to having so few idols (one, two or three) the friars proceeded to string up many of the Indians, having tied their wrists together with cord, and thus hoisted them from the ground, telling them that they must confess all the idols they had, and where they were. The Indians continued saying they had no more . . . and so the friars ordered great stones attached to their feet, and so they were left to hang for a space, and if they still did not admit to a greater quantity of idols they were flogged as they hung there, and had burning wax splashed on their bodies.[72]

These violent interrogations resembled inquisitorial proceedings, but the missionaries proceeded without judicial oversight. The Mayans were never charged with crimes or tried. Instead they were subjected to violence collectively on a large scale.

In effect, the Franciscans were leading a war. Over a three-month period 4,500 indigenous people were tortured and 157 died under questioning or soon thereafter. The proceedings sparked controversy among the Spanish because the Franciscans had dispensed with formal legal procedure. The friars' defenders argued that there were few judges available and the scale of the problem was beyond the capacity of courts. "If we had proceeded with all according to the order of the law, it would be impossible to finish with the province of Manı́ alone in twenty years, and meanwhile they would all become idolaters and go to hell."[73] Unable to rely on courts to prosecute disobedient indigenous people, the Franciscans performed tortures that resembled those that would have been applied, generally on a smaller scale, in a criminal process in Europe.

Other imperial officials similarly borrowed and adapted forms of violence associated with criminal practice and deployed them in wartime in America. During their wars in Brazil in the 1640s, the Dutch and the Portuguese treated each other according to standard European norms governing warfare, but colonial leaders on both sides pretended they had a right to the loyalty of indigenous Brazilians, and so they threatened to treat opposing indigenous warriors as criminals. The Dutch were unwilling to pay the diplomatic and strategic cost of pursuing a policy of execution, but the Portuguese hanged Tupi war captives as rebels and strung up their bodies around the walls of a captured Dutch fort.[74]

In 1623, Kongo's King Dom Pedro sent a letter to the Vatican complaining that the Portuguese governor of Luanda, João Correira de Sousa, had allied himself with the Imbangala and invaded his kingdom with "an army of more than two hundred thousand . . . who fed on human flesh." The Portuguese and their allies had "ravaged and destroyed a number of provinces where an infinite number of Christians had been killed and eaten. In addition, many had been reduced to slavery." Exaggerating for dramatic effect, Dom Pedro claimed that in one province "all had been killed and eaten." Correira justified his alliance with the Imbangala by rejecting Dom Pedro's claim to the throne and charging the king's supporters with rebellion.[75]

To punish indigenous peoples as rebels, some imperial leaders chose from a range of violent acts sanctioned by criminal procedure, while others borrowed selectively, and often inventively, from an inventory of perceived atrocities allegedly committed by the indigenous peoples themselves. During their war against Algonkian peoples near New Amsterdam in the 1640s, Dutch soldiers engaged in their own kind of mimicry. Farmers in the Dutch colony reported seeing the aftermath of one episode of bloodshed: a line of wounded indigenous men and women "running past . . . with their hands cut off; others had their legs cut off. Some carried their bowels in their arms; others had such horrible cuts, hacks and wounds, that the like can never have happened elsewhere."[76] The farmers initially thought that Mohawk warriors had attacked these people, but the perpetrators were Dutch. The mayhem resulted from the colonial governor's frustration at not being able to proceed against the indigenous people through the instruments of European-style criminal procedure. Following the killing of a colonist, he had asked his council, "Is it not right and proper to punish the scandalous murder . . . and in case the Indians do not surrender the murderer to our demand is it not right to destroy the whole village to which he belongs?"[77] The Dutch ultimately attacked several villages.[78]

A few years earlier Grotius had insisted optimistically that in wartime "children, women, old men, priests, scholars [and] husbandmen are to be spared."[79] Gouge largely agreed, declaring that "Women, children, the sick and the aged, are in the number of enemies . . . but these are enemies who make no resistance, and consequently give us no right to treat their persons ill."[80] Guidelines like these were difficult to observe during sieges and attacks on towns and villages, and when the forces of one empire took colonial territory from another they frequently apprehended and transported colonial populations including women and children.[81] Similarly, colonial armies facing indigenous resistance often plotted to remove or exterminate entire communities. For their part, many indigenous Americans had engaged in campaigns to destroy rival villages, and after European colonists arrived in the Americas indigenous warriors frequently fought to restrict or reduce the spread of colonial settlement.[82] Some tried to eliminate colonies altogether. Those efforts inevitably targeted women and children as well as men.

Before the New Englanders with their indigenous allies burned the village at Mystic in 1636, a Pequot delegation had asked a group of colonial soldiers whether they killed women and children. The soldiers had replied menacingly, "they should see that hereafter."[83] The Pequot's question reflected a widespread dread of violence against people who were poorly equipped to defend themselves. Another participant in the Pequot War observed that the colonists were "loth to destroy women and children," and so were "the Indians belonging to that place."[84] Nonetheless, Pequot warriors killed women and children, though in much smaller numbers than the colonists did. In a raid on Wethersfield, Connecticut, a Pequot war party killed a woman and her child and took two young women captive.[85] They used the women's clothing as sails on their canoes in an apparent effort to taunt the colonists.[86] From childhood, New England boys were taught that military service demonstrated manhood and that good soldiers should fight to defend the other members of their families. By displaying the women's clothing, the Pequot warriors demonstrated that they knew how to upset the New Englanders.[87]

Similar dynamics operated in other parts of the Americas. In northern Chile in the seventeenth century, Araucanian warriors paraded and humiliated Spanish women they had captured in wartime, and they intentionally kept Spanish settlers on their guard by spreading vague rumors of impending and ongoing attacks.[88] In threatened colonial outposts in eighteenth-century Brazil, settlers mobilized to defend their communities against raids by indigenous warriors that they described as campaigns of arson, theft, and murder.[89] In New France, Jesuit publicists railed against the cruelty of Haudenosaunee war parties. In contrast to Chilean, Brazilian and Anglo-American writers who tended to emphasize violence against colonists, French Jesuits focused on the suffering of indigenous Americans who had converted to Christianity. According to Paul Ragueneau, after Haudenosaunee warriors overran the village of Tionnontaté in 1649,

> It was a scene of incredible cruelty. The enemy snatched from a Mother her infants, that they might be thrown into the fire; other children beheld sick Mothers beaten to death at their feet or groaning in the flames, permission, in either case, being denied them to show the least compassion. It was a crime to shed a tear, these barbarians demanding that their prisoners should go into captivity as if they were marching to their triumph. A poor Christian Mother, who wept for the death of her infant, was killed on the spot, because she still loved, and could not stifle soon enough her Natural feelings.[90]

The Jesuits celebrated these dead Christians as martyrs and stoked rage against the Haudenosaunee.[91]

In a variety of colonial contexts, Europeans observers expressed horror at the ways indigenous American warriors directed violence against women. Indigenous responses to colonial violence are less easy to document, but there is strong evidence of sharp differences over rape. Colonists charged indigenous Americans with rape in wartime, but tellingly, several colonial commentators in North America registered surprise and admitted that indigenous warriors committed no rapes at all. According to New Englander William Hubbard, in the 1670s during King Philip's War indigenous warriors did not engage in "any uncivil carriage to any of the females, nor ever attempted the chastity of any of them." Mary Rowlandson and Cotton Mather confirmed Hubbard's observation, and by the 1740s William Douglass had reached a general conclusion that indigenous warriors "never offer violence to our women captives."[92]

These writers' surprise is revealing. European treatises on warfare condemned rape, but there is ample evidence that European soldiers raped women.[93] This was a common complaint of wartime adversaries and a source of disciplinary trouble for commanding officers. On rare occasions, commanders like James Wolfe in Canada threatened mass rape as a way to intimidate their opponents.[94]

Indigenous American women in the early modern era produced few if any written protests against rape, but documents written by Europeans contain hints of the frequency of the practice. During the Pequot War in 1637, for example, John Winthrop described an encounter with a woman who had been taken captive. She pleaded with him for mercy. "One of her first requests," he reported, "was that the English would not abuse her body."[95] During the Spanish conquest of Alta California in the eighteenth century, soldiers committed rape repeatedly. According to Junipero Serra, the head of the California missions,

> In the morning, six or seven soldiers would set out together . . . and go to the distant *rancherias* even many leagues away. When both men and women at the sight of them would take off running . . . the soldiers, adept as they are at lassoing cows and mules, would lasso Indian women, who then became prey to their unbridled lust. Several Indian men who tried to defend the women were shot to death.[96]

Indigenous Californians resisted the Spanish soldiers at the scene of the rapes. In other places warriors regrouped and took organized punitive action, launching retributive raids after campaigns involving rape. After French soldiers raped Carib women on Dominica in 1653, Carib warriors retaliated by destroying a French settlement on the nearby island of Marie-Galante.[97]

Since the fifteenth century many elements of warfare in the Atlantic world served to alienate people from each other, helping define racial categories that would become starker as the centuries progressed. Exaggerated assessments

Fig. 7.5 Christian Richter, mid-seventeenth century. A European soldier attacking a woman. Richter worked in Weimar between 1613 and 1667, and this image reflects German experience during the Thirty Years' War. Staatliche Graphische Sammlung München.

of the stealth, acrobatic ability, and military process of indigenous warriors served to make them terrifying to Europeans. Rumors of large-scale, routine cannibalism, directed against Europeans as well as Africans and indigenous Americans, encouraged people on both sides of the ocean to see each other as heartless and dangerous, and associate conflict with personal annihilation. The exchange and display of heads and other body parts, outside the context of any shared understanding of the meaning of the gesture, had a similar effect, and so did torture whenever the adversaries did not agree about the purpose of the exercise. Incidents of mass rape polarized opposing forces, encouraging rapists to brutalize and dehumanize the people who opposed them, as well as their families. The victims of rape along with their defenders were likely to view rapists as brutes.

From the perspective of European imperial leaders who imagined themselves to be representatives of order, a frustrating irony was at work. Their engagements with the peoples of Africa and the Americas often promoted moral chaos, and sometimes in moments of crisis colonial officials thought they might be able to solve their problems by eliminating entire indigenous populations. Leaders of the Virginia colony embraced genocidal rhetoric in 1622 following the Powhattan attack. Company officials vowed to destroy their indigenous opponents, "rooting them out for being longer a people upon the face of the earth."[98] In 1679, after decades of maintaining complex relations with Carib warriors, French colonial officials on Martinique and Dominica resolved to "destroy" the Caribs entirely. They drew up an elaborate plan and calculated the cost of the ships and weaponry necessary for a campaign that would have taken them around much of the Caribbean.[99] Both the English in Virginia and the French on Dominica claimed that they had been provoked militarily, but they also justified their plans in economic terms. Virginia Governor Francis Wyatt argued that the "expulsion of the savages" would open up "the free range of the country for increase of cattle."[100] Jean-Baptiste Patoulet, the Intendant-General of the French Antilles, promoted attacking the Caribs by highlighting their value as slaves.[101]

But it was always easier to imagine genocide than to carry it out. In one of the most ambitious genocidal schemes in North American history, in 1763 Jeffery Amherst distributed blankets that had been used by smallpox patients to indigenous Americans as gifts. If his plan had been successful, he would have spread contagion indiscriminately among indigenous Americans, potentially on a massive scale. He intended to kill without ritual, by guile, anonymously, without any pretense that he was sending an instructive message. But his effort proved futile, since smallpox, we now know, is rarely if ever transmitted through cloth.[102]

Amherst developed his plan in a moment of deep frustration. Along with other British officials, he had hoped that Britain's military success against the French in Canada had altered the balance of power in North America so that Britain would no longer have to negotiate with indigenous Americans as they had done in the past. British delegations would no longer have to offer presents to indigenous leaders or sit with them respectfully at treating gatherings. But after the war of 1763, the restoration of order required compromise. The British reversed course and returned to a policy of cultivating and carefully nurturing alliances.[103]

Virtually every time a military leader dreamed of genocide, the effort failed, because all of the colonists' lethal technologies had limitations. After two major wars against indigenous peoples in 1644 and 1676, Virginia had greater success working within a network of alliances with Algonkian, Siouan, and Iroquoian peoples to maintain peace and facilitate colonial expansion.[104] In the 1680s the French government favored a similar diplomatic policy toward the Caribs and other indigenous peoples of the Caribbean basin, since Louis XIV refused to authorize or fund the colonists' plan for genocide.[105] In most places on the mainland of North and South America, indigenous peoples retained military power. They outnumbered colonists in many regions and were able to exploit rivalries between Europeans to win allies, gain diplomatic leverage, and supplies. Few indigenous populations were ever driven to extinction. On the other hand, though the European empires frequently wrecked each other's colonies in the Americas, indigenous warriors seldom overran established colonies. The Pueblo destroyed most of New Mexico in 1680, but that was an exception. The colonies survived, but the colonial settlers on their frontiers remained vulnerable. Some scholars have argued that these circumstances gave rise to a distinctive approach to warfare among the colonists in the region that became the United States, a moralistic, retaliatory "American way of war."[106] A sense of constant insecurity also troubled other regions where colonial settlers felt surrounded and threatened by indigenous peoples.[107]

For their part, indigenous communities suffered their own harrowing disorientations. Scholars have long debated whether warfare in the Americas became deadlier as a result of colonization. According to an old view, prior to the arrival of Europeans the ethics of feuding, emphasizing the importance of individual deaths, kept overall wartime mortality rates low. Warriors tortured captives slowly and prized parts of their bodies as trophies because combat deaths were rare. More recently archaeologists and historians have argued that the wars fought in the Americas before colonization killed at least as many people on a per capita basis as those that followed, but it is difficult to conduct a body count and, to perform the analysis effectively, war-related deaths would have to be disentangled from the impact of disease, dispossession, forced labor, and migration.[108]

Europeans carried new pathogens to the Americas in the fifteenth and sixteenth centuries, introducing the indigenous people to smallpox, measles, flu, and other diseases. Epidemics swept through villages, towns and nations.[109] Passing from person to person, contagion often traveled faster than Europeans could. Some people fell sick before they had ever confronted a colonist or soldier. But in places like the Caribbean islands and Mexico, illness arrived at the moment of contact with European expeditionary forces. A description of the Mexican city of Tlatelolco, composed in the Nahuatl language in the 1520s or 1530s, links the destruction of human bodies to the damage in the landscape:

> Broken bones littered the road; crushed heads, roofless houses. Walls were made red with blood. Worms crawled through the noses in the

streets; the house walls were slippery with brains. The water was dyed
red with blood. Thus we went along; we drank brackish water.[110]

As this description of Tlatelolco suggests, disease, warfare, and decay infused the
process of conquest and colonization so thoroughly their various demographic
impacts cannot be isolated.[111] The deprivation and stress of conflict increased
everyone's susceptibility to disease, but it was obvious from the moment the
epidemics struck that they did not affect all people equally. European observers
watched indigenous people suffer and explained it as a miracle, while indigenous Americans responded with dread. For the first generation of Americans to
meet the Spanish, it was difficult to separate illness from the experience of war.
Almost from the moment the Spanish arrived in the Americas, disorientation,
heightened fear, and confusion became common features of American warfare.

Slavery and Warfare on Land

During the eighteenth century, Carib warriors in South America sold indigenous captives to Dutch colonists. According to a contemporary account, the
Caribs made "incursions on the interior Indians for the sake of making prisoners
who are afterwards sold to the inhabitants of the Dutch colonies."

> Upon these occasions they surround the scattered houses of these
> Indians, in the night, while they were sleeping without apprehension of
> danger and make them all prisoners. The men, however, who would be
> apt to escape if they were sold to slavery, are usually put to death, while
> the women, and children of both sexes, are reserved for sale.[1]

Killing the male captives served the military needs of Caribs and met the
demands of the Dutch, who preferred to buy young and female indigenous
Americans as slaves and purchase enslaved adult men from Africa. This process
of sex selection, and the Caribs' and colonists' preferences, reflect the influence
of warfare and military considerations in redistributing enslaved populations
around the early modern Atlantic world.

Among the Aztecs in the sixteenth century adult men who were captured in
war often faced ritual execution, while women and children were less ceremoni-
ously consigned to slavery.[2] In early modern war zones generally, when captives
were held near the place where they were taken, pragmatic considerations favored the preservation of women and children because adult men were often
more dangerous and difficult to hold. If men escaped death at the hands of their
captors, they might subsequently find themselves left behind after their female
relatives and children were carried away and enslaved. In the lower Mississippi
Valley in the early eighteenth century, travelers to Taena villages encountered
hundreds of single men. They had been passed over by raiders who had taken
most of the women and children captive.[3]

Detailed records of the slave trade out of Africa reveal a stark gender divide
and age pattern. The majority of captives shipped away from the continent were

Atlantic Wars. Geoffrey Plank, Oxford University Press (2020). © Oxford University Press.
DOI: 10.1093/oso/9780190860455.001.0001

males between the ages of fourteen and thirty.[4] Extrapolating from these records it appears that women were nearly three times more likely than men to be kept in Africa as slaves, and children were vastly more likely to be retained. This pattern reflected African preferences as well as European demand.[5] In most regions that supplied war captives to Europeans, the majority of the local enslaved population was female. In Kongo nobles distinguished themselves by maintaining dozens or even hundreds of wives, many of whom were acquired as slaves.[6] In West Africa in 1785, Paul Erdman Isert, a German surgeon working for the Baltic Guinea Company, described a king ostentatiously greeting Europeans. He was followed by a retinue of women.

> After having made us wait for him for more than half an hour, the mighty person himself appeared with a very numerous following of musicians and women. The latter kept the flies away with fans made of palm leaves, as well as thus wafting fresh air around him. A large umbrella was held twirling over his head.[7]

In addition to providing personal and ceremonial services, enslaved women performed hard manual work, processing fish, for example, or working as porters.[8] On his visit to Ouidah in 1773, Robert Norris met the king's "master of the horse" who was responsible for "the superintendence of the plantations, which provide the king's household with provisions; and to see that the women who are to cultivate them are not remiss in the discharge of their duty."[9] Many societies across the Atlantic world held more women than men in slavery.

In valuing adult male slaves over women, early modern transatlantic slave traders broke with a pattern of behavior that remained common in Africa and the Americas and had prevailed in Europe in antiquity.[10] The slave traders understood that holding men in slavery required a greater mobilization of military force. In taking men from Africa, they displayed confidence in their ability to control them as captives. They judged that the risks involved could be offset by the men's presumed superior ability to perform heavy labor.

But since there were strong men in Europe and the Americas, why did they go to Africa to acquire men? To explain why the traders preferred Africa as a source for male slaves, we need to examine the peculiarities of the European experience with slavery. Iceland is a good place to start.

In the summer of 1627 four corsair ships left North Africa to raid Iceland and take captives. Three of the ships sailed from Algiers, and one from Salé on Africa's Atlantic coast. One of the ships attacked coastal settlements on the western side of the island, while the remaining three, working together, attacked the eastern and southern coast as well as the Westman Islands south of mainland Iceland. At the Westman Islands, the largest of the ships anchored far off the shore, safe in deep water. Its purpose was only to carry men and supplies, to bring soldiers to Iceland and carry captives away.[11] Over the course of one month, the raiders killed approximately forty Icelanders and captured four hundred others to be sold in Africa as slaves. Ólafur Egilsson was seized in the Westman Islands. According to his account the raiders "rushed with violent speed across the island, like hunting hounds, howling like wolves, and the weak women and children could not escape. . . . Only a few of the people who were the strongest, or had nothing to carry, or did not pay attention to anybody else, managed to avoid capture."[12]

The captain of one of the ships had been born in the Netherlands. His original name was Jan Jansen, but he became known as Murat Reis after he began sailing with North African corsairs. He had acquired his first military experience serving on Dutch privateers in the war against Spain. Around 1618 he had been captured by North African raiders in the Canary Islands and converted to Islam. Reis had rare and valuable knowledge of naval warfare, and he rose to prominence among the corsairs of Salé.[13] According to some accounts Reis planned and oversaw the raid on Iceland. Other men of European birth served on the ships. According to Egilsson, the crews included men from England, Germany, Scandinavia, and Spain. Most of these men had been forced to work as crew members and were "sometimes beaten as a reward."[14]

Many of these European crew members were held as slaves, but others had secured their freedom by converting to Islam. Egilsson condemned the converts as apostates and villains. He claimed that they were "by far the worst of people, and cruelly brutal to Christians. It was they who bound those taken captive and wounded and killed people."[15] The pilot of one of the ships was Danish. Some claimed that he had refused to convert to Islam, but since he had valuable knowledge of the Icelandic coastline, he had been able to convince his masters to free him if he guided them safely to land.[16] European captives with naval experience were particularly prized among the corsairs, but some of the Europeans in the raiding party distinguished themselves by fighting on land. Eglissson was captured by Englishmen.

> We struggled, along with the others, for a long time until we were beaten and struck with the butts of their spears and had to give in. Most of those attacking us were English, and I have since wondered that they did not kill us all with their beatings.[17]

The English who beat Egilsson into submission may have included fishermen taken from vessels captured by the corsairs only a few days earlier.[18]

Egilsson and the other Icelanders who were seized in 1627 thought that the English and other Europeans who participated in the raid violated an array of

conventions governing how Christians should treat one another. Slavery had
been common in Iceland and Europe during the Middle Ages, but by the seventeenth century the islanders, like people throughout Western Europe, rarely
placed each other in perpetual bondage except as a punishment for crime.
During the Thirty Years' War, the French sent Spanish and Portuguese war
captives to row Mediterranean galleys, and they kept them in bondage after
hostilities ended, but it was unusual for Europeans to employ prisoners of war
in this way. Learned opinion was moving steadily against the practice.[19] Dutch
philosopher Hugo Grotius acknowledged that war captives had been enslaved
since antiquity, but he declared that "Christians have generally agreed that such
as are taken in war between them should not become servants, to be sold, to be
forced to work, and suffer the like servile things."[20] While European Christians
increasingly opposed the enslavement of Christian European war captives, judicial authorities continued to sentence men and women to long terms of bound
labor as punishment. Alleged rebels like some royalist English, Welsh, Scottish,
and Irish prisoners seized in the civil wars of the 1640s were summarily designated criminals and transported to North America and the Caribbean.[21] Convict
labor was widespread in Europe and Europe's transatlantic empires throughout
the sixteenth, seventeenth, and eighteenth centuries. Death sentences were
commuted to long terms of bound service to provide labor for the colonies and
oarsmen for galleys. In the 1680s, facing a labor shortage, the French bought
convicts from Savoy to row in their Mediterranean fleet.[22] In the eighteenth century the French purchased convicts from Poland and Spain for their galleys.[23]

The governments of Western Europe generally insisted that their own
subjects should never suffer perpetual bound service unless they had been formally condemned and identified as worthy of subordination. But as the events
in Iceland in 1627 suggested, people in Europe remained vulnerable to enslavement. In the early seventeenth century there may have been as many as a hundred thousand Europeans held as slaves in Muslim North Africa and the Middle
East.[24] Overall in North Africa, the mortality rate among European slaves was
approximately 17 percent per year. Fewer than 5 percent of these men, women
and children were ever ransomed and returned.[25] Eight years after the four hundred Icelanders were taken in 1627, 330 had died.[26] Thirty-four of the survivors
were ransomed, and only twenty-seven found a way back to Iceland.[27] The capture, enslavement and sale of Christian Europeans provoked outrage across the
continent. Captives like Egilsson emphasized their innocence and argued that
they had done nothing to deserve their fate. They vilified the corsairs, especially
the free Europeans who often commanded and guided the slave-raiding crews.
Egilsson described them as "servants of Satan, the father of all ungodliness."[28]

The communal indignation expressed by Egilsson and many others helped
Christian Europeans justify their ongoing trade in Muslim North African

captives, with a particular focus on men who had served on corsair ships. From a common Christian European perspective these rowers, sailors, and fighters deserved punishment and subjection, but they were also highly valued as slaves. Just as the corsairs prized Christian captives with sailing skills, Christian Europeans sought out Muslim men seized from galleys because they were assumed to possess special strength and skill.

The Spanish crown claimed title to all Muslim prisoners of war taken at sea. On Spanish galleys, enslaved Muslim rowers worked alongside convicts. They were often assigned the position at the end of the oar where the rowing was most difficult. Enslaved Muslim men and some who had converted from Islam to Christianity assumed positions of responsibility on Spanish galleys, helping to guard convicts and care for them when they were sick.[29] Other enslaved Muslim captives, including men, women, and children, were employed as domestic servants, and some men were sold to work in the Almadén mercury mine.[30] Elsewhere in the Mediterranean, at Livorno and Malta, thousands of enslaved Muslim men were sold to Spanish, French, Tuscan, Neapolitan, Genoese, and English buyers.[31] Women and children were available for sale at these markets, but a large proportion of the captives on offer were men who had worked on galleys and were destined to return to hard physical work and military service at sea. Christian Europe's Mediterranean slave trade placed special value on men.

The Mediterranean markets starkly categorized peoples along geographical and confessional lines. Only Muslims were available for purchase at Malta and Livorno, not Christian Europeans. This Christian policy mirrored Muslim strictures prohibiting Muslims from holding each other as slaves, except that Christians did not always free converts.[32] Across Christian Europe, controversy surrounded the impact of conversion on the status of the enslaved, but the religious exemption from enslavement applied first and foremost to people of European ancestry. There were few other instances in the early modern period when Christian Europeans expressed such solidarity and acted in accordance with their shared interests and beliefs. When Christian Europeans and colonists wanted slaves, they sought them in the places they identified as non-Christian parts of the world, in Africa and the Americas. Their consistency in this regard helped set the trajectory of the transatlantic slave trade.[33]

The Mediterranean slave trade encouraged Europeans to believe that only certain kinds of people should be held in slavery. The outcry surrounding the enslavement of Christian Europeans also drew attention to the process of enslavement and gave added force to old arguments that the propriety of holding war captives in slavery depended on the circumstances surrounding their capture. Christian commentators had long condemned unprovoked raids and the capture of apparently harmless victims. In addition to condemning corsairs, some Christian commentators applied this principle to censure the behavior of other

Christian Europeans in cases involving non-European war captives. In 1511 Friar Antonio de Montesinos gave a sermon in Santo Domingo objecting to the enslavement of the indigenous people of Hispaniola. Addressing a Spanish congregation, Montesinos pleaded,

> Tell me, by what right do you hold these Indians in such a cruel and horrible servitude? By what authority did you make unprovoked war on these people, living in peace and quiet on their land, and with unheard-of savagery kill and consume so great a number of them? Why do you keep them worn-out and down-trodden, without feeding them or tending their illnesses, so that they die—or rather you kill them—by reason of the heavy labour you lay upon them, to get gold every day?[34]

Montesinos gave voice to an uneasiness that had been spreading across the Spanish empire since 1495, when 12 ships arrived in Spain carrying 350 indigenous American captives. They were survivors from an original group of 550 who had been sent across the ocean from Hispaniola to be sold as slaves.[35] Queen Isabella intervened and blocked that sale, but fifty of the captives, men between the ages of twenty and forty, were later sent to the galleys, and the fate of the remainder is uncertain.[36] In 1503 Isabella decreed that the indigenous people of Hispaniola were "free and not servile," but paradoxically she also directed the governor of the Indies "to compel and force the said Indians to associate with the Christians of the island and to work on their buildings, and to gather and mine the gold and other metals, and to till the fields and produce food for the Christian inhabitants."[37] The Spanish crown would not categorically ban the enslavement of indigenous Americans until 1542, and by that time Spanish soldiers and colonists had captured and enslaved at least tens of thousands, and perhaps hundreds of thousands, of indigenous Americans.[38]

The protection offered the indigenous peoples of the Americas after 1542 was nothing like what was granted to Christian Europeans. The peculiarities of the Spanish policy highlight the importance of warfare in the evolving European ideology regarding slavery. In the Spanish empire it was still legal for colonists to purchase indigenous Americans who had been captured and enslaved by others. The Spanish also continued to use other elaborate mechanisms to force indigenous Americans to work, compulsory labor schemes that did not quite amount to slavery. Most Europeans and colonists accepted the legitimacy of forced labor systems including slavery, but many had qualms about participating directly in violent campaigns to capture and enslave people without just cause.

In 1637 during the Pequot War, New England soldiers adopted an informal policy of killing adult male war captives and enslaving women and children. In the words of Edward Johnson, "the squaws and some young youths they brought home with them," but "finding the men to be deeply guilty of the crimes they undertook the war for, they brought away only their heads as a token of their victory."[39] In one engagement New Englanders took 105 captives, including 24 adult men. They killed 22 of the men immediately, temporarily spared the lives of two to use them as guides, and led 81 women and children away as slaves.[40] Some of these captives were assigned to the New Englanders' indigenous allies, but most of them were delivered as slaves to colonial households. By the time the fighting ended New Englanders had enslaved approximately three hundred Pequots, mostly women and children. The colonists' Narragansett allies objected to this policy, pleading that captives who had not taken up arms should "be not enslaved, like those who are taken in war, but (as they say is their general custom) be used kindly, have houses and goods and fields given them."[41] The Naragansetts lost that argument, but in the next few years most of the enslaved women and children escaped from their assigned colonial homes.

In 1641 the Massachusetts General Court declared that "there shall never be a bond slavery, villeinage, or captivity among us unless it be lawful captives taken in just wars, and such strangers as willingly sell themselves or are sold to us."[42] The colonial settlers of Massachusetts were confident that their war against the Pequot had been just, and they continued to pursue the women and children who had run away and escaped slavery. During King Philip's War in 1675, New Englanders again enslaved war captives. During that conflict various colonial assemblies and law courts issued judgments and directives designed to reassure the soldiers and slaveholders of their right to seize indigenous Americans.[43]

Not just in New England but throughout the Americas, colonists voiced less concern, and demanded less reassurance, about holding Africans as slaves. Indeed, there may have been widespread ignorance about the process of enslavement in Africa. Writing in the 1680s, Jean Barbot remarked that "many Europeans believe that parents sell their own children, men their wives and relations," but such incidents were rare. According to Barbot, in places like Ouidah the people on sale were "generally prisoners of war, taken from their enemies like other booty," though he acknowledged that "perhaps some" had been "sold by their own countrymen in extreme want or upon a famine, as also some as a punishment of heinous crimes."[44]

Europeans seldom discussed the wars that led to the capture of Africans, and when they did they commented on them only in general terms and almost never suggested that any of the specific conflicts had been just. On the contrary, Europeans and colonists more frequently argued that Africans engaged in endless, random, self-destructive violence. In 1684 Thomas Tryon claimed that in Africa "those that are strongest and most numerous kill, slay and murder the other at their pleasure; and as for those that they save alive, 'tis not out of pity or kindness, but to gratify their own covetousness by making merchandize of them

Fig. 8.1 In 1793, the captain of British slave ship, Samuel Gamble, drew this picture of African captives being led to the coast for sale. Royal Museums Greenwich.

and exposing them to slavery."[45] Some colonists argued in favor of the transatlantic slave trade by asserting that it rescued Africans from their own wars.[46] The widespread claim that Africa's wars were brutal, perpetual, mercenary, and self-destructive reinforced an increasingly pervasive racial ideology suggesting that Africans, particularly those with dark skin, were incapable of rational self-government and therefore suited for slavery. Abolitionists eventually responded to this argument by suggesting that slave traders promoted warfare in Africa, but at least until the mid-eighteenth century the more common view was that since Europeans purchased people who had already been enslaved, they were not morally responsible for the process of capture and subjugation.[47]

Early in the sixteenth century, a Portuguese missionary in the Kingdom of Kongo named Father Fernandes purchased a Kongolese woman as a slave. He had sex with her, and she gave birth to a child. In 1514 King Afonso of Kongo sent a letter to the king of Portugal complaining about Fernandes. Afonso suggested that the missionary's behavior was typical of many Portuguese in Kongo. He said they "fill their houses with whores." In a series of letters to the kings of Portugal over the next several years, Afonso outlined how slavery should function in Kongo, including who should be enslaved, who should buy them and where they should be sold. He argued that Portuguese priests should be banned from buying any women and that the Portuguese in general should stop "taking our natives, sons of the land and sons of our noblemen and our vassals and our relatives."[48] Afonso thought that the Portuguese should purchase only non-Kongolese war captives as slaves.

For the rest of the sixteenth century and beyond, Afonso and his successors took measures to maintain separate slave markets in Kongo to protect their people from kidnapping, abuse, and exile. They monitored their ports carefully and demanded documentation on the status of people sold into the Atlantic market. On occasions when large numbers of Kongolese slaves were sold abroad, they took extraordinary measures to repatriate them. In the late 1570s and early 1580s during a wartime subsistence crisis, it was reported that "as a result of necessity, father sold son, and brother, brother so that each person obtained food in any manner they could."[49] After conditions improved, Kongo's King Àlvaro sent an emissary to São Tomé and Portugal to repurchase captives and bring them home. Throughout the sixteenth century, Kongo's kings sought to protect their own people from the transatlantic slave trade, even as they promoted the sale and export of foreign war captives as slaves. Most of the people sold out of Kongo before the early seventeenth century were either convicts or captives from outside the kingdom who had been taken in war.

Kongo's regulatory system disintegrated in the seventeenth century. American demand for slaves increased with the expansion of sugar production, and as the transatlantic slave trade grew it became more difficult to control. Then Kongo's political order collapsed. Rival rulers labeled their opponents rebels and threatened entire communities with enslavement. In 1653, following the killing of a missionary in the village of Ulolo, King Garcia II ordered "the village head arrested along with all of the inhabitants."[50] In incidents like these women and children were enslaved along with men. The cumulative effect transformed Kongo. In the 1650s and 1660s, according to one observer, half the population lived in slavery.[51] The wars also supplied transatlantic markets, as rival Kongolese factions sold local captives abroad. The people of Ulolo were taken to Luanda for sale to the Portuguese. In Kongo and elsewhere in Africa, warfare supplied the slave trade and the threat of enslavement and exile became an increasingly powerful instrument of war.

The expansion of the Atlantic slave trade forced many people to re-examine the value and purpose of slavery and its relationship to war. In Kongo in 1643, King Garcia II raised doubts about the viability and advisability of a labor system founded on constant violence. He regretted the suffering caused by the slave trade, and specifically complained that wars associated with slavery had helped fracture and shrink his kingdom.

> Instead of gold and silver and other goods which function elsewhere as money, the trade and the money here are persons, who are not in gold, nor in cloth, but who are creatures. It is our disgrace and that of our predecessors that we, in our simplicity, have given the opportunity to do many evils in our realm, and above all, that there are people who pretend that we never were lords over Angola and Matamba. The inequality of the arms has lost the lands over there to us and our rights are being lost through violence.[52]

Throughout the early modern period, the experience of combat and its consequences informed the debate over slavery and the slave trade. Opponents of the enslavement and sale of captives argued that these practices damaged social cohesion and perpetuated political instability and violence. Such concerns eventually led to calls for abolition, but before that occurred, wartime animosities and other dynamics associated with military conflict skewed the selection of people chosen for slavery.

Groups that seldom engaged in war, in the Arctic, for example, had neither the ability nor the desire to subordinate people and hold them in bondage. By contrast, most warring societies in Africa and the Americas held slaves. In some places, individuals could be born into the status or sold into it by their parents or kin. Wrongdoers were also frequently sentenced to slavery, but in most slaveholding societies a large proportion of the enslaved had been captured in war. Africans and indigenous Americans justified enslaving war captives by arguing that slavery was a gift to people who might otherwise have been killed—a fate better than death.[53] Some indigenous people in South America referred to war captives as pets, and the analogy is telling. South Americans turned wild animals into pets by killing their parents and assuming the parental role.[54] The process was violent but also assimilative. It brought young animals into the household and created emotional and spiritual bonds across normally rigid boundaries.[55] Many indigenous American peoples demonized and dehumanized their wartime adversaries, but the adoption and familiarization of captives also established ties between warring communities. As in

Fig. 8.2 King Garcia II of Kongo depicted with European missionaries. Beinecke Rare Book and Manuscript Library, Yale University.

Africa, in North and South America indigenous men and women frequently married enslaved war captives.

But almost everywhere in the Atlantic world, the relationship between warfare and slavery changed with the rise of transatlantic commerce. The Atlantic slave trade created incentives for keeping captives alive and selling them to be sent far from their original homes. This contributed to an escalation of conflict in regions that fed the slave trade. Atlantic trade also altered the consequences of defeat in war. Men, women, and children were routinely sent to masters who were unfamiliar with the military codes of conduct and social conventions that had set the terms of the captives' initial enslavement.

The experience of slavery in the American colonies varied greatly. Some enslaved men and women lived alone with their masters or in small groups. Some laborers and craftsmen in urban settings, and livestock keepers in remote regions, lived relatively independent lives.[56] At the other extreme, agricultural workers on large plantations often experienced a way of life that resembled the worst of military service. On sugar plantations they were housed in barracks, were worked in gangs, were supervised constantly, and were subjected to harsh and sometimes arbitrary physical punishment.[57] Men and women living in these conditions struggled to form and maintain families, and they often died young. Enslaved men and women arriving in the British West Indies in the mid-eighteenth century had a one-in-ten chance of dying within a year. Nearly one-fifth of newly arriving slaves died within three years.[58] Between 1626 and 1807, 387,000 enslaved men and women came to Barbados, but in 1834, when as part of the abolition process the British authorities counted the slaves, there were only 84,000.[59] Commenting on conditions in the Caribbean in the 1680s, Tryon observed, "it looks like the fields of Mars, where often recruits are re- quired to supply the place of the slaughtered soldiers."[60]

Slavery in the Americas provoked armed resistance. On Hispaniola in 1521, twenty Africans fled from a sugar plantation. News spread of an uprising, and soon the rebels attracted twenty more fugitives from other plantations. They attacked a cattle ranch, killing some of the Spanish and liberating people who had been held there as slaves, including twelve indigenous Americans. They seized food from the ranch, and then set buildings on fire before proceeding on their march. They attracted recruits along the road and mustered a force of 120 before a colonial army stopped them. Six fugitives were killed in a skirmish a few miles from the colonial capital, Santo Domingo, but most of the others escaped to the mountains where they joined a growing network of hidden camps and villages built by men and women who had escaped slavery. These refugees, or maroons, included indigenous Americans the Spanish had captured on other is- lands, African slaves who had been brought from Spain and the Canary Islands, and others who had been carried directly from Africa. Many of the 1521 fugitives were Muslim Wolofs, recently brought to Hispaniola from Senegal.

The social and political stability of Hispaniola had been shaken two years earlier when several groups of indigenous Taino islanders fled their assigned villages and took up arms against the Spanish. For the next decade, African and indigenous slaves fought alongside Taino warriors resisting Spanish rule. Fighting together in small units they raided the island's plantations and mines, terrorizing the Spanish and forcing many to evacuate the countryside. By 1534 there were four thousand fighting men resisting Spanish rule. In that year, the most powerful leader of the Taino resistance came to an accommodation with the Spanish, but many of the Africans refused to submit. They maintained their maroon communities, raising crops in the mountains, for another fourteen years.[61]

Recent archaeological finds confirm that during this upheaval Africans and indigenous Americans found refuge together and guarded each other, sheltering in caves in the mountains of Hispaniola.[62] In several other places similar alliances formed between indigenous American and African groups. Around the Bay of Bahia in eastern Brazil in the 1580s, sugar plantations were worked by enslaved indigenous Americans and increasing numbers of captives from Africa. Beginning in 1585 hundreds of these people began to follow religious leaders who preached that "God was coming now to free them from their captivity and to make them Lords of the white people."[63] Preachers promised that soon they would have food without working for it, that they would "fly to the sky," and that "they had no fear of the swords or of the chains because the iron would change to wax and would not harm them."[64] Fugitives from slavery, including indigenous Brazilians, Africans, and enslaved people born of African parents, built temples in the forest where they performed elaborate rituals and promoted a set of beliefs and practices that came to be known as Santidade. They may have developed their own language. The congregations grew by encouraging people to escape from slavery. On at least one occasion they made an accommodation with a plantation owner, but masters who opposed them faced attack.

Santitade followers burned houses, destroyed sugar mills, and set fire to crops. According to one plantation owner, "if the masters of the slaves prohibited their slaves from following the cult, the slaves rose up against their masters; they wounded and killed them and robbed and burned their estates. . . . They created a riot and a general uprising against the whites and they laid waste to everyone."[65] Eventually the colony mustered sufficient military force to defeat the movement. Most of the followers of Santidade were re-enslaved after their leaders were killed in front of their congregations. Nonetheless, a pattern of cooperative resistance had been established and it is possible that specific Santidade beliefs survived. In 1613 reports reached Madrid that in "two or three places" in Brazil there were "groups of Indians and African slaves who had fled their masters and joined together with others, and that they lived in idolatry, and that they called their communities santidades."[66] In the Caribbean, similarly, African men escaping slavery joined Carib groups. In 1675 the English governor of the Leeward Islands reported that plantations on St. Vincent, Dominica, and St. Lucia had been attacked by a combined force of nine hundred indigenous American and six hundred African warriors.[67]

The Carib war parties of the 1670s, like the Santidade movement earlier in Brazil, attracted Africans but they were not led by them. Other maroon groups displayed a more distinctly African character. On the Isthmus of Panama several maroon bands, collectively known as the Cimarrons, formed a federation in the 1550s. The Spanish fought them for many years, until the late 1570s and early 1580s when several of the Cimarron bands agreed to abandon their camps and settle in towns in exchange for an acknowledgment of freedom.[68] During the implementation of these agreements a census was taken which reveals much about the composition and organization of the Cimarron bands. Some of the leaders carried African-inflected names like Juan Jolofo (John Wolof) and Antón Mandinga. One of the bands had a leader who named himself after a king in West Africa who remained powerful in the 1580s. The leaders' names reflected their specific African origins, and it appears that the men who joined them generally

identified with the same African society or an allied group. For example, all of
Juan Jolofo's followers described themselves as either Wolof or Berbesí.[69]

In the seventeenth century former slaves in northeastern Brazil similarly referred to Africa when they described themselves. Beginning in 1605, refugees
from Brazil's coastal plantations established camps across a wide territory, between 45 and 75 miles inland from the Atlantic in an arc nearly 100 miles long.
The Portuguese called this area "Palmares" in reference to the palm trees that
grew there, but some of the inhabitants called it "Angola Junga," or little Angola.
In the 1670s the leader of Palmares was known as "Ganga-Zumba," an adaptation of the title "nganga a nzumbi," which had been used to designate religious
leaders among the Imbangala in central Africa. The inhabitants of the refugee
settlements adopted African rituals of respect when they approached Ganga-
Zumba, prostrating themselves while clapping their hands. They called their
fortified towns "mocambos" or "quilombos." These labels came from a Central
African military vocabulary. The term "kilombo" came into use only in the mid-
seventeenth century during Kongo's Civil Wars to designate an all-male military
camp. In KiMbundu, "mukambo" meant hideout.[70]

Operating in Brazil posed special challenges for the African warriors who
escaped to the quilombos, and they had to adapt, sometimes borrowing tactics
and technology from their allies and adversaries. Nonetheless, their approach
to warfare reflected their African origins. Like the Kilombos of the Imbangala
in Central Africa, the quilombos of Brazil were designed for combat. They were
surrounded by two rows of wooden palisades with a ditch lined with spikes between the wooden walls. The largest of these settlements was half a mile long
with six-foot-wide streets, which reported to contained 1,500 houses. Some
of quilombos took advantage of features of the landscape including hills and
woody marshes to provide additional defense. The inhabitants felled trees
and piled them outside the palisades to impede attackers, and they dug pit
traps. The Dutch made their first concerted attempt to destroy the quilombos
in 1640. Intermittently over the next several decades, Dutch and Portuguese
commanders launched several more large-scale military campaigns, but the
people of Palmares held off them until 1694. Throughout that period there were
also frequent smaller scale colonial expeditions designed to re-enslave men and
women, or destroy individual quilombos. Between 1654 and 1678 Palmares was
attacked on at least twenty separate occasions.[71]

African warriors who had been captured, enslaved, and carried across the
Atlantic brought with them a kind of military training and experience that boys
and men born into slavery in the Americas could not acquire. As late as 1833,
Lucumí men launched a military campaign in Cuba using weapons and tactics
that differed greatly from contemporary European or Spanish-American ways
of war. They carried makeshift shields, and used red umbrellas as symbols of

authority, rank, and power. Their commanders dressed in colorful clothing, and one wore a woman's dress. They rode horses and gave orders in the Lucumí language to warriors who sang songs and marched to the rhythm of a drum. The warriors' weapons included firearms, machetes, and spears. They proceeded systematically from one plantation to another, gathering recruits and killing nearly every white colonist they met.[72] Most of these men had been born in Africa and it is likely that many of them had arrived in Cuba with military experience. In preparation for another campaign in Cuba in 1844, an enslaved African man named Manuel Lucumí was appointed the principal drummer to rally enslaved men. He was assigned the task of "playing the main drum because in their homeland he always carried the war drums."[73] When enslaved African men and women banded together to fight their masters, they often rallied to the beat of war drums. More than a recruitment tool, the drums were signals making it possible for fighters to coordinate their actions. Large-scale operations required military discipline.

If the warriors succeeded in escaping their colonial masters and established their own autonomous maroon communities, they had to be prepared to defend themselves. Most large maroon settlements began as military camps, and they sustained themselves, in part, by raiding. Even if they survived for decades, they generally remained on alert and retained a distinctly military character. In the early 1730s a man named Seyrus escaped from slavery in Jamaica and lived for a while in a maroon settlement composed of three villages, collectively known as Nanny Town, in the mountains to the east of the island. There had been maroon settlements in those mountains since the 1650s, though perhaps not continuously. Jamaica's maroons evacuated their camps and villages and rebuilt in new locations to avoid recapture and punishment. When a British expedition entered and demolished Nanny Town in 1732, the soldiers took Seyrus prisoner and questioned him under torture. His testimony contains contradictions, but his words still offer one of the fullest descriptions of the internal workings of a Jamaican maroon community. According to Seyrus, the men and women who lived in Nanny Town had one "head man" who "orders everything, and if a man commits any crime he is instantly shot to death." Seyrus acknowledged, however, that the headman ignored a great deal of criminal behavior because his position was vulnerable. As Seyrus described it, "if the head man should commit any great crime, his soldiers (as they are called) shoot him and appoint another in his place."[74]

Other descriptions of maroon settlements in the western part of Jamaica depict a more formalized military structure. The leader of the western maroons, Cudjoe, had officers serving him.

> The chief employment of these captains was to exercise their respective men in the use of the lance, and small arms after the manner of

the Negroes on the coast of Guinea, to conduct the bold and active in robbing the plantations of slaves, arms, ammunition, etc., hunting wild hogs, and to direct the rest with the women in planting provisions and managing domestic affairs.[75]

Reports from Brazil suggest similar dynamics operated among the maroons there. In 1645 a prisoner taken by the Dutch reported that the "king" of one quilombo ruled with "severe justice." Whenever groups tried to leave his settlement without permission, he would send Brazilian-born maroons after them, and "when they were caught, they would be killed, such that fear reigned among them, especially the blacks from Angola."[76]

Maroon leaders were wary of exposure and the threat of attack, and to maintain secrecy and prevent subversion they sought to control the movements of people living in their settlements. They often resorted to violence to retain and control the inhabitants of their villages. They also used force to bring newcomers in. As some colonial slaveholders described it, they "stole slaves" to boost the maroon population. Like other military encampments around the world, maroon settlements generally had a severe gender imbalance. In general, women were less likely than men to fight or risk violence to escape and live among warriors. Since women were scarce among them, maroon warriors often targeted them for abduction. In 1739 the governor of Jamaica complained about the maroons, that "in all their plunderings they are industrious in procuring Negro women, girls and female children."[77] Reports from western Jamaica suggest that women seized by maroon warriors were shared among men, while in the east they were assigned one partner and supervised. According to Seyrus they were guarded "night and day."[78] The warriors of Palmares similarly abducted women, and all the people they seized, men and women alike, were treated as slaves.[79] But in other places some women rose to prominence among fugitives from slavery. A woman venerated as the "Mother of God" helped recruit fugitives into the Santidade movement.[80] Nanny Town was named after a formidable woman called Nanny who wore, according to one witness, "a girdle around her waist, with . . . nine or ten different knives hanging in sheaths to it, many of which I have no doubt have been plunged in human flesh and blood."[81] Nanny wielded some authority in her village, but like all other women hoping to escape colonial slavery and live among maroons, she confronted physical hardship and danger.

Only a small minority of the enslaved people brought to the Americas joined maroon settlements, but the fear that people held in slavery might take up arms against their masters put colonial slaveowners into a defensive posture which had implications for everyone living in or near slaveholding colonies. In 1680 French colonists on St. Kitts enacted regulations that banned enslaved people from gathering together, even for weddings, and authorized white colonists to fire upon and apprehend anyone participating in an unlicensed meeting. According to the statutes enacted in St. Kitts any enslaved person entering public space needed a letter of permission from his or her master. These provisions were later incorporated into the *Code Noir*, the slave code for the French empire.[82]

The *Code Noir* authorized progressively severe punishments for anyone attempting to escape from slavery. In the first instance, the offender was to have his or her outer ears cut off and a fleur de lys branded on one shoulder. For the second offence, a hamstring was cut, making walking painful and difficult, if not impossible. The punishment for a third offence was death.[83] English colonists similarly instituted pass systems, and in general the English colonies delegated most punishment to masters.[84] The Barbados slave code of 1661 served as a model for several English colonies. It prohibited masters from "wantonly" killing the people they held as slaves, but also stipulated that if any of those people died in the course of justified punishment their masters would not be held liable.[85] Following the Barbados example, Jamaica gave wide latitude to masters in the administration of punishment, but in 1717 the colonial legislature directed that dismemberment should be the exclusive prerogative of a special court system that the colony set up for the enslaved, and on occasion those courts ordered the slitting of nostrils and the amputation of ears and feet.[86] These punishments are noteworthy not only for their permanence and cruelty, but also because the slitting of nostrils and the amputation of limbs were not widely used as criminal punishments in Europe and were seldom if ever performed on free colonists in the Americas. Such discriminatory practices were common in many slave-holding colonies. People caught trying to escape slavery were sentenced to lose hands or feet in the British, Danish, Dutch, French, and Portuguese empires.[87] The penalties differentiated the enslaved and served as a public spectacle for the lifetime of the person punished. The hobbled and disfigured were meant to be seen, so that their appearances could serve as warnings to others.

Jamaica's courts sentenced men and women to death for unauthorized long absences, harboring fugitives while possessing arms, stealing livestock, and attacking slaveholders.[88] Dutch colonial courts in Surinam imposed the death penalty for similar offences as well as the purported crime of insulting a white colonist.[89] Like dismemberments, executions were organized for dramatic effect. In one case in Jamaica, when three enslaved people were put to death for killing their master, one of the offenders, a man named Dick, was hung in chains and left to die slowly. One of his accomplices, a man named Anthony, was "staked down and made fast to the ground and burnt till he be dead," and a third man, Frank, was hanged. Frank's body was decapitated after his death, and his head hung on a pole.[90] Suriname's executions were equally dramatic. After the enslaved workers on a coffee plantation took up arms, their alleged leader was drawn and quartered. Some of the other participants were burned alive, some were broken and killed on the rack, and some were hung from the gallows with a hook through their ribs.[91]

To apprehend and re-enslave fugitives and subject them to punishment, colonial slaveholders and their governments deployed a range of military forces. On Hispaniola in the 1520s, merchants, miners, and planters made voluntary contributions and loans to recruit and supply fighting men who spent weeks at a time searching for runaways and maroons in the mountains and countryside. Initially they fielded units of hundreds of soldiers, but they found greater success

Fig. 8.3 William Blake, "A Negro Hung Alive by the Ribs to the Gallows" (1796). Blake produced this print for the publication of John Gabriel Stedman's *Narrative of a Five Years Expedition against the Revolted Negroes of Surinam*. Stedman describes captured maroons hung by hooks through the ribs. © Victoria and Albert Museum, London.

placing smaller squadrons of ten or fifteen men at strategic points across the island. The troops included enslaved Africans and indigenous islanders along with other servants of the colonists.[92] Especially when troops had to be raised at short notice, commanders had to improvise, call for volunteers, make unconventional alliances, and sometimes even arm men they considered dangerous. In 1556 after the Viceroy of Peru appointed Captain Pedro de Ursúa to command an expedition against the Cimmerons of Panama, Ursúa struggled to find recruits, but eventually found suitable men in prison on the isthmus. He fielded an army of convicted rebels, men who two years earlier had taken up arms against the government of Peru.[93]

In the seventeenth century, colonists in Brazil hired men with experience fighting indigenous forces as contractors to lead campaigns against maroons. These men recruited a variety of men to fight with them, including Portuguese soldiers, allied indigenous warriors, and militiamen including free people of African descent and indigenous Brazilians.[94] In the second decade of the eighteenth century, perceiving new maroon threats, the governor of Brazil authorized anyone willing to fight them to launch an expedition on their own initiative.[95] Similarly, in Antigua in 1680, the English colonial government authorized the payment of a large prize to anyone who apprehended a fugitive from slavery.[96] Colonial slaveholders in Saint-Domingue relied on a police force called the maréchausée, composed entirely of free black men, to patrol for fugitives from slavery, apprehend them, and hand them over for punishment.[97] The British in Jamaica fielded slaves as well as free blacks in the specialized military units the colony fielded against maroons.[98] Barbados, South Carolina, North Carolina, and Virginia depended on militia units and specialized slave patrols composed almost entirely of white colonists to conduct periodic searches, monitor gatherings, enforce curfews, and muster in the event of any suspected insurrection.[99] British colonists on the mainland of North America also frequently called for assistance from indigenous Americans to help them apprehend fugitives from slavery.

On September 9, 1739, at 11:00 a.m., Lieutenant Governor William Bull of South Carolina summoned his colonial militia after encountering a small army of African men "marching in a daring manner out of the province, killing all they met and burning several houses as they passed along the road." By 4:00 p.m. the militia had assembled, ridden to meet the fugitives, dismounted, and engaged them in a gun battle. Bull was impressed by the militiamen's "expedition and bravery." They had killed forty fugitives, some in battle and others after capture. They had detained many of the fugitives in order to return them to their masters, but some had fled and dispersed into the countryside. Militiamen continued to pursue the remaining fugitives for several days, and Bull sent a plea to Chickasaw and Catawba leaders for help.[100]

In many parts of the Americas, colonial governments and plantation owners formed alliances with indigenous American warriors to deter escapes and suppress insurrections. Arawak and Warao warriors played an indispensable role as allies to the Dutch combating the largest revolt among the enslaved in the Caribbean before the Age of Revolution. In Berbice on the coast of South America, on February 27, 1763, enslaved men began marching from plantation to plantation seizing weapons and gathering recruits. They moved rapidly, reaching twenty plantations in a day. There had been 350 European colonists in Berbice at the start of the fighting. Most of them fled and lost contact with the colony's formerly enslaved population, between four thousand and five thousand men, women, and children. By the end of March there were only a few dozen Dutch colonists left, confined to small forts running short of food and water. Military reinforcement eventually arrived from Surinam, St. Eustatius, and Holland, but the newly arriving soldiers were susceptible to disease and of the six hundred soldiers who disembarked in January 1764, only twenty were in good health six months later. The Dutch were also restricted geographically. They could use their ships to patrol and control navigable streams, but without enslaved laborers to serve as porters they could not carry heavy equipment or supplies inland.

At various times since the 1680s, indigenous South American groups had signed treaties with the Dutch agreeing to help them recapture fugitives from slavery. In this moment of crisis, the Dutch invoked these treaties and called for assistance. Indigenous warriors conducted night-time patrols to protect Dutch outposts from ambush. On at least one occasion they attacked a farming settlement of former slaves, destroying crops and killing fifty-five including women and children. They patrolled rivers and creeks to prevent the fugitives from reaching fields where they might have been able to raise crops, and began a slow, methodical process of starving the former slaves back into submission. In the closing months of the conflict indigenous warriors received payments for each fugitive they captured or killed. To compensate and reward the warriors, the Dutch paid them for living slaves and for the severed right hands of those they killed. Many indigenous communities relied on trade with the Dutch and did not want to see them go. The indigenous people of the region also had their own reasons to be wary of the establishment of new maroon settlements. Maroons on the margins of nearby Surinam had raided their villages and abducted people, particularly women and children.[101]

In large sections of North and South America, the arrival of European colonists with enslaved Africans transformed indigenous American beliefs and practices regarding war captives and slavery. Conflict and the spread of epidemic disease weakened many indigenous communities, and in response groups like the Haudenosaunee escalated their efforts to take war captives for adoption. This sometimes led to spiraling conflict and helped create linguistically and culturally diverse communities where former war captives born in distant lands struggled to belong.[102] Indigenous warriors also sold captives to European colonists. In the seventeenth and eighteenth centuries several long-distance trade routes carried captives hundreds or even thousands of miles across North America to colonial ports. Men and women seized on the southern Great Plains were brought to Montreal where the word "Pawnee" became a local synonym for slave.[103] Charleston, South Carolina and New Orleans also became markets for indigenous war captives.[104] Furthermore, indigenous American groups also began to seize, keep, and purchase Africans and African Americans as slaves. Along the banks of the lower Oronoko River, after Arawak villagers began selling tobacco to the Spanish, the Arawak purchased enslaved men and women from Africa to work in the fields.[105] In southeastern North America in the late eighteenth and nineteenth centuries, many indigenous people became slaveholders and grew cash crops using Africans and African Americans as slaves.[106]

Indigenous groups in various parts of the Americas helped colonists recapture fugitives from slavery. The Portuguese in Brazil were heavily reliant on indigenous allies. Commenting on the relationship in 1633, a colonist in Paraíba named Duarte Gomes de Silveira wrote,

> There is no doubt that without Indians in Brazil there can be no Negroes of Guinea, or better said, there can be no Brazil, for without them ["Negroes"] nothing can be done and they are ten times more numerous than the whites; and if today it is costly to dominate them with the Indians whom they greatly fear. . . . What will happen without Indians? The next day they will revolt and it is a great risk to resist domestic enemies.[107]

The system of trade and agricultural production that brought Africans to work in the Americas depended on the systematic application of violence. Warfare supplied the transatlantic slave trade, and military forces in and around the colonies kept enslaved people from escaping. In colonies that depended on slave labor, some commentators like Duarte Gomes de Silveira worried that their economies would collapse if the masters lost control. For this reason alone, when people in slavery took up arms against their masters, it often seemed that the fate of entire communities hung in the balance. Colonists suffered from visceral fears in the face of what they thought was an existential threat. In 1692, the Portuguese quoted the inhabitants of Palmares calling out "Death to the whites and long live liberty."[108] Similarly, in South Carolina in 1739, colonists reported that the Africans were "calling out liberty" and "pursuing all the white people they met with, and killing man, woman and child."[109] In Cuba in 1798, 1806, and

1825, Africans were quoted asserting that they intended to kill "all the whites."[110] On many occasions when they rose up against their masters, enslaved men and women targeted men, women, and children of European descent. Maroon groups in some places feared and killed the white colonists they encountered. But maroons could be avoided, and indeed they often wanted to be avoided. At least until the late eighteenth century, the threat they posed was localized.

Violent conflict was intrinsic to slavery, embedded in its origins and part of its operations. Colonial military officials were often confident of their ability to control enslaved men, and some demonstrated this by arming them. In small numbers, enslaved soldiers served under arms in the earliest Spanish expeditions to the Americas.[111] In 1555, after the French seized Havana, the Spanish commander led at least two hundred enslaved men under arms to retake the city. Later in the sixteenth century, the Spanish garrisons in Santo Domingo and Cartagena included hundreds of men in slavery.[112] In the 1640s, during the wars between the Portuguese and the Dutch in Brazil, Portuguese military leaders armed enslaved men and took them into battle, promising to free them at the end of the conflict. When some of the masters complained, Queen Luisa of Portugal intervened and directed that the men could be freed only with their masters' consent.[113] The Spanish were more consistent in rewarding enslaved soldiers with freedom. The Spanish also offered freedom to men and women in other empires. In Florida they recruited men formerly enslaved in South Carolina to serve in the defense of St. Augustine.[114]

Despite their fear of mass escapes, armed rebellions, and the creation of hostile armed communities on the margins of their settlements, colonial officials often forged alliances with maroons to exploit their military capabilities. On Hispaniola in 1533, the Spanish came to terms with Enriquillo, the leader of a resistance force that included indigenous islanders and formerly enslaved Africans. Under the terms of the agreement, Enriquillo and his followers agreed to detain any fugitives from slavery they encountered in the future and to return them to the Spanish for punishment and re-enslavement.[115] In 1582, Spanish colonial officials reached an agreement with Luis Mazambique, a leader among the Cimarrons, recruiting Mazambique to lead expeditions three times a year into the mountains of Panama to destroy refugee communities and re-enslave the inhabitants.[116] Cudjoe entered into a similar pact with the British on Jamaica, and a man named Santiago formed this kind of alliance with the French in Saint Domingue.[117] In order to maintain slavery in the colonies, plantation owners and imperial officials negotiated and forged alliances with a wide variety of military leaders. As a consequence, some men who might have at one time seemed destined for perpetual slavery acquired a measure of power and respect within the European-led empires.

In 1553 a merchant from Seville sailing between Panama and Peru shipwrecked off the coast of South America. On board were several enslaved men, including one Cape Verdean, Alonso de Illescas, who had been baptized in Seville and carried his master's name. After the shipwreck, Alonso de Illescas and the other Africans abandoned their former masters. They eventually formed an autonomous community, fighting and terrorizing the local indigenous people. In 1577 a Spanish emissary came to see them. He met a variety of people living with Alonso de Illescas, including indigenous Americans, Africans, and people of mixed ancestry. In an effort to assert Spanish authority, he offered Alonso de Illescas a governorship. The emissary was disappointed after Alonso de Illescas declined, and he imagined the former slave rhetorically asking his fellow maroons, "How can you trust these Christians, since you know that their inclination is to take everything for themselves?"[118] The Spaniard considered this line of thinking unfair. He had acted on behalf of the Spanish king and had tried to be generous. For the next twenty-two years the maroons in the region resisted Spanish incursions. Then in 1599, three new leaders, identified as Don Francisco de Arobe and his sons Don Pedro and Don Domingo, came to Quito to receive gifts and swear allegiance to Spain.[119]

To mark the occasion a local judge commissioned a portrait of the three men which he sent to King Philip III. In an accompanying letter he identified the men as "barbarians" and declared that "up until now" they had been "invincible." He wrote, "They have been great warriors against the heathen Indians and other heathen provinces. They are greatly feared by them (the Indians) because they kill many of them and those that they capture become their slaves over whom they rule with terrible firmness and cruel punishment." The judge believed that the maroons' newly declared allegiance with Spain was a cause for celebration. He claimed that the maroons had never been "made subject" to the Spanish before, but of course, at one time Don Francisco de Arobe and his sons had been subject to the Spanish, or as least their parents and grandparents had been. They, or their parents and grandparents, had escaped Spanish slavery. By fighting they had earned themselves, at least in the assessment of some Spanish observers, respect.[120]

We will never know whether Alonso de Illesca ever asked, "How can you trust these Christians?," but the question would have been a good one. Similarly, it might have been worth asking the people of Quito who welcomed Don Francisco de Alonso and his sons, "How can you trust these people you identify as barbarians?" Ironically, it is likely that part of their answer would have centered on the very characteristics that made maroons frightening as neighbors. Their military skills, apparent ruthlessness, and readiness to capture and enslave people suggested that they could be useful partners in a violent imperial project. There was no indication in Quito that these men opposed slavery, or that their

Fig. 8.4 Sánchez Galque, *Los Tres Mulatos de Esmeraldas* (1599). Upon completion, this portrait of Don Francisco de Arobe and his sons Don Pedro and Don Domingo was sent to King Philip III of Spain. Museo de Amèrica, Madrid.

struggles had ever represented a fundamental challenge to the prevailing labor system. The slave trade would be challenged widely only in the closing decades of the eighteenth century. To understand the rise of opposition to the trade and slavery generally, and other political changes, it is necessary to examine broad shifts in the pattern of European imperialism across the Atlantic world chronologically, as the final part of this book does.

PART THREE

TRANSATLANTIC WARFARE

The First Phase of Atlantic Warfare, from the Fifteenth Century to 1688

The Atlantic world came into being only gradually. The Norse settlement on Greenland and the fishing grounds off Iceland drew Europeans toward the western side of the ocean during the Middle Ages. By the early sixteenth century northern mariners and fishermen were routinely visiting North America's east coast. During the fifteenth century Portuguese and Spanish traders, explorers, and colonists traveled south down the western coast of Africa, sometimes building forts. Spanish and Portuguese colonists also occupied several important island chains near Africa and in the temperate mid-Atlantic before a Spanish expedition reached the Caribbean in 1492. During this period of European expansion many of the hallmarks of Atlantic warfare emerged. Europeans fought against each other, exploited divisions within local communities, and joined military alliances with indigenous peoples. The combatants engaged in predatory raids, retaliatory attacks, and captive-taking.

In 1493 Pope Alexander VI drew an imaginary line through the oceans of the world. He asserted that the peoples beyond the line were "barbarous," and he charged the Spanish monarchs with the task of introducing them to order, civility, and Christianity. Though the Pope divided the Earth categorically by region, his purpose was integrative. In the long run he hoped to make the whole world more like Europe. But imperial expansion proved much more contentious, compromising, and violent than Alexander VI imagined it would be. By the mid-sixteenth century, European rulers were drawing lines through the ocean with the purpose of dissociating colonial warfare from European affairs. A new pragmatic understanding among diplomats developed, asserting that the land and waters of the Caribbean and North and South America lay "beyond the line," meaning that no act of violence or depredation on the American side of the Atlantic would be construed as a cause for full-scale war.

During the sixteenth century, and for most of the seventeenth century, small-scale skirmishes on the ocean and on the non-European coasts of the Atlantic

Atlantic Wars. Geoffrey Plank, Oxford University Press (2020). © Oxford University Press.
DOI: 10.1093/oso/9780190860455.001.0001

rarely escalated into transatlantic war. European attempts to pursue large-scale transatlantic military campaigns rarely succeeded, because expeditionary forces sent from Europe almost invariably became mired in a tangle of regional or local battles. European commentators began to associate the Americas and Africa with relentless war. Some blamed the greed and cruelty of colonists. Others argued that the indefensible territorial claims of the Spanish and the Portuguese had made peaceful international relations outside of Europe impossible. Many Europeans also suggested that war prevailed on distant Atlantic shores because the indigenous peoples were heathens and savages, incapable of maintaining peace.

While European philosophers, political leaders and diplomats advanced theories to explain the pattern of warfare around the Atlantic, within each colony governors, soldiers, merchants, missionaries, and settlers grappled with the complex requirements of local politics as they tried to secure alliances and ward off aggression from nearby adversaries. The colonists' struggles usually made sense within the context of their immediate surroundings. They often had little to do with the grandiose schemes of Europe's political leaders.

Traditional heroic narratives of the "Age of Exploration" emphasize the Portuguese, Italians, and Spanish, paying particular attention to the ambitions, character flaws, accomplishments, and failures of popes and princes, kings and queens, and explorers like Christopher Columbus. This concentration on famous individuals from the Mediterranean region can distract from the continuities of life and conflict in places like Iceland, Labrador, and the North Atlantic fishing grounds. Events in and around the northern seas foreshadowed developments elsewhere.

For hundreds of years after the first settlement of Iceland at the end of the eighth century, Icelandic and European ships traveled a variety of routes between the island and the Faroe Islands, the Shetlands, the Orkneys, Scandinavia, Britain, and Ireland. As sailing technology evolved and ocean-going ships became larger, Iceland's trade began to follow fewer paths. Norway came to dominate Icelandic commerce, as its ships were more efficient than smaller Icelandic skiffs. With a shortage of wood, Iceland could not compete in ship-building. Large Norwegian ships were restricted geographically because of their need for port facilities, and eventually the kingdom's principal port, Bergen, became the vital link connecting Iceland to the rest of the world.

A Danish visitor to Bergen around the year 1200 described his ship's entrance into the city:

> With keen keel they plowed the crest of the foaming deep and sailed
> in a swift course between skerries and capes until they reached the city
> and laid the prows up to the pier in the presence of a great crowd. At

once brisk men came running with ropes, towed the ships to a safe place, and made them fast with great skill. The city is the richest and most noted in the country.... It is full of supplies; dried codfish is found in such masses that it is beyond measure and number. There you can see a stream of ships and people that come from all quarters: people from Iceland and Greenland, Englishmen, Germans, Danes, Swedes, Gotlanders, and others whom it would take a long time to mention. There is an abundance of honey, wheat, good clothes, and also silver and other goods. You can get enough of everything.[1]

Norway formally annexed Iceland in 1264, and by the end of the thirteenth century the Norwegians were taking so much fish that some Icelanders claimed that they had been left hungry.[2]

Iceland's dependence on Norwegian trade made the islanders vulnerable not only to exploitation, but also to neglect. In the second half of the fourteenth century Norway expanded its North Sea fishery and its interest in Iceland declined.[3] In the summer of 1412 a group of Icelanders saw a strange fishing vessel off the south coast. They rowed out to investigate and identified the crew as English. A few weeks later five of the English fishermen came ashore complaining that there was not enough food on their ship. While those men were still on shore their mates abandoned them and sailed back to England, and so the five English fishermen spent the next winter lodging in homes scattered across southern Iceland.[4] More English arrived in 1413, this time with written permission from the King of Norway. They collected the five men who had overwintered, and they fished. As many as thirty fishing vessels arrived in that first full season of English fishing off Iceland.

Within a matter of weeks, trouble began. A few English fishermen sailed to the north of Iceland and seized cattle without permission. They could not speak Icelandic and did not know how to negotiate a purchase, and so they left money behind in an apparent effort to compensate for the islanders' loss of livestock. Other English fishermen farther south were not so scrupulous and took cattle without attempting to make payment.[5] English fishing ships returned in 1414 and 1415, and in 1415 the fishermen stole fish from Icelanders on at least two occasions.[6]

In 1425, after twelve years of suffering the misbehavior of English fishermen, Hannes Palsson, the governor of Iceland, tried to arrest a group of them offshore on the Westman Islands. The English defended themselves with bows and arrows and defeated the governor's landing party. They captured Palsson and carried him to England.[7] Palsson sent a petition from jail to the King of England listing dozens of crimes committed by English fishermen over the previous five years. The fishermen had raided farms, killed farmers, and looted churches. One crew

from Hull committed at least half of the offenses. Kidnapping figured promi-
nently in Palsson's list of grievances. One wealthy Icelander was held for ransom.
Children were stolen, or purchased at a small price and carried off as slaves.[8]

Palsson's petition did not put an end to these depredations. In 1429 eight
Icelandic children, five boys and three girls, were offered for sale in Norfolk as
slaves. It is unclear whether those children had been purchased or kidnapped,
but their arrival in England became a diplomatic incident, and in 1430, apparently in a conciliatory gesture toward Norway, the men who had carried the children to Norfolk were ordered to return them to their original homes.[9]

Despite these disturbances, many Icelanders sold fish to the English be-
cause there was little trade with Norway and the English offered grain and
other goods that were in short supply. The Kings of Norway, now united with
Denmark, issued a series of contradictory decrees regarding the legality of the
English presence in Iceland, but their pronouncements were generally ignored.
When challenged by the Danish king for trading with the English, one group of
Icelanders responded that they were hungry and traded only with those English
who came "in peace." They boasted that they fought against the unruly ones.
"We have punished those men on doggers and fishing boats who have robbed
and created a disturbance in the harbours."[10] The scuffles continued, but over
the next several decades the English expanded their influence so much that by
the 1460s England's King Edward IV referred to the island as "our Iceland."[11]
Then there was another crisis. In 1467 a party of fishermen from Norfolk landed
near the site of present-day Reykjavik and killed Bjorn Thorleifsson, the Danish
governor of Iceland. They dumped his body in the sea, looted his farm before
burning it, and held his son for ransom. Thorleifsson's widow escaped, made
her way to Denmark, and complained. The Danish retaliated by seizing English
ships, initiating five years of war.[12]

Historians commonly refer to the fifteenth century in Iceland as "the English
century," a label that effectively isolates this era of violence, suggesting that
something radical changed later, perhaps as early as the 1460s, but certainly by
1497 when the Venetian John Cabot, inspired by Columbus and sailing with
a commission from England's King Henry VII, discovered Newfoundland and
its fishing banks. But there was no sharp transition between the era of English
activity in Iceland and the age of European exploration in North America.
Developments on Iceland had a direct bearing on the course of events along the
American coast.

Cabot's crew included several Bristol fishermen who had previously worked
in the waters off Iceland, and they claimed that the seas off Newfoundland were
"covered with fish which are caught not merely with nets but with baskets."
They predicted that the English would "fetch so many fish" off Newfoundland
that "this kingdom will have no more need of Iceland."[13] If those fishermen's

predictions had proven true, there would have been a sharp divide between the fifteenth and sixteenth centuries, a break occasioned by Europe's rediscovery of the "New World" and the beginning of large-scale transatlantic commerce. But their prediction did not come to pass. Trade statistics reveal that England's catch off Newfoundland only supplemented the haul English fishermen continued to take in Icelandic waters. Indeed, England's fishery off Iceland continued to expand well into the seventeenth century.[14] The fishery was changing, but only gradually, and the gradual shifts reveal a great deal about the ongoing evolution of international relations, colonial expansion, and the pattern of warfare in the early modern Atlantic world.

In the sixteenth century, English fishing vessels began to operate more autonomously and farther from shore, landing on Iceland only for a few days at a time and then mostly just to gather water and provisions. They bought fewer fish and caught more, salting their catch on board. They also faced growing international competition. First came merchants and fishermen from the Hanseatic League, who started arriving in the fifteenth century and eventually captured a large share of Iceland's commerce. Then came fishermen from the Bay of Biscay, Portugal, and Holland. The fishermen were armed and ready to fight when they came into contact, but no nation had the capacity to drive their competitors from the ocean. In 1578 the English imperial promoter Richard Hakluyt asked Anthony Parkhurst to list the number of rival fishermen working in the North Atlantic. Parkhurst protested that it was impossible to say because each ship worked "not near the other by 200 leagues." This was an exaggeration, but Parkhurst was right that the fishermen seldom saw each other. Nonetheless, he provided an estimate suggesting that in addition to the English there were 100 Spanish ships on the water, 20 or 30 Basque whalers, 50 Portuguese vessels and 150 from Brittany and France.[15]

As Europeans were jostling with each other on the North Atlantic, another expansive people arrived from the opposite direction and came to dominate hundreds of miles of coast in North America. In less than three hundred years from around 1200, the ancestors of the modern Inuit extended their territories from Elsmere Island in the high Arctic to the Gulf of St. Lawrence. They traveled in extended-family bands of up to fifty members. With dog sleds, bows and arrows, open boats called umiaks, and elaborate harpoons, they were better equipped than their predecessors to hunt marine mammals in an increasingly cold environment. Their technology also gave them military advantages. DNA studies suggest that they did not intermarry with the earlier inhabitants of Labrador, nor did they have children with them in any other way. They simply displaced them. No written documents from this period exist. There may have been violent clashes between the newcomers and the earlier inhabitants, but they did not have bows and arrows and it is possible that many of them withdrew to avoid conflict, retreating to less promising territories where in the long run they were unable to support themselves.[16]

When Europeans began arriving off the coast of North America in the sixteenth century, many Inuit bands recognized an opportunity and entered trade. A vivid account of such an exchange comes from Baffin Island in 1576 when the English explorer Martin Frobisher, communicating only through gestures, gave bells and other metal items to an Inuit band in exchange for furs. The first meeting was friendly, and five men from Frobisher's crew left his ship to spend more time with the Inuit. They never returned. Perhaps those five men preferred the food, shelter, and company that the Inuit offered over what was available on their ship, but Frobisher suspected that they had been kidnapped. Using a bell as a lure, he drew an Inuit man close his ship, seized him, and carried him to England.[17] Frobisher returned to Baffin Island with a much larger crew a year later. On that occasion he and his men were prospecting for gold, but Frobisher also hoped to retrieve the five men he had lost. Under Frobisher's direction, the crew fought the Inuit on Baffin Island. They killed several men and took an Inuit man, a young woman, and a child as hostages. Frobisher's crew struggled to communicate with their captives and their efforts to bargain for the return of the five missing men failed. In the end the ships retreated, taking the three Inuit to England.[18]

Like the "English century" in Iceland, Frobisher's expeditions to the Arctic are usually viewed as a short-lived episode that concluded ingloriously and abruptly. The "gold" he brought home proved to be useless pyrite, and his dream of establishing a wealthy, large, permanent colony in Labrador foundered. His experience serves as an object lesson in the hubris and incompetence of sixteenth-century English imperialists. But his story takes on additional meaning in the context of Labrador. After his withdrawal the Inuit retained their uncontested command of that coast, but the English presence in the region continued, and rival fleets of seasonal fishermen and whalers arrived every year from most of the nations of western Europe.

As Frobisher's experience indicates, there was occasion for conflict as well as trade along North America's coast. European sailors, fishermen, and whalers were vulnerable on shore, and their seasonal camps were looted in wintertime. Frustrated, angry, and hoping to deter scavenging, fishermen punished the local people, inaugurating cycles of reprisal. In 1609, forty Frenchmen were killed on the coast of Labrador.[19] In 1623 Samuel Champlain gave voice to widespread animosities when he described the Inuit as "small men with very ugly faces and deep-set eyes, wicked and treacherous in the highest degree. They clothe themselves in the skins of seals; their boats are of leather and in them they go about prowling and making war. They have killed a number of St. Malo men who had previously often paid them back in double measure."[20]

Fig. 9.1 Anonymous watercolor from the 1580s or 1590s depicting a skirmish in Labrador between Englishmen on Martin Frobisher's expedition and Inuit warriors. British Museum.

Inuit bands resisted colonization and controlled the interior of Labrador well into the eighteenth century. They faced challenges on the margins of their territories, but they also reached accommodations with Europeans to facilitate trade. On an island called Petit Mécatina in the Gulf of St. Lawrence archaeologists have discovered a village with mixed architecture including an unmistakably Inuit house alongside buildings of Basque design. They found the remains of an iron smithy in the village, and houses and middens containing a mix of Inuit and European goods including antler spear points, soapstone lamps, and olive jars. It appears that a community of Europeans and Inuit survived for several years on the island, living together seasonally, but the place was abandoned in a hurry. In 1728, a party of French and indigenous warriors from the south landed at a place they called "Esquimaux Harbour," almost certainly the settlement at Petit Mécatina, and killed all the members of two Inuit families.[21]

There are striking similarities in the pattern of interaction that the English established with the people of Iceland in the fifteenth century and subsequent European relations with the aboriginal peoples of the Arctic from the late fifteenth century onward. A few sailors and fishermen abandoned their ships and crews and stayed in America like the five hungry English who overwintered in Iceland in 1412. Some spent the rest of their lives in America. European encounters with indigenous Americans were usually briefer than that, with fishermen, whalers, and indigenous people trying to profit from each other. Some engaged in trade using hand gestures and displays of goods or they found intermediaries who could translate. Just as frequently, rival groups of fishermen, whalers, Inuit, and other indigenous peoples pilfered from each other and punished one another, falling into a rhythm of raid and retribution.

Archaeological evidence and contemporary commentary make it clear that the northernmost American coasts were the scene of frequent fighting in the sixteenth and seventeenth centuries, but most of those battles are poorly documented. We have a much better record of the Portuguese ventures down the coast of Africa and the Spanish voyages of exploration and conquest because the royal courts of Portugal and Spain vigorously promoted imperial expansion. They celebrated their projects and invested significant resources in conquest, colonization, and trade. But the Portuguese and Spanish never fully controlled their purported empires. The establishment of Portuguese and Spanish outposts in the temperate, subtropical, and tropical Atlantic in the fifteenth and sixteenth centuries was just as chaotic as the European ventures farther north and provoked at least as much violence.

To secure and defend their overseas empires the Portuguese and Spanish adopted tactics that they had deployed against the Muslim-ruled territories on their borders in Europe, but the purpose and impact of their efforts changed almost beyond recognition when they were applied in lands across the sea. In 1415 when the Portuguese built their first fort in Africa, at Ceuta on the Strait of Gibraltar, they were pursuing the same strategy they had followed for years on the borders of Portugal. The fortification of Ceuta followed a logic that was well established in Europe, where forts were commonly used to defend territory and secure conquests. The Portuguese were seizing and fortifying Muslim-ruled territory pre-emptively, simultaneously expanding their own dominions and attempting to contain the power of Castile. In the 1460s, much farther south on the Atlantic coast of the Sahara, the Portuguese built another fort. This second fort had a different purpose and was logistically much more difficult to build. Surrounded by sand and dry ground, without any local source of stone or wood, the Portuguese shipped in the necessary building materials. They also imported provisions and would have to do so indefinitely. They also knew they would never be able to govern the desert. From their perspective, their fort was an isolated haven. It created a safe harbor for ships and a sanctuary for mariners, soldiers, and traders on a barren and dangerous coast. It also served as a well-guarded warehouse.[22]

As the Portuguese sailed south down the African coast, they entered dynamic and changing political, commercial and military environments. The continuing spread of Islam south of the Sahara had altered political structures and social relations, encouraging the creation of new military hierarchies and long-distance trade in gold and captives.[23] Military leaders associated with the Empire of Mali dominated the westernmost parts of Africa, patrolling a vast territory from the mouth of the Senegal to the Niger River. After suffering badly in several skirmishes in the 1450s the Portuguese sought peaceful relations with Mali's rulers, and they would later seek a similar accommodation with the leaders of the Songhai Empire.[24] Initially the Portuguese hoped to trade for gold, but soon they recognized the additional profits they could earn through the slave trade.

From their fort on the coast, and from heavily armed ships, the Portuguese traded with African merchants. They exchanged cloth, metal, and other items for gold, ivory, and captives. During the 1460s Portuguese ships continued to explore the African coastline, but it was only in the 1470s that they realized they could circumvent the Empire of Mali by sail. When the Portuguese arrived at Africa's "Gold Coast," the news spread quickly and dozens of ships from several European nations followed suit. They fought each other like the fishermen and traders off Iceland, and they competed for trade. To fortify Portugal's position and strengthen its claim to the region's trade, in 1481 a fleet set sail with six hundred men and building materials including worked stone, ironwork, bricks, lime, nails, and timber for the third Portuguese fort in Africa, São Jorge da Mina.[25]

Mina, as it came to be known, sat next to a deep harbor with two linked Akan villages on either side. Those villages owed allegiance to two different kingdoms, Komenda and Fetu. Before constructing their fort, the Portuguese distributed gifts to placate the local leaders, and over the next several years they established profitable trading relations with partners in both villages, as well as with the leaders of their respective kingdoms. In 1514 the villagers joined together and built new houses closer to the Portuguese fort, severing their allegiances to Komenda and Fetu. The leaders of Kamenda and Fetu valued their trade with the Portuguese and so they suffered the loss of jurisdiction without a fight, but the Portuguese remained vulnerable to them militarily.[26]

European commentators described the construction of São Jorge da Mina as a momentous, transformative event for Africa. Writing in 1506, Duarte Pacheco

Pereira asserted that "in all Guinea, this was the first solid building to be built since the creation of the world."[27] Pereira was wrong about Africa's built environment prior to the 1480s, but his statement conveys a sense of the fort's ideological significance in its European, imperial context. Columbus visited Mina in the 1480s, and the experience helped convince him of the importance of initiating urban settlement as a basis for colonization. Along with the earlier Portuguese fort at Arguin in the Sahara, the Minas fort seemed to inaugurate a new form of imperialism, one that prioritized fortified trading posts, the defense of supply lines, and the constant maintenance of the infrastructure necessary for long-distance trade.

The Portuguese did not occupy much of Africa. In 1555, English writer Richard Eden mocked the very notion that the Portuguese could exclude English or other European traders from the coasts between their widely spaced forts. By the "erecting of certain fortresses or rather blockhouses among naked people," the Portuguese "think themselves worthy to be lords of half the world."[28]

Fig. 9.2 1609 Line Engraving by Johan Theodor de Bry, depicting the Portuguese fort at Sao Jorge de Mina. Universitätbibliothek Universität Heidelberg.

Nonetheless, Portugal extended its string of outposts down the coast of Africa and from there to various points around the Indian Ocean. Their strategic bases gave them a competitive advantage for the duration of the sixteenth century. Despite what Eden said, the English could barely compete with them.

The Spanish adopted their own version of Portugal's imperial model. Like the Portuguese, they celebrated fortified coastal ports both for the logistical advantages they provided and as markers of civilization. The practical advantages of building coastal forts were demonstrated clearly in the 1520s when French privateers began to attack Spanish shipping in the Caribbean, but their symbolic importance had become evident earlier. Far more than the Portuguese in Africa, the Spanish in America founded fortified towns as a way of asserting authority over surrounding regions. In perhaps the most celebrated example of this, in 1519 Hernán Cortés "founded" Vera Cruz on the coast of Mexico before he marched inland and met the Aztecs. The original founding of Vera Cruz was a fiction. Cortés ordered the destruction of his ships so that he could deploy their crews as soldiers and prevent his men from deserting by sea. He had no immediate need for port facilities and built very little on the site. Nonetheless, he believed that establishing a town "with a judiciary and council," even if that town was only aspirational in 1519, transformed the landscape and signaled Spain's right and ability to govern that part of Mesoamerica.[29]

Even more than the construction of São Jorge da Mina, Cortés's expedition into Mexico has been seen for centuries as a turning point in the history of the world, particularly among those who praise the accomplishments of Europeans. Hernán Cortés stands alongside Christopher Columbus and Francisco Pizarro, occupying pride of place among the early modern military leaders whose careers and actions are assumed to have been pivotal and globally consequential. The Spanish crown granted the conquistadors a great deal of autonomy to administer justice, conduct military operations, seize land, and requisition labor. These arrangements followed legal precedents that had been established during the wars between the Iberian Christian kingdoms and the Muslim-ruled territories to their south, but this delegation of authority had much more radical implications when applied across the ocean. The crown had no capacity to supervise the conquistadors closely, and the Spanish in general knew that without ocean-going ships the indigenous peoples of the Americas would never be able to cross the ocean to retaliate against Spain. Thus, the conquistadors had greater license to work independently, even recklessly, and as a group they viewed their royal grants as prizes and personal property. They moved opportunistically, exploited divisions within indigenous societies and within their own ranks, betrayed one another frequently, and sought short-term personal gains in the form of titles and riches. The Spanish forces were generally small, and their most violent engagements often stemmed from petty feuds, but the cumulative consequences of their actions were enormous.[30]

For generations before the Spanish arrived, Mesoamerica had been riven by discord. In a little over a century the Aztec Empire had gained power, population and riches through military force, claiming tribute from communities across an expanding territory. Tributary communities were generally left to govern themselves, but they had to pay for the upkeep of the empire, which grew dramatically. The Aztec capital, Tenochtitlan, had grown from a small village at the end of the fourteenth century to a city of approximately two hundred thousand when Cortés arrived. Many local people resented the Aztec's demands and exactions, and when the Spanish came they welcomed them as potential allies. After the Aztec and Spanish descended into warfare, several indigenous communities joined the Spanish in the fight.

In 1560, the leaders of Huejotzingo described the assistance the people of their region gave Cortés and his men following their arrival on the continent. "No one intimidated us," they said, "no one forced us." They had been glad to see the Spanish arrive.

> Truly we fed and served them; some arrived sick so that we carried them in our arms and on our backs, and we served them in many other ways. . . . When a Spaniard was afflicted, at once we would manage to reach him, like no one else. . . . And when they began their conquest and war making, then also we well prepared ourselves to aid them, for out came all of our war gear, our arms and provisions and all our equipment, and we not merely named someone, we went in person, we who rule, and we brought all our nobles and all of our vassals to aid the Spaniards. We helped not only in warfare, but also we gave them everything they needed; we fed and clothed them, and we would carry in our arms and on our backs those whom they wounded in war or who were very ill, and we did all the tasks in preparing for war. And so that they could fight the Mexica with boats, we worked hard; we gave the Spaniards the wood and pitch with which they built the boats.[31]

The council of Huejotzingo made this statement in an address to King Philip II of Spain as part of a petition for financial relief. Crafting their statement with political aims in mind, the councilmen exaggerated their community's loyalty and service, and simplified the story they told. They claimed that God had inspired them to choose the Spanish side. In fact, the leaders of Huejotzingo had recognized the value of allying with Cortés against the Aztec Empire. They had wanted to fight the Aztecs, and as it happened they chose the winning side. Their community had not merely survived the war, it had shared in the victory.

Across the territories of the old Aztec and Inca empires, Spanish military success did not immediately or uniformly result in a transfer of authority from indigenous American to European hands. On the contrary, the defeat of large centralized indigenous empires empowered many local communities. In places like Huejotzingo, local autonomy eroded only gradually in the wake of a succession of epidemics and a steady influx of immigrants and captives from the Caribbean, Europe, and Africa. In some places indigenous communities eventually lost the ability to fight, but the Spanish Empire continued to face military resistance.

Fig. 9.3 Drawing from the sixteenth-century Historia de Tlaxcala, depicting Cortés meeting his future ally Xicotencatl. Benson Latin American Collection, LLILAS Benson Latin American Studies and Collection, University of Texas at Austin.

The fighting was sporadic and confined to regions. At no time was there a single military contest on a continental scale, no one war of conquest pitting the might of the Spanish Empire against all of the indigenous peoples of North and South America. In most parts of the Americas the trend was toward fragmentation and relatively small-scale battles, as old polities collapsed. This change was perhaps most pronounced on the outer fringes of colonial influence, in territories seldom visited by Europeans. Complex societies in the Amazon basin disintegrated and scattered, abandoning their old agricultural settlements.[32] In the lands that the Spanish called "Florida," a vast region encompassing most of the present-day American South, large temple complexes fell into decay, trade routes connecting people across hundreds of miles stopped operating, and military power shifted from chiefs commanding forces sometimes numbering in the thousands to smaller, more mobile bands. In some parts of southeastern North America villages dispersed, and hamlets and farmsteads were established without fortification in scattered locations. Elsewhere, in zones of greater conflict, villagers lived together behind palisades.[33] Following the arrival of Europeans in North America, the introduction of new epidemic diseases, depopulation, and other environmental changes hastened the collapse of the old military order.[34] Villages freed from the influence of old temple complexes formed new alliances, and eventually new nations arose including the Choctaw and Cherokee. But even after these nations formed, intermittent, localized warfare continued between rival communities.[35]

Despite the disorder that followed the first European ventures into North and South America, powerful leaders in Europe believed that Columbus and his successors could bring peace to the continents. In 1493 Pope Alexander VI responded to Columbus's first transatlantic voyage by declaring that God was pleased. The Pope indicated that with God's help "the Catholic faith and the Christian religion" would "be exalted and be everywhere increased and spread, that the health of souls be cared for and that barbarous nations be overthrown and brought to the faith." To advance that process he granted Spain authority over "all islands and mainlands found and to be found, discovered and to be discovered towards the west and south" of a line through the middle of the Atlantic.[36]

This was an extraordinary assertion of authority. The Pope assumed not only that Christians should govern all "barbarous nations," but also that the church could regulate the overseas ventures of Europe's kings. Within months these assumptions were challenged. The Portuguese objected to the vagueness of the decree and sought legal protection for their own expanding empire. In 1494 a hasty negotiation between Portugal, Spain, and the Papacy resulted in the Treaty of Tordesillas, which divided the non-Christian world in half and at least in theory granted Spain most of the Americas while giving Africa and the lands surrounding the Indian Ocean to Portugal. The treaty had immediate tangible effects. It channeled the overseas conflict between Spain and Portugal to two bands of ocean and islands surrounding the difficult-to-locate longitudinal lines that the treaty-makers had used to divide the world.[37] In the meantime within their delegated hemispheres, the Spanish and the Portuguese continued to claim that they would bring order, civility, and Christian charity to the heathen peoples of the world. The Spanish claimed that they ruled the Americas through a chain of command decreed originally by Jesus when he appointed his apostle Peter to succeed him. The Popes had inherited Peter's authority, and they in turn had authorized Spanish rule in the Americas.[38]

Colonial governors, missionaries, and conquistadors began promoting this vision of order under the authority of the Roman Catholic Church during a time of upheaval in Europe. The Protestant Reformation was only one of several sources of violent discord among Europeans. State formation, international rivalry, and innovations in military technology encouraged war. Beyond religious differences, the states of Europe north of the Pyrenees had many reasons to challenge Spain's and Portugal's exclusive imperial claims. Strategic and economic interests encouraged François I of France to authorize attacks on Spanish shipping on the Atlantic and in the Caribbean in the 1520s.[39] French Protestants played a prominent role in establishing Fort Coligny in Brazil in 1555, but they were interested in more than the advance of Protestantism, and when the Portuguese came to destroy Fort Coligny they were defending more than Catholicism.[40]

Nonetheless, the Reformation altered perceptions and destroyed any pretense of European harmony. In 1562, another group of French Protestants challenged the Spanish in North America by establishing an outpost on the southeast coast of North America, eventually building a fort and settlement they called La Caroline. Like their compatriots earlier in Brazil, these colonists had mixed motivations, but the outbreak of the French wars of religion affected their project profoundly. With France in turmoil, the Protestant leaders of the colony had difficulty securing supplies, and they tried to gain sponsorship from England's Protestant Queen Elizabeth I.[41] Intrigue within England stymied that effort, but the overture reflected a change in the perceived function of La Caroline. It was not merely a French base for operations against Spain, nor was it simply the beginning of a new French imperial presence in North America. La Caroline became, at least briefly in the imagination of some of its promoters, part of an international, transatlantic effort to advance the Protestant interest against the Catholic.

The Spanish responded decisively against La Caroline. They may or may not have had sectarian motivations, but the behavior of their commanders provided Protestant commentators with evidence that the conflict between the

French and Spanish empires had become a religious war. Pedro Menendez de Avilas, the Spanish commander who oversaw the destruction of La Caroline, supervised the killing of hundreds of colonists, and in a dramatic climax after the Spanish had taken the fort, he ordered the execution of 150 more Frenchmen who had been captured trying to flee. A priest who accompanied the Spanish troops later reported that he had intervened after Menendez had ordered the executions, reminding him that some of the French colonists may have been Catholic. Following the priest's intervention, "ten or twelve" of the captives were identified as Catholic and spared. Most of the remainder were killed.[42] Some historians have cited the killing of the Protestants as the American equivalent of the St. Bartholomew's Day Massacre. Some have highlighted this event as the inauguration of centuries of religious strife in the colonies.[43] From the sixteenth century on hostility between Catholics and Protestants inflamed many local conflicts, but like the original Spanish colonial vision, which suggested that Christianity confronted heathenism across North and South America, the purportedly global confrontation between Catholics and Protestants failed to result in any single, coordinated, coherent campaign.

Of all the European wars before 1688, the ones with most widespread immediate impact on the Atlantic world were the Dutch wars of independence. The Dutch revolt against the Catholic Hapsburg Empire began in 1568 and transformed the United Provinces into a global power. The Dutch fought the combined forces of Portugal and Spain, which were united from 1580 through 1640. Targeting the Portuguese, in 1596 Dutch privateers tried to seize São Jorge da Mina. Dutch forces would return to Mina in 1606 and 1625, before successfully taking it in 1637.[44] Targeting the Spanish in 1605, the leaders of another Dutch expedition tried to instigate an uprising in Santo Domingo.[45] As early as the 1590s the Dutch had joined the international flotilla fishing and battling off the coasts of Newfoundland, and by 1606 Dutch traders had sailed up the Gulf of St. Lawrence and entered the North American fur trade.[46] Rival groups of Europeans had been competing and occasionally fighting each other in North America since the fifteenth century, but the Dutch arrived in the region at a pivotal moment. In the early seventeenth century, several bodies of colonists founded permanent armed outposts, including the French at Port Royal, Acadia in 1604 and Quebec in 1608, and the English at Jamestown in 1607 and Plymouth in 1620. The Dutch established their own colony of New Netherland on the Hudson River in 1614.

Twenty years after the founding of New Netherland, Harmen Meyndertsz van den Bogaert left the Dutch fort on the present-day site of Albany and traveled with two companions through land controlled by the Mohawks and the Oneidas. In his journal he described a densely settled region. He passed through villages and larger settlements he called "castles" within a few hours' walking distance of each other. At one "castle," a palisaded hilltop with sixty-six longhouses, Bogaert reported that "one of the councillors came to ask me what we were doing in his country and what we brought him for gifts." After Bogaert responded that he had nothing to offer, the man responded, "that we were worth nothing because we brought no gifts." The "councillor" reminded Bogaert that the French in Canada provided gifts, and he showed Bogaert some items they had received from a French delegation earlier in the year. Bogaert and his companions changed tack, and a few days later they delivered gifts to the man they identified as the castle's "chief."[47] Their gifts did not include pistols or muskets, but soon the Dutch would be delivering firearms to the people of the region, and by the 1660s Dutch traders were providing the Mohawk specially made weapons, manufactured in Holland with indigenous Americans in mind. Armed with Dutch muskets, the Mohawk and other nations of the Haudenosaunee expanded their influence over a wide section of eastern North America. They fought for hunting grounds and furs, received furs as tribute, and took war captives in an ultimately self-defeating effort to maintain their population. Shortly after Bogaert's visit, the indigenous peoples of the region were struck by smallpox.[48]

The Dutch began the colonization of the Hudson River Valley during a twelve-year truce between the United Provinces and the Hapsburg Empire. After the truce expired in 1621, the Dutch West Indian Company received its charter and launched aggressive action against the Spanish and Portuguese overseas. In 1624 the company sent an expeditionary force across the Atlantic to surprise and seize São Salvador da Bahia, the capital of the Portuguese colony. The Portuguese retook Salvador in 1625, but the Dutch returned in 1630 and against Portuguese opposition established a colony in the northern part of Brazil which the Dutch called "New Holland." In 1620s and 1630s the West India Company also attacked Puerto Rico and other Spanish colonies around the Caribbean, and claimed possession of Tortuga, Tobago, and other islands and coastal settlements, helping to inaugurate a century of imperial conflict in the region as Spanish, Dutch, English, French, Danish, and other European colonists sporadically attacked and deported each other from military outposts, towns and plantations.[49]

The conflict in the Caribbean eroded Spain's claim to sovereignty over half the world. As early as the 1559, Spanish diplomats had acknowledged the near-impossibility of policing a hemisphere. At Cateau-Cambrésis they assured the French that skirmishes in the Caribbean were to be expected, and they would not cite combat there to justify war in Europe. By the mid-seventeenth century the Spanish put this arrangement in writing, in treaties with the Dutch and the English. They did not give up their territorial claim to the Caribbean and most of the Americas, but with so many European powers contesting their sovereignty over the region, it made no sense to suggest that every foreign colonial effort constituted a cause for war. Spain therefore admitted that warfare might continue in and around the American colonies even when the nations of Europe were at peace.[50]

This concession affected indigenous peoples alongside colonists and Europeans. In the 1630s one furious Spanish governor argued that the Dutch were capable of forging strong ties with indigenous American peoples because they did not care about civility, Christianity, or civilization. "The license of their lives has made them masters of all those islands from which all their merchandize is drawn. . . . The Indians embrace their company, because they imitate the barbarity of their lives and allow them to enjoy full liberty without constraint of tribute, labour, or the sweet yoke of the Gospel."[51] Though the governor was exaggerating for dramatic effect, there was an element of truth in his assessment of the Dutch. Compared to earlier colonial groups they were much less likely to send missionaries to work among indigenous people and were much less likely to establish government over them. The Dutch often showed indigenous peoples outward respect. This stance reflected pragmatic military and economic considerations. Everywhere the Dutch went in North and South America, the Caribbean, and Africa, they entered competitive colonial environments, and compared to other colonial groups they were few in number. For the sake of survival and to make their colonies pay, Dutch governors, merchants, and military leaders participated in complex diplomatic exchanges. Their circumstances compelled them to comply with indigenous protocols and adjust their policies in response to local concerns.[52] They were not guided by any general policy of toleration or benevolence. Especially in Brazil, Dutch colonial promoters and missionaries dreamed of transforming the lives of indigenous people, Christianizing them, and incorporating them into colonial society. The Dutch were also quite capable of large-scale retributive, demonstrative, and exploitative violence. In the early 1640s Governor Willem Kieft of New Netherland oversaw the wholesale destruction and massacre of several Munsee villages. More broadly, by the mid-seventeenth century the Dutch had become the leading slave traders of the Atlantic world. They held that position until the English eclipsed them toward the end of the seventeenth century.

When the Dutch garrison withdrew from São Salvador da Bahia in 1625, they took with them thirteen Potiguar men, indigenous Brazilians. They brought the men to Amsterdam, where they studied Dutch, honed their skills as translators, and advised the directors of the West India Company on the geography and politics of Brazil. In 1630, in preparation for their second invasion of Brazil, the company formally declared that the Portiguars would enjoy the status of "free subjects" under Dutch rule. The company's directors hoped that the men they had trained in Amsterdam would translate this message and help the Dutch rally the Potiguars to their side. Later that year at least three of the translators returned to Brazil in the service of the West India Company, but despite the efforts of the three men, the Portiguars proved far warier than expected. The company arrived with an impressive show of force. Sixty-five Dutch warships sailed into harbor of Pernambuco, and hundreds of soldiers landed. The Dutch squadron battled through rows of Portuguese sailing ships. Dutch cannon-fire battered down the walls of the Portuguese fort, and the Portuguese surrendered.[53] Nonetheless, the Portiguars did not rise in support of the Dutch. It is likely that many of them remembered the precipitous Dutch retreat from Salvador in 1625. They may have considered the Dutch unreliable as allies.[54]

While the West India Company had the capacity to oust the Portuguese from their fort in Pernambuco, the governors of New Holland remained anxious to secure indigenous support for their efforts to expand their territories, develop new trade routes, and continue their campaigns against the Spanish and Portuguese Empires. Thus in 1631 the Dutch governor of New Holland welcomed the arrival of Marica Latira, an emissary from "a nation of *Wilden* named Tapuyas" in the province of Rio Grande do Norte to the north. A few months later, another messenger arrived from the northern province and told the Dutch that they wanted to "become as one people with us." Encouraged by these messages, in 1633 the West India Company launched a successful invasion of Rio Grande do Norte and drove the Portuguese garrison out. The Dutch were disappointed that the Tapuyas failed to arrive to assist them in the campaign, but soon thereafter Nhaduí, the indigenous leader who had sent the second emissary to the West India Company, arrived with 1,500 men, women, and children. They received gifts from the company and eventually settled near the Dutch fort in the northern province.[55] In the coming years the Dutch would continue to take strategic advice from indigenous people. In 1641, for example, the Dutch responded positively to an invitation to attack the Portuguese in Maranhão, still farther north in Brazil. In that campaign, the West India Company troops received support from eighty indigenous fighters.[56] By the 1640s the Dutch in New Holland were accustomed to fighting alongside indigenous Brazilian allies. They received the greatest support from Brasilianen, indigenous people who had lived for years alongside the Portuguese. In one campaign the company's Dutch troops had as many as a thousand Brasilianen with them as well as warriors from other indigenous communities.[57] Various indigenous leaders in Brazil recognized that the Dutch could help them oust the Portuguese. For their part, West India Company officials believed not only that they needed local allies, but also that indigenous Brazilian warriors had special skills, and that in certain kinds of operations they could outperform the Dutch.

Since the late sixteenth century, and especially after the resumption of hostilities in 1621, the Dutch struggle against the Hapsburgs had a global dimension, extending across the Atlantic into the Caribbean and Brazil, south into

Africa, and beyond into the Indian Ocean. The scale of this conflict encouraged
the Dutch to generalize and think abstractly, not just about the economic and
military strengths and vulnerabilities of widely dispersed colonies, but also
about the character, skills, and weaknesses of the indigenous peoples who
surrounded them. Drawing on fantastic, gruesome, second-hand reports, in the
1620s Dutch chronicler Nicholaes van Wassenaer composed a detailed comparison of cannibalism as practiced in the Americas, Africa, and the East Indies.[58]
Such comparisons served mostly to denigrate indigenous peoples and exalt
European culture by comparison, justifying colonial expansion. But when they
generalized about the military practices of indigenous peoples around the world

Fig. 9.4 Albert Eckhout's idealized portrait of an indigenous Brazilian warrior,
1643. Photograph by John Lee of the painting in the National Museum of Denmark.

the Dutch were not always derogatory. On the contrary, some military leaders within the West India Company believed that Brazil's indigenous peoples had transferable skills that could help them in Africa.

In 1641, encouraged by reports that the new King of Kongo, Garcia II, would give them support, the Dutch West India Company launched a campaign to drive the Portuguese from their largest colony in Africa, Angola. The expedition sailed from Brazil. Along with Dutch sailors and soldiers, the ships carried 240 Brasilianen, including men who had been recruited as warriors, and women who supported the men logistically. The expedition succeeded in taking the Portuguese fort at Luanda, and the West India Company held it for seven years, but the project accomplished less than expected. The directors of the West India Company had planned to cultivate and exploit an alliance with Garcia II, secure hegemony over the region, and take control of the slave trade. They intended not only to acquire African captives for the Dutch colonies in America, but also to cut off the supply of captive laborers in the Spanish and Portuguese empires, imagining that the economies of both empires would collapse. The Dutch never achieved that kind of hegemony.

According to a member of the Dutch fleet, the inhabitants of Luanda "gathered together about twenty-five thousand Negros or Black-Moores & some thousand whites, to resist our forces."[59] After the Dutch entered Luanda this resistance army withdrew and reinforced Portuguese strongholds elsewhere in the region. In the meantime, with few translators or emissaries with knowledge of Angola, the Dutch had difficulty maintaining Luanda's slave trade, which declined to a fraction of what it had been under Portuguese rule.[60] The Brasilianen were little help. Some died of exposure or in naval combat before reaching land. Others were killed fighting in Angola and further afield in São Tomé, but even more died of disease. In 1642 when the Dutch carried the survivors back to Brazil, fewer than a hundred remained alive.[61] To survive and make a profit in Angola the Dutch needed local allies, and one possible solution was to reach an agreement with members of Angola's Portuguese community to revive old channels of commerce. The Dutch tried this gambit, but their African allies opposed them. Garcia II was determined to oust the Portuguese, and so was Queen Njinga of Ndongo, another powerful Dutch ally. After several years of tangled diplomacy, in 1647 the West India Company agreed to follow Njinga's guidance, but unfortunately for the Dutch, their joint expedition against the Portuguese inland from Luanda depleted their garrison just when a Portuguese war fleet arrived from Rio de Janeiro. The Dutch commander in Luanda, sensing his own vulnerability and perhaps overestimating Portuguese strength, surrendered.[62]

The West India Company's withdrawal from Luanda in 1648 was the start of a fundamental transformation in the nature of Dutch imperialism. The West India Company was expelled from Brazil in 1654, and New Netherland fell to the English in 1664. The Dutch briefly took New Netherland back in 1673 but returned it to the English in the Treaty of Breda in 1674. Dutch merchants continued to grow rich in the Atlantic after that date. The Dutch retained Mina and various other posts on the coast of Africa, as well as Surinam and a few islands in the Caribbean, but their dream of a large transatlantic empire was gone. It is easy to see something peculiarly Dutch about their fate, to imagine that they were culturally destined to favor commerce over conquest. But the collapse of the Dutch projects in Brazil and Angola fit a pattern found in nearly all imperial ventures across the Atlantic in the seventeenth century. Grand schemes foundered in this era. When Oliver Cromwell resolved to attack the Spanish Empire in America in 1654, his scheme closely resembled the earlier strategies of the Dutch, and his huge effort accomplished very little except that the English acquired sovereignty over Jamaica. Cromwell was disappointed. He considered Jamaica a paltry prize, and in the short term the English barely controlled the island. They would be fighting the island's maroons for decades to come.[63]

In 1678, four years after the Dutch finally ceded New Netherland to the English, a group of sachems from the Onondaga met with commissioners from the new government of New York and summarized the history of their previous relations with the Dutch. According to the commissioners' notes, the sachems declared that the Onondaga and the Dutch had established an "ancient brotherhood" which had "subsisted since the first instance of navigation being used here," in other words since the Dutch first sailed up the Hudson River. The sachems oversimplified the history of Dutch–Onondaga relations, but they had a diplomatic purpose in doing so. They were inviting the English to take the place of the Dutch, encouraging them to behave in the way they suggested the Dutch had done. The sachems insisted that their brotherhood with the English would continue as it had with the Dutch. The note-takers reported that the sachems told the New York delegation that they "rejoice and now renew the ancient covenant and make the chain bright."[64]

During the previous three years, the Onondaga and other Haudenosaunee nations had demonstrated to the English the value of maintaining good relations. Most of the Haudenosaunee had remained neutral in 1675 and 1676 when other indigenous Americans had taken up arms against English colonists in Virginia and New England. Warriors from one of the Haudenosaunee nations, the Mohawk, had joined the fight in New England, in effect taking the side of the English.[65] By 1678, the Haudenosaunee had emerged as the English empire's most militarily powerful allies among the indigenous peoples of North America. From the Hudson River to the Chesapeake Bay, other indigenous groups faced a new political reality. In the Delaware River Valley, south and west of the Hudson, the Lenape had exerted considerable military power for decades, defending their territory and confining Swedish and Dutch colonists to a set of small outposts.[66] In the 1670s, however, the Lenape's posture changed, and they began to self-consciously present themselves as "women," that is, as people dedicated to peace. This may have been an assertion of diplomatic prowess and privilege, but it was also clearly a laying-down of arms. The Lenape delegated their warrior functions to the Haudenosaunee. In the meantime, the surrender of New Netherland had removed the Dutch claim of sovereignty over the Lenape homeland and facilitated the arrival of English colonists. Large numbers began to arrive in the late 1670s and the most prominent among them were Quakers.

The Quakers were avowed pacifists and scrupulous in their commercial dealings. They were anxious to avoid any appearance of fraud or deceit. Arriving in America with grants from the English king Charles II, they watched each other closely as they entered the Delaware Valley and criticized each other if it appeared that they were failing to negotiate with the Lenape in a peaceful and open manner.[67] The Quaker proprietor of Pennsylvania, William Penn, sent a letter to "the kings of the Indians" prior to his arrival to assure them that he was "very sensible of the unkindness and injustice that hath been too much exercised towards you" by other Europeans. Penn assured them, "I am not such a man." He wrote, "I have great love and regard towards you, and I desire to win and gain your love and friendship by a kind, just and peaceable life."[68] The Lenape were also inclined to avoid conflict. They sold Penn land and accommodated the arrival of thousands of Pennsylvania colonists without a fight. Nearly every other successful colonial project in the early modern era had relied on military assistance from indigenous groups. Most colonies entered armed alliances, but Pennsylvania lacked a formal military establishment and instead received protection from a highly ritualized, meticulously maintained network of indigenous American diplomacy.[69] Sachems, councilors, translators, and go-betweens representing the Haudenosaunee, the Lenape, and other groups allowed Pennsylvania to survive and expand for more than seventy years without war on its frontiers. The leaders of other English colonists chafed at these arrangements, but the Quakers celebrated them, and described their colony as a miracle.

Like many earlier European advocates of colonization, Penn and the other promoters of Pennsylvania oversimplified the politics of the Americas by describing it in schematic terms. While some of their predecessors had suggested that their colonies were engaged in a great struggle between Christianity and heathenism, or Protestantism and Catholicism, Penn and his supporters presented themselves as champions of peace overthrowing the dominion of war. In Pennsylvania they sought to prove that people of various nations and languages could live and work together in harmony, and they believed that this project had the potential to change the world. Some of Pennsylvania's early colonists believed that they had freed themselves from the punishment that God had imposed on humanity following the construction of the Tower of Babel.[70]

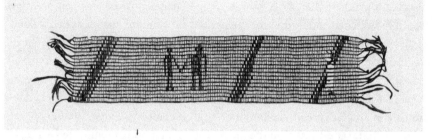

Fig. 9.5 Wampum belt traditionally associated with the treaty or treaties negotiated between the Lenape and William Penn in the early 1680s. From Frank Gouldsmith Speck and William C. Orchard, *The Penn Wampum Belts* (New York, 1925). British Library.

Penn named his colonial capital Philadelphia after the righteous city described in the Book of Revelation that was destined to survive God's wrath at the end of human history. Viewed in this light, Pennsylvania may have been the most ambitious colonial project ever conceived, but the colony was not as exceptional as its promoters imagined it to be. Pennsylvania remained part of the English empire, with its future tied to the military fortunes of the other colonies and their allies including the nations of the Haudenosaunee. Local tensions gradually increased from the 1680s on as the rapid influx of colonizing settlers, Quakers and non-Quakers alike, displaced people on a large scale. In the 1750s Pennsylvania became a war zone. By that time, the pattern of warfare across the Atlantic world had changed.[71]

Between the fifteenth century and the 1680s, the grand imperial ambitions of European political leaders were repeatedly frustrated across the Atlantic. The Danes and English could not enforce their competing claims to sovereignty over Iceland and its fishery. On a grander scale, the Popes and the Kings and Queens of Portugal and Spain never had the power to divide up Africa, the Americas, and the islands of the Atlantic and Caribbean neatly. The French, English, Dutch, and other Europeans disrupted the efforts of the Spanish and Portuguese even as their own grand schemes to establish domination foundered. In the meantime, soldiers and warriors, colonists, bound laborers, and indigenous peoples forged their own alliances and entered battles locally, responding to, and seeking to shape, regional power dynamics. Even as imperial leaders mapped out campaigns on an oceanic scale, the fighting in each zone of combat proceeded according to its own logic and timetable. But as the people of Pennsylvania would learn in 1754, in the eighteenth century wars spread increasingly quickly and comprehensively across the Atlantic, from Europe to the colonies and in the other direction, sometimes affecting nearly all the peoples of the ocean basin at once.

Ocean-Spanning Wars, 1688–1776

Warfare comprehensively reshaped European politics in the period between 1688 and 1776. Armies and navies expanded, and governments reformed financial institutions and tax structures in order to pay for them. Scribes proliferated and new bureaucratic networks developed to channel expenditure. Warily watching each other, states maintained large forces even in peacetime, and monarchs, ministers, and their military advisors established new commissioning and disciplinary procedures in part to retain political control over the military. There were precedents for these developments. Elements of the new "fiscal-military state" appeared first in Spain in the sixteenth century, and in Holland and Sweden in the first half of the seventeenth. But after 1688 the new military-political order spread across Europe, contributing to the centralization of government in small and large states alike.[1] Dynastic controversies erupted into armed struggle as royal houses adapted to the new political order, defended their sovereignty, and asserted themselves within Europe's evolving state system. The result was a seemingly relentless series of wars with countries shifting alliances and facing a changing, diverse range of adversaries. Successively over six decades, rival claimants to the thrones of England, Spain, Poland, and Austria recruited allies and transformed their domestic disputes into widespread conflicts.

More was at stake in these "wars of succession" than the identity of any particular king or queen. In the midst of the tangle of diplomacy and warfare, many political leaders in Britain and Europe came to believe that they were pursuing a single coherent objective: the maintenance of a balance of power. They argued that warfare, or at least the threat of armed conflict, was an essential component of a new European system protecting the sovereignty of all of the continent's states. According to some eighteenth-century commentators, this was all for the common good.[2]

Looking back, many historians have argued that European leaders in this period were ready to engage in war so frequently because the continent's manner of fighting had become less destructive. According to this view the professionalization of Europe's armies, improved logistics, the imposition of military discipline,

Atlantic Wars. Geoffrey Plank, Oxford University Press (2020). © Oxford University Press.
DOI: 10.1093/oso/9780190860455.001.0001

and increased respect for international rules of war meant that wars had become less devastating for civilian populations. This perception stems largely from the absence of armed conflict in the geographical centers of two of Europe's most powerful states, England and France. Elsewhere, in regions where armies engaged with one another, for example in Spain during the War of the Spanish Succession and in Flanders during the War of the Austrian Succession, soldiers still laid waste to the countryside and subsisted on plunder.[3] War remained destructive. Much of the most important commentary produced in this period emphasizes the human and financial cost of warfare rather than its sustainability. By the 1740s, some critics were questioning the rationality of a political system that seemed to perpetuate needless violence.

In order to fully understand these critiques it is necessary to acknowledge the traumatic experience of warfare and at the same time adopt a perspective that crosses the Atlantic Ocean. Despite all the claims that the series of wars that began in 1688 were fought to protect the balance of power in Europe, the wars themselves were not confined to that continent. On the contrary, they served to demonstrate that Europe was fully integrated into the Atlantic world. In the final decades of the seventeenth century faster communication and a much a greater investment of European and colonial resources allowed for sustained warfare on a transatlantic scale. The European powers began to fight more frequently and vigorously over their overseas empires, with wars between Europe's imperial powers occasioning battles simultaneously in several parts of their transatlantic territories. As the wars grew longer, more extensive, and costlier, American affairs began to alter the politics of Europe in new ways. Indeed, in 1739 and 1754, colonial conflicts served as the initial flashpoints turning imperial rivalry into full-scale war and plunging Europe itself into armed struggle. Appreciating what was happening requires looking beyond the concerns of the European leaders and paying attention to the full range of actors including indigenous Americans, Africans, colonists, and captives who influenced the outbreak and spread of war. The escalation of conflict sometimes reflected the ambitions of European governments, but often it stemmed from their inability to control and restrain violence in and around their colonies. The large-scale imperial wars that began after 1688 altered political dynamics across the Atlantic world.

From the moment Europeans entered the Atlantic, colonization and trade had occasioned widespread sporadic conflict. Indeed the Atlantic economy, as it developed, depended upon nearly continuous armed struggle in some places, particularly in parts of western and central Africa.[4] The routinization of warfare and the distance separating the various outposts of Atlantic trade prevented most conflicts from generating any sense of transatlantic crisis. The incidence of localized conflict continued through the eighteenth century unabated. The discovery of gold in the Minas Gerais region of Brazil, for example, initiated more than a century of intermittent combat involving Portuguese authorities, armed settlers and prospectors, indigenous American warriors, and African maroons.[5] Wars like these were an intrinsic component of the Atlantic economy, but they were little noticed outside the regions immediately affected. The fighting may have been harrowing for those directly concerned, but there was generally little expectation that small-scale struggles would spread beyond their immediate regions and escalate into warfare on an intercontinental scale.

Alongside localized conflicts, Atlantic history from the beginning was also punctuated by European-led military expeditions designed to conquer colonies and redirect trade. In the sixteenth and seventeenth centuries the conquistadors and their Protestant imitators launched campaigns that were designed to have permanent large-scale effects, and the same could be said concerning the commercially minded European adventurers who launched attacks to seize territory in the Americas. Increasingly in the second half of the seventeenth century, such campaigns were centrally led. During the sequence of Anglo-Dutch Wars that began in 1652, and in the English campaign against Spanish-ruled Hispaniola and Jamaica in 1654, the Atlantic seemed to grow smaller, as strategic decisions made in Europe disrupted the lives of people in the Americas on a large scale in a short time frame. The Anglo-Dutch wars occasioned consequential battles in widely scattered colonial territories and reflected the grand imperial aspirations of political leaders in England, the Netherlands, and France.

Nonetheless, though some centuries-old patterns persisted, imperial warfare changed fundamentally after 1688. The scale, extent, and duration of conflicts grew, and the repetitious sequence of imperial wars fostered a sense within many communities that war and peace were experiences shared on both sides of the ocean, binding people together across great distances, bridging economic, religious, and cultural divides. The Atlantic was becoming a single political arena, with distinct eras defined by the rhythm of imperial warfare. This development was recognized by increasingly diverse numbers of people in Africa, the Americas, and Europe as the eighteenth century progressed. On occasion, the imperial wars gave rise to a sense of shared allegiance between peoples separated by thousands of miles of ocean. Equally importantly, many people came to believe that they were taking great risks and making enormous sacrifices for a distant stranger's cause. Eventually a desire to break free from the cycle of imperial warfare animated reformers and revolutionaries on nearly every shore of the Atlantic.

In 1688, Louis XIV sent troops into the Rhineland for what he expected to be a short campaign.[6] The Dutch ruler William of Orange recognized that this deployment would keep the French distracted at least temporarily. Seizing the opportunity and taking up an invitation he had received from members of the English parliament, he sailed for England, where alongside his wife Mary he ousted Mary's father King James II from the throne. James fled to France, where Louis XIV offered him protection. Soon the English and the French were at war, in large part because James intended to return to power in England by force of arms. The war put European governments to great expense and transformed the lives of many people. During the war years from 1689 to 1697, military spending consumed 74 percent of English government expenditure, and France fielded an army of over four hundred thousand men.[7] When the war ended, after nine years of fighting, William still reigned in England and the borders of Europe had not significantly changed.[8]

In Europe the conflict came to be known as the War of the League of Augsburg in reference to the complex alliance of European powers arrayed against France. Many of the adversaries interpreted the struggle in religious terms because Louis and James were Catholic, and both men increasingly came to view themselves as champions of the Catholic faith. For his part William, as leader of the Dutch Republic, had long seen himself as a defender of Protestantism fighting against the oppressive power of Catholic France. Critically, however, the war did not simply divide Europe along sectarian lines. William and Mary had Catholic allies, including the Hapsburgs in Spain.

Across the Atlantic the war assumed more complex dimensions, because in some places, for example in the Caribbean and around the easternmost colonial settlements in New England, the formal declaration of war between the French and English Empires enflamed conflicts that were already underway. In the Leeward Islands the English and the French had long been jostling for control of various islands. On several occasions in the 1680s, even when England and France were officially at peace, English forces had seized and transported French colonists from the islands of St. Lucia, St. Vincent, and Dominica. St. Kitts was the most fiercely contested island because England and France both maintained colonies there, and also because the English side of St. Kitts was home to a frequently restive Irish population. In 1666, during the second Anglo-Dutch War, Irish servants attacked their masters and ransacked their home plantations, creating an opening for the French to overrun the English part of the island and deport eight hundred colonists. Something similar happened in 1689. Irish servants rose up when they first heard the news of tumult in England. Months later, after the announcement of formal hostilities between England and France, the French overran St. Kitts. In 1690 and 1691 the English counterattacked, dispossessing French settlers on St. Kitts and other islands. The English confiscated land and hundreds of enslaved Africans and transported approximately 1,800 French colonists to Hispaniola.[9]

In several other theaters around the Caribbean the war that formally began in 1688 continued and intensified old patterns of hostility. Raids on shipping and coastal communities had long been a component of the Caribbean economy, but the costs and dangers of trade rose significantly during the war years of the 1690s. Privateers from rival empires seized dozens of ships and enormous quantities of cargo.[10] They also ransacked coastal settlements. The contents of planters' homes as well as the enslaved workers on their plantations became prizes. In 1693 the English took thousands of enslaved laborers from French-owned plantations on Martinique, and in a single operation in 1694, French privateers supported by naval vessels took three thousand workers away from their English masters on Jamaica.[11]

Similarly, along the Gold Coast in Africa, the war that formally began in 1688 intensified a violent struggle that was already underway. Rival European slave traders had long been jockeying over access to the slave trade. Before the commencement of formal hostilities, the English and the French had both frequented the market at Ouidah, but after 1688, with newly licensed French privateers operating off the Atlantic coast and the threat of large-scale French attacks looming, the English decided to keep French traders away, and built new fortifications. The French stopped coming to Ouidah, and two years later, fortu-itously from the English perspective, an African mercenary army acting under the direction of the King of Allada destroyed the nearby Dutch outpost at Offra, reinforcing English dominance over the slave trade on that coast. It is very un-likely that the King of Allada intended to take sides in the imperial conflict raging at the time, but in the short run he helped secure one of the English empire's most valuable wartime gains.[12]

As had happened in earlier conflicts throughout the Atlantic world, during the War of the League of Augsburg combatants often assisted each other opportun-istically or inadvertently, despite their having very different long-term strategic goals. On the eastern fringes of New England, for example, the eastern Abenaki had already taken up arms against English colonial settlements in 1688, before the formal declaration of hostilities in Europe. Though the New Englanders suspected French influence, the Abenaki were acting on their own initiative, with their own resources, and for their own aims. After the subsequent declaration of war between England and France, the Abenaki received some French assistance including a contingent of 50 Canadian soldiers, and they were able to expand their campaign. At the high point of their success they had driven the English out of most of present-day Maine and controlled territory within 70 miles of Boston. The eastern Abenaki were allies of France, but they were not fighting as agents of the French empire. On the contrary, they were quite clear in describing their limited territorial aims, and they insisted upon their autonomy.[13]

If one examines specific theaters of conflict in detail, especially outside of Europe, the War of the League of Augsburg appears to have been an accumulation of discrete, loosely connected conflicts, involving a diverse array of competing adversaries, with each group pursuing its own objectives. Nonetheless, one of the important features of the war was the desire of political leaders on both sides of the Atlantic to simplify things, and offer stark, almost dualistic appraisals of the consequences of defeat or victory. In French Canada, for example, the governor of Montreal Louis-Hector de Callière responded to the news of England's revolution of 1688 by predicting that the Dutch and English colonists in New York would find common cause with the New Englanders. Acting in unison as Protestants, they would jointly attack Canada's Catholics. De Callière predicted that the Protestant warriors would recruit indigenous American allies, and "fall on us, [and] burn and sack our settlements." He concluded that "the only means to avoid this misfortune" was "to anticipate it."[14] The governor put forward an ambitious plan to conquer New York. Louis XIV and his ministers responded positively to de Callière's proposal. In June 1689 they ordered the seizure of New York, and directed the governor-general of New France to condemn part of New York's Protestant population to forced labor and to expel the remainder to Pennsylvania or New England.[15] Similar unrealized visions of conquest affected the thinking of royal ministers, colonial officials, and military officers in the English Empire. At around the same time that the French ordered the conquest of New York, the English Privy Council authorized the seizure of every French-ruled island in the Caribbean.[16]

These projects may have been excessively ambitious, but at least they were territorially limited. In the early years of the War of the League of Augsburg, some leaders within the English colonies were thinking in grander terms. In the early months of the war Edwin Stede, the Lieutenant Governor of Barbados, reported that he had seen a prophesy predicting that the English and Dutch under William III were going to conquer France. To advance that goal, he believed that English, Dutch and colonial forces should engage the French simultaneously in as many theaters as possible, including the Caribbean and North America.[17] Just as Stede had hoped they would, in 1690 the provisional governments of New York and Massachusetts launched a hugely expensive expedition designed to conquer French Canada.[18] New England Puritan minister Cotton Mather, an ardent supporter of the attack, claimed not only that the future of North America was at stake, but that a successful campaign could usher in Christ's thousand-year reign on earth. The soldiers would need divine assistance, but "If our God will wrest America out the hands of its old landlord Satan, and give these utmost ends of the Earth to our Lord Jesus, then our present conflicts will shortly be blown over, and something better than a Golden Age will arrive."[19]

Disease and dissension, particularly among New York's Haudenosaunee allies, halted the Canada expedition. Mather's perspective changed after this failure, and his commentary at the end of the war reveals much about its general impact in the worst-affected parts of North America. In a sermon delivered in 1697 Mather emphasized the sweep of devastation that the war had caused.

He was still thinking providentially, but feeling chastened, and now he argued that God had punished Massachusetts for its collective sins. His outlook owed much to New England's Puritan past, but in a telling passage that reflected the changing religious, social, and political circumstances of the colonies, he pleaded, "Do not now imagine, that it is only the more strict and severe doctrine of a non-conformist that now smites your consciences."[20] He made it clear that he believed that Anglicans, Presbyterians, and other Protestants would have to work together to achieve righteousness, secure God's favor, and defeat Catholic influence in North America. In the recent war, all of those groups had suffered. Mather listed what the New Englanders had lost in the imperial conflict, and he argued that the burden had been almost universally shared.

Mather described the toll in material terms. He lamented the cost of fielding troops, which, he claimed, "put us to such vast charges" that if the New Englanders had been able to buy their adversaries "for an hundred pound an head [sic], we should have made a saving bargain of it."[21] Measuring the economic damage resulting from the conflict, he observed that "the expensive part of the war hath been a scourge of adversity upon those who could not be reached by destructive part of it."[22] Those with property in the zone of combat had suffered more. Farms had been abandoned along one hundred miles of shoreline in Maine. "Clusters of towns (besides lesser villages)" had been "brought low."[23] The destruction had ruined the fortunes of rich men, who discovered suddenly that "all their treasures have been treasures of snow; one summer has melted all away to nothing."[24] Poor men, for their part, had been "plunged still into deeper poverty."[25] But more than property had been lost. "Several hundreds of our neighbours, first and last, have been carried into captivity."[26] Men with "grey hairs" had been killed, as had women and infants.[27]

According to Mather, "Ten years of our war have set many ten hundreds of persons a mourning over their dead friends; we have seen everywhere the mourners go about the streets. Now, I durst make you this offer; that if you can find three persons who have met with no matter of sadness and sorrow in these ten years, with the names of them, we'll fetch your dead friends to life again."[28] He emphasized the deaths of children, old people, and women, but acknowledged that it was "chiefly" the "young men" who had faced the "fury of war."[29] "Fathers have been burying their sons all the country over. Many of us have had our sons, even those very sons of whom we said, 'This same shall comfort us,' we have had them violently snatched away from us, and cropped in the very flower of their youth."[30] With regard to the "widows and orphans" and "those that have had many mouths to feed," their "straits," "wants," and "cares" were beyond imagination or expression. Mather claimed that their ordeal was beyond the comprehension even of the sufferers themselves.[31]

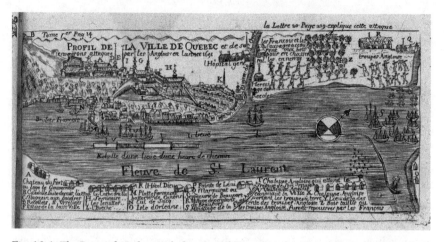

Fig. 10.1 The Baron de Lahontan's drawing of the stymied 1690 attack on Quebec. The New England fleet and its indigenous American allies in canoes can be seen on the far right. Courtesy of the John Carter Brown Library.

Mather saw that wartime experience had bound the colonists together and given them more reason to stay alert to developments in Europe. Partly as a consequence of the dynamics he described, the War of the League of Augsburg accelerated a process of imperial integration that also gained impetus from William and Mary's efforts to restructure colonial government and regulate trade. This process of integration reached beyond the formal boundaries of the English empire. Mather was not overtly concerned with the war's impact on the people he identified as enemies, but the litany of woes he recited for the New Englanders had corollaries within indigenous American communities and in the French colonial societies of Newfoundland, Acadia, and Canada. To be sure, even in the English colonies of North America there were regions that escaped the ravages of war, but throughout the Americas the conflict had shown people that they had self-interested reasons to pay close attention to Europe. That message would be reinforced five years later, when in 1702 the European empires began another cycle of war.

Like the War of the League of Augsburg before it, the War of the Spanish Succession (1702–1713) began in Europe, in this case over rival claims from the Hapsburg and Bourbon royal families to the Spanish throne. England supported the Hapsburgs, France the Bourbons, and the two sides devoted much more energy and resources to the fight over Spain than France had ever done on behalf of England's deposed King James II. A great deal was at stake: not just the future of Spain, but Spain's American empire too.[32] In Europe and especially in Britain, the War of the Spanish Succession is remembered for large battles. On several occasions armies numbering in the tens of thousands confronted each other on open fields and fought for days. The British army under the Duke of Marlborough secured celebrated victories at Blenheim, Ramillies, Oudenaard, and Malplaquet, but despite those successes the war ended with an elaborate compromise.[33]

War weariness and frustration had been building since the end of the previous war, contributing to a widespread re-evaluation of European and colonial affairs. Rather than viewing compromise as a disappointment, many commentators, rulers, and diplomats came to celebrate it. The idea that no single power should dominate Europe gained currency in the late 1690s and gathered strength toward the end of the War of the Spanish Succession.[34] Compromise would never be easy because old antagonisms lingered, but in order to maintain a balance of power, kings, ministers, and diplomats were ready to shift alliances, work cooperatively with former adversaries, overlook confessional differences, and make concessions. This outlook transformed European politics and had an equally significant influence on diplomacy and warfare on the western side of the Atlantic. The rigorous negotiations that ended the War of the Spanish Succession gave rise to a creative reassessment of the meaning and value of colonial possessions. The peace treaties concluded in 1713 drew precise distinctions between sovereignty over territory, sovereignty over people, access to resources, and the right to trade. The agreements stipulated that the Bourbons would hold the throne of Spain, but also opened up parts of the overseas Spanish empire to limited international commerce.

European concerns motivated the men who initiated the War of the Spanish Succession and those who negotiated its end in 1713, but other interests were at stake in the fighting in the Americas. In English colonies the war revived old hostilities toward the Catholic French. Furthermore, since the Spanish colonies almost uniformly accepted the Bourbon's claim to the Spanish throne, it was easy for English colonists to assume that the Catholic Spaniards, like the French, were their enemies.[35] Therefore the war had a religious dimension in the Americas that was not quite so clearly defined in Europe.

The declaration of war released pent-up tensions, and in some parts of the Americas it resulted in a rapid escalation of violence. In and around Spanish Florida, for example, an array of indigenous American groups, occasionally allied with the English and the Spanish, had long been skirmishing, seizing captives, and jockeying for territory and trade. In May 1702, just as the colonists were learning that war had been declared in Europe, Muskhogean warriors plundered and destroyed the Spanish mission at Timucua. When a body of Apalachee warriors, along with some Spanish, marched north out of Florida in retaliation, they were ambushed, with the loss of over five hundred men. A few months later English forces from South Carolina, with support from hundreds of allied indigenous American fighting men, laid siege to the Spanish fort at St. Augustine. The siege failed, but over the subsequent months and years the English and their indigenous American allies overran most of Spanish Florida, killing or displacing thousands of people who had lived in and around Florida's Franciscan missions. Some of the displaced people surrendered and moved to the outskirts of English settlements in South Carolina. Others sought refuge on the margins of the new French colony of Louisiana. Many more were enslaved. By the time the war ended in 1713 the British and their indigenous American allies had reduced the Spanish presence in Florida to two small, fortified posts.[36]

The English on St. Kitts responded even more quickly and decisively when they received news that war had been declared between England and France. They drove the French from the island, sending 1,200 French colonial refugees to Martinique.[37] The war provided colonists throughout the Americas with a chance to revive old antagonisms and settle territorial conflicts by force of arms. In South America after Portugal's entry into the war, Bourbon Spanish forces, fighting alongside Jesuit-trained Guaraní militia, took action in an effort to resolve a long-standing dispute over the north bank of the Rio de la Plata. They crossed the river and laid siege to Colónia do Sacramento, and after four months the Portuguese evacuated the town.[38]

Fig. 10.2 Jan Van Huchtenberg, The Second Battle of Hochstädt (Blenheim), 1704. Licenced by the Ministero per i beni et le attività culturavi—Torino, Musei Reali—Galleria Sabauda.

In the northern parts of North America, in an unusually well-coordinated operation, a contingent of French soldiers and Abenaki warriors attacked the fortified town of Deerfield in western Massachusetts, killing fifty of the approximately 300 residents and carrying away 112 captives.[39] Farther east in the winter of 1708, French forces seized the British fishing settlement of St. John's on Newfoundland, and destroyed it before retreating the following spring.[40] Both of these operations reflected long-standing tensions that were local or regional in scale. The Deerfield raid was an escalation in a long sequence of reciprocal raids and counterattacks involving captive-taking in and around northern New England. Similarly, the destruction of St. John's brought a series of violent confrontations between Newfoundland's French and British fishermen to a climax. Though these were in some respects local battles, especially within the British empire they were interpreted as part of a confrontation between empires on a continental scale.

Since 1689, New Englanders had grown accustomed to thinking of their purported enemies as a single bloc. The French colony of Acadia played no part in the Deerfield raid, but for those New Englanders who believed that all of the French and their indigenous American allies were in league against them, Acadia became an appropriate target for retribution. A retaliatory raid in 1704 reportedly left only five houses standing in the colony. This was the first of three attacks on Acadia launched from New England during the War of the Spanish Succession. After a failed effort to conquer the colony in 1707, the New Englanders succeeded in 1710 with British naval support.[41] Then they set their sights on Canada, and a successful lobbying campaign secured an unprecedented level of British involvement. In the summer of 1711 thousands of British soldiers arrived in Boston to take part in the expedition. Seventy sailing vessels carrying 7,500 troops left Boston for Canada, but on a windy, foggy night in the Gulf of St. Lawrence, several of the transport ships struck rocks. More than 700 soldiers and officers drowned, along with 150 sailors, 35 women, and some children. Five hundred others were rescued from the water, but the project had failed.[42]

The British ministers who authorized the 1711 expedition against Canada briefly shared the New Englanders' desire to simplify the map of North America by ousting the French. But after the failure of that project, in the negotiations at Utrecht that ended the war, French, Spanish, and British negotiators entered into a series of creative compromises. Britain conceded that Spain would have a Bourbon king, but also secured a limited right to trade with Spanish colonists in the Caribbean. Regarding Newfoundland, the French dropped their claim to sovereignty on the island in exchange for fishing rights along its northern shore and an arrangement that gave the resident French colonists a year to choose whether to remain as British subjects or emigrate.[43] The French similarly acknowledged British sovereignty over Acadia, but only after the British agreed to give the Acadian colonists a year to decide whether to become subjects or leave. Elsewhere on the mainland of North America, the negotiators agreed that indigenous Americans could travel freely between French-claimed and British-claimed territories, and they promised to convene a commission that would assign imperial masters to all the communities they identified as wandering tribes.[44] The commission never met. The agreements that ended the War of the Spanish Succession left many issues unresolved.

In the medium term, the ambiguous provisions of the Treaty of Utrecht may have facilitated local accommodations. With encouragement from both the French and the British, the French colonists on Newfoundland abandoned their settlement and moved en masse to Louisbourg, France's new, fortified fishing port on Cape Breton Island. The Acadians, by contrast, refused to accept either of the choices given them under the terms of the treaty. For several years they remained in their homes without swearing allegiance to the British crown. In 1720s and 1730s they took an oath of allegiance to Britain, but only on the condition that they would not be compelled to take up arms against the French.[45] In the medium term, French and British colonists alike found ways to profit from these ad hoc arrangements. A vigorous colonial trade developed between the Acadians, the New Englanders, and the French at Louisbourg.

Along several coasts of the Atlantic, the period from 1713 to 1739 were years of stability and prosperity, providing a shared experience of peacetime as a counterpoint to the earlier era of war. To be sure, there were important armed conflicts during these years. There were wars in Europe including the War of the Quadruple Alliance and the War of the Polish Succession, but none of these conflicts spread or escalated as the previous imperial wars had done. On the contrary, their limited nature and the intricacy of the dynastic and territorial negotiations that surrounded them gave strength to the burgeoning idea that military force underlay Europe's balance of power. There were also major wars outside of Europe between 1713 and 1739. The Yamasee War in and around South Carolina devastated that region.[46] Similarly, the Fox Wars upended life for many in the upper Mississippi Valley.[47] Still, in many parts of the Atlantic world these were decades of relative peace. Groups as diverse as the fishermen off Newfoundland, the Haudenosaunee, and the French planters of Saint Domingue thrived.

It is important to remember, however, that just as imperial wars affected people differently depending on their region and status, so the benefits of peace were unequally shared. There may not have been a major imperial war between 1713 and 1739, but many peoples' lives around the Atlantic Ocean continued to be wracked by almost incessant violence. This was particularly so among those who were directly affected by the slave trade. The ill-fated voyage of the slave ship *Scipio* in 1729 and 1730 illustrates much about the constancy of violence, and the way it contributed to growing political instability across the Atlantic world over the course of the eighteenth century.[48]

The *Scipio* left Bristol in the winter of 1729 and sailed to Elem Kalabary in the Bight of Biafra, a former fishing village that had been thoroughly rebuilt, repeopled, and reorganized to pursue and endure warfare and slaving. Known as New Calabar in English, Elem Kalabary stood on an island or hill rising out of the tidal, marshy delta of the Niger River.[49] Its leaders commanded twenty- and thirty-man war canoes, which served both military and commercial purposes. The canoes and their crews defended the town and also carried and distributed trade goods and captives. Elem Kalabary had been engaged in the Atlantic slave trade since the fifteenth century.

The *Scipio*'s captain was an experienced slaver named Edward Roach. This was Roach's third slaving voyage since 1727.[50] His principal contact in Elem Kalabari was the commander of a war canoe he called Tom Ancora and who was probably Amakoro, the son of the king of Elem Kalabari.[51] Roach came to Elem Kalabary to purchase hundreds of captives, but before he entered into negotiations for that many, he bought "a fine black girl for his own use." When the time came to acquire the main body of captives Roach invited Amakoro on board his ship, and at the end of the negotiations Amakoro poured himself a mug of brandy and surprised the captain by putting his arm around the young woman that Roach had bought for himself. Roach responded with fury and rammed his cane down Amakoro's throat, knocking out some of his teeth. After this incident, Roach's ability to trade in Elem Kalabary had been put in jeopardy, and so he came ashore the next day to apologize. He visited Amakoro and seemed to reach a new accommodation with him, but soon after he returned to his ship he fell sick, and members of his crew suspected that he had been poisoned.

Roach oversaw the loading of 275 captives onto the *Scipio* and guided the ship away from Elem Kalabari, but he was growing increasingly feverish. His hands and feet swelled to monstrous proportions, and he spent his last days in his cabin fumbling at his window trying desperately to position himself to breathe fresh air. The men confined below deck endured even greater heat and close conditions without the benefit of windows, and with the added trauma of hearing each other die. More than sixty of the captives died before the *Scipio* reached the Caribbean. Knowing that Roach was incapacitated, the captives attempted an insurrection a few days after leaving the coast. The apparent leader of this effort was a man the sailors called Adam. Adam and his supporters pushed the ship's cook into a vat of boiling rice, stabbed the boatswain, and threw him overboard. Then one of the crew members shot Adam through the head. This display of force convinced the rest of the enslaved men to submit to authority, and instead of contending with the armed crew they retreated to the hold. Nonetheless, from that moment forward the sailors were terrified.

The *Scipio* reached Jamaica under the command of its first mate James Seabonds. The surviving captives were sold in the market in Kingston, and when the sailors ventured below deck they discovered that the ship was overrun with rats. Though they interpreted this as an "ill omen," they loaded new cargo and set sail again, this time for Cuba. Before they reached the island, they were stopped by a large Cuban ship. Despite Seabonds's pleas, the crew of the *Scipio* recognized that they were outgunned and outnumbered and refused to offer resistance. Sixty armed men looted the *Scipio* and took away its navigational equipment before allowing it to sail northward. Proceeding blindly under the command of an inexperienced sailor, the ship struck rocks off the Bahamas, leaving its skel-etal crew shipwrecked on an uninhabited island. They were rescued three weeks later by pirates who had come to salvage everything of value from the remains of the wreck.

The local character and small scale of the struggles that beset the *Scipio* fit patterns that had been established in the sixteenth and seventeenth centuries, and few of those who suffered on the ship could have imagined that their ordeals would be cited to justify or trigger any large-scale, oceanic, or global conflict. The expedition left almost everyone on board isolated and neglected, cut off from both their familiar communities and the wider world. Nonetheless, in ways that none of them could have appreciated at the time, their troubles became part of a transatlantic political drama, tightening bonds between continents and leading to an increasingly synchronized ebb and flow of warfare across the ocean.

Formally, from the perspective of the courts of Europe, the *Scipio* had left Bristol in wartime, but had arrived in the Caribbean during a period of interna-tional peace. Britain and Spain had gone to war in 1727, and after more than two years of mostly ineffective action the two empires had concluded a peace agree-ment in November 1729. During the imperial war, like many other ship captains in the Spanish Caribbean, Juan Fandiño had acquired a letter of marque for the duration of the conflict giving him authority to act as a privateer for Spain. When confronted later about his attack on the *Scipio*, Fandiño insisted that he had been ignorant of the 1729 peace agreement, and that he and his men had plundered the *Scipio* with authority, under to the terms of his letter of marque and the normal standards of behavior governing wartime privateers.[52] In making this argument, Fandiño invoked local custom and the practical impossibility of closely regulating the violence surrounding Caribbean trade. He did not deny the authority of any agreements reached by Europe's diplomats, but he asked for adjustment and flexibility in the context of the colonies. Such arguments, how-ever, were increasingly dismissed by members of the British public who insisted that fundamental principles were at stake.

Since 1713, the Spanish and British had repeatedly engaged in disputes over the protocols governing Caribbean commerce. Under the terms of the agreements concluded at Utrecht, Britain claimed a special right to sell captive men, women, and children in the Spanish colonies. Spain interpreted this right narrowly, and insisted on its own right to inspect British vessels to make sure they were not exceeding the quotas set by the international agreement. Some British merchants, by contrast, interpreted the 1713 treaties as a ratification of their broader claim to liberty of commerce as the birth right of free-born Englishmen.

A series of violent altercations between British and Spanish vessels in the Caribbean in the late 1720s and early 1730s was aggressively publicized in the British press, contributing to a popular sense of grievance throughout the United Kingdom and its empire, which eventually inspired a clamor for war.[53] During this agitation the name of the *Scipio* appeared on elaborate lists of alleged outrages, each of which were cited as a cause for retribution.[54] Merchants in the British colonies joined ship owners from across Britain, petitioning Parliament to take action against Spain. Prime Minister Robert Walpole was reluctant to take formal military action and tried to reach an accommodation with the Spanish, but eventually he gave in to public pressure and declared war. A British fleet bombarded the Spanish colonial town of Portobello, on the Caribbean coast of Panama, in the autumn of 1739. According to reports appearing in the Massachusetts newspapers, the fleet fired "incessantly," sending seven or eight cannon balls into Portobello every minute for over an hour. The barrage put the town's defenders "in panic," and they ransomed Portobello "at a great price." Let loose upon the ruins, every sailor in the fleet "enriched himself with plunder."[55] Several months later, encouraged by this apparent success, the British laid siege to the better-defended Spanish port of Cartagena, in an operation that New Englanders would long remember as a disaster.

The Anglo-Spanish war that began in 1739 was the first imperial conflict to draw large numbers of soldiers from Britain's North American colonies away from their home regions for service overseas. Some indigent men were forced into service by the local overseers of the poor. Others were enslaved men assigned to the military by their masters. But the bulk of the New Englanders were farmers and tradesmen who were enticed by the terms of enlistment and the promise of plunder, and also motivated by a wave of imperial patriotism fuelled by expressions of rage against the Spanish.[56] Between 1740 and 1742, 3,000 colonials joined more than 6,000 regular British soldiers in the campaign against the Spanish colonies in the Caribbean. Hundreds of enslaved men from Jamaica supported them as auxiliaries.[57] Of these men, more than 1,800 colonials and over 5,000 regular British soldiers died.[58] Most of them died of disease. Their deaths left a demographic void in parts of the British empire, particularly in Boston, Massachusetts, where for years widows and orphans swelled the ranks of the poor.[59]

Boston suffered economically for nearly a decade. Portobello, on the other hand, never recovered.[60] While the war selectively took adult males from Boston, it cut down the inhabitants of Portobello more indiscriminately, leaving widowers as well as widows, childless parents as well as orphans. Yet physical pain is experienced individually and cannot be quantified or compared using numbers. Tobias Smollett served as a surgeon's mate in the British fleet off Cartagena, and years later he offered this description of the scene on board the hospital ships. The sick and wounded were

> pent up between decks ... where they had not room to sit up right; they wallowed in filth; myriads of maggots were hatched in the putrefaction of their sores, which had no other dressing than that of being washed by themselves with their allowance of brandy; and nothing was heard but groans, lamentations, and the language of despair invoking death to deliver them from their miseries.[61]

The Atlantic economy in the eighteenth century was infused with large-scale, organized, lethal violence, to such an extent that one must ask whether there were periods that might be meaningfully described as peace. The men Smollett observed suffered intensely, but so too did the men and women who ten years earlier had experienced deprivation, injury, and death as consequence of the sailing of the *Scipio*, including the cook who was scalded in his rice pot, the boatswain who was stabbed and drowned in the Atlantic, the sixty who died in the hold of the ship, and the enslaved survivors including the "fine young black girl" whose names and specific fate are unknown, but who in all likelihood were all sold as slaves in Jamaica. It would be easy to conclude, as Fandiño suggested in defense of his privateering attack on the *Scipio*, that the distinction between wartime and peace was a diplomatic formality, negotiated in the courts of Europe beyond the immediate cognizance of the inhabitants of the rest of the Atlantic world. The formal sequence of European phases of wartime and peace was artificial and failed to encompass or describe the full range of experiences across the competing empires. Nonetheless, that alternating rhythm reflected an increasingly important reality. While European wars had long affected colonial developments, during the eighteenth century, colonial conflicts increasingly roiled Europe and reverberated back to affect widely scattered colonized zones.

Britain's declaration of war against Spain in 1739 was the first in a cascade. Within a few years most of the major powers in Europe were fighting. In Europe between 1740 and 1748, a range of regional conflicts were combined to form a grand confrontation known to posterity as the War of the Austrian Succession. In North America, by contrast, the Anglo-Spanish war and the Anglo-French war remained distinct. Each began dramatically following a formal declaration of war. Quickly after Britain declared war against Spain in 1739, Georgia Governor James Oglethorpe mustered a large-scale attack on Spanish Florida. He raised an army from South Carolina and Georgia, and recruited militia from local communities. He deployed seven warships and called for assistance from indigenous American allies. His subsequent siege of St. Augustine failed, but the action damaged, depopulated, or destroyed several communities that had been established in the region since the last war, including an isolated settlement of Scottish Highlanders and a fortified community of formerly enslaved laborers who had escaped British-colonial plantations to find refuge near St. Augustine.[62] France's declaration of war against Britain in 1744 triggered equally swift action in the northeast of North America, as French forces deployed from Louisbourg, with the support of Mi'kmaq warriors, plundered and destroyed Canso, a fishing settlement on the Atlantic coast of Nova Scotia.[63]

Nova Scotia and Cape Breton Island were the scenes of some of the most dramatic events in the conflict. In 1745, a New England expedition, with some support from the Royal Navy, seized Louisbourg. One year later, the French

Fig. 10.3 The ruins of Portobello as they appeared in 1910. From Alfred B. Hall and Clarence Lyon Chester, *Panama and the Canal* (New York: Newson and Company, 1914), 30. Library of Congress.

launched more than sixty ships carrying approximately 11,000 men with the aim of retaking Louisbourg, conquering Nova Scotia, and harrowing the coasts of New England. The fleet met rough weather in the Atlantic and disease struck the officers, troops, and crew. Most of them managed to land in Nova Scotia, but they were debilitated and unable to enter combat. Hunger, suicide, and drowning carried some of the men away, but an array of illnesses including typhus and scurvy killed most of them. By the time the remnant force had returned to France, the total number of dead was approaching eight thousand.[64] In North America there was a widespread sense of futility surrounding most of the action in the War of the Austrian Succession, and frustration grew following the conclusion of the peace treaty in 1748 which officially restored the imperial boundary lines to those that had been agreed at Utrecht in 1713. Tensions persisted, and in several places across the continent colonists and indigenous Americans anticipated and prepared for a resumption of armed conflict.

In general, the inhabitants of North America did not celebrate the balance of power that the Europeans were maintaining. Nor did they belong to the military culture that was evolving as part of the new European state system. Under the new order imagined for "military Europe," soldiers and officers from different nations were expected sometimes to fight alongside each other and at other times against each other according to the political necessities of the day.[65] During the War of the Austrian Succession, indigenous Americans were among the first to question whether they were willing to fight on those terms. In the Ohio Valley and Great Lakes region, indigenous American allies of the French initially joined forces and attacked British traders across the region. But then significant numbers of France's erstwhile allies turned against the French. In general they did so not because they supported the British empire, but because they felt ill served by their old allies. As one disaffected warrior expressed it, the French "would always get their [the Wyandots'] young men to go to war against their enemies, and would use them as their own people, that is like slaves."[66] Responding to the views of such men, some French military officers feared that the indigenous peoples of North America had entered into a general pact "not to kill one another, and to let the whites act against each other."[67] This was inaccurate, but there was a kernel of truth in the assessment. Though there was no general agreement among indigenous Americans in 1747, the idea of refusing to participate in imperial wars would eventually gain adherents and would play an important role in shaping the conduct and legacy of the Seven Years' War. More broadly in the long run, disillusionment with the wartime machinations of imperial leaders would contribute to revolutionary sentiments on both sides of the Atlantic.

The outbreak of war in North America in 1754 was not a surprise to anyone, but no one expected the conflict to spread as far as it did. Like the Anglo-Spanish war of 1739, the conflict started in the colonies and escalated into a major

European and imperial war. Relatively small-scale skirmishes between French and British forces in the upper Ohio River Valley initiated a series of widening confrontations which eventually engaged forces from nearly every European power from Portugal to Russia, and occasioned battles across the Americas and in other places as distant as India and the Philippines. On some shores of the Atlantic—in Cuba, for example—the imperial conflict arrived suddenly, unsettling relatively stable social and political arrangements. In other places, like Senegal, the war intensified, redirected, and added meaning to long-standing battles between local groups.

Senegal, already devastated by famine, was torn apart by civil war in the 1750s. In 1757, following the death of Emir Amar Wuld Ali Shandhora, Shandhora's heir, Mokthar Wuld Amar, fought to seize control of local trade routes. His forces ranged across the Senegal River valley and blocked access to the French fort at the mouth of the river, Saint-Louis de Senegal. Amar cut off the French because they were trading with his African rivals. It is not clear whether he wanted to create an opening for the British empire. In 1758 a British expeditionary force took advantage of the situation and seized the French fort, claiming that Amar had planned to grant Britain a monopoly on local trade. Amar may not have intended any such thing, but as a result of these skirmishes the British empire acquired an outpost on the mainland of West Africa that it would hold for the next twenty-one years.[68]

In contrast to the Senegal Valley, where local conflicts escalated, drew in imperial forces, and gradually became part of a wider transatlantic struggle, the Seven Years' War came to Cuba abruptly, ending a long period of relative peace. For eight years the Spanish Empire managed to stay out of the Seven Years' War, and during that time Cuba's defenses were neglected. Britain and Spain entered into formal hostilities only in January 1762, and several more months passed before the British raised a force to attack Cuba. The fleet sailed from England, and the soldiers and sailors on board knew very little about the Spanish-ruled island. After they arrived in the Caribbean they were joined by others who may have known the region slightly better, including some white West Indians, a contingent of mainland British colonial soldiers, and hundreds of enslaved men and free blacks mobilized from the British West Indies. The attacking forces vastly outnumbered the defenders, and they were composed entirely of people who had traveled to reach the zone of combat. The island's geography and peculiar social dynamics were new to them. For Cuba, this was an entirely imperial, as opposed to a locally generated, war.[69]

While the discrete engagements of the Seven Years' War may have had disparate origins and locally distinctive implications, viewed as a whole the war contributed to a growing pool of shared experience and encouraged wide-ranging debates about the allocation of power and resources across the Atlantic world. In

Senegal, at the end of the war, the British took responsibility, at least in theory, for governing a complex, mixed community of people variously speaking Wolof, French, and English, and adhering to an array of local and transatlantic spiritual traditions including Protestantism, Catholicism, and Islam.[70] The British governors in the Senegal Valley, supported by a variety of imperial promoters, developed plans to transform the region, but all their schemes failed because an insufficient number of English-speaking Protestant settlers were attracted to Africa to effect significant change. Locally, the most important impact of the seizure of Saint-Louis de Senegal was an increase in warfare and raiding upriver in response to the British demand for captives. Nonetheless, Britain's seizure of the fort, and the subsequent debates over the future of the nascent colony of Senegambia, raised momentous questions throughout the British empire concerning Britain's ability to colonize in Africa. These discussions continued over several decades and ultimately helped inspire the British campaign to end the transatlantic slave trade.[71]

The British returned Cuba to Spain as part of the negotiated settlement of the war, leaving the Spanish to grapple with the implications of the imperial conflict for the future of the island. Spanish officials resolved that they needed to spend more in infrastructure and defense and import a large number of enslaved workers. The events of the Seven Years' War secured Spanish investment in Cuba, which helped tie the island to the Spanish empire long after most Spain's American colonies gained independence. Another legacy of the war was a renewed dedication to slavery. The colony would hold men and women in slavery long after the practice had been formally abolished in most of the Atlantic world.[72]

Not just in Cuba and Senegambia, but also in Canada, Florida, Louisiana, and other scattered places around the Atlantic, the Seven Years' War inspired wide-ranging debates over labor regimes, forced migration, the structure and purpose of the transatlantic empires, and the rights of colonial and conquered populations.[73] Some of these debates involved efforts to resolve issues that had been left hanging since the Treaty of Utrecht in 1713. The Acadians, for example, were caught in the crossfire of the Seven Years' War, and neither the French nor the British respected their professed intention to avoid military service. After the British captured a few Acadian men fighting alongside the French, the governor of Nova Scotia demanded that the Acadians take an unconditional oath of allegiance to the British crown, without any promise that they could avoid participating in combat. When they refused to swear allegiance on those terms, the governor ordered the forcible removal of the entire population.

In the interior of North America, the scattered protests of the 1740s anticipated a much more widespread, creative exchange of ideas among indigenous Americans concerning their relationship to the competing empires and the propriety of their participation in any imperial wars. In the 1760s a religious leader among the Munsee named Papunhank renounced all war. Reaching out to political leaders and others in Pennsylvania, he told them to "look upon all mankind as one and so become as one family."[74] Papunhank preached to colonists as well as indigenous people in his effort to promote an inclusive peace. By contrast, Delaware prophet Neolin called on his followers to distance themselves from Europeans and colonists, and to reject imported technologies. Neolin placed special emphasis on the avoidance of firearms, proposing instead that indigenous Americans should hunt and fight only with weapons made from wood and stone.[75] Neolin is often credited with helping to inspire a war in 1763, when a widely dispersed alliance of indigenous American warriors launched simultaneous attacks against the British in the Great Lakes region and Ohio River Valley. Those warriors used firearms. They were not ready to abandon entirely the military technology and culture that they and their predecessors had developed over the previous 150 years. Nonetheless, their grievance against the military infrastructure of the British Empire was reflected in their choice of targets. Rather than sacking scattered farms or other civilian settlements, they concentrated on forts.[76]

Neolin imagined a future in which the colonists would go away and leave the indigenous peoples of America to mind their own affairs. For decades, anthropologists and historians have been fascinated by the apparent irrationality of this vision and have suggested that it was borne out of desperation.[77] The idea of evacuating colonies and permanently reversing the process of colonization makes more sense, however, if seen in the context of the recently ended war. A combined force of British soldiers and New Englanders had just expelled the Acadians and destroyed nearly every building in the former French colony. Additionally, even as Neolin was speaking, Spanish Florida was experiencing a more peaceful but equally comprehensive evacuation. Following the erasure of Spanish Florida British officials, colonial promoters and colonists drew up an array of plans for the emptied territory, and many of their proposals appear in retrospect to have been just as fanciful as Neolin's scheme.[78] In the 1760s indigenous American prophets and British imperial officials were grappling with the same issues and responding to common experiences as they were drawing up plans for the continent. Too often these groups are studied separately.

Papunhank's pacifism came as a response to the same war that traumatized Pennsylvania's Quakers and forced them to re-examine the meaning of their commitment to peace. Many Quakers were happy to hear Papunhank deliver his message, because it seemed to advance ideas that they were already developing. One of those was Anthony Benezet. In his first antislavery tract in 1759, Benezet had begun by reminding his readers of the suffering they had experienced in the Seven Years' War, and particularly the traumas experienced by colonists captured by indigenous Americans. He wrote,

> In ancient times it was the practice of many nations, when at war with each other, to sell the prisoners they made in battle, in order to defray the expenses of the war. This unchristian or rather inhuman practice, after many ages continuance, is at length generally abolished by the Christian powers of Europe, but still continues among some of the nations of Asia and Africa, and to our sad experience, we find it also practiced by the natives of America. In the present war, how many of our country men are dragged to bondage and sold for slaves, how many mourn, a husband, a wife, a child, a parent, or some near relation taken from them?

Benezet demanded, "while our hearts are affected for our brethren and relations, while we feel for our own flesh and blood, let us extend our thoughts to others," and specifically to families in Africa.[79]

Benezet argued that African nations often went to war with the sole purpose of acquiring captives and that European slave traders encouraged this practice. Thus he insisted that Africa's two greatest problems, warfare and slavery, were linked. Benezet's broad moral stance against warfare and his specific analysis of the slave trade attracted attention among political leaders in Britain and the colonies, among philosophes in France, and among black and white abolitionists on both sides of the Atlantic. As a unapologetic veteran of Britain's royal navy, the former slave and abolitionist Olaudah Equiano was no pacifist, but he read Benezet's work carefully and cited it in his autobiography to fill out his discussion of the slave trade's impact on Africa.

The Quakers, particularly those of Pennsylvania, played an important role in mid-eighteenth-century debates over the purpose, conduct, and consequences of war. In France, Enlightenment philosophers praised Quaker pacifism and religious toleration, and their idealized vision of Quaker society eventually helped inspire France's first abolitionists.[80] For some French writers the success of Pennsylvania before the Seven Years' War had proved that an alternative model for social relations was possible, and specifically that it was possible to prosper without war.

The Philosophes did not, however, denounce warfare in abstract, universal terms.[81] Their complaints were directed specifically against the pattern of warfare that had developed in the eighteenth century. They were critical of dynastic wars, with their apparent pettiness, frequency, and destructiveness. The recent wars seemed to demonstrate that a monarch's ambitions could run directly against the interests of his or her subjects. Montesquieu asserted, "The spirit of monarchy is war and expansion; the spirit of republics is peace and moderation."[82]

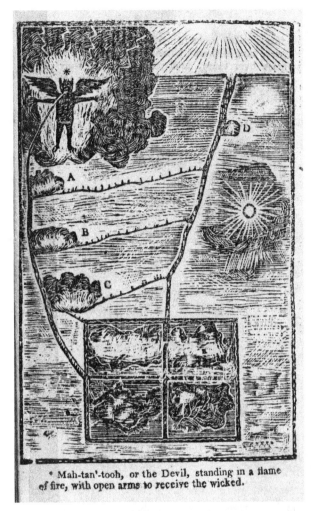

* Mah-tan'-tooh, or the Devil, standing in a flame
of fire, with open arms to receive the wicked.

Fig. 10.4 A drawing by a contemporary depicting Neolin's prophesy. Indigenous Americans who followed the wrong path, for example by fighting in the style of Europeans, were destined for Hell. Beinecke Rare Book and Manuscript Library, Yale University.

Like most other writers of the French Enlightenment, Voltaire supported the use of military force by soldiers who were fighting to defend their homes and families, their safety, their rights, or their nation.[83] He believed that soldiers should fight for their own collective cause. Critically, he and his like-minded contemporaries condemned religious warfare, and in doing so they adopted a universalist perspective which considered the impact of wars on all the affected parties, including combatants and noncombatants on both sides of any sectarian divide. In *Candide* Voltaire vividly recounted wartime suffering and suggested that the Seven Years' War was little more than an aggregation of piratical raids, senseless violent contests between dynastic houses, and colonial battles over worthless territory. In a famous passage discussing the war, Voltaire's scholar Martin addresses the question of whether the English were "as crazy as the French." Martin says, "You're aware that these two countries are at war, fighting over a few acres of snow, somewhere in the vicinity of Canada, and that they've already spent, on this lovely scuffle, far more than the whole of Canada is worth. Telling you more precisely whether one country or the other contains a larger number of lunatics—well, I'm not smart enough for that."[84] Voltaire was alert to the escalating cost of eighteenth-century warfare, costs that seemed to exceed any possible gain.

Though the Seven Years' War began in North America, the imperial powers expended most of their resources, in terms of manpower and money, on the continent of Europe. The cost of this long, extensive conflict challenged the fiscal stability of several European states, with long-lasting political consequences. In France, a sense of shared sacrifice simultaneously stoked nationalistic fervor, frustration, and disillusionment with Louis XV. As the war dragged on, and losses mounted, the French in general grew weary of their imperial project in North America, to such an extent that after Canada was ceded to the British in 1763, the colony was virtually erased from France's collective memory.[85] Meanwhile in Britain a growing sense of national proprietorship over the North American colonies led to potentially contradictory impulses: for the British to take a stronger hand in colonial government, and to require the colonists to contribute more to the cost.[86] For generations historians have linked the events and controversies surrounding the Seven Years' War to the convulsions of the subsequent revolutionary age.[87] Much of the politics of the revolutionary era grew out of the shared experience of war, as voices were raised against the European empires' increasingly elaborate manner of conducting military operations simultaneously in widely scattered zones of combat.

In 1776 in *Common Sense*, Thomas Paine argued against monarchy as a political system, and one of his principal claims was that dynasties served only their own interests and plunged their subjects into needless wars. Echoing Montesquieu, Paine wrote, "In the early ages of the world . . . there were no kings; the consequence of which was there were no wars; it is the pride of kings which throw mankind into confusion." After recounting centuries of Biblical and English history, Paine concluded, "In short, monarchy and succession have laid (not this or that kingdom only) but the world in blood and ashes."[88] Implicitly, Paine imagined a more peaceful, republican future, but he was not a pacifist. On the contrary, *Common Sense* was a call to arms. Paine was a recent immigrant to Pennsylvania when he wrote *Common Sense*, and he was already engaged in an extensive debate with his pacifist Quaker neighbors over the propriety of resorting to military action. Six months before the publication of *Common Sense* he had drawn a distinction between mercenary warfare and defensive war. Berating the British, he wrote, "From the House of Commons the troops of Britain have been exhorted to fight, not for the defense of their natural rights, not to repel the invasion or the insult of enemies; but on the vilest of all pretences, gold." Unjustly attacked by such disreputable soldiers, America's patriots were justified in fighting to defend their homes and property as well as their "spiritual freedom and political liberty."[89] Paine's way of analyzing the morality of warfare was not entirely new, but the distinction he drew acquired greater resonance in the revolutionary age. Good soldiers fought only to defend their rights. This was an idea that would help dismantle the eighteenth-century Atlantic world.

Revolution

Growing up in South Carolina in the 1760s and 1770s, Boston King was a child of the eighteenth-century Atlantic world. His father had arrived as a slave from across the ocean, converted to Christianity, learned to read, and became a driver on a plantation. His mother was enslaved on the same plantation. She made clothes for her masters and worked as a healer using a variety of remedies, including some she had learned from neighboring indigenous Americans. The war for US independence disrupted King's world, first tearing him from his childhood home and then exposing widening fissures in the social, economic, political, and military ties that for centuries had bound the peoples of Africa, the Americas, and Europe together.[1]

According to King's account, he first experienced the Revolutionary War as an irritant upsetting his working relationships. Early in the war he was hired out to work with a carpenter. Wartime military expenditure in South Carolina and the interruption of trade out of Charleston drove up the cost of nails, which tempted one of King's coworkers to steal a pile of them. King was wrongly accused of this theft and beaten so thoroughly that he could not return to work for three weeks. A few months later a horse went missing and King was so frightened of the possible consequences that he fled his master and sought the British army's protection. In effect, he had decided to accept an offer made by General George Clinton in 1779. In anticipation of the British army's campaign in the American South, Clinton had sought to weaken the Patriots by offering "full security" to any of the people they held as slaves.[2] King reported that the British soldiers received him "readily." He wrote that from that moment, "I began to feel the happiness of liberty, of which I knew nothing before." But his experience of liberation was mixed with sadness, because he had moved permanently away from his all of his former friends, and now had to live among "strangers."[3]

King found companions among the British soldiers and eventually became a servant to two officers, but his career with the army was punctuated by violations of trust. After he contracted smallpox he learned that "All the blacks affected with that disease were ordered to be carried a mile from the camp, lest

Atlantic Wars. Geoffrey Plank, Oxford University Press (2020). © Oxford University Press.
DOI: 10.1093/oso/9780190860455.001.0001

the soldiers should be infected and disabled from marching." They were not treated well in quarantine. "We lay sometimes a whole day without anything to eat or drink."[4] On another occasion King had been sent out fishing when the troops received marching orders. They left him behind. King set off to rejoin the army accompanied by a loyalist man named Lewes who initially promised to take King where he wanted to go. "You will see your regiment before 7 o'clock tonight," Lewes had said. But before the day was out Lewes announced that he wanted King to stay and work for him. Lewes started the conversation almost politely, asking "How will you like me to be your master?" But when King protested Lewes became rougher. "If you do not behave well," he warned, "I will put you in irons, and give you a dozen stripes every morning."[5] King discovered that Lewes was a horse thief. He fled back alone to his regiment, informed against Lewes, and watched with some satisfaction as British soldiers burned down his house as punishment.

This incident earned King some credit with the officers. They subsequently gave him a dangerous assignment carrying a secret message between British camps. The officers promised King "great rewards" for this work because he would be traveling through Patriot-held territory. If King was captured, he would have faced punishment and re-enslavement. King walked more than twenty miles to deliver the message, and the Patriots nearly caught him, but he received only a paltry reward. "Colonel Small gave me three shillings and many fine promises," he remembered.[6] Shortly thereafter King left the regiment to work on a privateer. He participated in one successful naval engagement, but when his ship reached British-occupied New York he disembarked and left military service behind.

In New York King met and married a woman named Violet who had escaped from slavery in North Carolina, but he could not stay with her constantly because the only work he found was on a pilot boat guiding ships in and out of New York harbor.[7] On one voyage the vessel strayed too far out to sea and drifted for days, causing the crew to nearly starve. They were rescued by a whaling ship that took them to Patriot-held New Jersey. There King was once again among "strangers" with opposing lines of armed men separating him from his family, and he feared re-enslavement. For days he paced the banks of the Hudson River, watching the tides and the actions of the soldiers patrolling the shore. Eventually he found a small boat and when no one was watching and the currents were right, he rowed to Staten Island. From there he proceeded to Manhattan. "When I arrived at New York," he wrote, "my friends rejoiced to see me once more restored to liberty."[8] But New York was not secure.

In 1783 Britain acknowledged US independence. In King's words, the "horrors and devastation" of the war were over. The news "diffused universal joy among all parties," he wrote, "except us." The former slaves worried that they would be returned to their original status and their fears grew as they saw "old masters coming from Virginia, North Carolina, and other parts, and seizing upon their slaves in the streets of New York, or even dragging them out of their beds."[9] The British once again offered King an escape. They carried him with Violet and three thousand other former slaves from New York to Nova Scotia.

The black loyalists, as these migrants came to be known, were part of an ambitious new imperial project. Until the Revolutionary War the British had never been able to assert full authority over Nova Scotia. For decades the leaders of the colony had intermittently fought and negotiated with the Mi'kmaq, Wulstukwiuk, and other indigenous peoples. After 1783, thirty thousand new settlers arrived in the province. In the words of John G. Reid, the foundations of indigenous power in the region were "swept away" by "the sudden force of numbers brought by the Loyalist migration."[10] King was part of that migration, but he did not comment on the indigenous peoples in his memoirs. Instead he described Nova Scotia as a wilderness where he felt alone and deprived. "I thought I was not worthy to be among the people of God, nor even to dwell in my own house, but was fit only to reside among the beasts of the forest."[11] After their arrival in Nova Scotia, Violet experienced a religious awakening. Boston King's anguish eventually precipitated his own conversion, and with Violet's encouragement he became a Methodist preacher attending to the needs of former slaves. They also began to dream of crossing the Atlantic to the land of their ancestors, but in the 1780s they had "not the least prospect . . . of ever seeing Africa."[12] Summarizing the first thirty years of his life, Boston King wrote, "I had suffered greatly from the cruelty and injustice of the Whites, which induced me to look upon them, in general, as our enemies."[13]

In other parts of the Atlantic world in the revolutionary era such sentiments led to violence, but in 1792 Boston King and Violet found allies among the white directors of the Sierra Leone Company who recruited them and more than a thousand others to participate in yet another imperial project, this time in Africa. From Boston King's perspective, the Sierra Leone enterprise was different from earlier colonial projects, "their intention being, as far as possible in their power, to put a stop to the abominable slave trade."[14] Colonization in Africa refocused Boston King's energies and allowed him to accept a working alliance with British imperial promoters. Like many of the other Christian abolitionists of his generation, he thought that Africa could be colonized extensively and, in a new way, peacefully.

Operating from different premises, many other people involved in the revolutionary struggle voiced objections to various kinds of intercultural cooperation. In 1776 in the Declaration of Independence, the United States Continental Congress condemned George III and his government for hiring mercenaries, forcing colonial seamen to enlist against their wills, encouraging insurrections among the enslaved, and fighting in alliance with indigenous Americans. Attributing the entire British war effort to the king, the Congress complained,

> He has plundered our seas, ravaged our coasts, burnt our towns, and destroyed the lives of our people. He is at this time transporting large armies of foreign mercenaries to complete the works of death, desolation and tyranny already begun with circumstances of cruelty and perfidy scarcely paralleled in the most barbarous ages, and totally unworthy [of] the head of a civilized nation. He has constrained our fellow citizens taken captive on the high seas to bear arms against their country, to become executioners of their friends and brethren, or to fall themselves by their hands. He has excited domestic insurrections amongst us, and endeavoured to bring on the inhabitants of our frontiers, the merciless Indian savages whose known rule of warfare is an undistinguished destruction of all ages, sexes and conditions.

Thomas Jefferson was the original author of these words, and following his direction, at the moment of its founding, the United States denounced mercenary warfare and military ties between "civilized" and "savage" peoples. The representatives of the new nation also decried tactics that upset its social order and integrity, including the forcible recruitment of local people to fight against their "friends and brethren," and efforts to encourage enslaved men like Boston King to flee their masters. The Patriots' concerns reflected the delicacy of their position in 1776. They were trying to protect a nation they had only just called into existence. Their war was not simply a defensive action, but also an instrument for social and political change.

Over the next few decades, not just in the United States but across the Atlantic world, questions related to military service gained urgency as insurgents, soldiers, and political leaders resorted to warfare as an instrument of reform. Some combatants had radical intentions from the moment they took up arms, but in many cases the ideological implications of military service became apparent only over time. On December 18, 1777, a man who identified himself as "José Tupac Amaru, Cacique of the pueblos of Surimana, Pampamarca and Tungasuca" appeared before a council of royal officials in Lima. He claimed to be speaking on behalf of all the caciques, or traditional indigenous leaders, in Tinta province, Peru. Tupac Amaru delivered a protest against the mistreatment of "those Indians, who are your subjects, due to the imponderable toils that they suffer" in "Potosí, more than 200 leagues distant." The "Pueblos," he explained, were "forced to travel to such a distant mine, take their women and children with them and make a painful farewell to their relatives and their home." Some died on the road. Others were killed or severely injured working in the silver mines and never returned to their villages. Tupac Amaru asked the *Audencia* of Lima to protect the interests of Peru's indigenous people, even at the expense of others. He suggested that there were better ways to operate mines and proposed specifically that the miners "provide themselves with blacks" to do the work.[15] Tupac Amaru respected royal authority in 1777. He was working within official channels in his efforts on behalf of the indigenous peoples of Peru and had sent several petitions to various imperial officials.

Elsewhere in the Andes other indigenous leaders were pursuing similar campaigns.[16] In 1778 Tomás Katari, an Aymara-speaking protestor with no command of Spanish, began an extended series of protests, traveling from Potosí as far as Buenos Aires complaining about the mistreatment of indigenous peoples. When Katari returned to his home in the town of Macha in present-day Bolivia, he was flogged and jailed. His supporters rallied and managed to free him. After he was rearrested, they took a hostage and demanded Katari's freedom. When his jailers refused, they killed their hostage, seized another, and successfully obtained Katari's release.[17] Protests that had begun with legal petitioning had descended into violence.

The war in the Andes in the early 1780s was deadlier than the war of US independence. Between August 1780 and the cessation of hostilities in the Andes in January 1782, approximately one hundred thousand would die. Tupac Amaru was not involved in Tomás Katari's protests, but in November 1780 he orchestrated an elaborate ritual signaling his own revolutionary intentions. With a small contingent of supporters, he kidnapped a tax collector and compelled him to write letters summoning scores of Spanish officials to Tungasuca, where Tupac Amaru lived. At the same time, he and several other caciques brought thousands of indigenous people into the town. After everyone was assembled, the town crier, speaking Quechua, proclaimed that indigenous people would no longer be forced to labor in the mines or textile mills, and that several taxes and regulations had been abolished. Then in a great procession, the tax collector was led to a gallows accompanied by a man he had held as a slave, and that man hanged him.[18]

Even after this action, Tupac Amaru continued to insist that he was loyal to the Spanish crown. He argued that the imperial taxation regime and the renewed imposition of forced labor, which colonial officials had enforced after 1763, were unauthorized innovations violating centuries-old principles of Spanish governance.[19] In keeping with this belief, he sought to recruit a diverse coalition of supporters including colonists of European descent, people of mixed race, enslaved Africans and people of African descent, and members of a variety of indigenous groups.[20] But he also, critically, invoked Inca authority. He claimed direct descent from Inca rulers. Indeed the name Tupac Amaru had belonged to one of the Incas' last emperors. In his role as a military and political leader, he issued complex and potentially contradictory pronouncements, but many of his followers understood his program in simple terms. They believed they were engaged in something almost magical. The Inca empire had returned.[21]

The war stirred racial and communal animosity. Immigrants from Spain, and Spanish colonists generally, fled from Tupac Amaru and his supporters, spreading stories of cannibalism and mass slaughter.[22] In some places the actions of the revolutionaries seemed to confirm their fears. In November 1780, in one of their first major engagements, Tupac Amaru's supporters faced a mixed force of royalist colonists and indigenous Peruvians, and by the time the fighting had ended all 578 colonial fighters were dead.[23] A few weeks later in Calca, the insurgents reportedly killed "everyone who had a shirt." Some of them raped Spanish women. It was said that some of them raped corpses, and they mutilated the bodies of the dead.[24] In Checacupe, near Cuzco, a raiding party killed Spaniards including women and children, as well as the local priest.[25] Farther south, beyond Tupac Amaru's direct influence, revolutionaries killed hundreds, and reportedly "no one who had any trace of European background was spared."[26] An indigenous leader called Tupac Catari sent an edict to his supporters in the region of Lake Titicaca directing them to kill all Spanish officials with their wives and children. His order also imposed death on "anyone who is or appears to be a Spaniard, or who at least is dressed in imitation of the Spaniards."[27] Tupac Catari sought not only to eliminate the agents of Spanish imperialism but also their offspring and associates and to eradicate nearly every trace of Spanish influence in the region.

Positioning himself as a liberator, Tupac Amaru promised to advance the interests of all the people of Peru including enslaved people of African descent. But in the midst of the violence it was difficult to distinguish liberation from coercion. He offered enslaved people freedom, but even as he did so he threatened them with reprisals if they failed to follow his commands.

> As everybody has experienced rough treatment from the Europeans, they should all come, without exception, and support my position by totally deserting the Spaniards, even if they were slaves to their masters with the added benefit that they will be freed of their servitude and slavery to which they were subjected. And if they do not abide by this proclamation they will experience the most severe punishment that I can impose.[28]

There was an element of bluster in this pronouncement. Though Tupac Amaru's forces were powerful, they never entered the regions where most of Peru's people of African descent lived. Facing coercive pressure from their masters and government, enslaved black Peruvians were far more likely to fight for the imperial authorities than for the insurrection. Indeed, despite Tupac Amaru's desire to recruit from all parts of Peruvian society, the forces arrayed against him better represented a cross-section of Peru.[29] The largest contingent of soldiers and militiamen fighting in defense of the colonial government were indigenous Peruvians, and they were joined by people of mixed race, blacks, people of Spanish ancestry, and Spaniards.

The imperial forces punished the revolutionaries severely. On occasion they refused to take prisoners, and after some engagements they performed mass executions, killing hundreds or even thousands at a time.[30] They dramatized the administration of justice, particularly following the capture of Tupac Amaru in April 1781. Tupac Amaru was put on trial alongside several others including his wife Micaela Bastidas, who had served as his advisor and deputy through the campaign. They were both convicted and sentenced to death. Tupac Amaru was forced to watch the executioners clumsily strangle Micaela with a rope. The executioners then cut out his tongue. They tied his arms and legs to four horses, but no one on the scene had ever quartered a prisoner before, and they could not get the horses to dislodge his limbs. They beheaded him instead, and to complete the ceremony they led his ten-year-old son to see the headless corpse.[31]

Tupac Amaru and his family received far more attention than most of the other men and women captured by the colonial forces. One week after Tupac Amaru was captured, Jóse del Valle led troops into the town of Santa Rosa. Del Valle summoned all the town's men into the central square, and then ordered the execution of every fifth man. His soldiers killed old men alongside those of fighting age, and supporters of the colonial regime as well as revolutionaries. Del Valle had heard that Santa Rosa was a "rebel town," and he wanted to terrify and weaken its inhabitants and deliver a message.[32] In response to the revolutionaries' campaigns against Spaniards, colonial authorities denigrated Peru's indigenous cultures. Following the execution of Tupac Amaru, the colonial government tried to ban traditional clothing, the Quechua language, musical instruments, and hereditary offices.[33]

Peru had not been a major theater of combat between the European-led empires in the eighteenth century. Nonetheless, its economy and politics had been deeply affected by the endemic violence attending transatlantic trade and the century's major imperial wars. Like most other colonies in the Americas, Peru imported enslaved laborers from Africa, and Tupac Amaru challenged the future of slavery. He and his supporters also protested the practice of forcing indigenous people to labor, and in so doing they struck against silver mining and the silver trade, the most important economic link tying Peru to Europe. The revolutionaries' other professed grievances stemmed from innovations in imperial governance that had been instituted by the Spanish crown in response to Spain's poor performance in the Seven Years' War. Peru had experienced that war from a distance, but its shock waves had destabilized colonial society.

In other Atlantic regions where people had more direct experience with the wars between the empires, revolutionaries protested more explicitly against the eighteenth-century pattern of warfare.

In the first year of the revolution in France, the National Assembly renounced wars of conquest. During the debate leading up to that resolution, one assemblyman unconsciously echoed the sentiments of indigenous American warriors in the Ohio Valley who had complained about French imperial policy nearly forty years earlier. "Until this day . . . empires were owned as pieces of private property, and whole peoples given as dowries like herds of sheep."[34] Another assemblyman denounced Louis XIV by describing him as a "vain, superstitious and despotic king who [had] breathed nothing but war and waged it with barbarity."[35] The majority of the National Assembly asserted that the representatives of the people would be wiser than any monarch had been. The "people" would only support fighting for self-defense. If all the world were republican peace would prevail. As one assemblyman put it, "May all nations be as free as we wish to be, and there will be no more war."[36]

Despite the expression of such hopes, one noteworthy feature of the revolutions in both the United States and France was their ultimate denunciation of pacifism. The leaders of both revolutionary movements felt challenged, sensed their own fragility and believed that their survival depended on their ability to mobilize and justify military action. The communitarian ethos of the revolutions brought those who questioned military service under suspicion. More generally, the revolutionaries frequently vilified those who challenged their principles. In some theaters in the closing years of the War of Independence in the United States, and more famously on occasion during the French Revolution, distinctions between combatants and noncombatants dissolved. Violence escalated as loyalists and counterrevolutionaries rallied to defend the old order, their property, and their lives.[37]

Grand ambitions to change the world by force of arms do not always inspire massive violence, but there are many ways in which revolutionary action can spiral into widespread bloodshed. Such campaigns often entail the rejection of customary or judicial mechanisms for maintaining order. Revolutionaries often believe they are operating without clear precedents or traditions establishing constraints on violent action. In confrontations between revolutionary and reactionary forces, individuals on both sides may sense their own moral superiority and show contempt for their adversaries. Anger, fear, and the desire for vengeance feed on each other. Additionally, revolutionaries frequently deploy violence as an instrument to effect social change.

Like many other colonies around the Atlantic World, Saint Domingue faced a series of crises following the end of the Seven Years' War. White planters resisted paying more for the colony's defenses, while impoverished white colonists, many of them refugees from the colonies France had lost during the war, resented the demands of militia service. The colony's growing community of free blacks, by contrast, supplied large numbers of willing militiamen, many of whom viewed military service as a promising path toward social advancement.[38] During the War of Independence in the United States, hundreds of black militiamen from Saint Domingue served with French soldiers on the side of the Patriots. When Boston King ran to catch up with the British army, the forces arriving behind him included free black militiamen from Saint Domingue. From King's perspective those men were fighting on behalf of South Carolina's Patriot slaveholders, but according to many in Saint Domingue they were just being "good Frenchmen." Their service demonstrated, in the words of one newspaper, "the zeal and the goodwill of citizens of every condition."[39] In Paris in 1789, revolutionary leaders like Abbé Henri Gregoire cited the achievements of the free black militia, including their service in the United States during the War of Independence. and their role combating rebellions among the enslaved in Saint Domingue, to support granting them full rights as citizens of France.[40]

Within weeks of the start of the French Revolution, France's National Assembly began debating the status of free blacks in Saint Domingue. Arguing on their own behalf, some free blacks invoked revolutionary principles, asserting that they had "inalienable rights based on nature and the social contract" and that "all men are born and remain free and equal."[41] When the enslaved in the colony rose in arms in August 1791, some similarly invoked the liberal values of the French Revolution. But there were other ways to advocate for freedom, and the complexity of French and colonial politics demonstrated the limited value of liberal rhetoric. Many of the most articulate proponents of the purported values of the French Revolution supported the continuation of slavery or other systems of forced labor.

At the start of the insurrection in 1791 hundreds of white landowners and workers had fled the affected countryside with their families, in effect liberating their workers and leaving newly freed people in control of large territories. This provided the insurgents an opportunity to organize and arm themselves and demonstrated what terror could accomplish. The French colonial authorities responded by trying to terrorize the enslaved, encouraging cycles of reprisal and escalation. A newspaper in 1791 reported, "The country is filled with dead bodies, which lie unburied. The negroes have left the whites, with stakes, &c. driven through them into the ground; and the white troops, who now take no prisoners, but kill everything black or yellow, leave the negroes dead upon the field."[42] Reports from this period suggested that a bitter, simple race war had begun, but the conflict was never so simple. Some former slaves received assistance from the Spanish in the adjacent colony of Santo Domingo, and from the outset the white French colonists knew that they were outnumbered. They sought support from others, including free and enslaved people of African descent.

The complicated politics of Saint Domingue became even more so in 1793 following the execution of Louis XVI and the outbreak of war with Spain and Britain. Spanish colonial officials in Santo Domingo sent troops into Saint Domingue and promised any enslaved men who joined their forces freedom and land. Under threat, the republican leaders of the French colony answered with a promise of their own. They offered any enslaved men who enlisted with them liberty "in the name of the Republic, and declared that all those who took up arms for her would become the equals of their former masters."[43] Enslaved men who enlisted for military service had been promised freedom before, but this time was different. Many of the "slaves" in question had already freed themselves by taking up arms on their own initiative. This gave them bargaining power which they could exploit either by asserting their own autonomy or by pitting the commanders of competing empires against each other.

In June 1793 a man named Macaya led a body of soldiers in an attack on Cap François, the northern capital of the colony. After the city had been sacked, he retreated with his troops into nearby mountains, and then broke with his former French republican allies. Macaya explained that he had always been a monarchist, and he went on to profess simultaneous allegiance to three kings: the King of Kongo, the King of Spain, and the King of France. As a former slave and now a soldier, he expected those kings to protect his interests, but he believed that they would do more than that. He compared them to the kings in the Bible who had been led by a star to adore Jesus Christ. Some republican revolutionaries complained bitterly about the prevalence of monarchical belief among Saint Domingue's enslaved people and former slaves. "It is the kings who want slaves," they declared. "It is the kings of Guinea who sell them to the white kings."[44] African, European, and distinctly Caribbean groups argued with and learned from each other even as they formed alliances, used and betrayed one another. Their arguments as well as their actions reflected the complex dynamics of the revolution. In the midst of the conflict it was almost impossible for anyone to consistently follow a guiding light or star of Bethlehem. Macaya shifted alliances several times during the war. Three years after professing his allegiance to the kings of Spain and France, he returned to Cap François and proposed killing the entire white population.[45]

In contrast to the Spanish, who had been aiding the insurrection covertly almost from the beginning, the British commanders who arrived in Saint Domingue in September 1793 were wary of promoting general emancipation. British policymakers feared that a precedent might be set and that the revolt might spread and undermine the security and economic viability of Britain's colonies, particularly Jamaica. At the same time, however, Britain's military commanders recognized that enslaved men and self-liberated former slaves constituted the bulk of Saint Domingue's potential military manpower. Therefore, they started to recruit among the enslaved, but they adopted a cautious approach. They asked slaveholders to assign some men to military service and eventually introduced levies in the territories they controlled, occasionally for example conscripting one-fifteenth of each plantation's enslaved labor force.[46]

For as long as Britain remained in the conflict, that is until 1798, Britain's policies gained support from the Saint Domingue's slaveholders. The enslaved, by contrast, continued to weigh competing appeals. Pressing their advantage, some former slaves challenged the logic of freeing armed men while leaving noncombatants in slavery. Black men in Saint Domingue were quoted on the floor of the French National Assembly asking "Is it the fault of our women ... that they have not been able to arm themselves for France? Should one punish the weakness of their sex? After all, they share our feelings. What is more, they will inspire our children and work to feed our warriors. As for our children, they are our possessions, our blood."[47] In the late summer of 1793 French Republican leaders in Saint Domingue declared an end to slavery in the colony, and in 1794 the French republic outlawed slavery throughout its empire. But even after that, many in Saint Domingue remained skeptical, questioning the consistency and durability of such pledges.

Toussaint Louverture emerged as Saint Domingue's principal leader in the late 1790s. He denounced uncompensated labor but to maintain economic output he supported forcing field workers to stay on plantations growing cash crops for a share of the profit. In 1802 the French captured Louverture, and Jean-Jacques Dessalines succeeded him. Dessalines resisted Napoleon's efforts to reintroduce slavery by force of arms, but he continued to promote his own forced-labor schemes. When Macaya resisted Dessalines, Dessalines sent men to raid his camp. They brought back "women and children and prisoners." "I had a few hung, and others shot," Dessalines reported. He hoped that "in ten years" the people of the region would remember the "lesson."[48]

As Dessalines predicted, the violence of the Haitian Revolution would be remembered for generations, but not entirely in the way he hoped. Dessalines has been memorialized as a vengeful, impulsive tyrant, and the conflict that brought him to power has long been associated with merciless, almost indiscriminate racial violence. According to an eyewitness account recorded years later, in 1802 Dessalines rallied his soldiers by telling them "when the French are reduced to small, small numbers, we will harass them and beat them; we will burn the harvests and then take to the hills. They will be forced to leave. Then I will make you independent."[49]

In a desperate effort to ward off that imagined fate, French commanders in the closing months of the conflict plotted their own forms of genocide. They ordered the execution of thousands of prisoners and oversaw the drowning of women and children. General Victor-Emmanuel Leclerc argued for a "war of extermination" and wrote Napoleon declaring, "We must destroy all the blacks of the mountains—men and women—and spare only children under twelve years of age. We must destroy half of those in the plains and must not leave a single coloured person in the colony who has worn an epaulette."[50] On both sides of the Atlantic, when armies were deployed to conquer territory or maintain order in regions with potentially restive populations, an ideologically charged understanding of military service frequently contributed to incidents of mass slaughter. In Europe during the Napoleonic wars, the French destroyed towns and killed thousands of men, women, and children in Belgium, Germany, Switzerland, Holland, Italy, Spain, and Russia. Napoleon declared that in a conquered country "kindness is not humaneness." On at least one occasion he privately expressed hope that the inhabitants of a newly conquered region would rise up against the French so his soldiers could make an example of them. "As long as you have not made an example," he wrote, "you will not be master."[51] When Napoleon's officers directed mass killings, they invariably claimed that they had been provoked and they described the targeted population as "brigands" "fanatics," "vagabonds," or "beasts." But their own violence could be indiscriminate. Later in the decade several French officers would call for a "war of extermination" in Spain.

In 1804 the French military withdrew from Saint Domingue and Haiti declared its independence, but the massacres continued. It was reported that in the town of Jérémie Dessalines drew up a list of all the white inhabitants, and three days later nearly three-quarters of them, more than three hundred people, were dead.[52] Even those who took inspiration from the Haitian Revolution associated it with punitive, disabling destruction. In Barbados in the spring of 1816, an enslaved woman named Nancy Grigg argued that the people of her island should follow the example of the Haitians and rise up to take their freedom. "The only way to get it," she explained, "was to fight for it, otherwise they would not get it; the way they were to do, was to set fire, as that was the way they did it in Santo Domingo."[53]

Grigg's comments show how in the wake of the Haitian Revolution, the debate over slavery was also a debate over the application of organized violence. That had always been the case, but the collapse of Saint Domingue's slave regime altered perspectives, especially in the British Empire. Some opponents of slavery like Griggs advocated warfare, and partly in response, more defenders of slavery positioned themselves as advocates of peace.

As the events in Saint Domingue indicate, from the 1790s well into the nineteenth century the British Empire was a constant and powerful defender of slavery in the Caribbean. On occasion British military commanders offered freedom to slaves in war zones, for example in North America during the War of

Independence in the United States and in Saint Domingue during the Haitian Revolution, but they did so strategically. Their wartime proclamations carefully specified which men were to be granted freedom, and they operated with the aim of weakening Britain's opponents and recruiting valuable manpower while at the same time preserving the support of loyal slaveholders and keeping the slave labor system intact, especially in the Caribbean where slavery generated the greatest profit. Between 1787 and 1807 Britain engaged in an extended debate over the transatlantic slave trade, and though the British sometimes celebrate this period as the time when they turned against slavery, the most prominent figures on both sides of the argument insisted that slave labor should remain an important feature of the British imperial economy. Most of those who would later be praised as abolitionists aimed not to end slavery but to make it work better. If their project had succeeded, slavery would have continued, eventually with the entire enslaved population born into that status.

In the early months of the insurrection among the enslaved in Saint Domingue, celebrated abolitionist Thomas Clarkson consulted in Paris with free blacks from the French colony and concluded that there would have been no uprising if the slaveholders had employed only locally born people as slaves. Clarkson argued that men and women captured in Africa and carried across the ocean arrived with "dissatisfied and exasperated minds." The laborers' "discontent and feeling of resentment" gave their masters no alternative but to treat them roughly. "We cannot keep people in a state of subjection to us who acknowledge no obligation to serve us but by breaking their spirits and treating them as creatures of another species." For this reason, he argued, Africans held as slaves in the Caribbean were routinely mistreated and therefore frequently rebelled. In support of this assertion he cited historian Edward Long, who claimed that "all the insurrections of the slaves that he could ever trace in the islands were begun by the imported Africans and never by the creole, or island-born slaves."[54] By halting the transatlantic slave trade, abolitionists like Clarkson intended to disassociate slavery from warfare in Africa and the traumas of the Middle Passage. They also thought that blocking the slaveholders' access to African suppliers would give them an incentive to treat their workers well. Reliant for the future on the natural increase of the enslaved workforce, masters would protect their workers' health, encourage wholesome family life, and avoid the application of harsh discipline. This, in turn, would reduce the workers' incentive to escape or revolt. The abolitionists were optimistic in 1807, but Grigg's discontent nine years later reflected a widespread and growing recognition that the British government's prohibition of the transatlantic slave trade had not been enough to ensure peace.

Under the influence of revolutionary-era slave-trade abolitionists, the British Empire adopted policies that aimed simultaneously at lessening the risk of

DESALINES.

Fig. 11.1 A portrait of Jean-Jacques Dessalines published in Mexico in 1806. Courtesy of the John Carter Brown Library.

insurrection in the colonies and disassociating American slavery from African violence. In Africa itself Britain's policy was not to repress warfare, captive-taking, or slavery, but as far as possible to seal off those practices from the direct involvement of Europeans. After the British outlawed the transatlantic slave trade, Freetown, the capitol of Sierra Leone, became a valuable port for British ships intercepting slaving vessels. The colony also became a landing site for the men, women, and children rescued from those ships.[55] But the colonial government never assumed a leading role in combating slavery in Africa. Even within its own jurisdiction, the British protectorate of Sierra Leone did not outlaw slavery until 1928.[56]

The United States banned the transatlantic slave trade at the same time that the British empire did. Other nations eventually followed suit. Naval patrols enforced the ban along the westernmost coasts of West Africa, but farther east and south Portuguese slaving ships and others continued to carry enslaved men and women from the Bights of Benin and Biafara, Kongo and Angola. Indeed, the trade from central Africa expanded in the early nineteenth century, and more than 1,900,000 people were forcibly shipped across the ocean between 1801 and 1850. In the meantime, the disruption of well-established transatlantic trading networks unsettled regional politics. Some slave-trading kingdoms like Oyo disintegrated, inaugurating a long period of war. Though many old slave markets had closed, captives from these wars were still sold to European traders. Yoruba-speaking warriors from the vicinity of Oyo were sold in Cuba and Brazil, where some of them organized uprisings against their masters.[57] During this period of upheaval in West Africa the Kingdom of Asante struggled to ship its war captives away, and as an alternative increasingly executed them. In the long term, an over-abundance of captives throughout the region led to a search for new ways to deploy slave labor, in gold mining, for example, and in palm oil production for European and American markets.[58]

Like Britain, the United States sought to distance itself from the apparent violence of the African slave trade. US and British policy in this regard had similar objectives, to dissociate those nations from African slaving practices and to preserve peace among those who continued to work as slaves within US and British jurisdictions. From the 1770s, several US states aspired to become lands of freedom, but few political leaders were ready to risk abrupt change. The United States banned slavery in some territories where it had never been legally established, but for the rest of the eighteenth century and beyond, in states with functioning slave systems the most common model for emancipation was selective and gradual. The policy was to retain slavery while reducing the number of people in bondage. State governments extended the process of emancipation over generations, ostensibly to facilitate a smooth economic transition and allow time for the enslaved and their children to prepare for work in a new labor system. The overall aim was to avoid social disruption and maintain domestic peace. Most of the northern states adopted this policy, and similar proposals for gradual abolition had significant support among slaveholders in the South until the early nineteenth century. But for many white southerners, the Haitian Revolution served as an object lesson in the danger of trying to live side by side with former slaves. Thomas Jefferson opposed the insurrection in Saint Domingue from its inception, and as president in 1804 he refused to recognize Haiti's independence. He called Haitians "cannibals of the terrible republic" and warned that they would spread violence into the United States.[59] Thereafter,

Fig. 11.2 Freetown, Sierra Leone in 1803. From Thomas Masterman Winterbottom, *An Account of the native Africans in the neighbourhood of Sierra Leone; to which is added an account of the present state of medicine among them* (1803). British Library.

he and other like-minded white southerners supported gradual abolition only through the mechanism of colonizing Africa with former slaves.

Jefferson feared that the Haitian Revolution would destabilize the United States, and it was not the only foreign conflict to scare him. During the years of Jefferson's presidency Napoleon proclaimed himself emperor of France, positioning himself as a national hero while continuing to pursue his extraordinarily successful military career. Under Napoleon's direction France became "La Grande Nation" with conquests across Europe. By 1815 his wars had left four million dead.[60] The pro-British policies of Jefferson's predecessor in the 1790s, John Adams, had culminated in a "Quasi-war" with France, dividing the United States and strengthening a growing apprehension that if the country confronted any European power militarily, the resulting conflict would undermine the autonomy of the new nation, threaten its territorial integrity, and corrupt its republican principles. Acknowledging these dangers, for most of the period of the Napoleonic wars, Jefferson and his successor James Madison struggled to remain neutral. They experimented with trade embargos in an effort to discover ways to resolve international conflicts without resort to warfare.[61] Jefferson's ambitious anti-militarism was part of a hemispheric trend. In contrast to the eighteenth-century imperial wars, the Napoleonic wars had the long-term effect of disassociating American military affairs from those of Europe.

After Napoleon's forces invaded Portugal in 1807, the Portuguese royal house of Braganza fled to Brazil with thousands of followers and made Rio de Janeiro their capital. In 1808, after Napoleon's allies in Spain arrested King Ferdinand VII, Spain's colonists in the Americas declared their continued allegiance to the imprisoned monarch, and for the next several years governed in his name without any direction from Spain. During those years several colonies adopted liberal reforms and promoted local autonomy, but the process was often violently disrupted as colonial forces battled each other. When Ferdinand returned to power in Spain in 1814, he sent an army of ten thousand across the Atlantic to start an unsuccessful, years-long campaign to re-establish order under Spanish authority. The ensuing wars divided the Spanish-speaking peoples of North and South America and helped give rise to a new military culture. Both Ferdinand's forces and their opponents enlisted rich and poor colonists, indigenous men, free people of color, African-born and American-born men held in slavery. Commanders of all ideological stripes employed the old recruitment practice of offering freedom to any enslaved men who joined their armies.[62] But even when the officers professed egalitarian principles their units were intrinsically hierarchical, with *creoles*, American-born whites, holding the highest offices. In the aftermath of the wars, in the newly independent republics, impoverished whites, indigenous men, and free and enslaved people of color found work in and around military bases and within the ranks. Creole elites rallied to the army as a source of order and local pride, while the commanders, *caudillos*, exercised patronage power and generally dominated politics.[63]

Like many in the United States, revolutionaries in the former Spanish colonies sought more than a simple, legal separation from their old imperial masters. Their avowed rejection of European influence had an emotional component. As early as 1812 an English traveler in Venezuela encountered "a species of fanatical hatred of Europeans, who are termed ferocious, cruel, and perfidious, whilst the Americans are magnanimous, mild and just."[64] Sentiments like these could have fatal consequences. In 1813, Simón Bolívar, leading revolutionary forces in Venezuela, ordered the execution of any Spaniard who refused to support his revolution, and within months hundreds died.[65] Despite such efforts, the revolutionaries could never keep Europeans away. There were loyalist factions in many places, and Spain's large island colonies of Cuba, Santo Domingo, and Puerto Rico remained part of the Spanish empire even as the mainland colonies rebelled. Britain retained its Caribbean colonies, along with the string of settlements in North America that would eventually join to form Canada. Other European empires remained in the Caribbean, and perhaps most importantly, Britain was the dominant naval power throughout the Atlantic.

The revolutionary era had opened with a demonstration of the limits of naval power, when the British blockade of Boston Harbor failed to secure obedience from the Patriots. The Massachusetts economy had matured and diversified over the previous century, allowing the supporters of the Provincial Congress to withstand an interruption of Atlantic trade. The British navy learned a similar lesson after its commanders sought to capitalize on Britain's victory at Trafalgar by seizing outposts on the shores of the Spanish empire in the Americas. A British expeditionary force dispatched from the Cape of Good Hope occupied Buenos Aires in 1806 only to face violent, organized popular resistance. Within two months, a local volunteer army of eight thousand men including whites and blacks, Spaniards and Creoles, had surrounded and ousted the British.[66] In 1807 a second British expedition attacked across the river at Montevideo, and again the British were defeated quickly. These episodes had lasting legacies, because they inspired within the two cities' populations a defiant civic pride even before the inauguration of their independence struggles against Spain. But in the long run the people of the region did not simply unite against the intrusion of British, Spanish, or other European influences. Buenos Aires and Montevideo had long been rivals, and the nascent revolutionary movements on the two sides of the Rio de la Plata gave rise not to one republic but two. Divisions between the revolutionaries created openings for the British, allowing them to play an important role in Spanish American politics generally, and in Uruguay in particular, for years to come.[67]

The War of Independence in the United States, the war in the Andes in the early 1780s, the French Revolution, the Haitian Revolution, and the wars for independence in the former Spanish colonies on the mainland of North and South America were distinct events, but they had common origins. In the thirteen rebellious British colonies and Peru, war-related changes to imperial policy following the Seven Years' War gave impetus to protest movements that escalated into revolution. French participation in the war of US independence contributed to the financial crisis that led to revolution in France in 1789. The subsequent wars of the French Revolution and the Napoleonic Wars further destabilized politics throughout the Americas and provided an opening for revolution in San Domingue and parts of the Spanish Empire.

The partial dissolution of the British, Spanish, and Portuguese empires signaled the end of the early modern era of ocean-spanning Atlantic warfare. On occasion in the nineteenth century, Britain, Spain, and France intervened militarily in American affairs. Similarly, some American peoples, particularly Canadians, participated in Europe's wars. But the transatlantic pattern of warfare had changed. After the revolutionary era wars seldom occasioned combat on both sides of the Atlantic simultaneously or spread from one side of the ocean to the other, and gradually a new structure of formal and informal international agreements emerged to discourage the British and other European powers from providing military aid to indigenous peoples living outside the borders of their existing empires.

Though some indigenous Americans had fought for the Patriots in the War of Independence, after the fighting ended most of the military leaders of the United States proceeded on the assumption that as a group, indigenous Americans had violently opposed the formation of the new nation. According to a logic common throughout the country's political leadership, the indigenous Americans had fought with the British and lost. Therefore, they were vanquished, and their lands had been conquered. During the war itself units of the Continental Army had overrun Haudenosaunee villages in northern New York, burning crops, destroying villages, and displacing thousands. After the war ended and for decades thereafter, US army commanders reserved for themselves the option of pursuing similar campaigns in the Ohio Valley, the southern Great Lakes region, and the South. But in a fateful set of engagements in the 1780s and 1790s, indigenous American confederacies successfully defended themselves against the US army, and partly as a consequence the federal government became more inclined to negotiate, seek allies among indigenous leaders, and acknowledge that indigenous Americans retained autonomy, sovereignty, and land.

Representatives of the British empire, including military commanders, soldiers, traders, colonial officials based in Canada, and diplomats and ministers in London, played an important role in this formative period of US–indigenous relations. Until 1794, the British army retained forts in the western region that Britain had formally ceded to the United States. Those forts served as trading posts where indigenous groups received supplies including weapons. Indigenous American warriors and refugees sought shelter in those forts during times of conflict with the United States. Even after the British army evacuated the region, traders from Canada continued to supply warriors in US-claimed territory, much to the consternation of political leaders and commentators in the United States. Britain's persistent ties to the indigenous peoples of the trans-Appalachian west became a rallying cry, helping lead the United States to war with Britain in 1812. During that war the British allied themselves with Tecumseh, a visionary Shawnee military leader who advocated independence for indigenous peoples across a wide section of the present-day American Midwest and South. As late as 1814, in their peace negotiations with the United States, the British demanded the creation of an autonomous indigenous American state carved out of present-day Minnesota, Wisconsin, Iowa, Missouri, Illinois, Indiana, and Ohio.[68] But a few months later the British abandoned their indigenous allies, and in the Treaty of Ghent they foreswore any engagement in indigenous American affairs within the US borders. In effect, they left the indigenous peoples to the mercy of the federal government. The Treaty of Ghent only related to lands claimed by the United States, but in the Monroe Doctrine in 1823, the federal government tried unilaterally to extend its understanding of national sovereignty by declaring opposition to any effort by any European power to found new colonies in the Western Hemisphere. In 1823 the United States had neither the military power nor the diplomatic leverage to force its will on Europe's major powers. Nonetheless, the Monroe Doctrine roughly predicted the future. In widely separated regions there was a growing common interest in suppressing transatlantic military operations. In some places this reflected deeply felt emotional and ideological commitments. Anti-imperial and anti-European convictions across the Americas operated alongside racial animosities and stereotypical beliefs that associated distant continents with unsavory military practices.

In widely scattered regions of the Atlantic world, revolutionary struggles transformed military culture as revolutionaries and their opponents increasingly associated fighting with ideological commitment. Political leaders exalted patriotic and loyal soldiers over mercenaries, opportunists, and foreign interventionists who entered combat without a legitimate stake in the fight. Oppositional thinking, sometimes pitting indigenous peoples against Europeans, or revolutionary white Americans against Europeans, or black Haitians against whites, made it difficult for many people to acknowledge that members of disparate communities could simultaneously cooperate, retain independence, and remain principled. The defense of new national boundaries across the Americas gave added impetus to the general trend disfavoring alliances between colonial powers and maroons, enslaved people or indigenous groups. In the nineteenth century, when they fought against internationally recognized colonial or national governments, maroons, enslaved people, and indigenous Americans found it increasingly difficult to recruit wartime allies from abroad.

Their isolation was reinforced by changes in the military balance of power at sea. The new American governments and the old European imperial powers tightened their dominance of the ocean. The new revolutionary-era military ethic discouraged privateering. The expansion of transatlantic trade after 1815 generally lowered the price of trade goods, making piracy and privateering less profitable.[69] Commerce raiding declined, and with the risk of attack diminishing, merchant vessels were less likely to arm themselves. In the meantime, national and imperial governments continued to invest in navies, and the increasing sophistication and specialization of warships reinforced their dominance. The British Royal Navy became the pre-eminent naval force on the Atlantic.

After centuries of encouraging the shipment of African captives across the ocean, American political leaders and European colonial powers in Africa redirected their energies. With Britain in the lead, between 1807 and 1850, various governments and imperial authorities on both sides of the ocean began to intercept and prohibit the shipment of captives across the Atlantic. In doing so, they broke a strong, long-standing link between American and African warfare.

Francisco Ferreira Gomes was born in Brazil in the late eighteenth century.[70] According to some reports he was born enslaved and his father purchased his freedom. His father had been a lieutenant in a battalion operating along the coast of central Africa around the Portuguese-ruled city of Benguela. Officers like his father sometimes augmented their income by working as merchants carrying captives, produce, and manufactured goods between Africa, Europe, and Brazil. Gomes's parents may have met when his father was visiting Rio de Janeiro for trade. Gomes spent his childhood in Brazil, but at the age of fifteen he moved to Benguela, and soon thereafter he joined his father's battalion. By the 1820s he was a wealthy man. He invested in at least two merchant ships and entered the slave trade. During his career he participated financially in the sale of nearly seven thousand Angolan captives in Brazil. Gomes was also politically active, and in 1824 he was accused of conspiring to kidnap the Portuguese governor of Benguela, seize the port, and "hoist the flag of the empire of Brazil."[71] He and his coconspirators were said to have support from the soldiers of Benguela as well as merchants and the crews of sailing vessels operating along the coast of Angola. Some claimed that the merchants had solicited military aid from Rio de Janeiro.

Brazil had declared its independence only two years earlier, and the allegations against Gomes were an echo of that event. But his accusers were also alarmed by other precedents. They warned that Gomes was dangerous because he was black and so were the soldiers who supported him. They claimed that the conspirators aimed to install a government similar to the regime in Haiti. It was said that

Fig. 11.3 A US cartoon from 1812 depicting Britain's alliance with indigenous Americans. Library of Congress.

they planned to kill large numbers of Portuguese. One witness asserted that Gomes intended to "wash his feet in the blood of European loyalists."[72] These accusations exposed fears and racial animosities that had hardened in the context of the Atlantic revolutions. Whether or not the stories were accurate, it is clear that Gomes and his supporters drew distinctions between whites. According to his accusers, Gomes claimed fidelity to the Emperor of Brazil and sought support from white Brazilians. His aim, they said, was to liberate Portugal's Atlantic African outposts from European rule while at the same time maintaining the vital economic and political connections linking Brazil with Angola.

Brazilian independence had disrupted the old political order, but in a revolutionary climate of communal animosity it was difficult to establish new lines of authority while upholding the alliances and partnerships that had sustained the slave trade. Gomes was accused of treason, but ultimately factional politics sabotaged the case against him. He was arrested and taken on board one of his own ships to the Angolan capital of Luanda where the clergy and others suspected the colonial authorities in Benguela of freemasonry and sedition. After reviewing the evidence against Gomes, they said they could not find "the slightest proof" of the charges against him.[73] Gomes was released, recovered his assets, returned to Benguela, became a judge in a court overseeing commercial disputes, and resumed his participation in the slave trade. In 1834 he retired and returned to Rio de Janeiro.

The old Atlantic World did not collapse in a single moment. Brazil did not abolish slavery until 1888, and Angola did not secure its independence from Portugal until 1975, but even in the 1820s the tremors of revolution and abolition had spread to those countries. In Brazil, Angola, and on every other shore of the Atlantic, there were widespread expectations, hopes, and fears that the transatlantic military networks that had shaped the lives of Gomes and countless others were breaking apart.

Conclusion

The lands surrounding the Atlantic were changed more thoroughly than any other part of the world during the early modern era. Millions of people from Africa and Europe crossed the ocean. Epidemics spread across the Americas and decimated many indigenous communities. American cities collapsed and new cities were built. Large tracts of forest were cleared in colonized regions, while in other places cleared land turned to forest. Hitherto unknown species of livestock arrived in the Americas, while crops spread from one side of the ocean to the other. Transatlantic commerce altered the economy on every shore, drawing wealth and capital increasingly to Europe and some European colonies and outposts.

Warfare drove these developments. Since the time of the Vikings, competition and conflict among Europeans had spurred on the development of European sailing technology. Merchant ships, whalers, and fishing vessels doubled as warships. As these ships and specialized naval vessels grew larger, they required greater investment in port facilities and increasingly elaborate mechanisms to recruit, feed, arm, and control sailors. Europeans and colonists held supremacy at sea not because they were united, but rather because they were continuously fighting each other and investing in offensive and defensive naval capabilities. Though disunited, they controlled nearly all the ships on the Atlantic throughout the early modern era, which allowed them to direct the flow of commerce and migration.

From the fifteenth through the eighteenth century, Europeans did not achieve similar military supremacy on land in Africa or the Americas. Early modern European armies depended on gunpowder and horses, and these were not easy to use in many Atlantic environments. Capital investment, which had given Europeans a formidable advantage at sea, was less decisive in land warfare in and around the colonies. Hand-held firearms changed hands easily, and locally constructed alternatives such as arrows, spears, and pit-traps were often effective weapons against colonial forces.

The eighteenth-century revolutions did not upset European and colonial dominance at sea, and despite the anti-imperial rhetoric of many revolutionaries,

Atlantic Wars. Geoffrey Plank, Oxford University Press (2020). © Oxford University Press.
DOI: 10.1093/oso/9780190860455.001.0001

they had the long-term effect of consolidating European and colonial power on land in the Americas and ultimately in Africa as well. In the early modern era, the Europeans and their descendants gained naval supremacy on the Atlantic by fighting each other. By contrast, they gained power on land in Africa and the Americas in the nineteenth century through a series of formal and informal postrevolutionary mutual agreements.

After the revolutions, European and American military culture promoted the concentration of power. In parts of Europe and the Americas, military service became a sign of loyalty associated with citizenship and political allegiance. The effect was polarizing, encouraging wartime political leaders, officers, and soldiers to denigrate their opponents as ideologically deviant and culturally inferior. In Europe the violence of the revolutionary era subsided after the defeat of the French Empire and the erection of a more stable continental state system. But many of the dynamics that had led to massacres in Europe during the French Revolution and Napoleonic wars would resurface later in the context of efforts to displace or destroy minorities within the boundaries of modern European multinational empires and nation-states.[1]

Western and central Africa suffered endemic violence through most of the nineteenth century, and for a variety of reasons guns became the weapons of choice in most regional conflicts. The Africans' reliance on these weapons increased their dependence on European merchants and left them vulnerable when gun technology changed. In the closing decades of the nineteenth century, European forces arrived to conquer territory and establish new colonies. Soldiers began arriving from Europe with breach-loader rifles, and by the 1890s some came with machine guns. Africans could resist only with inferior firearms.[2]

In the nineteenth century in large parts of the Americas the descendants of Europeans secured nearly uncontested military supremacy on land. Several technological, demographic, and political changes contributed to this shift, including an increase in the volume of European migration to the Americas; the construction of roads, canals, and railroads facilitating the movement of large armies and immigrant settlers; and the expansion of weapons industries working closely with national governments.[3]

In the northern United States, the dominant ideology in the nineteenth century promoted patriotism and free labor markets. Citizens of the new republic celebrated contractualism, personal responsibility, and the rejection of physical coercion in the operation of the economy. Encouraged by these values, millions of Europeans moved to the United States.[4] Cheap abundant labor expanded the resource base of the US economy as immigrants occupied land to farm and mine. Even in the eighteenth century, British colonists in North America had been richer on average than their counterparts in the Spanish colonies, but in the nineteenth century the economic divergence between the United States and other nations in the Western Hemisphere increased in aggregate terms.[5] This divergence had military implications, as demonstrated in 1846 when Mexico and the United States went to war. With a larger, well-equipped, and disciplined army, Mexico appeared to be better prepared, but with its greater wealth and manpower, the United States was able to mobilize quickly on an unprecedented scale and secured an unexpected, overwhelming victory.[6] The country was poorly prepared to govern the territory it conquered from Mexico. Arguments over slavery in the region led to the Civil War, which in turn occasioned two more mass mobilizations, north and south. Despite northern fears of British intervention on behalf of the Confederacy and wartime proposals for a US invasion of Canada, the conflict did not become an international one. Following the defeat of the Confederacy, the United States deployed its army in a campaign to pacify the west. With overwhelming force and little fear of foreign intervention, the US army sought not only to quell resistance among indigenous Americans, but to eradicate some indigenous cultures.[7]

Across the Americas, the events of the Revolutionary era resulted in the widespread adoption of a military culture that favored the regular armies of empires and nation-states and discouraged cross-border alliances between regular forces and enslaved men and women, refugees from slavery, or indigenous Americans. Postrevolutionary international arrangements promoted political stability while reinforcing the power of colonists and their descendants. The enslaved continued to resist and escape from slavery and indigenous Americans continued to fight colonization, but when they resorted to arms their struggles were generally confined within territorial boundaries. In most of the Western Hemisphere the abolition of slavery came by legislation, official proclamation, or constitutional amendment, separately within each internationally recognized jurisdiction. Similarly, with fewer military allies indigenous Americans were less able to defend themselves in battle, and eventually they saw their status and future deliberated and decided upon in the law courts and legislatures of various American empires, colonies, and nation-states.

Revolutionaries in the eighteenth century had challenged the prevailing norms of Atlantic warfare. An array of groups including indigenous Americans, black and white abolitionists, and some French revolutionaries objected to alliance networks that seemed to force societies into war against their interests. Many also objected to the practice of fighting for profit. Pirates, plunderers, and mercenaries faced rebuke, alongside African slave traders. The new revolutionary-era ethic of warfare undermined the legitimacy of the transatlantic slave trade.

According to some eighteenth-century commentators, the apparent irrationality, cruelty, and injustice of the prevailing pattern of warfare gave all the people affected by it a common cause. The Munsee prophet Papunhank suggested that instead of fighting everyone should "look upon all mankind as one and so become as one family."[8] But the events of the Revolutionary era divided people, often hardening animosities and reinforcing prejudices that dated back to the fifteenth century. With the abolition of the transatlantic slave trade, the European empires and American nation-states severed long-standing relationships that slavers had maintained with African partners. As slavery was gradually outlawed in the Americas, the survival of the practice in Africa made it easier for European and American commentators to describe the exploitation of captives as a sign of deficiencies in the African character. Writing in 1839, British abolitionist Thomas Fowell Buxton argued that the expansion of "legitimate commerce" between Europeans and Africans would introduce "civilization, peace, and Christianity to the unenlightened, warlike, heathen tribes who now so fearfully prey on each other."[9] Buxton was aware of the role Europeans had played for centuries encouraging the slave trade, but he had served in the British parliament during the debates over the abolition of slavery in the British empire, and he believed that the British, in particular, had taken important strides toward improving their policies and behavior. For the next century, reformers repeatedly insisted that societies that maintained slavery were primitive, ignorant, anarchic, and brutal. That argument was cited to promote colonial rule in Africa.[10]

In the Andes during wars of the early 1780s and in Saint Domingue in the 1790s and early nineteenth century, revolutionary forces brought terror to many communities. This was not unusual for the era. Revolutionary struggles across the Americas and in Europe occasioned communal violence. Volunteer forces were often poorly disciplined. Imbued with a sense of ideological purpose and fearing retribution if they failed to act, they plundered and humiliated their opponents, sometimes attacking entire communities, committing massacres and forcing men, women and children to flee. But within the European empires and among the citizens of the newly formed American republics, such atrocities had a special resonance if the alleged perpetrators rallied under indigenous American or black leadership.

The revolutionary fighters in the Andes and on Saint Domingue hoped to restructure their societies. Their aims were revolutionary, but white commentators, remembering stories that had circulated around the Atlantic since the fifteenth century, argued that their military campaigns were not innovative at all. They claimed that the followers of Tupac Amaru and the warriors of the Haitian Revolution were engaged in the same kind of horrific violence that had long plagued the Atlantic world. Similar arguments were made against Tecumseh and his followers between 1809 and 1814. Though Tecumseh intended to lead a revolution, he was presented within the United States as a primitive man heading a regressive, hostile force. For many citizens of the new republic, the revolutionary impulse to break the old pattern of Atlantic warfare required indigenous

Americans and other alleged savages to give up their military autonomy and serve the national government or disarm.

The widespread adoption of a new military culture in the late eighteenth century did not erase memories of earlier violence, but history was simplified to meet the needs, express the fears, and support the reform agendas of the colonists, citizens, and supporters of the resilient European empires and the nineteenth-century American nation-states. Reformers and imperialists suggested that Europeans had improved themselves during the early modern period while others had not, and that suspect racial groups had always been the instigators of the worst forms of violence. This distorted vision of the past obscured fundamental truths about the early modern pattern of Atlantic warfare.

Violent military recruitment, shifts in alliances and interests, and accidents of war mixed the warriors, sailors, and soldiers of the early modern Atlantic world. During his career a European sailor might enter combat under a succession of different flags, and fight alongside men abducted from Africa and the Americas. Africans and indigenous Americans served on European naval and private vessels, and some fought in European and colonial armies. Men who escaped from slavery, like Juan Jolofo on the isthmus of Panama and Cudjoe on Jamaica, reached agreements with colonial authorities and secured their freedom by joining slave patrols. Autonomous indigenous American groups similarly fought in alliances defending and securing the interests of colonial slaveholders. When Europeans established colonies in the Americas or did business in Africa, they almost always needed assistance from African or indigenous American military leaders, and the success of their ventures depended on cross-cultural cooperation. Colonies needed alliances in order to survive, and many of the most profitable European outposts including the trading posts on the western coast of Africa and the sugar plantations in the Caribbean depended on a continuous stream of war captives.

Christian Europeans exempted themselves from slavery. Some indigenous American and African societies were devastated while capital and resources accumulated in Europe. The violence of the early modern era laid the foundations for the racial hierarchy that was erected in the nineteenth century. But from the fifteenth century to the Age of Revolution, warfare did not divide the peoples of the Atlantic world simply along clear, consistent lines. Often instead, in horrible ways, it brought them together.

NOTES

Introduction

1. Donald H. Holly Jr., *History in the Making: The Archaeology of the Eastern Subarctic* (Lanham, MD: Rowman & Littlefield, 2013), 43; Sharla Chittick, "Pride and Prejudices, Practices and Perceptions: A Comparative Case Stidy in North Atlantic Environmental History" (PhD diss., University of Stirling, 2011), 51–56.
2. Bernard Bailyn, *Atlantic History: Concept and Contours* (Cambridge, MA: Harvard University Press, 2005).
3. See Karen Ordahl Kupperman, *The Atlantic in World History* (New York: Oxford University Press, 2012) and John K. Thornton, *A Cultural History of the Atlantic World* (Cambridge: Cambridge University Press, 2011); Thomas Benjamin, *The Atlantic World: Europeans, Africans, and Their Shared History, 1400–1900* (Cambridge: Cambridge University Press, 2009); Douglas Egerton, Alison Games, Jane Landers, Kris Lane, and Donald Wright, *The Atlantic World: A History, 1400–1888* (Malden, MA: Wiley-Blackwell, 2007); Nicholas Canny and Philip Morgan, eds., *The Oxford Handbook of the Atlantic World, 1450–1850* (Oxford: Oxford University Press, 2011); Joseph C. Miller, ed., *The Princeton Companion to Atlantic History* (Princeton, NJ: Princeton University Press, 2015); David Armitage and Michael J. Braddick, eds., *The British Atlantic World, 1500–1800* (New York: Palgrave Macmillan, 2009).
4. H. Thomas Rossby and Peter Miller, "Ocean Eddies in the 1539 Carta Marina by Olaus Magnus," *Oceanography* 16 (2003): 77–88.
5. Ari Thorgillson, *Book of the Icelanders*, quoted in Kirsten A. Seaver, "'Pygmies of the Far North,'" *Journal of World History* 19 (2008): 63–87, 70; William W. Fitzhugh, "Puffins, Ringed Pins and Runestones: The Viking Passage to America," in *Vikings: The North Atlantic Saga*, ed. William W. Fitzhugh and Elisabeth I. Ward (Washington, DC: Smithsonian Institution Press, 2000), 11–25, 19–20; Andrew J. Dugmore, Christian Keller, and Thomas H. McGovern, "Norse Greenland Settlement: Reflections on Climate Change, Trade, and the Contrasting Fates of Human Settlements in the North Atlantic Islands," *Arctic Anthropology* 44 (2007): 12–36, 17.
6. Dugmore et al., "Norse Greenland Settlement," 19; Hans Christian Gulløv, "The Nature of Contact between Native Greenlanders and Norse," *Journal of the North Atlantic* 1 (2008): 16–24; Patricia D. Sutherland, "The Norse and Native North Americans," in *Vikings*, ed. Fitzhugh and Ward, 238–47.
7. Hans Christian Gulløv, "Natives and Norse in Greenland," in *Vikings*, ed. Fitzhugh and Ward, 318–26, 322.
8. Kirsten Thisted, "On Narrative Expectations: Greenlandic Oral Traditions about the Cultural Encounter between Inuit and Norsemen," *Scandinavian Studies* 73 (2001): 253–96, 288–89; Finn Gad, *The History of Greenland: Earliest Times to 1700*, vol. 1 (Montreal: McGill-Queen's University Press, 2014), 158–60.
9. Thisted, "On Narrative Expectations."

10. M. A. P. Renouf, Michael A. Teal, and Trevor Bell, "In the Woods: The Cow Head Complex Occupation of the Gould Site, Port aux Choix," in *The Cultural Landscapes of Port aux Choix: Precontact Hunter Gatherers of Northwestern Newfoundland*, ed. M. A. P. Renouf (Boston: Springer, 2011), 251–69.

11. Birgitta Linderoth Wallace, "The Viking Settlement at L'Anse aux Meadows," in *Vikings*, ed. Fitzhugh and Ward, 208–16.

12. Keneva Kunz, trans., "Eirik the Red's Saga," *The Sagas of Icelanders: A Selection*, ed. Robert Kellogg (New York: Penguin, 2000), 653–74, 669–70.

13. Keneva Kunz, trans., "The Saga of the Greenlanders," in *Sagas of Icelanders*, ed. Kellogg, 636–52, 642–43.

14. Kunz, "Saga of the Greenlanders," 646–48.

15. Kunz, "Eirik the Red's Saga," 672.

16. Kunz, trans., "Eirik the Red's Saga," 667.

17. Janel M. Fontaine, "Early Medieval Slave-trading in the Archaeological Record: Comparative Methodologies," *Early Medieval Europe* 25 (2017): 466–88; Ruth Mazo Karras, *Slavery and Society in Medieval Scandinavia* (New Haven, CT: Yale University Press, 1988), 47–49.

18. See Neil S. Price, "'Laid Waste, Plundered and Burned': Vikings in Frankia," in *Vikings*, ed. Fitzhugh and Ward, 116–26.

19. Kunz, trans., "Saga of the Greenlanders," 636–38.

20. Kunz, trans., "Eirik the Red's Saga," 671.

21. Kunz, trans., "Eirik the Red's Saga," 671.

22. Kunz, trans., "Saga of the Greenlanders," 648.

Chapter 1

1. Richard T. Callaghan, "Archaeological Views of Caribbean Seafaring," in *The Oxford Handbook of Caribbean Archaeology*, ed. William F. Keegan, Corinne L. Hofman, and Reniel Rodríguez Ramos (Oxford: Oxford University Press, 2013), 283–95.

2. Brian M. Fagan, *Ancient North America: The Archaeology of a Continent* (London: Thames and Hudson, 1995), 182–84, 198, 202–12.

3. Jack Forbes, *Africans and Native Americans: The Language of Race and the Evolution of Red-Black Peoples*, 2d ed. (Urbana: University of Illinois Press, 1993), 7–8.

4. Thornton, *Cultural History of the Atlantic World*, 19.

5. Reuben Gold Thwaites, ed., *The Jesuit Relations and Allied Documents*, vol. 5 (Cleveland: Burrows Brothers, 1908), 105–09, 117–19.

6. Evan Haefeli, "On First Contact and Apotheosis: Manitou and Men in North America," *Ethnohistory* 54 (2007): 407–43; Andrew Lipman, *The Saltwater Frontier: Indians and the Contest for the American Coast* (New Haven, CT: Yale University Press, 2015), 51–53.

7. John L. Nickalls, ed., *The Journal of George Fox* (Cambridge: Cambridge University Press, 1952), 624.

8. G. H. Loskiel, *History of the Mission of the United Brethren Among the Indians in North America* trans. G. I. La Trobe (London, 1794), Part I, pp. 123–24.

9. Silas T. Rand, *Legends of the Micmacs* (New York, 1894), 225.

10. See, for example, Ottaba Cugoano, *Thoughts and Sentiments on the Evil of Slavery* (London, 1787), 9–10; Mahommah Gardo Baquaqua and Samuel Moore, *Biography of Mahommah G. Baquaqua* (Detroit, 1854), 41.

11. Petition from Belinda, dated Boston, February 1782, in Vincent Carretta, ed., *Unchained Voices: An Anthology of Black Authors in the English-Speaking World of the 18th Century* (Lexington: University of Kentucky Press, 1996), 142–43.

12. *A Narrative of the Life of James Albert Ukawsaw Gronniosaw* (2d. ed., n.d.), 9.

13. Kwasi Konadu, *The Akan Diaspora in the Americas* (New York: Oxford University Press, 2010), 58.

14. N. A. M. Rodger, *The Safeguard of the Sea: A Naval History of Britain, Volume One, 660–1649* (London: Harper Collins, 1997), 32–35.

15. See Alex Roland, "Secrecy, Technology and War: Greek Fire and the Defense of Byzantium, 678–1204," *Technology and Culture* 33 (1992): 655–79.

16. Felipe Fernández-Armesto, "Naval Warfare after the Viking Age, 1100–1500," in *Medieval Warfare: A History*, ed. Maurice Keen (Oxford: Oxford University Press, 1999), 23–252, 236.

17. Rodger, *Safeguard of the Sea*, 98–99. On the relationships between Sluys and Bruges see James Murray, *Bruges, Cradle of Capitalism, 1280–1390* (Cambridge: Cambridge University Press, 2005), 28–38.

18. John E. Dotson, "Ship Types and Fleet Composition at Genoa and Venice in the Early Thirteenth Century," in *Logistics of Warfare in the Age of the Crusades*, ed. John H. Pryor (Aldershot: Ashgate, 2006), 63–75; Fernández-Armesto, "Naval Warfare after the Viking Age," 236.

19. See Samuel Eliot Morison, *Admiral of the Ocean Sea: A Life of Christopher Columbus* (Boston: Little, Brown, 1942), 112–31.

20. John F. Guilmartin Jr., "The Earliest Shipboard Gunpowder Ordnance: An Analysis of its Technical Parameters and Tactical Capabilities," *Journal of Military History* 71 (2007): 649–69.

21. Louis Sicking, "Naval Warfare in Europe, 1330–1680," in *European Warfare, 1350–1750*, ed. Frank Tallett and D. B. J. Trim (Cambridge: Cambridge Univeristy Press, 2010), 236–63, 244–47.

22. Rodger, *Safeguard of the Sea*, 170.

23. Rodger, *Safeguard of the Sea*, 251.

24. Fernández-Armesto, *The Spanish Armada: The Experience of War in 1588* (Oxford: Oxford University Press, 1988), 128–29.

25. Fernández-Armesto, "Naval Warfare after the Viking Age," 247–51.

26. Ian Friel, *Maritime History of Britain and Ireland* (London: British Museum Press, 2003), 57. 59, 64–65.

27. Richard W. Unger, "Warships and Cargo Ships in Medieval Europe," *Technology and Culture* 22 (1981): 233–52.

28. Brad Loewen and Vincent Delmas, "The Basques in the Gulf of St. Lawrence and Adjacent Shores," *Canadian Journal of Archaeology* 36 (2012): 213–66, 213–21.

29. Willis Stevens, Daniel LaRoche, Douglas Bryce, and R. James Ringer, "Evidence of Shipboard Activities," in *The Underwater Archaeology of Red Bay: Basque Shipbuilding and Whaling in the 16th Century*, 5 vols., ed. Robert Grenier, Marc-André Bernier, and Willis Stevens (Ottawa: Parks Canada, 2007), 4:123–68, 156–62.

30. Loewen and Delmas, "The Basques in the Gulf of St. Lawrence and Adjacent Shores," 224.

31. Loewen and Delmas, "Basques in the Gulf of St. Lawrence," 219. See also Carla Rahn Phillips, *Six Galleons for the King of Spain: Imperial Defense in the Early Seventeenth Century* (Baltimore: Johns Hopkins University Press, 1986), 20–24.

32. Brad Loewen, "Conclusion: The Archaeology of a Ship," in *Underwater Archaeology of Red Bay*, ed. Grenier, Bernier, and Stevens, 315–16.

33. Richard Barker, Brad Loewen, and Christopher Dobbs, "Hull Design of the *Mary Rose*," in *Mary Rose, Your Noblest Shippe: Anatomy of a Tudor Warship*, ed. Peter Marsden (Portsmouth: Mary Rose Trust, 2009), 35–65, 43–47.

34. Margaret Ellen Newell, "The Birth of New England in the Atlantic Economy: From the Beginning to 1770," in *Engines of Enterprise: An Economic History of New England*, ed. Peter Temin (Cambridge, MA: Harvard University Press, 2000), 11–68, 45.

35. On the general question of timber supply see Paul Warde, "Fear of Wood Shortage and the Reality of Woodland in Europe, c.1450–1850," *History Workshop Journal* 62 (2006): 29–57, 40–41.

36. John E. Dotson, "Ship Types and Fleet Composition at Genoa and Venice," 75; Rodger, *Safeguard of the Sea*, 25.

37. Michel Mollat du Jourdin, *Europe and the Sea*, trans. Teresa Lavender Fagan (Oxford: Blackwell, 1993), 74.

38. See Lauren Benton, *A Search for Sovereignty: Law and Geography in European Empires, 1400–1900* (Cambridge: Cambridge University Press, 2010), 43–45.

39. A. W. Lawrence, *Trade Castles and Forts of West Africa* (London: Jonathan Cape, 1963). See also George F. Brooks, *Eurafricans in Western Africa* (Athens: Ohio University Press, 2003).

40. Paul Gilroy, *The Black Atlantic: Modernity and Double Consciousness* (Cambridge, MA: Harvard University Press, 1993), 4.

41. Ulrich Schmidt, *The Conquest of the River Plate* trans. Luis L. Domingez (London: Hakluyt Society, 1896), 9.

42. Benton, *Search for Sovereignty*, chapter 2.

43. Philip P. Boucher, *France and the American Tropics to 1700: Tropics of Discontent?* (Baltimore: Johns Hopkins University Press, 2008), 41–42.

44. David Wheat, "Mediterranean Slavery, New World Transformations: Galley Slaves in the Spanish Caribbean, 1578–1635," *Slavery and Abolition* 31 (2010): 327–44.

45. Phillips, *Six Galleons*, 9–18.

46. C. R. Boxer, *The Portuguese Seaborne Empire, 1415–1825* (Exeter: Carcanet, 1991), 205–27; Lawrence, *Trade Castles and Forts*, 30–36; Jan Glete, *War and the State in Early Modern Europe: Spain, the Dutch Republic and Sweden as Fiscal-Military States* (London: Routledge, 2002), 86; Armando da Silva Saturnino Monteiro, "The Decline and Fall of Portuguese Seapower, 1583–1663," *Journal of Military History* 65 (2001): 9–20.

47. Sicking, "Naval Warfare in Europe, 1330–1680," 239–40.

48. Phillips, *Six Galleons*, 20.

49. Kenneth R. Andrews, *Elizabethan Privateering: English Privateering during the Spanish War, 1585–1603* (Cambridge: Cambridge University Press, 1964); Kenneth R. Andrews, *The Spanish Caribbean: Trade and Plunder, 1530–1630* (New Haven, CT: Yale University Press, 1978), 148–51.

50. On the organization of the Dutch Navy see Marjolein 't Hart, *The Dutch Wars of Independence: Warfare and Commerce in the Netherlands, 1570–1680* (New York: Routledge, 2014), 126–47.

51. Jaap R. Bruijn, *The Dutch Navy of the Seventeenth and Eighteenth Centuries* (Columbia: University of South Carolina Press, 1993), 17–28.

52. Monteiro, "The Decline and Fall of Portuguese Seapower;" Glete, *War and the State*, 110–15, 162–71.

53. Richard W. Unger, "Warships and Cargo Ships in Medieval Europe;" Phillips, *Six Galleons*, 23–24.

54. Jonathan I. Israel, *Dutch Primacy in World Trade, 1585–1740* (Oxford: Oxford University Press, 1989).

55. Glete, *War and the State*.

56. David Goodman, *Spanish Naval Power, 1589–1665: Reconstruction and Defeat* (Cambridge: Cambridge University Press, 1996); Monteiro, "The Decline and Fall of Portuguese Seapower."

57. Bruijn, *Dutch Navy*, 69.

58. N. A. M. Rodger, *The Command of the Ocean: A Naval History of Britain, 1649–1815* (London: Penguin, 2004), 217.

59. James Pritchard, *In Search of Empire: The French in the Americas, 1670–1730* (Cambridge: Cambridge University Press, 2004), 267–300; Boucher, *France and the American Tropics*, 194–201.

60. N. A. M. Rodger, "From the 'Military Revolution' to the 'Fiscal-Naval State'," *Journal for Maritime Research* 13 (2011): 119–28. See also Daniel A. Baugh, "Great Britain's 'Blue Water' Policy, 1689–1815," *International History Review* 10 (1988): 33–58.

61. J. S. Bromley, *Corsairs and Navies, 1660–1760* (London: Hambledon Press, 1987); Carl E. Swanson, *Predators and Prizes: American Privateering and Imperial Warfare, 1739–1748* (Columbia: University of South Carolina Press, 1991).

62. Rodger, *Command of the Ocean*, 218.

63. James Pritchard, "From Shipwright to Naval Constructor: The Professionalization of 18th-Century French Naval Shipbuilders," *Technology and Culture* 28 (1987): 1–25.

64. Rodger, *Command of the Ocean*, 413.

65. William M. Fowler Jr., *Rebels Under Sail: The American Navy during the Revolution* (New York: Scribner's, 1976); Jonathan R. Dull, *The French Navy and American Independence* (Princeton, NJ: Princeton University Press, 1975).

66. See generally Troy Bickham, *The Weight of Vengeance: The United States, the British Empire, and the War of 1812* (New York: Oxford University Press, 2012).

67. G. R. Crone, ed., *The Voyages of Cadamosto* (London: Hakluyt Society, 1937), 51.

68. Christopher Columbus to Luis de Santángel, February 15, 1493, in *Wild Majesty: Encounters with Caribs from Columbus to the Present Day, an Anthology*, ed. Peter Hulme and Neil L. Whitehead (Oxford: Clarendon Press, 1992), 13.

69. Diego Álvarez Chanca, quoted in *Wild Majesty*, ed. Hulme and Whitehead, 32, 33.

70. Forbes, *Africans and Native Americans*, 11.

71. C. Harvey Gardiner, "The First Shipping Constructed in New Spain," *The Americas* 10 (1954): 409–19.

72. Woodrow Borah, *Early Colonial Trade and Navigation between Mexico and Peru* (Berkeley: University of California Press, 1954), 2, 5–6.

73. Joseph A. Goldenberg, *Shipbuilding in Colonial America* (Charlottesville: University Press of Virginia, 1976), 63.

74. Boxer, *Portuguese Seaborne Empire*, 210–11.

75. Toni L. Carrell and Donald H. Keith, "Replicating a Ship of Discovery: *Santa Clara*, a Sixteenth-Century Caravel," *International Journal of Nautical Archaeology* 21 (1992): 281–94.

76. Eric Robert Taylor, *If We Must Die: Shipboard Insurrections in the Era of the Atlantic Slave Trade* (Baton Rouge: Louisiana State University Press, 2006), 119–138.

77. Matthew R. Bahar, *Storm of the Sea: Indians and Empires in the Atlantic's Age of Sail* (New York: Oxford University Press, 2019), 89–97.

Chapter 2

1. Pablo E. Pérez-Mallaína, *Spain's Men of the Sea: Daily Life on the Indies Fleets in the Sixteenth Century*, trans. Carla Rahn Phillips (Baltimore: Johns Hopkins University Press, 1998), 66.

2. Diego Garcia de Palacio, quoted in Pérez-Mallaína, *Spain's Men of the Sea*, 65.

3. Pérez-Mallaína, *Spain's Men of the Sea*, 26.

4. Bruijn, *Dutch Navy*, 200–01.

5. James Pritchard, *Louis XV's Navy, 1748–1762: A Study of Organization and Administration* (Montreal: McGill-Queen's University Press, 1987), 82.

6. Bruijn, *Dutch Navy*, 202.

7. Testimony dated August 21, 1593, quoted in Pérez-Mallaína, *Spain's Men of the Sea*, 28.

8. Pérez-Mallaína, *Spain's Men of the Sea*, 27–28.

9. Pritchard, *Louis XV's Navy*, 75.

10. Edward Barlow, *Barlow's Journal* (London: Hurst and Blackett, 1934), vol. 1, p. 33.

11. Barnaby Slush, *The Navy Royal, or a Sea-cook Turned Projector* (London, 1709), 3.

12. Pérez-Mallaína, *Spain's Men of the Sea*, 50.

13. N. A. M. Rodger, *The Wooden World: An Anatomy of the Georgian Navy* (London: Collins, 1986), 348–51; Pritchard, *Louis XV's Navy*, 85.

14. Pérez-Mallaína, *Spain's Men of the Sea*, 76–77.

15. Rodger, *Wooden World*, 39.

16. Slush, *Navy Royal*, 9.

17. David Erskine, ed., *Augustus Hervey's Journal* (London: Chatham Publishing, 2002), 176.

18. Rodger, *Wooden World*, 214.

19. Bruijn, *Dutch Navy*, 204.

20. Pritchard, *Louis XV's Navy*, 87.

21. Rodger, *Wooden World*, 237–44. On the Revolutionary era, see Niklas Frykman, "Connections between Mutinies in European Navies," *International Review of Social History* 58 (2013): 87–107.

22. Pritchard, *Louis XV's Navy*, 87.

23. Bruijn, *Dutch Navy*, 206.

24. Fernández-Armesto, *Spanish Armada*, 52–54.

25. Luc François Nau quoted in James Pritchard, *Anatomy of a Naval Disaster: The 1746 French Naval Expedition to North America* (Montreal: McGill-Queen's University Press, 1995), 99.

26. Rodger, *Wooden World*, 61.

27. Pérez-Mallaína, *Spain's Men of the Sea*, 165.

28. Rodger, *Wooden World*, 75–78.

29. Phillips, *Six Galleons*, 93–103; Bruijn, *Dutch Navy*, 50, 116–19; Glete, *War and the State*, 133, 166; Pritchard, *Louis XV's Navy, 1748–1762*, 179–83; Daniel A. Baugh, *British Naval Administration in the Age of Walpole* (Princeton, NJ: Princeton University Press, 1965), 386–451.

30. Baugh, *British Naval Administration*, 387.

31. Bruijn, *Dutch Navy*, 117, 119.

32. Pritchard, *Louis XV's Navy*, 179; Pritchard, *Anatomy of a Naval Disaster*.

33. Rodger, *Wooden World*, 71.

34. Baugh, *British Naval Administration*, 375.

35. Phillips, *Six Galleons*, 173.

36. Pérez-Mallaína, *Spain's Men of the Sea*, 30–33; Bruijn, *Dutch Navy*, 40–53, 111–28; Rodger, *Wooden World*, 129, 252–302. The French were less successful than others in making a career as a naval officer more attractive than private service. See Pritchard, *Louis XV's Navy*, 55–70.

37. Rodger, *Wooden World*, 87–98; Bruijn, *Dutch Navy*, 57, 138.

38. Bruijn, *Dutch Navy*, 198.

39. E. H. W. Meyerstein, ed., *Adventures by Sea of Edward Coxere* (Oxford: Clarendon Press, 1945), 4–5.

40. Meyerstein, ed., *Adventures by Sea of Edward Coxere*, 5–19.

41. Guy Chet, *The Ocean is a Wilderness: Atlantic Piracy and the Limits of State Authority, 1688–1856* (Amherst: University of Massachusetts Press, 2014).

42. John Churchman, *Account of the Gospel Labours and Christian Experiences of a Faithful Minister of Christ, John Churchman* (Philadelphia, 1779), 204–06.

43. Phillips, *Six Galleons*, 20.

44. "Arguments in Favour of Establishing Wednesday as an Additional Fish Day, February 1563," in *Tudor Economic Documents*, 3 vols., ed R. H. Tawney and Eileen Power (London, 1924), 104–10.

45. Pritchard, *Louis XV's Navy*, 75, 209.

46. Rodger, *Wooden World*, 124–26.

47. Nicholas Rogers, *The Press Gang: Naval Impressment and its Opponents in Georgian Britain* (New York: Continuum, 2007), 96.

48. Bruijn, *Dutch Navy*, 49–50, 135; Rodger, *Wooden World*, 129.

49. Bruijn, *Dutch Navy*, 129.

50. Pérez-Mallaína, *Spain's Men of the Sea*, 200.

51. Bruijn, *Dutch Navy*, 130.

52. Kevin Costello, "Habeas Corpus and Naval and Military Impressment, 1756–1816," *Journal of Legal History* 29 (2008): 215–51, 216; Rodger, *Wooden World*, 150.

53. Rodger, *Wooden World*, 168.

54. Rogers, *Press Gang*, 83.

55. Barlow, *Barlow's Journal*, vol. 1, p. 146.

56. Edward Boscawen, quoted in Rodger, *Wooden World*, 104.

57. John Lax and William Pencak, "The Knowles Riot and the Crisis of the 1740's in Massachusetts," *Perspectives in American History* 10 (1976): 163–216; see also Denver Brunsman, "The Knowles Atlantic Impressment Riots of the 1740s," *Early American Studies* 5 (2007): 324–66.

58. *London Evening Post*, July 31, 1759.

59. Rodger, *The Wooden World*, 175–76.

60. Barlow, *Barlow's Journal*, vol. 1, p. 146.

61. Benton, *Search for Sovereignty*, 51–52, n.26.

62. Pérez-Mallaína, *Spain's Men of the Sea*, 41.

63. David Wheat, *Atlantic Africa and the Spanish Caribbean, 1570–1640* (Chapel Hill: University of North Carolina Press, 2016), 231.

64. Randy J. Sparks, *Where the Negroes are Masters: An African Port in the Era of the Slave Trade* (Cambridge, MA: Harvard University Press, 2014), 190.

65. Rogers, *Press Gang*, 92.

66. Bruijn, *Dutch Navy*, 55.

67. Bruijn, *Dutch Navy*, 133, 201.

68. Pérez-Mallaína, *Spain's Men of the Sea*, 56.

69. Charles M. Hough, ed., *Reports of Cases in the Vice Admiralty of the Province of New York* (New Haven, CT: Yale University Press, 1925), 29–31; *Pennsylvania Journal*, May 16 and May 30, 1745; *Boston Evening Post*, May 20, 1745; *American Weekly Mercury*, May 23, 1745.

70. Daniel Horsmanden, *A Journal of the Proceedings in the Detection of the Conspiracy formed by some White People, in Conjunction with Negro and other Slaves for Burning the City of New York* (New York, 1744), 78. See Jill Lepore, *New York Burning: Liberty, Slavery, and Conspiracy in Eighteenth-Century Manhattan* (New York: Vintage, 2005); Peter Linebaugh and Marcus Rediker, *The Many-Headed Hydra: Sailors, Slaves, Commoner, and the Hidden History of the Revolutionary Atlantic* (Boston: Beacon Press, 2000), 174–210.

71. Olaudah Equiano, *The Interesting Narrative of the Life of Olaudah Equiano* (London, 1789), 171–79.

72. Gisli Palsson, *The Man Who Stole Himself: The Slave Odyssey of Hans Jonathan* (Chicago: University of Chicago Press, 2016), 81.

73. Palsson, *Man who Stole Himself*, 75–114.

74. Pritchard, *Louis XV's Navy*, 86; Bruijn, *Dutch Navy*, 203–04; Rodger, *Wooden World*, 201–02.

75. Barlow, *Barlow's Journal*, vol. 1, 115.

76. Nicholas Rogers, *Mayhem: Postwar Crime and Violence in Britain, 1748–1753* (New Haven, CT: Yale University Press, 2013), 36–37.

77. Pérez-Mallaína, *Spain's Men of the Sea*, 16.

78. Benjamin L. Carp, *Rebels Rising: Cities and the American Revolution* (New York: Oxford University Press, 2007), 27.

79. Pérez-Mallaína, *Spain's Men of the Sea*, 25.

80. Pérez-Mallaína, *Spain's Men of the Sea*, 8; Rogers, *Mayhem*, 38–39.

81. Chet, *Ocean is a Wilderness*, 66–91.

82. Pérez-Mallaína, *Spain's Men of the Sea*, 169.

83. Rogers, *Mayhem*, 41–42.

84. Pérez-Mallaína, *Spain's Men of the Sea*, 217.

85. Edward Ward, *The Wooden World Dissected* (London, 1707), 100; see Pérez-Mallaína, *Spain's Men of the Sea*, 169; Rodger, *Wooden World*, 207–09.

86. Barlow, *Barlow's Journal*, vol. 1, p. 31.

87. Edward Barlow, Journal, JOD/4/210 and JOD/4/213, National Maritime Museum. For more on these journal entries see Maev Kennedy, "Sailor's Rape Confession Uncovered in Seventeenth-Century Journal," *The Guardian*, September 18, 2018.

88. Clare A. Lyons, *Sex among the Rabble: An Intimate History of Gender and Power in the Age of Revolution, Philadelphia, 1730–1830* (Chapel Hill: University of North Carolina Press, 2006), 55.

89. Rodger, *Wooden World*, 80.

90. Ward, *Wooden World Dissected*, 96.

91. B. R. Burg, *Boys at Sea: Sodomy, Indecency, and Courts Martial in Nelson's Navy* (New York: Palgrave, 2007), 42–43.

92. See for example Pérez-Mallaína, *Spain's Men of the Sea*, 171–72.

93. Pérez-Mallaína, *Spain's Men of the Sea*, 217.

94. For Hans Staden's full story see Eve M. Duffy and Alida C. Metcalf, *The Return of Hans Staden: A Go-Between in the Atlantic World* (Baltimore: Johns Hopkins University Press, 2013), 12–76.

95. Hans Staden, *The Captivity of Hans Stade of Hesse*, Albert Tootal, trans. (London: Hakluyt Society, 1874), 73.

96. Staden, *Captivity of Hans Stade*, 13.

97. See H. E. Martel, "Hans Staden's Captive Soul: Identity, Imperialism, and Rumors of Cannibalism in Sixteenth-Century Brazil," *Journal of World History* 17 (2006): 51–69; Duffy and Metcalf, *Return of Hans Staden*, 77–102.

98. Arne Bialuschewski, "Slaves of the Buccaneers: Mayas in Captivity in the Second Half of the Seventeenth Century," *Ethnohistory* 64 (2017): 41–63.

99. Bialuschewski, "Slaves of the Buccaneers," 45.

100. Pérez-Mallaína, *Spain's Men of the Sea*, 74. A registry in the US in the 1790s generated even more dramatic results. See Simon Newman, "Reading the Bodies of Early American Seafarers," *William and Mary Quarterly* 55 (1998): 59–82, 67.
101. Pritchard, *Anatomy of a Naval Disaster*.
102. Pritchard, *Louis XV's Navy*, 83–84.
103. Stephen F. Gradish, *The Manning of the British Navy during the Seven Years' War* (London: Royal Historical Society, 1980), 212.
104. Pérez-Mallaína, *Spain's Men of the Sea*, 242. For a discussion of sailor religiosity in a later, Anglo-American context see Christopher P. Magra, "Faith at Sea: Exploring Maritime Religiosity in the Eighteenth Century," *International Journal of Maritime History* 19 (2007): 87–106.
105. For the dominant imperial interpretation of the workings of providence see Jorge Cañizares-Esguerra, *Puritan Conquistadors: Iberianizing the Atlantic, 1550–1700* (Stanford, CA: Stanford University Press, 2006).
106. See Steve Mentz, "God's Storms: Shipwreck and the Meanings of Ocean in Early Modern England and America," in *Shipwreck in Art and Literature: Images and Interpretations from Antiquity to the Present Day*, ed. Carl Thompson (New York: Routledge, 2013), 77–91.

Chapter 3

1. J. Franklin Jameson, *Narratives of New Netherland, 1609–1664* (New York: Scribner's, 1909), 19.
2. Jameson, *Narratives of New Netherland*, 26.
3. J. Thornton, *Africa and Africans in the Making of the Atlantic World, 1400–1800*, 2d ed. (Cambridge: Cambridge University Press, 1998), 37–38.
4. In *The Saltwater Frontier: Indians and the Contest for the American Coast* (New Haven, CT: Yale University Press, 2015), Andrew Lipman surveys several decades of conflict on the North American coast from New Jersey to Cape Cod in the seventeenth century, and he does not cite any instance in which indigenous American warriors, facing armed resistance, used canoes successfully to attack and seize a sailing vessel. For a possibly exceptional incident see [Alexander Oliver Exquemelin], *The History of the Bucaniers of America* (London, 1699), 54.
5. Pérez-Mallaína, *Spain's Men of the Sea*, 183.
6. Fernández-Armesto, *Spanish Armada*, 144–45.
7. Sicking, "Naval Warfare in Europe, 1330–1680," 254.
8. Pérez-Mallaína, *Spain's Men of the Sea*, 184–85.
9. See Daniel K. Benjamin and Anca Tifrea, "Learning by Dying: Combat Performance in the Age of Sail," *Journal of Economic History* 67 (2007): 968–1000.
10. Colin J. M. Martin, "Incendiary Weapons from the Spanish Armada Wreck *La Trinidad Valencera*, 1588," *International Journal of Nautical Archaeology* 23 (1994): 207–17.
11. Cotton Mather, *Decennium Luctuosum: An History of Remarkable Occurances in the Long War* (Boston, 1699), 94.
12. Jan Glete, *Warfare at Sea, 1500–1650: Maritime Conflicts and the Transformation of Europe* (London: Routledge, 2000), 195, n.26.
13. Thomas Lurting, *The Fighting Sailor turn'd Peaceable Christian* (London, 1710), 7–10.
14. B. McL. Ranft, ed., *The Vernon Papers* (London: Navy Records Society, 1958), 295–96.
15. Fernández-Armesto, *Spanish Armada*, 193.
16. Rodger, *Wooden World*, 56.
17. Equiano, *Interesting Narrative*, 148–50.
18. William Spavens, *The Narrative of William Spavens, Chatham Pensioner, Written by Himself* (Louth, 1796).
19. Rodger, *Wooden World*, 59–60.
20. Equiano, *Interesting Narrative*, 148–49.
21. Maarten Harpertszoon Tromp's account of his council, as told to Dom Francisco Manuel and translated by C. R. Boxer, in Boxer, *The Journal of Maarten Harpertszoon Tromp, 1639* (Cambridge: Cambridge University Press, 1930), 209.

22. John F. Guilmartin Jr., "The Military Revolution in Warfare at Sea during the Early Modern Era: Technological Origins, Operational Outcomes, and Strategic Consequences," *Journal for Maritime Research* 13 (2011): 129–37, 134; Rodger, *Command of the Ocean*, 217.

23. Michael A. Palmer, "'The Soul's Right Hand': Command and Control in the Age of Fighting Sail, 1652–1827," *Journal of Military History* 61 (1997): 679–705, 680.

24. See Robert Stradling, "Catastrophe and Recovery: The Defeat of Spain, 1639–43," *History* 64 (1979): 205–19; Stradling, *The Armada of Flanders: Spanish Maritime Policy and European War, 1568–1668* (Cambridge: Cambridge University Press, 1992), 106–10.

25. Horatio Nelson to Earl Spencer, November 6, 1799, in Nicholas Harris Nicolas, ed., *The Dispatches and Letters of Vice Admiral Lord Viscount Nelson*, vol. 4 (London, 1844), 90.

26. Alison Sandman, "Spanish Nautical Cartography in the Renaissance," in *The History of Cartography, Volume Three: Cartography in the European Renaissance*, ed. David Woodward (Chicago: University of Chicago Press, 2007), 1095–142.

27. See Dava Sobel, *Longitude: The True Story of a Lone Genius who Solved the Greatest Scientific Problem of his Time* (London: Fourth Estate, 1996).

28. Olivier Chaline, "Strategy Seen from the Quarterdeck in the Eighteenth-Century French Navy," in *Strategy and the Sea: Essays in Honour of John B. Hattendorf*, ed. N. A. M. Rodger, J. Ross Dancy, Benjamin Darnell, and Evan Wilson (Suffolk: Boydell and Brewer, 2016), 19–27, 23.

29. Wim Klooster, *The Dutch Moment: War, Trade and Settlement in the Seventeenth Century Atlantic World* (Ithaca, NY: Cornell University Press, 2016), 43.

30. Rodger, *Command of the Ocean*, 76–77.

31. Jakob Seerup, "Danish and Swedish Flag disputes with the British in the Channel," in *Strategy and the Sea*, ed. Rodger et al., 28–36, 34.

32. Erskine, ed., *Augustus Hervey's Journal*, 46–47.

33. Alonso de Palencia, *Cuarta dédada de Alonso de Palencia* (excerpts), trans. by P. E. H. Hair, in Hair, *The Founding of the Castelo de Sãa Jorge da Mina: An Analysis of the Sources* (Madison: University of Wisconsin African Studies Program, 1994), 118–25, 123–24.

34. Harry Kelsey, *Sir Francis Drake: The Queen's Pirate* (New Haven, CT: Yale University Press, 1998), 95.

35. Olive Anderson, "The Establishment of British Supremacy at Sea and the Exchange of Naval Prisoners of War, 1689–1783," *English Historical Review* 75 (1960): 77–89.

36. Pritchard, *Louis XV's Navy*, 81.

37. Anderson, "Establishment of British Supremacy at Sea," 77.

38. Renaud Morieux, "Diplomacy from Below and Belonging: Fishermen and Cross-Channel Relations in the Eighteenth Century," *Past and Present* (2009): 83–125.

39. Anderson, "Establishment of British Supremacy at Sea," 81.

40. Rodger, *Wooden World*, 160.

41. William Dampier, *A New Voyage Round the World* (London, 1702), 1:26, 44–45.

42. Benton, *Search for Sovereignty*, 112–20.

43. *The Trials of Five Persons for Piracy, Felony, and Robbery* (Boston, 1726), 8.

44. Marcus Rediker, *Villains of All Nations: Atlantic Pirates in the Golden Age* (London: Verso, 2012), 13–16.

45. *Trials of Five Persons*, 28.

46. *Trials of Five Persons*, 9, 22.

47. *Trials of Five Persons*, 9.

48. *Trials of Five Persons*, 11.

49. *Trials of Five Persons*, 24.

50. *Trials of Five Persons*, 14.

51. *Trials of Five Persons*, 9.

52. Peter Earle, *The Pirate Wars* (London: Metheun, 2003), 206; Rediker, *Villains of All Nations*, 163.

53. Chet, *Ocean is a Wilderness*.

54. See, for example, *The Tryals of Sixteen Persons for Piracy* (Boston, 1726); Marcus Rediker, *Villains of All Nations: Atlantic Pirates in the Golden Age* (London: Verso, 2004), 2–4.

55. *A Collection of Voyages and Travels, Some Now Printed from Original Manuscripts, others Now Published in English, in Six Volumes* (London, 1732), 5:546.
56. David Richardson, "Shipboard Revolts, African Authority, and the Atlantic Slave Trade," *William and Mary Quarterly* 58 (2001): 69–92, 74.
57. Cugoano, *Thoughts and Sentiments*, 10.
58. Richardson, "Shipboard Revolts," 74.
59. Taylor, *If We Must Die*, 75–76.
60. William Snelgrave, *A New Account of Some Parts of Guinea and the Slave Trade* (London, 1734), 186–91.
61. Richardson, "Shipboard Revolts," 72.

Chapter 4

1. David B. Quinn, *England and the Azores, 1581–1582: Three Letters* (Lisbon: Junta de Investigaçoes Cientificas de Ultramar, 1979), 207–08.
2. Alan James, "A French Armada? The Azores Campaigns, 1580–1583," *Historical Journal* 55 (2012): 1–20.
3. James, "A French Armada?," 5.
4. *Calendar of State Papers, Foreign, May-December 1582* (London, 1909), 345–46.
5. *Calendar of State Papers, Foreign, May-December 1582* (London, 1909), 346–47.
6. James, "A French Armada?," 17, n.69.
7. Fernández-Armesto, *Spanish Armada*, 135–39.
8. *Collection of Voyages and Travels*, 5:457.
9. *Collection of Voyages and Travels*, 5: 458.
10. *Collection of Voyages and Travels*, 5: 458.
11. *Collection of Voyages and Travels*, 5: 460.
12. Donald G. Shomette and Robert D. Haslach, *Raid on America: The Dutch Naval Campaign of 1672–1684* (Columbia: University of South Carolina Press, 1988), 80–82.
13. Wallace T. MacCaffrey, *Elizabeth I: War and Politics, 1588–1603* (Princeton, NJ: Princeton University Press, 1992), 117–18; Klooster, *Dutch Moment*, 26.
14. Klooster, *Dutch Moment*, 49.
15. Klooster, *Dutch Moment: War*, 49.
16. George Edmundson, "The Dutch Power in Brazil (Continued)," *English Historical Review* 14 (1899): 676–99, 686–87.
17. A. J. B. Johnston, *Endgame 1758: The Promise, the Glory, and the Despair of Louisbourg's Last Decade* (Lincoln: University of Nebraska Press, 2007), 184–272.
18. [Exquemelin], *History of the Bucaniers*, 59.
19. [Exquemelin], *History of the Bucaniers*, 60.
20. [Exquemelin], *History of the Bucaniers*, 60.
21. [Exquemelin], *History of the Bucaniers*, 57.
22. [Exquemelin], *History of the Bucaniers*, 57.
23. [Exquemelin], *History of the Bucaniers*, 60.
24. [Exquemelin], *History of the Bucaniers*, 67.
25. Johannes Postma, "Surinam and its Atlantic Connections, 1667–1795," in *Riches from Atlantic Commerce: Dutch Transatlantic Trade and Shipping, 1585–1817*, ed. Johannes Postman and Victor Enthoven (Leiden: Brill, 2003), 287–322, 299.
26. Victor Enthoven, "'That Abominable Nest of Pirates': St. Eustatius and the North Americans, 1680–1780," *Early American Studies* 10 (2012): 239–301, 270.
27. See, for example, A. J. O'Shaughnessey, *An Empire Divided: The American Revolution and the British Caribbean* (Philadelphia: University of Pennsylvania Press, 2000), 49–50.
28. Enthoven, "Abominable Nest," 276–82.
29. Mark Meuwese, *Brothers in Arms, Partners in Trade: Dutch-Indigenous Alliances in the Atlantic World, 1595–1674* (Leiden: Brill, 2012), 290–95.
30. Meuwese, *Brothers in Arms*, 296–301.
31. For the French position in this conflict, see Boucher, *France and the American Tropics*, 194–201.

32. Shomette and Haslach, *Raid on America*, 157.
33. Shomette and Haslach, *Raid on America*, 161.
34. Shomette and Haslach, *Raid on America*, 157–74.
35. Fred Anderson, *Crucible of War: The Seven Years' War and the Fate of Empire in British North America, 1754–1766* (New York: Knopf, 2000), 237, 257, 395.
36. Jonathan R. Dull, *The French Navy and the Seven Years' War* (Lincoln: University of Nebraska Press, 2005), 143.
37. Roger Sidney Marsters, "Approaches to Empire: Hydrographic Knowledge and British State Activity in Northeastern North America, 1711–1783," (PhD diss., Dalhousie University, 2012), 107–220.
38. See generally Phillip Alfred Buckner and John G. Reid, eds., *Revisiting 1759: The Conquest of Canada in Historical Perspective* (Toronto: University of Toronto Press, 2012).
39. Marshall Smelser, *The Campaign for the Sugar Islands, 1759* (Chapel Hill: University of North Carolina Press, 1955); Dull, *The French Navy and the Seven Years' War*, 138–39.
40. Richard Gardiner, *An Account of the Expedition to the West Indies* 2d ed. (London, 1760), 4, n.
41. Anderson, *Crucible of War*, 501.
42. For the military context of his episode, see J. Frederick Fausz, "An 'Abundance of Blood Shed on Both Sides': England's First Indian War, 1609–1614," *Virginia Magazine of History and Biography* 98 (1990): 3–56.
43. William Strachey quoted in Samuel Purchas, *Haklutus Posthumous, or Purchas His Pilgrimes*, vol. 19 (Glasgow, 1906), 45.
44. Strachey quoted in Purchas, *Haklutus Posthumous*, 19:53.
45. Strachey quoted in Purchas, *Haklutus Posthumous*, 19:54.
46. For an account of this action see George Edmundson, "The Dutch Power in Brazil (1624–1654), Part I: The Struggle for Bahia (1624–1627)," *English Historical Review* 11 (1896): 231–59, 244–45.
47. Stuart B. Schwartz, "The Voyage of the Vassals: Royal Power, Noble Obligations, and Merchant Capital before the Portuguese Restoration of Independence, 1624–1640," *American Historical Review* 96 (1991): 735–62; Klooster, *Dutch Moment: War*, 40–41.
48. Schwartz, "Voyage of the Vassals."
49. Chris M. Hand, *The Siege of Beauséjour, 1755* (Fredericton, NB: Goose Lane, 2004), 46–47.
50. Opinion of Council [of Nova Scotia] respecting the French inhabitants, July 28, 1755, CO 217/16, 24, The National Archives, Kew.
51. Charles Lawrence to Robert Monckton, July 31, 1755, in *The Northcliffe Collection, Presented to the Government of Canada by Sir Leicester Harmsworth* (Ottawa, 1926), 80–83, 83. See also Charles Lawrence to Robert Monkton, August 8, 1755, in *Northcliffe Collection*, 83–85, 84.
52. Instructions to Robert Monckton, August 11, 1755, in *Northcliffe Collection*, 85–87, 85.
53. For a good, detailed account of this operation see Paul Delaney, "The Acadians Deported from Chignecto to 'Les Carolines' in 1755: Their Origins, Identities and Subsequent Movements," in *Du Grand Dérangement à la déportation: Nouvelles perspectives historiques*, ed. Ronnie-Gilles LeBlanc (Moncton, N.B.: Chaire d'études acadiennes, 2005), 247–389.
54. John McGrath, "Polemic and History in French Brazil, 1555–1560," *Sixteenth Century Journal* 27 (1996): 385–97, 394–95.
55. Duffy and Metcalf, *Return of Hans Staden*, 139–40; Donald W. Forsyth, "The Beginnings of Brazilian Anthropology: Jesuits and Tupinamba Cannibalism," *Journal of Anthropological Research* 39 (1983): 147–78, 159; John Hemming, *Red Gold: The Conquest of the Brazilian Indians* (London: MacMillan, 1978), 125; Philip B. Boucher, "Revisioning the 'French Atlantic,' or, How to Think about the French Presence in the Atlantic, 1550–1625," in *The Atlantic World and Virginia, 1550–1624*, ed. Peter C. Mancall (Chapel Hill: University of North Carolina Press, 2007), 274–306, 284.
56. "Summary by the Marques de Montesclaros of the History of the Portuguese Conquest of Maranhão and Pará 1613–16," in *English and Irish Settlement on the River Amazon, 1550–1646*, ed. Joyce Lorimer (London: Hakluyt Society, 1989), 167–69, 168.
57. "Summary by the Marques de Montesclaros," 167–69.
58. Phillips, *Six Galleons*, 184–86.

59. Cornelius Ch. Goslinga, *The Dutch in the Caribbean and on the Wild Coast, 1580–1680* (Gainesville: University of Florida Press, 1971), 132–34.

60. Karen Kupperman, *Providence Island, 1630–1641: The Other Puritan Colony* (Cambridge: Cambridge University Press, 1993), 336–38.

61. Shomette and Haslach, *Raid on America*, 91.

62. John G. Reid, "Imperial Intrusions, 1686–1720," in *The Atlantic Region to Confederation: A History*, ed. Phillip A. Buckner and John G. Reid (Toronto: University of Toronto Press, 1994), 78–103, 83–84.

63. Peter E. Pope, *Fish Into Wine: The Newfoundland Plantation in the Seventeenth Century* (Chapel Hill: University of North Carolina Press, 2004), 409.

64. A. J. B. Johnston, *Control and Order in French Colonial Louisbourg, 1713–1758* (East Lansing: Michigan State University Press, 2001), 88–89.

65. Johnston, *Endgame*, 274–76.

66. Philip Lawson, *The Imperial Challenge: Quebec and Britain in the Age of the American Revolution* (Montreal: McGill-Queens University Press, 1989). See also Christopher L. Brown, "Empire without Slaves: British Concepts of Emancipation before the American Revolution," *William and Mary Quarterly* 56 (1999): 273–306.

67. Kupperman, *Providence Island*, 338.

68. Thomas Spencer, *A True and Faithful Relation of the Proceedings of the Forces of their Majesties K. William and Q. Mary* (London, 1691), 11; Boucher, *France and the American Tropics*, 218.

69. Clifford Lewis, "Some Recently Discovered Extracts from the List Minutes of the Virginia Council and General Court, 1642–1645," *William and Mary Quarterly* 20 (1940): 62–78, 69; C. S. Everett, "'They Shall be Slaves for their Lives': Indian Slavery in Colonial Virginia," in *Indian Slavery in Colonial America*, ed. Alan Gallay (Lincoln: University of Nebraska Press, 2009), 67–108, 69–70.

70. Linford D. Fisher, "'Dangerous Designes': The 1676 Barbados Act to Prohibit New England Indian Slave Importation," *William and Mary Quarterly* 71 (2014): 99–124, 108.

71. Fisher, "Dangerous Designes," 109.

72. Fisher, "Dangerous Designes," 115.

73. Fisher, "Dangerous Designes," 113.

74. Alan Gallay, *The Indian Slave Trade: The Rise of the English Empire in the American South* (New Haven, CT: Yale University Press, 2004), 299.

75. Gerónimo Valés to the King of Spain, December 9, 1711, in *Missions to the Calusa*, ed. John H. Hann (Gainesville: University of Florida Press, 1991), 335–39.

76. Olivier Pétré-Grenouilleau, "Maritime Powers, Colonial Powers: The Role of Migration (c.1492–1792)," in *Migration, Trade and Slavery in an Expanding World: Essays in Honour of Peter Emmer*, ed. Wim Klooster (Leiden: Brill, 2009), 45–71, 48.

77. Simon J. Hogerzeil and David Richardson, "Slave Purchasing Strategies and Shipboard Mortality: Day to Day Evidence from the Dutch African Trade, 1751–1797," *Journal of Economic History* 67 (2007): 160–90.

78. Apart from the total migration figures cited by Pétré-Grenouilleau, the numbers in this paragraph come from the Transatlantic Slave Trade Database at www.slavevoyages.org. The total migration numbers in the database are very close to those cited by Pétré-Grenouilleau, but do not exactly match.

79. Snelgrave, *New Account*, 186–87.

Chapter 5

1. Meuwese, *Brothers in Arms*, 144.

2. Samuel de Champlain, *Voyages of Samuel de Champlain*, trans. Edmund F. Slafter (Boston: Prince Society, 1878), Vol. 2, Ch. 9.

3. Gomes Eannes de Azurara, *The Chronicle of the Discovery and Conquest of Guinea*, trans. Charles Raymond Beazley and Edgar Prestage (London: Hakluyt Society, 1894), Vol. 2, p. 255.

4. See Clifford J. Rogers, ed., *The Military Revolution Debate: Readings on the Military Transformation of Early Modern Europe* (Boulder, CO: Westview, 1995).

5. See J. E. Inikori, "The Import of Firearms into West Africa, 1750–1807: A Quantitative Analysis," *Journal of African History* 18 (1977): 339–68; W. A. Richards, "The Import of Firearms into West Africa in the Eighteenth Century," *Journal of African History* 21: (1980) 43–59.

6. See for example David L. Silverman, *Thundersticks: Firearms and the Violent Transformation of Native America* (Cambridge, MA: Harvard University Press, 2016).

7. Fernando del Pulgar, quoted in Weston F. Cook, "The Cannon Conquest of Nasrid Spain and the End of the Reconquista," *Journal of Military History* 57 (1993): 43–70, 63.

8. Wayne E. Lee, *Waging War: Conflict, Culture, and Innovation in World History* (New York: Oxford University Press, 2016), ch. 7.

9. *The New Method of Fortification as Practiced by Monsieur Vauban, Engineer General of France* (London, 1702), 86.

10. John A. Lynn, "The *Trace Italienne* and the Growth of Armies: The French Case," *Journal of Miltary History* 55 (1991): 297–330.

11. Lee, *Waging War*, 235–36; Bert S. Hall, *Weapons and Warfare in Renaissance Europe* (Baltimore: Johns Hopkins University Press, 1997).

12. Hall, *Weapons and Warfare*, 178.

13. See Murray Pittock, *Culloden* (Oxford: Oxford University Press, 2016).

14. Geoffrey Parker, "The Limits to Revolutions in Military Affairs: Maurice of Nassau, the Battle of Nieuwpoort (1600), and the Legacy," *Journal of Military History* 71 (2007): 331–72.

15. Geoffrey Parker, *The Military Revolution: Military Innovation and the Rise of the West, 1500–1800* (Cambridge: Cambridge University Press, 1988), 1.

16. Lynn, "*Trace Italienne*," 299.

17. Richard J. Reid, *Warfare in African History* (Cambridge: Cambridge University Press, 2012), 60–61; John K. Thornton, *Warfare in Atlantic Africa, 1500–1800* (London: UCL Press, 1999), 27.

18. Reid, *Warfare in African History*, 62; Thornton, *Warfare in Atlantic Africa*, 31.

19. Thornton, *Africa and Africans*, 120.

20. Paul E. Lovejoy, *Transformations in Slavery: A History of Slavery in Africa* (Cambridge: Cambridge University Press, 2012), 106.

21. Thornton, *Warfare in Atlantic Africa*, 86–87.

22. Reid, *Warfare in African History*, 98.

23. Graham Connah, "Contained Communities in Tropical Africa," in *City Walls: The Urban Enceinte in Global Perspective*, ed. James D. Lacey (Cambridge: Cambridge University Press, 2000), 19–45, 32–36.

24. Martin A. Klein, "The Slave Trade and Decentralised Societies," *Journal of African History* 42 (2001): 49–65, 53–54.

25. Connah, "Contained Communities," 32–36.

26. Walter Hawthorne, "The Production of Slaves where there was no State: The Guinea-Bissau Region, 1450–1815," *Slavery and Abolition* 20 (1999): 97–124.

27. John Mawe, *Travels in the Interior of Brazil* (London, 1812), 192. For context see Hal Langfur, "Moved by Terror: Frontier Violence as Cultural Exchange in Late-Colonial Brazil," *Ethnohistory* 52 (2005): 255–89.

28. Robert Charles Padden, "Cultural Change and Military Resistance in Araucanian Chile, 1550–1730," *Southwestern Journal of Anthropology* 13 (1957): 103–21, 109.

29. Silverman, *Thundersticks*, 30–31.

30. Padden, "Cultural Change and Military Resistance," 108–12.

31. Silverman, *Thundersticks*, 28.

32. Wayne E. Lee, "Fortify, Fight, or Flee: Tuscarora and Cherokee Defensive Warfare and Military Culture Adaptation," *Journal of Military History* 68 (2004): 713–70, 715–17.

33. David E. Jones, *Native American Armor, Shields, and Fortifications* (Austin: University of Texas Press, 2004), 58–62.

34. Robert Rogers, quoted in Armstrong Starkey, *European and Native American Warfare, 1675–1815* (Norman: University of Oklahoma Press, 1998), 19.

35. Alf Hornborg and Jonathan D. Hill, eds., *Ethnicity in Ancient Amazonia: Reconstructing Past Identities from Archaeology, Linguistics, and Ethnohistory* (Boulder: University Press of Colorado, 2011).

36. Craig S. Keener, "An Ethnohistorical Analysis of Iroquois Assault Tactics Used Against Fortified Settlements of the Northeast in the Seventeenth Century," *Ethnohistory* 46 (1999): 777–807, 786.

37. Lee, "Fortify, Fight, or Flee," 740–43.

38. Bruce G. Trigger, "Early Native North American Responses to European Contact: Romantic versus Rationalistic Interpretations," *Journal of American History* 77 (1991): 1195–215, 1207.

39. Hawthorne, "Production of Slaves," 108–10.

40. L. M. Pole, "Decline or Survival? Iron Production in West Africa from the Seventeenth to the Twentieth Centuries," *Journal of African History* 23 (1982): 503–13.

41. Enrique Rodríguez-Alegría, "Narratives of Conquest, Colonialism, and Cutting-Edge Technology," *American Anthropologist* 110 (2008): 33–43, 40.

42. Philip Nichols, *Sir Francis Drake Revived* (London, 1626), 13.

43. Nichols, *Sir Francis Drake*, 19.

44. Neil Whitehead, "The Snake Warriors—Sons of the Tiger's Teeth: A Descriptive Analysis of Carib Warfare ca. 1500–1820," in *The Anthropology of War*, ed. Jonathan Haas (Cambridge: Cambridge Univeristy Press, 1990), 146–70, 150.

45. Antonio Galvano, quoted in Robert Kerr, *A General History and Collection of Voyages and Travels Arranged in Systematic Order* vol. 2 (Edinburgh, 1811), 54. See also Antonio Galvano, *The Discoveries of the World, from their First Original unto the Year of our Lord 1555* (London: Hakluyt Society, 1862), 86.

46. Nichols, *Sir Francis Drake*, 19.

47. Reuben Gold Thwaites, ed., *Jesuit Relations and Allied Documents* (Cleveland: Burrows Brothers, 1896–1900), 61:83.

48. Francis Moore, *Travels into the Inland Parts of Africa* (London, 1738), 68.

49. Leonard A. Cole, "The Poison Weapons Taboo: Biology, Culture, Policy," *Politics and the Life Sciences* 17 (1998): 119–32, 120–21.

50. See Thomas Morton, *New English Canaan* (London, 1637), 45; John Underhill, *Newes from America* (London, 1638), 34.

51. Bernardo de Vargas Machuca, *The Indian Militia and Description of the Indies*, ed. Kris Lane, trans. Timothy F. Johnson (Durham, NC: Duke University Press, 2008), 77.

52. Bernardino de Sahagún, *General History of the Things of New Spain*, trans. Arthur J. O. Anderson and Charles E. Dibble, Vol. 12 (Santa Fe, NM: School of American Research, 1965), 20.

53. Vargas Machuca, *Indian Militia*, 77.

54. John Grier Varner and Jeannette Johnson Varner, *Dogs of the Conquest* (Norman: University of Oklahoma Press, 1983), 5–7.

55. Edward Waterhouse, *A Declaration of the State of the Colony and Affaires in Virginia* (London, 1622), 24.

56. Mark A. Mastromarino, "Teaching Old Dogs New Tricks: The English Mastiff and the Anglo-American Experience," *The Historian* 49 (1986): 10–25, 21, n.29.

57. James Homer Williams, "Great Doggs and Mischievous Cattle: Domesticated Animals and Indian-European Relations in New Netherland and New York," *New York History* 76 (1995): 245–64, 261.

58. Guy Chet, *Conquering the American Wilderness: The Triumph of European Warfare in the Colonial Northeast* (Amherst: University of Massachusetts Press, 2003); Mastromarino, "Teaching Old Dogs New Tricks."

59. Mary Rowlandson, *The Soveraignty and Goodness of God* (Boston, 1682), 3.

60. Thomas Church, *Entertaining Passages Relating to Philip's War* (Boston, 1716), 93.

61. Crone, ed., *Voyages of Cadamosto*, 35–36; Robin Law, *The Horse in West African Society* (Oxford: Oxford University Press, 1980), 51.

62. Law, *The Horse in West African Society*, 5–7.

63. Law, *Horse in West African Society*, 93–96.

64. Law, *Horse in West African Society*, 126–33.

65. James L. A. Webb, "The Horse and Slave Trade Between the Western Sahara and Senegambia," *Journal of African History* 34 (1993): 221–46.

66. Snelgrave, *New Account*, 56, 121–22.

67. Law, *Horse in West African Society*, 76–82.

68. Carolyn Jane Anderson, "State Imperatives: Military Mapping in Scotland, 1689–1770," *Scottish Geographical Journal* 125 (2009): 4–24, 14; Geoffrey Plank, *Rebellion and Savagery: The Jacobite Rising of 1745 and the British Empire* (Philadelphia: University of Pennsylvania Press, 2006), 19.
69. Parker, *Military Revolution*, 69–70.
70. James B. Wood, *The King's Army: Warfare, Soldiers, and Society During the Wars of Religion in France, 1562–1576* (Cambridge: Cambridge University Press, 1996), 160.
71. Parker, *Military Revolution*, 77–78.
72. John A. Lynn, *Giant of the Grand Siècle: The French Army, 1610–1715* (Cambridge: Cambridge University Press, 1997), 127–30.
73. Charles Hudson, *Knights of Spain, Warriors of the Sun: Hernando de Soto and the South's Ancient Chiefdoms* (Athens: University of Georgia Press, 1997), 67.
74. Hudson, *Knights of Spain*, 237–44.
75. Hudson, *Knights of Spain*, 387–94.
76. Hal Langfur, *The Forbidden Lands: Colonial Identity, Frontier Violence, and the Persistence of Brazil's Eastern Indians, 1750–1830* (Stanford, CA: Stanford University Press, 2006), 141.
77. Chet, *Conquering the American Wilderness*, 121–23.
78. Pekka Hämäläinen, *The Comanche Empire* (New Haven, CT: Yale University Press, 2008), 23.
79. Dan Flores, "Bison Ecology and Bison Diplomacy: The Southern Plains from 1800 to 1850," *Journal of American History* 78 (1991): 465–85, 481.
80. Hämäläinen, *Comanche Empire*, 26.
81. Richard White, "The Winning of the West: The Expansion of the Western Sioux in the Eighteenth and Nineteenth Centuries," *Journal of American History* 65 (1978): 319–43.
82. For lists of Carib landings see Philip B. Boucher, *Cannibal Encounters: Europeans and Island Caribs, 1492–1763* (Baltimore: Johns Hopkins University Press, 1992),17; Karl H. Schwerin, "Carib Warfare and Slaving," *Atropologica* 99–100 (2003): 45–72, 48–52.
83. Boucher, *Cannibal Encounters*, 35.
84. Frank Lestringant, *Cannibals: The Discovery and Representation of the Cannibal from Columbus to Jules Verne*, trans. Rosemary Morris (Berkeley: University of California Press, 1997), 15–31.
85. Robert Smith, "The Canoe in West African History," *Journal of African History* 11 (1970): 515–33, 526–27. Sparks 562.
86. Lipman, *Saltwater Frontier*, 75.
87. Vargas Machuca, *Indian Militia*, 99.
88. N. A. T. Hall, "Maritime Maroons: 'Grand Marronage' from the Danish West Indies," *William and Mary Quarterly* 42 (1985): 476–98, 482.
89. Bruce T. McCully, "Catastrophe in the Wilderness: New Light on the Canada Expedition of 1709," *William and Mary Quarterly* 11 (1954): 441–56, 448.
90. McCully, "Catastrophe in the Wilderness," 449.
91. McCully, "Catastrophe in the Wilderness," 451.
92. McCully, "Catastrophe in the Wilderness," 449.
93. McCully, "Catastrophe in the Wilderness," 451.
94. McCully, "Catastrophe in the Wilderness," 454.
95. Daniel K. Richter, "War and Culture: The Iroquois Experience," *William and Mary Quarterly* 40 (1983): 528–59, 539–40; Keith F. Otterbein, "Why the Iroquois Won: An Analysis of Iroquois Military Tactics," *Ethnohistory* 11 (1964): 56–63, 59–60.
96. *Collection of Voyages*, 5:266.
97. *Collection of Voyages*, 5:382.

Chapter 6

1. Bartolomé de Las Casas, *A Short Account of the Destruction of the Indies*, trans. Nigel Griffin (London: Penguin, 1992), 14.
2. Las Casas, *Short Account*, 11.
3. Michele Da Cuneo, *News of the Islands of the Hesperian Ocean Discovered by don Christopher Columbus of Genoa* (1495), trans. Theodore J. Cachey Jr., in *Italian Reports on America,*

1493–1522, ed. Geoffrey Symocox and Luciano Formisano (Turnhout, Belgium: Brepols, 2002), 50–63, 52.

4. William F. Keegan, "'No Man [or Woman] is an Island': Elements of Taino Social Organization," in *The Indigenous People of the Caribbean*, ed. Samuel M. Wilson (Gainesville: University Press of Florida, 1997), 107–17, 116–17; Henry Petijean Roget, "The Taino Vision: A Study in the Exchange of Misunderstanding," in *The Indigenous People of the Caribbean*, ed. Wilson, 169–75, 166–67.

5. Da Cuneo, *News of the Islands*, 58.

6. Kathleen Deagan, "Reconsidering Taino Social Dynamics after Spanish Conquest: Gender and Class in Culture Contact Studies," *American Antiquity* 69 (2004): 597–626; William F. Keegan and Morgan D. Maclachlan, "The Evolution of Avuncular Chiefdoms: A Reconstruction of Taino Kinship and Politics," *American Anthropologist* 91 (1989): 613–30.

7. Irving Rouse, *The Tainos: Rise and Decline of the People who Greeted Columbus* (New Haven, CT: Yale University Press, 1992), 150–58.

8. On the survival of communities see Deagan, "Reconsidering Taino Social Dynamics."

9. Friars of San Gerónimo to Cardinal Cisneros, January 20, 1517, in *Colección de documentos inéditos relativos al descubrimiento, conquista y colonización de las posesiones españoles en América y Occeanía*, ed. J. F. Pacheco, F. de Cárdenas y L. Torres de Mendoza (Madrid, 1864), 269.

10. John K. Thornton, *Cultural History*, 191.

11. Da Cuneo, *News of the Islands*, 52.

12. On the definition of warfare see R. Brian Ferguson, "Explaining War," in *The Anthropology of War*, ed. Jonathan Haas (Cambridge: Cambridge University Press, 1990), 26–55, 26.

13. Steven A. Leblanc, "Warfare and the Development of Social Complexity: Some Demographic and Environmental Factors," in *The Archaeology of Warfare: Prehistories of Raiding and Conquest*, ed. Elizabeth N. Arkush and Mark W. Allen (Gainesville: University Press of Florida, 2006), 437–68, 442–43.

14. Jean R. Soderlund, *Lenape Country: Delaware Valley Society before William Penn* (Philadelphia: University of Pennsylvania Press, 2015); Gunlög Fur, *A Nation of Women: Gender and Colonial Encounters among the Delaware Indians* (Philadelphia: University of Pennsylvania Press, 2009).

15. David Silverman, *Faith and Boundaries: Colonists, Christianity and Community among the Wampanoag Indians of Martha's Vineyard, 1600–1871* (Cambridge: Cambridge University Press, 2005).

16. André Corvisier, *Armies and Societies in Europe, 1494–1789*, trans. Abigal T. Siddall (Bloomington: Indiana University Press, 1979), 11.

17. Juan Alberto Román Berrelleza and Ximena Chávez Balderas, "The Role of Children in the Ritual Practices of the Great Temple of Tenochtitlan and the Great Temple of Tlatelolco," in *The Social Experience of Childhood in Ancient Mesoamerica*, ed. Traci Arden and Scott R. Hutson (Boulder: University Press of Colorado, 2006), 233–48, 236.

18. Ross Hassig, *Aztec Warfare: Imperial Expansion and Political Control* (Norman: University of Oklahoma Press, 1996), 30–36; Rosemary A. Joyce, "Girling the Girl and Boying the Boy: The Production of Adulthood in Ancient Mesoamerica," *World Archaeology* 31 (2000): 473–83, 479–80.

19. Roger Ascham, *The Scholemaster* (London, 1571), 19.

20. Marta Ajmar-Wollheim, "Geography and the Environment," in *A Cultural History of Childhood and Family in the Early Modern Age*, ed. Sandra Cavallo and Silvia Evangelisti (London: Bloomsbury, 2014), 69–94, 86–87.

21. Joyce, "Girling the Girl," 476.

22. Neil Lancelot Whitehead, "The Snake Warriors—Sons of the Tiger Teeth: A Descriptive Analysis of Carib Warfare, 1500–1820," in *The Anthropology of War*, ed. Jonathan Haas (Cambridge: Cambridge University Press, 1990), 146–70, 152–53.

23. Thornton, *Warfare in Atlantic Africa*, 90.

24. Thornton, *Warfare in Atlantic Africa*, 91–92; Stanley B. Alpers, *Amazons of Black Sparta: the Women Warriors of Dahomey* (London: Hurst and Company, 1998).

25. Thornton, *Warfare in Atlantic Africa*, 102, 116–17.

26. Thornton, *Warfare in Atlantic Africa*, 117.

27. John Keegan, *A History of Warfare* (London: Pimlico, 2004), 227–28.
28. William H. Marquardt, "The Emergence and Demise of the Calusa," in *Societies in Eclipse: Archaeology of the Eastern Woodland Indians, A.D. 1400–1700*, ed. David S. Brose, C. Wesley Cowan, and Robert C. Mainfort Jr. (Washington, DC: Smithsonian Institution, 2001), 157–72, 168.
29. Thornton, *Warfare in Atlantic Africa*, 37
30. Thornton, *Warfare in Atlantic Africa*, 64.
31. Thornton, *Warfare in Atlantic Africa*, 65.
32. Thornton, *Warfare in Atlantic Africa*, 91.
33. Lynn, *Giant of the Grand Siècle*, 354–56.
34. *Considerations upon the Different Modes of Finding Recruits for the Army* (London, 1775), 5.
35. Parker, *Military Revolution*, 48–49.
36. Lynn, *Giant of the Grand Siècle*, 352.
37. G. Davies, ed., *Autobiography of Thomas Raymond and Memoires of the Family of Guise of Elmore, Gloucestershire* (London, 1917), 35.
38. Thornton, *Warfare in Atlantic Africa*, 57–58.
39. Thornton, *Warfare in Atlantic Africa*, 37.
40. Thornton, *Warfare in Atlantic Africa*, 10.
41. Lee, *Waging War*, 85.
42. Thomas Brainerd, *The Life of John Brainerd the Brother of David Brainerd, and his Successor as Missionary to the Indians of New Jersey* (Philadelphia, 1865), 232.
43. *London Magazine* 9 (1740) 152.
44. John Thornton, "African Dimensions of the Stono Rebellion," *American Historical Review* 96 (1991): 1101–13.
45. Humphrey Bland, *A Treatise of Military Discipline*, 2nd ed. (London, 1727), 12–13, See Matthew McCormack, "Dance and Drill: Polite Accomplishments and Military Masculinities in Georgian Britain," *Cultural and Social History* 8 (2011): 215–330; William H. McNeill, *Keeping together in Time: Dance and Drill in Human History* (Cambridge, MA: Harvard University Press, 1995).
46. See for example J. A. Houlding, *Fit for Service: The Training of the British Army, 1715–1795* (Oxford: Clarendon Press, 1981), 261–64.
47. Harald Kleinschmidt, "Using the Gun: Manual Drill and the Proliferation of Portable Firearms," *Journal of Military History* 63 (1999): 601–30, 607.
48. John Keegan, *The Face of Battle* (New York: Viking, 1976), 297.
49. Thornton, *Warfare in Atlantic Africa*, 107.
50. Hämäläinen, *Comanche Empire*, 279–80.
51. William Douglass, *A Summary, Historical and Political, of the First Planting, Progressive Improvements, and Present State of the British Settlements in North America*, vol. 1 (Boston, 1750), 155.
52. Cadwallader Colden, *The History of the Five Indian Nations Depending on the Province of New-York in America* (New York, 1727), iii–iv.
53. Wayne E. Lee, "Peace Chiefs and Blood Revenge: Patterns of Restraint in Native American Warfare, 1500–1800," *Journal of Military History* 71 (2007): 701–41, 720–22.
54. Whitehead, "Snake Warriors," 153–54.
55. Thornton, *Warfare in Atlantic Africa*, 35, 37.
56. Alan J. Guy, *Oeconomy and Discipline: Officership and Administration in the British Army, 1714–63* (Manchester; Manchester University Press, 1985).
57. Davies, ed., *Autobiography of Thomas Raymond*, 35, 37.
58. Davies, ed., *Autobiography of Thomas Raymond*, 38, 40.
59. Lynn, *Giant of the Grand Siècle*, 398.
60. Lynn, *Giant of the Grand Siècle*, 405.
61. Fred Anderson, *A People's Army: Massachusetts Soldiers and Society in the Seven Years' War* (New York: Norton, 1984), 138.
62. Whitehead, "Snake Warriors," 154–55.
63. Thornton, *Warfare in Atlantic Africa*, 37.
64. Thornton, *Warfare in Atlantic Africa*, 64.

65. Thornton, *Warfare in Atlantic Africa*, 119–20.
66. Thornton, *Warfare in Atlantic Africa*, 117.
67. David H. Dye, *War Paths, Peace Paths: An Archaeology of Cooperation and Conflict in Native Eastern North America* (New York: Altamira Press, 2009).
68. James F. Brooks, *Captives and Cousins: Slavery, Kinship and Community in the Southwest Borderlands* (Chapel Hill: University of North Carolina Press, 2002); Hämäläinen, *Comanche Empire*.
69. Josiah Harmer to the Secretary of War, November 4, 1790, *American State Papers: Documents, Legislative and Executive, of the Congress of the United States, Vol. 4* (Washington, DC, 1832), 104.
70. Thornton, *Warfare in Atlantic Africa*, 38.
71. Thornton, *Warfare in Atlantic Africa*, 118.
72. Thornton, *Warfare in Atlantic Africa*, 69.
73. Thornton, *Warfare in Atlantic Africa*, 38.
74. Ida Altman, "Conquest, Coercion, and Collaboration: Indian Allies and the Campaigns in Nueva Galicia," in *Indian Conquistadors: Indigenous Allies in the Conquest of Mesoamerica*, ed. Laura E. Matthew and Michel R. Oudijk (Norman: University of Oklahoma Press, 2007), 145–74, 150–51.
75. Martin Vaan Creveld, *Supplying War: Logistics from Wallenstein to Patton* (Cambridge: Cambridge University Press, 1977), 5–6.
76. Davies, ed., *Autobiography of Thomas Raymond*, 39.
77. Davies, ed., *Autobiography of Thomas Raymond*, 43.
78. John A. Lynn II, *Women, Armies and Warfare in Early Modern Europe* (Cambridge: Cambridge University Press, 2008).
79. See Geoffrey Plank, "Making Gibraltar British in the Eighteenth Century," *History* 98 (2013): 346–69.
80. A. J. B. Johnston, *Control and Order in French Colonial Louisbourg, 1713–1758* (East Lansing: Michigan State University Press, 2001), 187.
81. Johnston, *Control and Order*, 183.
82. Lynn, *Women, Armies and Warfare*.
83. *Considerations upon the Different Modes*, 3.
84. Thornton, *Warfare in Atlantic Africa*, 68.
85. William R. Fitzgerald, "Contact, Neutral Iroquoian Transformation, and the Little Ice Age," in *Societies in Eclipse*, ed. Brose, Cowan, and Mainfort, 37–47, 39–40.
86. Geoffrey Plank, "Deploying Tribes and Clans: Mohawks in Nova Scotia and Scottish Highlanders in Georgia," in *Empires and Indigenes: Intercultural Alliance, Imperial Expansion, and Warfare in the Early Modern World*, ed. Wayne E. Lee (New York: New York University Press, 2012), 221–50.
87. See Gregory Evans Dowd, *War Under Heaven: Pontiac, the Indian Nations, and the British Empire* (Baltimore: Johns Hopkins University Press, 2002), 51.
88. A. O. Thompson, *Flying to Freedom: African Runaways and Maroons in the Americas* (Kingston: University of the West Indies Press, 2006), pp. 144–74, 265–94; M. Caton, *Testing the Chains: Resistance to Slavery in the British West Indies* (Ithaca, NY: Cornell University Press, 1982); M. C. Campbell, *The Maroons of Jamaica, 1655–1796: A History of Resistance, Collaboration and Betrayal* (Granby, MA: Bergin and Garvey, 1988); W. Hoogbergen, *The Boni Maroon Wars in Suriname* (New York: Brill, 1990); Richard Price, ed., *Maroon Societies: Rebel Slave Communities in the Americas* (Baltimore: Johns Hopkins University Press, 1979); Benton, *Law and Colonial Cultures*, 59–66.
89. Matthew Restall, "Black Conquistadors: Armed Africans in Early Spanish America," *The Americas* 57 (2000): 171–205, 181.
90. Jane Landers, "Transforming Bondsmen into Vassals: Arming Slaves in Colonial Spanish America," in *Arming Slaves: From Classical Times to the Modern Age*, ed. Christopher Leslie Brown and Philip D. Morgan (New Haven, CT: Yale University Press, 2008), 120–45, 121–22.
91. Hendrik Kraay, "Arming Slaves in Brazil from the Seventeenth Century to the Nineteenth Century," in *Arming Slaves*, ed. Brown and Morgan, 146–79, 155.

92. Johnson Green, *The Life and Confession of Johnson Green* (Worcester, MA, 1786).
93. *An Alarm to the Patriots* (London, 1749), 50.
94. Nicholas Rogers, *Mayhem: Postwar Crime and Violence in Britain, 1749–1753* (New Haven, CT: Yale University Press, 2012).
95. See John Phillips Resch, *Suffering Soldiers: Revolutionary War Veterans, Moral Sentiment, and Political Culture in the Early Republic* (Amherst: University of Massachusetts Press, 1999).
96. Lee, "Peace Chiefs and Blood Revenge," 722.
97. Blacksnake, quoted in Anthony F. C. Wallace, *The Death and Rebirth of the Seneca* (New York: Knopf, 1973), 121.
98. Blacksnake, quoted in Wallace, *Death and Rebirth*, 146.
99. Wallace, *Death and Rebirth*, 234.
100. Bulfinch Lamb, quoted in William Smith, *A New Voyage to Guinea* (London, 1744), 173.
101. *Parliamentary History of England from the Earliest Period to 1803, vol. 28* (London, 1816), 84–85.
102. See John Atkins, *A Voyage to Guinea, Brasil, and the West Indies* (London, 1735), 119–22.
103. William Smith, *A New Voyage to Guinea* (London, 1744), 266.
104. Robin Law, "Dahomey and the Slave Trade: Reflections on the Historiography of the Rise of Dahomey," *Journal of African History* 27 (1986): 237–67.
105. John Landers, *The Field and the Forge: Population, Production and Power in the Pre-Industrial West* (Oxford: Oxford University Press, 2003), 346.
106. Landers, *Field and the Forge*, 339.
107. Landers, *Field and the Forge*, 344.
108. Jan Lindegren, "Men, Money, and Means," in *War and Competition between States*, ed. Philippe Contamine (Oxford: Clarendon Press, 2000), 129–62, 140.
109. De Ganne Memoir, in *The French Foundations, 1680–1693*, ed. Theodore Calvin Pease and Raymond C. Werner (Springfield: Illinois Historical Library, 1934), 329.
110. *Decouvertes et etablissements des francais dans l'ouest et dans le sud* (Paris, 1889) vol. 1, p. 542. See Susan Sleeper-Smith, *Indian Women and French Men: Rethinking Cultural Encounter in the Western Great Lakes* (Amherst: University of Massachusetts Press, 2001), 23.
111. John Thornton, "The Slave Trade in Eighteenth-century Angola: Effects on Demographic Structures," *Canadian Journal of African Studies* 14 (1980): 417–27.
112. Dye, *War Paths, Peace Paths*, 2–4.
113. Dye, *War Paths, Peace Paths*, 114–23; Daniel K. Richter, "War and Culture: The Iroquois Experience," *William and Mary Quarterly* 40 (1983): 528–59.

Chapter 7

1. Peter Russell, *Prince Henry 'the Navigator': A Life* (New Haven, CT: Yale University Press, 2000), 291–315.
2. G. R. Crone, ed., *The Voyages of Cadamosto and other Documents on Western Africa in the Second Half of the Fifteenth Century* (London: Hakluyt Society, 1937), 1.
3. Crone, ed., *Voyages of Cadamosto*, 31.
4. Crone, ed., *Voyages of Cadamosto*, 33–34.
5. Geoffrey Symcox and Blair Sullivan, eds., *Christopher Columbus and the Enterprise of the Indies: A Brief History with Documents* (Boston: Bedford, 2005), 172.
6. For background on Léry see Adam Asher Duker, "The Protestant Israelites of Sancerre: Jean de Léry and the Confessional Demarcation of Cannibalism," *Journal of Early Modern History* 18 (2014): 255–86. The quotation is from Jean de Léry, *History of a Voyage to the Land of Brazil*, trans. Janet Whatley (Berkeley: University of California Press, 1990), 118.
7. De Léry, *History of a Voyage*, 118.
8. Barbara Ehrenreich, *Blood Rites: Origins and History of the Passions of War* (London: Virago, 1997), 132–43.
9. Crone, ed., *Voyages of Cadamosto*, 58.
10. Crone, ed., *Voyages of Cadamosto*, 59.
11. Crone, ed., *Voyages of Cadamosto*, 60.

12. William D. Piersen, "White Cannibals, Black Martyrs: Fear, Depression, and Religious Faith as Causes of Suicide among New Slaves," *Journal of Negro History* 62 (1977): 147–59.

13. Francis Moore, *Travels into the Inland Parts of Africa* (London, 1738), 208. For Job Ben Solomon's story see Thomas Bluett, *Some Memoirs of the Life of Job the Son of Solomon* (London, 1734).

14. Mungo Park, *Travels into the Interior Districts of Africa* (London, 1799), 319.

15. *Collection of Voyages and Travels,* 5:327.

16. Snelgrave, *New Account,* 162–63.

17. Bryan Edwards, *The History Civil and Commercial of the British Colonies in the West Indies, Vol. 2* (London, 1801), 150–51.

18. Piersen, "White Cannibals," 149.

19. Ottobah Cugoano, *Thoughts and Sentiments,* 9.

20. Park, *Travels into the Interior,* 319.

21. *Collection of Voyages and Travels,* 5:327.

22. Edwards, *History Civil and Commercial,* 150–51.

23. *Collection of Voyages and Travels,* 5:327.

24. Letter from John Snoek, January 2, 1702, in William Bosman, *A New and Accurate Description of the Coast of Guinea* (London, 1705), 489.

25. John Thornton, "Cannibals, Witches and Slave Traders in the Atlantic World," *William and Mary Quarterly* 60 (2003): 273–94, 286–89.

26. Neil Lancelot Whitehead, "Carib Cannibalism: The Historical Evidence," *Journal de la Société des Américanistes* 70 (1984): 69–87; Dye, *War Paths, Peace Paths,* 161.

27. Duker, "Protestant Israelites," 268.

28. Frank Lestrignant, *Cannibals: The Discovery and Representation of the Cannibal from Columbus to Jules Verne* (Cambridge: Polity Press, 1997), 16.

29. Symcox and Sullivan, eds., *Christopher Columbus and the Enterprise of the Indies,* 172–73.

30. Andrew Battell, *The Strange Adventures of Andrew Battell* (London: Hakluyt Society, 1901), 21.

31. Letter from John Snoek, January 2, 1702, in Bosman, *A New and Accurate Description,* 487.

32. Elizabeth Hanson, *An Account of the Captivity of Elizabeth Hanson* (London, 1760), 17. For other possible bluffs see Robert Charles Padden, "Cultural Change and Military Resistance in Araucanian Chile, 1550–1730," *Southwestern Journal of Anthropology* 13 (1957): 103–21, 119–20; Martel, "Hans Staden's Captive Soul," 64–65.

33. S. N. Wasterlain, M. J. Neves and M. T. Ferreira, "Dental Modification in a Skeletal Sample of Enslaved Africans found at Lagos (Portugal)," *International Journal of Osteoarchaeology* 26 (2016): 621–32; Jerome S. Handler, "Determining African Birth from Skeletal Remains: A Note on Tooth Mutilation," *Historical Archaeology* 28 (1994): 113–19.

34. Josiah Coale, *The Books and Divers Epistles of the Faithful Servant of the Lord Josiah Coale* (London, 1671), 21–22; Henry Cadbury, ed., *Narrative Papers of George Fox, Unpublished or Uncorrected* (Richmond, IN: Friends United Press, 1972), 174.

35. Jonathan Dickenson, *God's Protecting Providence Man's Surest Help and Defence* (London, 1700). This pamphlet was heavily promoted by Quakers. For its publication history see Charles M. Andrews and Jonathan Dickenson, "God's Protecting Providence: A Journal by Jonathan Dickenson," *Florida Historical Quarterly* 21 (1942): 107–26.

36. Lestrignant, *Cannibals,* 28, 30.

37. Symcox and Sullivan, eds., *Christopher Columbus and the Enterprise of the Indies,* 172–73.

38. Whitehead, "Carib Cannibalism," 78.

39. Thwaites, ed., *Jesuit Relations and Allied Documents,* 13:59–79.

40. De Léry, *History of a Voyage;* see Duker, "Protestant Israelites," 266–67.

41. Andrew Lipman, "'A Meanes to Knitt them Together': The Exchange of Body Parts in the Pequot War," *William and Mary Quarterly* 65 (2008): 3–28, 14.

42. Lipman, "'Meanes to Knitt them Together,'" 17.

43. Lipman, "'Meanes to Knitt them Together,'" 3.

44. Ruben G. Mendoza, "The Devine Gourd Tree: Tzompantli Skull Racks, Decapitation Rituals, and Human Trophies in Ancient Mesoamerica," in *The Taking and Displaying of Human Body Parts as Trophies by Amerindians,* ed. Richard J. Chacon and David H. Dye (New York: Springer,

2007), 400–43; Christopher L. Moser, "Human Decapitation in Ancient Mesoamerica," *Studies in Pre-Columbian Art and Archaeology* 11 (1973): 5–72, 26–28.

45. Nicholas P. Canny, "The Ideology of English Colonization: From Ireland to America," *William and Mary Quarterly* 30 (1973): 575–98, 582.

46. Snelgrave, *New Account*, 31–32.

47. Inga Celendinnen, *The Cost of Courage in Aztec Society: Essays in Mesoamerican Society and Culture* (Cambridge: Cambridge University Press, 2010), 29–31.

48. Robin Law, "'My Head Belongs to the King': On the Political and Ritual Significance of Decapitation in Pre-Colonial Dahomey," *Journal of African History* 30 (1989): 399–415, 404.

49. Robin Law, "'My Head Belongs to the King,'" 406.

50. Proclamation of the Governor, Council, and Assembly of Massachusetts, May 27, 1696 (Boston, 1696).

51. Meuwese, *Brothers in Arms*, 292–94, 301.

52. "Sur l'Acadie, 1748," MGl, Archives des colonies, CIID, vol. 10, doc. 154; Louis le Prévost Duquesnelle to Antoine-Louis Rouillé, 16 August 1753, MG 1, Archives des colonies CIIB, vol. 33, doc. 197; "Divers dépense," Louisbourg, 31 December 1756, MG 1, Archives des colonies CIIB, vol. 36, doc. 241, National Archives of Canada.

53. For an example see John Knox, *Journal of Captain John Knox*, ed., Arthur G. Doughty (Toronto: Champlain Society, 1914), vol. I, p. 297.

54. Dye, *War Paths, Peace Paths*, 3–4.

55. Gabriel Sagard, quoted in Karen Anderson, *Chain her by One Foot: The Subjugation of Women in Seventeenth-Century New France* (London: Routledge, 1991), 171.

56. John Underhill, *Newes from America* (London, 1638), 38.

57. See Wayne E. Lee, *Barbarians and Brothers: Anglo-American Warfare, 1500–1865* (Oxford: Oxford University Press, 2011), 130–41, 154–55.

58. See Adam J. Hirsch, "The Collision of Military Cultures in Seventeenth-century New England," *Journal of American History* 74 (1988): 1187–212.

59. See Ronald Dale Karr, "'Why Should you be so Furious?': The Violence of the Pequot War," *Journal of American History* 85 (1998): 876–909.

60. Underhill, *Newes from America*, 35–36.

61. James Kendall Hosmer, ed., *Winthrop's Journal "History of New England," 1630–1649* (New York: Scribners, 1908), vol. 1, p. 194.

62. Outside the context of adoption, this topic has not been studied widely. For a survey of the textual evidence see Nathaniel Knowles, "The Torture of Captives by the Indians of Eastern North America," *Proceedings of the American Philosophical Society* 82 (1940): 151–225. See also Karen Anderson, *Chain her by One Foot: The Subjugation of Women in Seventeenth-Century New France* (London: Routledge, 1991), 169–78.

63. Lyndal Roper, *Oedipus and the Devil: Witchcraft, Religion and Sexuality in Early Modern Europe* (London: Routledge, 1994), 205.

64. Steven Pinker, *The Better Angels of our Nature: A History of Violence and Humanity* (New York: Penguin, 2012), 71–154; Norbert Elias, *The Civilizing Process: State Formation and Civilization* (Oxford: Oxford University Press, 1982).

65. Hugo Grotius, *The Illustrious Hugo Grotius of the Law of Warre and Peace* (London, 1654), 294.

66. For context see Geoffrey Parker, "Early Modern Europe," in *The Laws of War: Contraints on Warfare in the Western World*, ed. Michael Howard, George J. Andreopoulos, and Mark R. Shulman (New Haven, CT: Yale University Press, 1994), 40–58.

67. William Gouge, *God's Three Arrowes Plague, Famine, Sword, in Three Treatises* (London, 1631). See Karr, "'Why Should you be so Furious?'," 880.

68. Charles Lawrence, Orders for attacking Louisbourg, May 1758, Abercromby Papers 303, Huntington Library.

69. *Boston Newsletter*, August 27, 1724; *The Rebels Reward: or, English Courage Display'd* (Boston, 1724); Ian Saxine, *Properties of Empire: Indians, Colonists, and Land Speculators on the New England Frontier* (New York: New York University Press, 2019), 77, 154.

70. Resolution of the council of Nova Scotia, October 1, 1749, CO 217/9, 117; Edward Cornwallis, Proclamation, October 2, 1749, CO 217/9, 118, The National Archives, Kew.

71. Patricia Seed, "Taking Possession and Reading Texts: Establishing the Authority of Overseas Empires," *William and Mary Quarterly* 49 (1992): 183–209, 202–05.
72. Bartolome´ de Bohorque, quoted Celendinnen, *Cost of Courage*, 98.
73. Fray Diego de Landa, quoted in Celendinnen, *Cost of Courage*, 100.
74. Mark Meuwese, "Imperial Peace and Restraints in the Dutch-Iberian Wars for Brazil, 1624–1654," in *The Specter of Peace: Rethinking Violence and Power in the Colonial Atlantic*, ed. Michael Goode and John Smolenski (Leiden: Brill, 2018), 30–63, 52–53.
75. Summary of a Letter from Dom Pedro,1 King of Kongo, to Monsignor João Baptista Vivès, São Salvador, 23 November 1623, in Malyn Newitt, ed., *The Portuguese in West Africa, 1415–1670: A Documentary History* (Cambridge: Cambridge University Press, 2012), 178–81.
76. Broad Advice, or Dialogue about the Trade of the West India Company," trans. Henry Murphy, in *Collections of the New York Historical Society* 3 (1856): 256.
77. Edmund B. O'Callaghan, ed., *Documents Relative to the Colonial History of the State of New York*, 15 vols. (Albany, NY: Weed, Parson, 1853–1887), 1:414.
78. Evan Haefeli, "Keift's War and the Cultures of Violence in Colonial America," in *Lethal Imagination: Violence and Brutality in American History*, ed. Michael A. Bellesiles (New York: New York University Press, 1999), 17–40.
79. Grotius, *Illustrious Hugo Grotius*, 589.
80. Gouge, *God's Three Arrowes*. See Karr, " 'Why Should you be so Furious?'," 880.
81. See chapter 4.
82. On wars to destroy rival settlements see Craig S. Keener, "An Ethnohistorical Analysis of Iroquois Assault Tactics Used against Fortified Settlements of the Northeast in the Seventeenth Century," *Ethnohistory* 46 (1999): 777–807.
83. Charles Orr, ed., *History of the Pequot War* (Cleveland: Helman-Taylor, 1897), 132.
84. Orr, ed., *History of the Pequot War*, 38.
85. Steven T. Katz, "The Pequot War Reconsidered," *New England Quarterly* 64 (1991): 206–24, 210–11.
86. Orr, ed., *History of the Pequot War*, 62.
87. Ann M. Little, *Abraham in Arms: Gender and War in Colonial New England* (Philadelphia: University of Pennsylvania Press, 2007), 22–23.
88. Padden, "Cultural Change and Military Resistance," 119–20.
89. Langfur, *Forbidden Lands*, 169–74.
90. Thwaites, ed., *Jesuit Relations*, 35:111.
91. On martyrdom in this context see Allan Greer, "Colonial Saints: Gender, Race, and Hagiography in New France," *William and Mary Quarterly* 57 (2000): 323–48.
92. Sharon Block, *Rape and Sexual Power in Early America* (Chapel Hill: University of North Carolina Press, 2006), 221–22.
93. Grotius, *Illustrious Hugo Grotius*, 551–52; Lynn, *Women, Armies, and Warfare*, 153–59.
94. Plank, *Rebellion and Savagery*, 172.
95. Michael L. Fickes, "'They Could not Endure that Yoke': The Captivity of Pequot Women and Children after the War of 1637," *New England Quarterly* 73 (2000): 58–81, 70.
96. Junipero Serra, quoted in Antonia I. Castañeda, "Sexual Violence in the Politics and Policies of Conquest: Amerindian Women and the Spanish Conquest of Alta California," in *Building with our Hands: New Directions in Chicana Studies*, ed. Adela de la Torre and Beatriz M. Pesquera (Berkeley: University of California Press, 1993), 15–33, 15.
97. Boucher, *Cannibal Encounters*, 49.
98. Alden T. Vaughn, "'Expulsion of the Salvages': English Policy and the Virginia Massacre of 1622," *William and Mary Quarterly* 35 (1978): 57–84, 78.
99. Boucher, *Cannibal Encounters*, 88.
100. "Letter of Sir Francis Wyatt, Governor of Virginia, 1621–1626," *William and Mary Quarterly* 6 (1926): 114–21, 118.
101. Boucher, *Cannibal Encounters*, 88.
102. Elizabeth A. Fenn, "Biological Warfare in Eighteenth-century North America: Beyond Jeffery Amherst," *Journal of American History* 86 (2000): 1553–80.
103. Richard White, *The Middle Ground: Indians, Empires, and Republics in the Great Lakes Region, 1650–1815* (Cambridge: Cambridge University Press, 1991), 269–314.

104. Dylan Ruediger, "'In Peace with All, or at least in Warre with None': Tributary Subjects and the Negotiation of Political Subordination in Greater Virginia, 1676–1730," in *Specter of Peace*, ed. Goode and Smolenski, 64–94.

105. Boucher, *Cannibal Encounters*, 88.

106. Several scholars have emphasized the importance of this dynamic in US military history. See John Shy, "The American Military Experience: History and Learning," *Journal of Interdisciplinary History* 1 (1971): 205–28; Russell F. Weigley, *The American Way of War* (Bloomington: Indiana University Press, 1973); Brian M. Linn, "*The American Way of War* Revisited," *Journal of Military History* 66 (2002): 501–33; John Grenier, *The First Way of War: American Warmaking on the Frontier* (New York: Cambridge University Press, 2005); Fred Anderson and Andrew Cayton, *The Dominion of War: Empire and Liberty in North America* (New York: Penguin, 2005).

107. See, for example, Hal Langfur, "Moved by Terror: Frontier Violence as Cultural Exchange in Late-Colonial Brazil," *Ethnohistory* 52 (2005): 255–89.

108. Lawrence H. Keeley, *War Before Civilization: The Myth of the Peaceful Savage* (New York: Oxford University Press, 1996); Pinker, *Better Angels*, 40–56.

109. Noble David Cook, *Born to Die: Disease and New World Conquest, 1492–1650* (Cambridge: Cambridge University Press, 1998).

110. John F. Schwaller, "Research Note: Broken Spears or Broken Bones: Evolution of the Most Famous Line in Nahuatl," *The Americas* 66 (2009): 241–52, 249–50.

111. David S. Jones, "Virgin Soils Revisited," *William and Mary Quarterly* 60 (2003): 703–42.

Chapter 8

1. Edward Bancroft, *An Essay on the Natural History of Guiana* (London, 1766), 257–58.

2. Camilla Townsend, *Malintzin's Choices: An Indian Woman in the Conquest of Mexico* (Albuquerque: University of New Mexico Press, 2006), 20, 24.

3. Gallay, *Indian Slave Trade*, 116.

4. Paul E. Lovejoy, *Transformations in Slavery: A History of Slavery in Africa* (Cambridge: Cambridge University Press, 2012), 64.

5. See Robin Law, *The Slave Coast of West Africa, 1550–1750: The Impact of the Atlantic Slave Trade on an African Society* (Oxford: Clarendon Press, 1991), 66–67.

6. John K. Thornton, *The Kingdom of Kongo: Civil War and Transition, 1641–1718* (Madison: University of Wisconsin Press, 1983), 48–49.

7. Paul Erdmann Isert, *Letters on West Africa and the Slave Trade*, ed. Selena Axelrod Winsnes (Accra, Ghana: Sub-Saharan Publishers, 2007), 127.

8. Robin Law, *Ouidah: The Social History of a West African Slaving "'Port',"* 1727–1892 (Athens: Ohio University Press, 2004), 76–77.

9. Robert Morris, *Memoirs of the Reign of Bossa Ahadee* (London, 1789), 86. See Law, *Slave Coast of West Africa*, 272; see also Law, *Ouidah*, 76–77.

10. David Eltis and Stanley L. Engerman, "Dependence, Servility, and Coerced Labor in Time and Space," in *The Cambridge World History of Slavery*, vol. 3, ed. Eltis and Engerman (Cambridge: Cambridge University Press, 2017), 1–21, 4.

11. Ólafur Egilsson, *The Travels of Reverend Ólafur Egilsson*, trans. Karl Smári Hreinsson and Adam Nichols (Washington, DC: Catholic University Press, 2016), 15.

12. Egilsson, *Travels*, 9.

13. Egilsson, *Travels*, xxiii–xxiv.

14. Egilsson, *Travels*, 18.

15. Egilsson, *Travels*, 19.

16. Egilsson, *Travels*, xxii–xxiii.

17. Egilsson, *Travels*, 10.

18. Egilsson, *Travels*, xxvii–xxviii.

19. Paul Walden Bamford, "The Procurement of Oarsmen for French Galleys, 1660–1748," *American Historical Review* 65 (1959): 31–48, 40–41.

20. Grotius, *Illustrious Hugo Grotius*, 570.

21. See Carla Pestana, *The English Atlantic in an Age of Revolution, 1640–1661* (Cambridge, MA: Harvard University Press, 2004), 188.

22. Bamford, "Procurement of Oarsmen," 36.

23. Bamford, "Procurement of Oarsmen," 40.

24. William G. Clarence-Smith and David Eltis, "White Servitude," in *Cambridge World History of Slavery*, ed. Eltis and Engerman, 3:132–59, 133.

25. Robert C. Davis, *Christian Slaves, Muslim Masters: White Slavery in the Mediterranean, the Barbary Coast and Italy* (New York: Palgrave, 2004), 16–21.

26. Davis, *Christian Slaves, Muslim Masters*, 17.

27. Egilsson, *Travels*, xxxii.

28. Egilsson, *Travels*, 8.

29. Ruth Pike, *Penal Servitude in Early Modern Spain* (Madison: University of Wisconsin Press, 1983), 9, 24.

30. Pike, *Penal Servitude*, 28–29.

31. Bamford, "Procurement of Oarsmen," 33–34; G. E. Aylmer, "Slavery under Charles II: The Mediterranean and Tangier," *English Historical Review* 114 (1999): 378–88, 380.

32. On Muslim practice see Lovejoy, *Transformations in Slavery*, 29–36.

33. See David Eltis, *The Rise of African Slavery in the Americas* (Cambridge: Cambridge University Press, 2000), 1–28.

34. Antonio de Montesinos quoted by Bartolome de las Casas in J. H. Parry, Robert G. Keith, and Michael Jimenez, eds., *New Iberian World: A Documentary History of the Discovery and Settlement of Latin America to the Early Seventeenth Century* 5 vols. (New York: Times Books, 1984), 2:310.

35. Massimo Livi-Bacci, "Return to Hispaniola: Reassessing a Demographic Catastrophe," *Hispanic American Historical Review* 83 (2003): 3–51, 39–40.

36. Lesley Byrd Simpson, *The Encomienda in New Spain: The Beginning of Spanish Mexico* (Berkeley: University of California Press, 1950), 2–3.

37. Simpson, *Encomienda in New Spain*, 13.

38. Erin Woodruff Stone, "Indian Harvest: The Rise of the Indigenous Slave Trade and Diaspora from Española to the Circum-Caribbean, 1492–1542" (PhD diss., Vanderbilt University, 2014); William L. Sherman, *Forced Labour in Sixteenth-Century Central America* (Lincoln: University of Nebraska Press, 1979).

39. Edward Johnson quoted in Fickes, "'They Could Not Endure that Yoke,'" 62.

40. Fickes, "'They Could Not Endure that Yoke,'" 59–60.

41. Margaret Ellen Newell, *Brethren by Nature: New England Indians, Colonists, and the Origins of American Slavery* (Ithaca, NY: Cornell University Press, 2015), 38.

42. Fickes, "'They Could Not Endure that Yoke,'" 78.

43. Newell, *Brethren by Nature*, 144–54.

44. *Collection of Voyages*, 5:327.

45. Thomas Tryon, *Friendly Advice to the Gentlemen-Planters of the East and West Indies* (London, 1684), 81.

46. See, for example, Phillips P. Moulton, ed., *The Journal and Major Essays of John Woolman* (Richmond, IN: Friends United Press, 1971), 61.

47. Tryon's views on race and slavery were idiosyncratic and open to conflicting interpretations. See Geoffrey Plank, "Thomas Tryon, Sheep, and the Politics of Eden," *Cultural and Social History* 14 (2017): 565–81.

48. Linda M. Heywood, "Slavery and its Transformation in the Kingdom of Kongo, 1491–1800," *Journal of African History* 50 (2009): 1–22, 6.

49. Duarte Lopes, quoted in Heywood, "Slavery and its Transformation," 7.

50. Heywood, "Slavery and its Transformation," 15.

51. Antonio Cavazzi, cited in Heywood, "Slavery and its Transformation," 20.

52. Garcia II quoted in Jan Vansina, *Kingdoms of the Savannah* (Madison: University of Wisconsin Press, 1966), 142–43.

53. See Eltis and Engerman, "Dependence, Servility, and Coerced Labor," 4.

54. Neil L. Whitehead, "Indigenous Slavery in South America, 1492–1820," in *Cambridge World History of Slavery*, ed. Eltis and Engerman, 3:248–71, 248.

55. Carlos Fausto and David Rodgers, "Of Enemies and Pets: Warfare and Shamanism in Amazonia," *American Ethnologist* 26 (1999): 933–56.
56. For an evocative description of slavery in eighteenth-century New York see Jill Lapore, *New York Burning: Liberty, Slavery and Conspiracy in Eighteenth-Century Manhattan* (New York: Vintage, 2006). On livestock keepers see Philip D. Morgan, "Slaves and Livestock in Eighteenth-Century Jamaica: Vineyard Pen, 1750–1751," *William and Mary Quarterly* 52 (1995): 47–76; Andrew Sluyter, *Black Ranching Frontiers: African Cattle Herders of the Atlantic World, 1500–1900* (New Haven, CT: Yale University Press, 2012).
57. Important comparative works highlighting crops and their influence on the living conditions of slaves include Richard S. Dunn, *A Tale of Two Plantations: Slave Life and Labor in Jamaica and Virginia* (Cambridge, MA: Harvard University Press, 2014), and Philip D. Morgan, *Slave Counterpoint: Black Culture in the Eighteenth-century Chesapeake and Lowcountry* (Chapel Hill: University of North Carolina Press, 1998). See also Dale W. Tomich, *Through the Prism of Slavery: Labor, Capital, and World Economy* (Lanham, MD: Rowman & Littlefield, 2004).
58. David Eltis, Frank D. Lewis, and David Richardson, "Slave Prices, the African Slave Trade, and Productivity in the Caribbean, 1674–1807," *Economic History Review* 58 (2005): 673–700, 677, n.19.
59. Kenneth F. Kiple, *The Caribbean Slave: A Biological History* (Cambridge: Cambridge University Press, 1985), 106.
60. Tryon, *Friendly Advice*, 142.
61. Erin Woodruff Stone, "America's First Slave Revolt: Indians and African Slaves in Española, 1500–1534," *Ethnohistory* 60 (2013): 195–217; Ida Altman, "The Revolt of Enriquillo and the Historiography of Early Spanish America," *The Americas* 63 (2007): 587–614.
62. Stone, "America's First Slave Revolt," 206.
63. Alida C. Metcalf, "Millenarian Slaves? The Santidade de Jaguaripe and Slave Resistance in the Americas," *American Historical Review* 104 (1999): 1531–59, 1531.
64. Metcalf, "Millenarian Slaves?," 1552.
65. Metcalf, "Millenarian Slaves?," 1551.
66. Metcalf, "Millenarian Slaves?," 1552.
67. Fisher, "'Dangerous Designes,'" 118.
68. Ruth Pike, "Black Rebels: The Cimarrons of Sixteenth-century Panama," *The Americas* 64 (2007): 243–66.
69. Wheat, *Atlantic Africa*, 54–63.
70. Robert Nelson Anderson, "The Quilombo of Palmares: A New Overview of a Maroon State in Seventeenth-century Brazil," *Journal of Latin American Studies* 28 (1996): 545–66; Charles E. Orser and Pedro P.A. Funari, "Archaeology and Slave Resistance and Rebellion," *World Archaeology* 33 (2001): 61–72.
71. See generally Anderson, "Quilombo of Palmares;" on archaeology and fortification see Orser and Funari, "Archaeology and Slave Resistance," 67–68, and Stuart B. Schwartz, *Slaves, Peasants and Rebels: Reconsidering Brazilian Slavery* (Urbana: University of Illinois Press, 1992), 114–16.
72. Manuel Barcia, *West African Warfare in Bahia and Cuba: Soldier Slaves in the Atlantic World, 1807–1844* (Oxford: Oxford University Press, 2014), 106–07, 117, 150–51.
73. Barcia, *West African Warfare*, 111.
74. Barbara Klamon Kopytoff, "The Early Political Development of Jamaican Maroon Societies," *William and Mary Quarterly* 25 (1978): 287–307, 299.
75. James Knight, quoted in Kopytoff, "Early Political Development," 297.
76. Anderson, "Quilombo of Palmares," 551–52.
77. Kopytoff, "Early Political Development," 301.
78. Kopytoff, "Early Political Development," 304.
79. Schwartz, *Slaves, Peasants and Rebels*, 124.
80. Metcalf, "Millenarian Slaves?," 1531.
81. Philip Thicknesse, *Memoirs and Anecdotes of Philip Thicknesse, Late Lieutenant Governor of Land Guard Fort* (1788), 121–22.
82. Vernon Valentine Palmer, "The Origins and Authors of the Code Noir," 56 *Louisiana Law Review* (1995): 363–407, 376, 384.

83. Malick M. Ghachem, "Prosecuting Torture: The Strategic Ethics of Slavery in Pre-Revolutionary Saint-Domingue (Haiti)," *Law and History Review* 29 (2011): 985–1029, 993.
84. Sally E. Hadden, *Slave Patrols: Law and Violence in Virginia and the Carolinas* (Cambridge, MA: Harvard University Press, 2001), 11.
85. Diana Paton, "Punishment, Crime, and the Bodies of Slaves in Eighteenth-century Jamaica," *Journal of Social History* 34 (2001): 923–54, 926.
86. Paton, "Punishment, Crime, and the Bodies," 940.
87. For Danish and Portuguese examples see N. A. T. Hall, "Maritime Maroons: "'Grand Marronage' from the Danish West Indies," *William and Mary Quarterly* 42 (1985): 476–98, 484; Schwartz, *Slaves, Peasants and Rebels*, 120.
88. Paton, "Punishment, Crime, and the Bodies," 939.
89. Natalie Zemon Davis, "Judges, Masters, Diviners: Slaves' Experience of Criminal Justice in Colonial Suriname," *Law and History Review* 29 (2011): 925–84, 962.
90. Paton, "Punishment, Crime, and the Bodies," 931.
91. Davis, "Judges, Masters, Diviners," 970.
92. Altman, "Revolt of Enriquillo," 599–600.
93. Pike, "Black Rebels," 248.
94. Schwartz, *Slaves, Peasants and Rebels*, 108, 123.
95. Schwartz, *Slaves, Peasants and Rebels*, 119–120.
96. Hadden, *Slave Patrols*, 227–28, n.20.
97. Stewart R. King, "The Maréchausée of Saint-Domingue: Balancing the Ancién Regime and Modernity," *Journal of Colonialism and Colonial History* 5 (2004), DOI: 10.1353/cch.2004.0052.
98. Kopytoff, "Early Political Development," 294.
99. Hadden, *Slave Patrols*, 6–40.
100. William Bull to the Board of Trade, October 5, 1739, in *Calendar of State Papers Colonial, American and West Indies*, vol. 45 (London: Her Majesty's Stationary Office, 1994), document 404. For more on the Stono Rebellion see Thornton, "African Dimensions of the Stono Rebellion."
101. Marjoleine Kars, "'Cleansing the Land': Dutch-Amerindian Cooperation in the Suppression of the 1763 Slave Rebellion in Dutch Guiana," in *Empires and Indigenes*, ed. Lee, 251–75.
102. Richter, "War and Culture."
103. Brett Rushforth, *Bonds of Alliance: Indigenous and Atlantic Slaveries in New France* (Chapel Hill: University of North Carolina Press, 2012). See also Brooks, *Captives and Cousins*.
104. Richard White, *The Roots of Dependency: Subsistence, Environment, and Social Change among the Choctaws, Pawnees, and Navajos* (Lincoln: University of Nebraska Press, 1983), 1–146; Gallay, *Indian Slave Trade*.
105. Neil L. Whitehead, "Indigenous Slavery in South America," 257.
106. Christina Snyder, *Slavery in Indian Country: The Changing Face of Captivity in Early America* (Cambridge, MA: Harvard University Press, 2012).
107. Duarte Gomes de Silveira quoted in Schwartz, *Slaves, Peasants and Rebels*, 110.
108. Schwartz, *Slaves, Peasants and Rebels*, 108.
109. *London Magazine and Monthly Chronologer* 9 (1740) 152.
110. Manuel Barcia, "'To Kill All Whites': The Ethics of African Warfare in Bahia and Cuba, 1807–1844," *Journal of African Military History* 1 (2017): 72–92, 77–78.
111. Matthew Restall, "Black Conquistadors: Armed Africans in Early Spanish America," *The Americas* 57 (2000): 171–205.
112. Jane Landers, "Transforming Bondsmen into Vassals: Arming Slaves in Colonial Spanish America," in *Arming Slaves: From Classical Times to the Modern Age*, ed. Christopher Leslie Brown and Philip D. Morgan (New Haven, CT: Yale University Press, 2006), 122–23.
113. Hendrk Kraay, "Arming Slaves in Brazil from the Seventeenth Century to the Nineteenth Century," in *Arming Slaves*, ed. Brown and Morgan, 146–79, 155–56.
114. Matthew Restall, "Crossing to Safety? Frontier Flight in Eighteenth-Century Belize and Yucatan," *Hispanic American Historical Review* 94 (2014): 381–419; Jane Landers, "Gracia Real de Santa Teresa de Mose: A Free Black Town in Spanish Colonial Florida," *American Historical Review* 95 (1990): 9–30.

115. Altman, "Revolt of Enriquillo," 602.
116. Pike, "Black Rebels," 264–65.
117. Helen McKee, "From Violence to Alliance: Maroons and White Settlers in Jamaica, 1739–1795," *Slavery and Abolition* 39 (2018): 27–52; M. L. E. Moreau de Saint-Méry, "The Border Maroons of Saint-Domingue: The Maniel," in *Maroon Societies*, ed. Price, 135–48, 140.
118. Tom Cummins, "Three Gentlemen from Esmeraldas: A Portrait Fit for a King," in *Slave Portraiture in the Atlantic World*, ed. Agnes Lugo-Ortiz and Angela Rosenthal (Cambridge: Cambridge University Press, 2013), 119–45, 126.
119. Jane Landers, "Leadership and Authority in Maroon Settlements in Spanish America and Brazil," in *Africa and the Americas: Interconnections during the Slave Trade*, ed. José C. Curto and Renée Soulodre-La France (Trenton, NJ: African World Press, 2005), 173–84, 174–75.
120. Cummins, "Three Gentlemen from Esmeraldas," 130.

Chapter 9

1. Karen Larsen, *A History of Norway* (Princeton, NJ: Princeton University Press, 1948), 178.
2. Bruce E. Gelsinger, *Icelandic Enterprise: Commerce and Economy in the Middle Ages* (Columbia: University of South Carolina Press, 1981), 184.
3. Gelsinger, *Icelandic Enterprise*, 185.
4. G. J. Marcus, "The First English Voyages to Iceland," *Mariner's Mirror* 42 (1956): 313–18, 313–14.
5. Marcus, "First English Voyages," 314.
6. Marcus, "First English Voyages," 316.
7. E. M. Carus Wilson, "The Iceland Trade," in *Studies in English Trade in the Fifteenth Century*, ed. Eileen Power and M. M. Postan (London: Routledge & Kegan Paul, 1933), 155–82, 164.
8. Kirsten A. Seaver, *The Frozen Echo: Greenland and the Exploration of North America, ca. A.D. 1000–1500* (Stanford, CA: Stanford University Press, 1996), 178–79.
9. Wilson, "Iceland Trade," 167; Seaver, *Frozen Echo*, 179.
10. Gelsinger, *Icelandic Enterprise*, 192.
11. Anna Agnarsdóttir, "Iceland's 'English Century' and East Anglia's North Sea World," in *East Anglia and its North Sea World in the Middle Ages*, ed. David Bates and Robert Liddiard (Woodbridge: Boydell Press, 2013), 204–16, 204.
12. Gelsinger, *Icelandic Enterprise*, 193; Wilson, "Iceland Trade," 179–80; Seaver, *Frozen Echo*, 198.
13. Raimondo di Socini to the Duke of Milan, London, 18 December 1497, in H. P. Biggar, ed., *The Precursors of Jacques Cartier, 1497–1534* (Ottawa: Canadian Archives, 1911), 20.
14. Evan Jones, "England's Icelandic Fishery in the Early Modern Period," in *England's Sea Fisheries: The Commercial Sea Fisheries of England and Wales since 1300*, ed. David J. Starkey, Chris Read, and Neil Ashcroft (London: Chatham Publishing, 2000), 105–18.
15. Anthony Parkhurst to Richard Hakluyt, 1578, in E. G. R. Taylor, ed., *The Original Writings and Correspondence of the Two Richard Hakluyts* (London: Hakluyt Society, 1935), 1:127–34, 128–29.
16. Max Friesen, "Pan-Arctic Population Movements: The Early Paleo-Inuit and Thule Inuit Migrations," in *The Oxford Handbook of the Prehistoric Arctic*, ed. Max Friesen and Owen Mason (New York: Oxford University Press, 2016).
17. Vilhjalmur Stefansson, ed., *The Three Voyages of Martin Frobisher*, vol. 1 (London, 1938), 48–50.
18. Alden T. Vaughan, *Transatlantic Encounters: American Indians in Britain, 1500–1776* (Cambridge: Cambridge University Press,), 1–5.
19. Greg Mitchell, "The Inuit of Southern Labrador and their Conflicts with Europeans, to 1767," in *Exploring Atlantic Transitions: Archaeologies of Transience and Permanence in New Found Lands*, ed. Peter E. Pope and Shannon Lewis-Simpson (Woodbridge: Boydell, 2013), 320–30, 321–22.
20. H. P. Biggar, ed., *The Works of Samuel De Champlain* (Toronto: Champlain Society, 1933), 168.
21. William Fitzhugh, "Archaeology of the Inuit of Southern Labrador and the Quebec Lower North Shore," in *Oxford Handbook of the Prehistoric Arctic*, ed. Friesen and Mason, 932–60.

22. P. E. H. Hair, *The Founding of the Castelo de São Jorge da Mina: An Analysis of the Sources* (Madison: University of Wisconsin African Studies Program, 1994), 14; Boxer, *Portuguese Seaborne Empire*, 25.

23. Lovejoy, *Transformations in Slavery*, 24–44.

24. Thornton, *Warfare in Atlantic Africa*, 23; Thornton, *Cultural History*, 21–22.

25. Hair, *Founding of the Castelo*, 14. See also generally, John Vogt, *Portuguese Rule on the Gold Coast* (Athens: University of Georgia Press, 1979), 19–32.

26. Vogt, *Portuguese Rule*, 85–86; Meuwese, *Brothers in Arms*, 64–65.

27. Quoted in Hair, *Founding of the Castelo*, 1.

28. Richard Eden, *The Decades of the Newe World or West India . . .* in *The First Three English Books on America*, ed. Edward Arbor (Birmingham, 1885), 373.

29. Hernán Cortés to Charles V, 1519, in Stuart B. Schwartz, ed., *Victors and Vanquished: Spanish and Naua Views of the Conquest of Mexico* (New York: Bedford, 2000), 75–78, 76; see Matthew Restall, *Seven Myths of the Spanish Conquest* (Oxford: Oxford University Press, 2003), 20.

30. See Restall, *Seven Myths*.

31. City council of Huejotzingo to Philip II, 1560, in James Lockhart and Enrique Otte, eds., *Letters and People of the Spanish Indies: Sixteenth Century* (Cambridge: Cambridge University Press, 1976), 165–72, 167–68.

32. Alf Hornborg and Jonathan D. Hill, eds., *Ethnicity in Ancient Amazonia: Reconstructing Past Identities from Archaeology, Linguistics, and Ethnohistory* (Boulder: University Press of Colorado, 2011). On the military dimension of this transformation see Carlo Fausto, *Warfare and Shamanism in Amazonia*, trans. David Rodgers (Cambridge: Cambridge University Press, 2012), 18–23.

33. Lee, "Fortify, Fight, or Flee," 726–27.

34. Dye, *War Paths, Peace Paths*, 141–66.

35. Robbie Ethridge, "The Emergence of the Colonial South: Colonial Indian Slaving, the Fall of the Precontact Mississippian World, and the Emergence of a New Social Geography in the American South, 1540–1730," in *Native American Adoption, Captivity, and Slavery in Changing Contexts*, ed. Max Caroccie and Stephanie Platt (New York: Palgrave Macmillan, 2012), 47–64.

36. Alexander VI, "Inter Caetera," May 4, 1493. http://www.nativeweb.org/pages/legal/indig-inter-caetera.html

37. See Jerry Brotton, *Trading Territories: Mapping the Early Modern World* (London: Reaktion Books, 1997), 119–50.

38. See Patricia Seed, *Ceremonies of Possession in Europe's Conquest of the New World, 1492–1640* (Cambridge: Cambridge University Press, 1995), 69.

39. Boucher, *France and the American Tropics*, 41–42.

40. Silvia Castro Shannon, "Religious Struggle in France and Colonial Failure in Brazil, 1555–1615," *French Colonial History* 1 (2002): 51–62; John McGrath, "Polemic and History in French Brazil, 1550–1560," *Sixteenth Century Journal* 27 (1996): 385–97.

41. Karen Ordahl Kupperman, *The Jamestown Project* (Cambridge, MA: Harvard University Press, 2008), 45–46.

42. Francisco López de Mendoza Grajales, "Memoire of the Happy Result and Prosperous Voyage of the Fleet Commanded by the Adelantado Pedro Menendez de Aviles," in *Laudonniere and Fort Caroline: History and Documents*, ed. Charles E. Bennett (Tuscaloosa: University of Alabama Press, 2009), 141–63, 163.

43. Owen Stanwood, "Catholics, Protestants, and the Clash of Civilizations in Early America," in *The First Prejudice: Religious Tolerance and Intolerance in Early America*, ed. Chris Beneke and Christopher S. Grenda (Philadelphia: University of Pennsylvania Press, 2011), 218–40, 221–22.

44. Wim Klooster, *The Dutch Moment: War, Trade and Settlement in the Seventeenth Century Atlantic World* (Ithaca, NY: Cornell University Press, 2016), 26, 30, 42, 67.

45. Klooster, *Dutch Moment: War*, 29.

46. Klooster, *Dutch Moment*, 23; J. Braat, "Dutch Activities in the North and Arctic during the Sixteenth and Seventeenth Centuries," *Arctic* 37 (1984): 473–80.

47. Harmen Meyndertsz van den Bogaert, "A Journey into Mohawk and Oneida Country," in *In Mohawk Country: Early Narratives about a Native People*, ed. Dean R. Snow, Charles T. Gehring, and William A. Starna (Syracuse, N.Y.: Syracuse University Press, 1996), 1–13, 8–9.
48. Silverman, *Thundersticks*, 21–28.
49. Klooster, *Dutch Moment*, 33–73.
50. Eliga H. Gould, "Zones of Law, Zones of Violence: The Legal Geography of the British Atlantic, circa 1772," *William and Mary Quarterly* 60 (2003): 471–510, 480–81.
51. Statement of Don Juan Desloguren, 1637, quoted in *Venezuela-British Guiana Boundary Arbitration* (New York, 1899), 281.
52. See Meuwese, *Brothers in Arms*.
53. Klooster, *Dutch Moment*, 31, 49.
54. Meuwese, *Brothers in Arms*, 137–41.
55. Meuwese, *Brothers in Arms*, 141–43.
56. Meuwese, *Brothers in Arms*, 157.
57. Meuwese, *Brothers in Arms*, 151.
58. Klooster, *Dutch Moment*, 53–54.
59. N. N., *A Little True Forraine Newes* (London, 1642).
60. Meuwese, *Brothers in Arms*, 213.
61. Meuwese, *Brothers in Arms*, 155–56.
62. Linda M. Heywood and John K. Thornton, *Central Africans, Atlantic Creoles, and the Foundation of the Americas, 1585–1660* (Cambridge: Cambridge University Press, 2007), 145–52; Meuwese, *Brothers in Arms*, 201–27; Klooster, *Dutch Moment*, 82–83.
63. See Carla Gardina Pestana, "English Character and the Fiasco of the Western Design," *Early American Studies* 3 (2005): 1–31.
64. Daniel K. Richter, "Rediscovered Links in the Covenant Chain: Previously Unpublished Transcripts of New York Indian Treaty Minutes, 1677–1691," *Proceedings of the American Antiquarian Society* 92 (1982): 45–85, 76.
65. Daniel K. Richter, *The Ordeal of the Longhouse: The Peoples of the Iroquois League in the Era of European Colonization* (Chapel Hill: University of North Carolina Press, 1992), 135–37.
66. Jean R. Soderlund, *Lenape Country: Delaware Valley Society Before William Penn* (Philadelphia: University of Pennsylvania Press, 2015).
67. Geoffrey Plank, "Discipline and Divinity: Colonial Quakerism, Christianity, and 'Heathenism' in the Seventeenth Century." *Church History* 85 (2016): 502–28.
68. William Penn to the Kings of the Indians, October 18, 1681, in Richard Dunn and Mary Maples Dunn, eds., *The Papers of William Penn*, vol. 2 (Philadelphia: University of Pennsylvania Press, 1982), 128–29. See Daniel K. Richter, "Land and Words," in *Trade, Land, Power: The Struggle for Eastern North America*, ed. Richter (Philadelphia: University of Pennsylvania Press, 2013), 135–54.
69. James H. Merrell, *Into the American Woods: Negotiators on the Pennsylvania Frontier* (New York: Norton, 1999).
70. Patrick M. Erben, *A Harmony of the Spirits: Translation and the Language of Community in Early Pennsylvania* (Chapel Hill: University of North Carolina Press, 2012).
71. See Patrick Spero, *Frontier Country: The Politics of War in Early Pennsylvania* (Philadelphia: University of Pennsylvania Press, 2016).

Chapter 10

1. Glete, *War and the State*; John Brewer, *The Sinews of Power: War, Money and the English State, 1688–1783* (Cambridge, MA: Harvard University Press, 1990).
2. Eliga H. Gould, *The Persistence of Empire: British Political Culture in the Age of the American Revolution* (Chapel Hill: University of North Carolina Press, 2000), 3–14; Tony Claydon, *Europe and the Making of England, 1660–1760* (Cambridge: Cambridge University Press, 2007), 192–98.
3. Creveld, *Supplying War*, 5–39; John A. Lynn, "How War Fed War: The Tax of Violence and Contributions during the Grand Siècle," *Journal of Modern History* 65 (1993): 286–310.

4. See for example Kwame Yebao Daako, *Trade and Politics on the Gold Coast, 1600–1720* (Oxford: Clarendon Press, 1970).

5. Langfur, *Forbidden Lands.*

6. Lynn, *Giant of the Grand Siècle*, 18.

7. Brewer, *Sinews of Power*, 32; Lynn, *Giant of the Grand Siècle*, 47.

8. Guy Rowlands, "Louis XIV, Vittorio Amedeo and French Military Failure in Italy, 1688–96," *English Historical Review* 115 (2000): 534–69.

9. Owen Stanwood. *The Empire Reformed: English America in the Age of the Glorious Revolution* (Philadelphia: University of Pennsylvania Press, 2011), 87; Kristen Block and Jenny Shaw, "Subjects without an Empire: The Irish in the Early Modern Caribbean," *Past and Present* 210 (2011): 33–60; Hilary McD. Beckles, "'A Riotous and Unruly Lot': Irish Indentured Servants and Freemen in the English West Indies, 1644–1713," *William and Mary Quarterly* 47 (1990): 503–22; Boucher, *France and the American Tropics*, 218.

10. William Thomas Morgan, "The British West Indies during King William's War (1689–97)," *Journal of Modern History* 2 (1930): 378–409, 383, 394.

11. Morgan, "British West Indies during King William's War;" Boucher, *France and the American Tropics*, 220.

12. Robin Law, *The Slave Coast of West Africa*, 129–32; Robin Law, ed., *Correspondence from the Royal African Company's Factories at Offra and Whydah on the Slave Coast of West Africa in the Public Record Office, London, 1678–93* (Edinburgh: Centre of African Studies, Edinburgh University, 1990), 71–74.

13. Emerson W. Baker and John G. Reid, "Amerindian Power in the Early Modern Northeast: A Reappraisal," *William and Mary Quarterly* 61 (2004): 77–106.

14. O'Callaghan, ed., *Documents*, 1:286.

15. O'Callaghan. ed., *Documents*, 1:292–97.

16. Morgan, "British West Indies during King William's War," 385.

17. Edwin Stede to Jacob Leisler, January 27, 1690, Leisler Papers, New York University.

18. See Emerson W. Baker and John G. Reid, *The New England Knight: Sir William Phips, 1651–1695* (Toronto: University of Toronto Press, 1998), 86–109.

19. Cotton Mather, *The Present State of New England* (Boston, 1690), 35.

20. Cotton Mather, *Decennium Luctuosum* (Boston, 1699), 213–14.

21. Mather, *Decennium Luctuosum*, 235.

22. Mather, *Decennium Luctuosum*, 226.

23. Mather, *Decennium Luctuosum*, 203.

24. Mather, *Decennium Luctuosum*, 219.

25. Mather, *Decennium Luctuosum*, 219.

26. Mather, *Decennium Luctuosum*, 223.

27. Mather, *Decennium Luctuosum*, 220–22.

28. Mather, *Decennium Luctuosum*, 227.

29. Mather, *Decennium Luctuosum*, 221.

30. Mather, *Decennium Luctuosum*, 231.

31. Mather, *Decennium Luctuosum*, 220.

32. For a sense of the continuing value of the Spanish Empire see Carlos Marichal, "The Spanish-American Silver Peso: Export Commodity and Global Money of the Ancien Régime, 1550–1800," *From Silver to Cocaine: Latin American Commodity Chains and the Building of the World Economy, 1500–2000*, ed. Steven Topik, Carlos Marichal, and Zephyr Frank (Durham, NC: Duke University Press, 2006), 25–52.

33. James Ostwald, "The 'Decisive' Battle of Ramillies: Prerequisites for Decisiveness in Early Modern Warfare," *Journal of Military History* 64 (2000): 649–77.

34. Claydon, *Europe and the Making of England*, 192–98.

35. On the Spanish colonists' allegiance see J. H. Elliott, *Empires of the Atlantic World: Britain and Spain in America, 1492–1830* (New Haven, CT: Yale University Press, 2006), 229.

36. Steven J. Oatis, *A Colonial Complex: South Carolina's Frontiers in the Era of the Yamasee War, 1689–1730* (Lincoln: University of Nebraska Press, 2004), 42–82.

37. Capitulation Agreement, 1702; CO 152/5, 8, The National Archives.

38. Mario Rodriguez, "Dom Pedro of Braganza and Colónia do Sacramento, 1680–1705," *Hispanic American Historical Review* 38 (1958): 179–208, 207.

39. Evan Haefeli and Kevin Sweeney, *Captors and Captives: The 1704 French and Indian Raid on Deerfield* (Amherst: University of Massachusetts Press, 2003).

40. Reid, "Imperial Intrusions," 90.

41. Geoffrey Plank, "New England and the Conquest," in John G. Reid, Maurice Basque, Elizabeth Mancke, Barry Moody, Geoffrey Plank, and William Wicken, *The "Conquest" of Acadia, 1710: Imperial, Colonial and Aboriginal Constructions* (Toronto: University of Toronto Press, 2004), 67–85.

42. Adam Lyons, *The 1711 Expedition to Quebec: Politics and the Limitations of British Global Strategy* (London: Bloomsbury, 2013), 134.

43. John G. Reid, "Imperialism, Diplomacies, and the Conquest," in Reid et al, *"Conquest" of Acadia*, 101–23, 102–07; Jean-François Brière, "Pêche et Politique à Terre-Neuve au XVIIe Siècle: la France véritable gagnante du traité d'Uthrect?" *Canadian Historical Review* 64 (1983): 168–87.

44. Fred L. Israel, ed. *Major Peace Treaties of Modern History, 1648–1967* 5 vols. (New York: Chelsea House, 1967–1980), 1:209–11.

45. Plank, *Unsettled Conquest*, 40–67, 87–105.

46. See Oatis, *Colonial Complex.*

47. R. David Edmunds and Joseph L. Peyser, *The Fox Wars: The Mesquakie Challenge to New France* (Norman: University of Oklahoma Press, 1993).

48. Silas Told, *An Account of the Life, and Dealings of God with Silas Told* (London, 1785), 26–39.

49. John Barbot, *A Description of the Coasts of North and South Guinea* (London, 1746), 380.

50. David Richardson, ed., *Bristol, Africa and the Eighteenth-century Slave Trade to America* (Bristol: Bristol Record Society, 1986), 159, 171.

51. G. I. Jones, *The Trading States of the Oil Rivers: A Study of Political Development in Eastern Nigeria* (London: Oxford University Press, 1963), 138–39.

52. Cecil Headlam ed., *Calendar of State Papers Colonial, America and West Indies*, vol. 38 (London, 1938), 55.ii. For the legal context of this assertion see Benton, *Search for Sovereignty*, 112–16.

53. Richard Pares, *War and Trade in the West Indies, 1739–1763* (London: Frank Cass, 1963), 1–64; Kathleen Wilson, "Empire, Trade and Popular Politics in Mid-Hanoverian Britain: The Case of Admiral Vernon," *Past and Present* 121 (1988): 74–109; Gerald Jordan and Nicholas Rogers, "Admirals as Heroes: Patriotism and Liberty in Hanoverian England," *Journal of British Studies* 28 (1989): 210–24.

54. See, for example, *New York Weekly Journal*, August 7, 1738.

55. *Boston Evening Post*, April 14 and 28, 1740.

56. Richard Harding, *Amphibious Warfare in the Eighteenth Century: The British Expedition to the West Indies, 1740—742* (Woodbridge: Royal Historical Society, 1991), 70–77; David Syrett, "The Raising of American Troops for Service in the West Indies during the War of Austrian Succession, 1740–1," *Bulletin of the Institute of Historical Research* 73 (2000): 20–32; Gary Nash, *The Urban Crucible: Social Change, Political Consciousness, and the Origins of the American Revolution* (Cambridge, MA: Harvard University Press, 1979), 169–70.

57. Philip D. Morgan and Andrew Jackson O'Shaughnessy, "Arming Slaves in the American Revolution," in *Arming Slaves*, ed. Brown and Morgan, 180–208, 184.

58. Harding, *Amphibious Warfare in the Eighteenth Century*, 205.

59. Gary Nash, "Urban Wealth and Poverty in Pre-Revolutionary America," *Journal of Interdisciplinary History* 6 (1976): 545–84, 576.

60. Anthony McFarlane, *Columbia before Independence: Economy, Society and Politics under Bourbon Rule* (Cambridge: Cambridge University Press, 1993), 109, 113; Geoffrey J. Walker, *Spanish Politics and Imperial Trade, 1700–1789* (London: Palgrave, 1979), 208, 216–17.

61. Tobias Smollett, *A Compendium of Authentic and Entertaining Voyages* (2d ed., London, 1766), 5:338.

62. Landers, "Gracia Real de Santa Teresa de Mose," 19–20; Plank, "Deploying Tribes and Clans," 236–39.

63. Plank, *Unsettled Conquest*, 106–09.

64. Pritchard, *Anatomy of a Naval Disaster.*

65. See Stephen Conway, *Britain, Ireland, and Continental Europe in the Eighteenth Century* (Oxford: Oxford University Press, 2011), 266–91.

66. Journal of Conrad Weiser, *Colonial Records of Pennsylvania*, vol. 5, pp. 348–58, 350. See White, *Middle Ground*, 201.

67. White, *Middle Ground*, 196.

68. James L. A. Webb Jr., "The Mid-Eighteenth-Century Gum Arabic Trade and the British Conquest of Saint-Louis de Sènègal, 1758," *Journal of Imperial and Commonwealth History* 25 (1997): 37–58; James F. Searing, *West African Slavery and Atlantic Commerce: The Senegal River Valley, 1700–1860* (Cambridge: Cambridge University Press, 1993), 129–62.

69. Allan J. Kuethe, *Cuba, 1753–1815: Crown, Military and Society* (Knoxville: University of Tennessee Press, 1986), 3–20; Evelyn Powell Jennings, "War as the 'Forcing House of Change': State Slavery in Late Eighteenth-century Cuba," *William and Mary Quarterly* 62 (2005): 411–40; Daniel E. Walker, "Colony Versus Crown: Raising Black Troops for the British Siege on Havana, 1762," *Journal of Caribbean History* 33 (1999): 74–83.

70. Webb, "Mid-Eighteenth-Century Gum Arabic Trade."

71. Christopher Leslie Brown, *Moral Capital: Foundations of British Abolitionism* (Chapel Hill: University of North Carolina Press, 2006), 274–77.

72. See generally Kuethe, *Cuba*; Jennings, "War as the 'Forcing House of Change.'"

73. Christopher Brown, "Empire Without Slaves: British Concepts of Emancipation in the Age of the American Revolution," *William and Mary Quarterly* 56 (1999): 273–306; David Weber, *The Spanish Frontier in North America* (New Haven, CT: Yale University Press, 1992), 198–203.

74. John Woolman, "The substance of some conversation with Paponahoal the Indian Chief at AB in presence of Jo. W-n AB Etc.," *Pemberton Papers*, 13:23, Historical Society of Pennsylvania. See Richard W. Pointer, "An Almost Friend: Papunhank, Quakers, and the Search for Security amid Pennsylvania's Wars, 1754–1765," *Pennsylvania Magazine of History and Biography* 138 (2014): 237–68.

75. Archibald Loudon, *A Selection of the Most Interesting Narratives of Outrages Committed by the Indians in their Wars with the White People* (Carlisle, PA, 1808), 273.

76. Dowd, *War Under Heaven.*

77. See especially Anthony F. C. Wallace, "Revitalization Movements," *American Anthropologist* 58 (1956): 264–81. See also Gregory Evans Dowd, *A Spirited Resistance: The North American Indian Struggle for Unity, 1745–1815* (Baltimore: Johns Hopkins University Press, 1992); Alfred A. Cave, *Prophets of the Great Spirit: Native American Revitalization Movements in Eastern North America* (Lincoln: University of Nebraska Press, 2006); Lee Irwin, *Coming Down from Above: Prophecy, Resistance, and Renewal in Native American Religions* (Norman: University of Oklahoma Press, 2008).

78. See Brown, "Empire Without Slaves."

79. Anthony Benezet, *Observations on the Inslaving, Importing and Purchasing of Negroes* (Germantown, PA, 1759), 2.

80. Edith Philips, *The Good Quaker in French Legend* (Philadelphia: University of Pennsylvania Press, 1932). On French abolitionism see Marie-Jeanne Rossignol, "The Quaker Antislavery Commitment and How it Revolutionized French Antislavery through the Crèvecoeur-Brissot Friendship, 1782–1789," in *Quakers and Abolition*, ed. Brycchan Carey and Geoffrey Plank (Urbana: University of Illinois Press, 2014), 180–93.

81. Robert Niklaus, "The Pursuit of Peace in the Enlightenment," in *Essays on Diderot and the Enlightenment in Honor of Otis Fellows*, ed. John Pappas (Geneva: Droz, 1974), 231–45.

82. Montesquieu, *The Spirit of Laws*, trans. and ed. Anne Cohler, Basia Miller and Harold Stone (Cambridge: Cambridge University Press, 1989), 132.

83. Haydn Mason, "Voltaire and War," *British Journal for Eighteenth-century Studies* 4 (1981): 125–38.

84. Voltaire, *Candide, or Optimism*, trans. Burton Raffel (New Haven, CT: Yale University Press, 2005), 94.

85. Christian Ayne Crouch, *Nobility Lost: French and Canadian Martial Cultures, Indians, and the End of New France* (Ithaca, NY: Cornell University Press, 2014).

86. Gould, *Persistence of Empire.*

87. See for example Fred Anderson, *Crucible of War: The Seven Years' War and the Fate of Empire in British North America, 1754–1766* (New York: Knopf, 2000).
88. Thomas Paine, *Common Sense*, 2nd ed. (Philadelphia, 1776), 18, 29.
89. A Lover of Peace [Thomas Paine], "Thoughts on Defensive War," *Pennsylvania Magazine* 1 (July 1776): 313–14.

Chapter 11

1. "Memoirs of Mr. Boston King," *Methodist Magazine* (March 1798): 105–10; (April 1798): 157–61; (May 1798): 209–13; (June 1798): 261–65; Phyllis R. Blakeley, "Boston King: A Negro Loyalist Who Sought Refuge in Nova Scotia," *Dalhousie Review* 48 (1968): 347–56.
2. Sylvia R. Frey, *Water from the Rock: Black Resistance in a Revolutionary Age* (Princeton, NJ: Princeton University Press, 1991), 113.
3. "Memoirs of Mr. Boston King," 107.
4. "Memoirs of Mr. Boston King," 107.
5. "Memoirs of Mr. Boston King," 108.
6. "Memoirs of Mr. Boston King," 109.
7. Blakeley, "Boston King," 350.
8. "Memoirs of Mr. Boston King," 157.
9. "Memoirs of Mr. Boston King," 157.
10. John G. Reid, "Pax Britannica or Pax Indigena? Planter Nova Scotia (1760–1782) and Competing Strategies of Pacification," *Canadian Historical Review* 85 (2004): 669–92, 673.
11. "Memoirs of Mr. Boston King," 159.
12. "Memoirs of Mr. Boston King," 209.
13. "Memoirs of Mr. Boston King," 264.
14. "Memoirs of Mr. Boston King," 261.
15. Ward Stavig and Ella Schmidt, trans. and ed., *The Tupac Amaru and Catarista Rebellions: An Anthology of Sources* (Cambridge: Hackett Publishing, 2008), 21–22.
16. Charles F. Walker, *The Tupac Amaru Rebellion* (Cambridge, MA: Harvard University Press, 2014), 30–31.
17. Nicholas A. Robins, *Native Insurgencies and the Genocidal Impulse in the Americas* (Bloomington: Indiana University Press, 2005), 38–39; Walker, *Tupac Amaru Rebellion*, 169.
18. Walker, *Tupac Amaru Rebellion*, 3–4; Robins, *Native Insurgencies*, 40.
19. Walker, *Tupac Amaru Rebellion*, 146.
20. Ward Stavig, *The World of Tupac Amaru: Conflict, Community, and Identity in Colonial Peru* (Lincoln: University of Nebraska Press, 1984), 226.
21. Walker, *Tupac Amaru Rebellion*, 66.
22. Robins, *Native Insurgencies*, 41; Walker, *Tupac Amaru Rebellion*, 137–38, 176, 191.
23. Robins, *Native Insurgencies*, 40
24. Walker, *Tupac Amaru Rebellion*, 104; Stavig, *World of Tupac Amaru*, 242–43.
25. Walker, *Tupac Amaru Rebellion*, 151.
26. Walker, *Tupac Amaru Rebellion*, 175.
27. Stavig and Schmidt, trans. and ed., *Tupac Amaru and Catarista Rebellions*, 224–25.
28. Stavig and Schmidt, trans. and ed., *Tupac Amaru and Catarista Rebellions*, 68.
29. Walker, *Tupac Amaru Rebellion*, 132; Leon G. Campbell, "Social Structure of the Túpac Amaru Army in Cuzco, 1780–1781," *Hispanic American Historical Review* 61 (1981): 675–93.
30. Walker, *Tupac Amaru Rebellion*, 104, 144, 150, 176, 186.
31. Walker, *Tupac Amaru Rebellion*, 165.
32. Walker, *Tupac Amaru Rebellion*, 185.
33. Walker, *Tupac Amaru Rebellion*, 258.
34. Constantin-François Volney, quoted in David A. Bell, *The First Total War: Napoleon's Europe and the Birth of Modern Warfare* (London: Bloomsbury, 2007), 203.
35. Jérôme Pétion de Villaneuve, quoted in Bell, *First Total War*, 102.
36. Jacques Jallet, quoted in Bell, *First Total War*, 98.
37. Wayne Lee, *Crowds and Soldiers in Revolutionary North Carolina: The Culture of Violence in Riot and War* (Gainesville: University Press of Florida, 2001); John Markoff,

"Violence, Emancipation, and Democracy: The Countryside and the French Revolution," *American Historical Review* 100 (1995): 360–86; Brian J. Singer, "Violence in the French Revolution: Forms of Ingestion/Forms of Expulsion," *Social Research* 56 (1989): 263–93.

38. Wim Klooster, *Revolutions in the Atlantic World: A Comparative History* (New York: New York University Press, 2009), 84–88.

39. John D. Garrigus, "Catalyst or Catastrophe? Saint-Domingue's Free Men of Color and the Battle of Savannah, 1779–1782," *Review/Revista Interamericana* 22 (1992): 109–25, 116.

40. Laurent Dubois, *Avengers of the New World: The Story of the Haitian Revolution* (Cambridge, MA: Harvard University Press, 2005), 67–68.

41. Free Citizens of Color, "Address to the National Assembly, October 22, 1789," in *Slave Revolution in the Caribbean 1789–1804: A Brief History with Documents*, ed. Laurent Dubois and John D. Garrigus (Boston: Bedford/St. Martins, 2006), 69.

42. *Philadelphia General Advertiser*, quoted in Dubois, *Avengers of the New World*, 116.

43. Dubois and Garrigus, eds., *Slave Revolution in the Caribbean*, 158.

44. Etienne Polverel and Léger Félicité Sonthanax, quoted in Dubois, *Avengers of the New World*, 159.

45. David Patrick Geggus, *Slavery, War, and Revolution: The British Occupation of Saint Domingue, 1793–1798* (Oxford: Clarendon Press, 1982), 203; John K. Thornton, "'I Am the Subject of the King of Congo': African Political Ideology and the Haitian Revolution," *Journal of World History* 4 (1993): 181–214, 207.

46. Geggus, *Slavery, War, and Revolution*, 315.

47. Louis Dufay, quoted in Klooster, *Revolutions in the Atlantic World*, 103.

48. Thornton, "'I Am the Subject of the King,'" 213; Dubois and Garrigus, eds., *Slave Revolution in the Caribbean*, 282.

49. Dubois and Garrigus, eds., *Slave Revolution in the Caribbean*, 273.

50. Dubois and Garrigus, eds., *Slave Revolution in the Caribbean*, 291–92.

51. Philip G. Dwyer, "Violence and the Revolutionary and Napoleonic Wars: Massacre, Conquest, and the Imperial Enterprise," *Journal of Genocide Research* 15 (2013): 117–31, 122.

52. Klooster, *Revolutions in the Atlantic World*, 111.

53. Gad Heuman, "From Slavery to Freedom: Blacks in the Nineteenth-century British West Indies," in *Black Experience and the Empire*, ed. Philip D. Morgan and Sean Hawkins (Oxford: Oxford University Press, 2004), 141–65, 145.

54. Thomas Clarkson, *The True State of the Case Respecting the Insurrection in St. Domingo* (Ipswich, 1792), 3.

55. Christopher Fyfe, *A History of Sierra Leone* (Oxford: Oxford University Press, 1963), 105–24, 136–39.

56. John Grace, *Domestic Slavery in West Africa, with Particular Reference to the Sierra Leone Protectorate, 1896–1927* (London: Frederick Muller, 1975), 220–62.

57. Barcia, *West African Warfare*; Reid, *Warfare in African History*, 111.

58. See Lovejoy, *Transformations in Slavery*, chapters 7 and 8.

59. Tim Matthewson, "Jefferson and Haiti," *Journal of Southern History* 61 (1995): 209–48, 217.

60. Charles J. Esdaile, *The Wars of Napoleon* (New York: Longman, 1995), 300.

61. D. McCoy, *The Elusive Republic: Political Economy in Jeffersonian America* (Chapel Hill: University of North Carolina Press, 1980), 209–35; J. C. A. Stagg, *Mr. Madison's War: Politics, Diplomacy, and Warfare in the Early American Republic, 1783–1830* (Princeton, NJ: Princeton University Press, 1983), 22–25.

62. Klooster, *Revolutions in the Atlantic World*, 151–55.

63. John Lynch, *The Spanish American Revolutions, 1808–1826* (London: Weidenfeld and Nicolson, 1973), 342–47.

64. Robert Semple, *Sketch of the Present State of Caracas* (London, 1812), 147.

65. Lynch, *Spanish American Revolutions*, 202–06.

66. Klooster, *Revolutions in the Atlantic World*, 128–29; Lynch, *Spanish American Revolutions*, 39–40.

67. Peter Winn, "British Informal Empire in Uruguay in the Nineteenth Century," *Past and Present* 73 (1976): 100–26. On the longstanding rivalry between Buenos Aires and Montevideo, see

Fabricio Prado, *Edge of Empire: Atlantic Networks and Revolution in Bourbon Rio de la Plata* (Berkeley: University of California Press, 2015).

68. Troy Bickham, *The Weight of Vengeance: The United States, the British Empire, and the War of 1812* (Oxford: Oxford University Press, 2012), 245.
69. See Chet, *Ocean is a Wilderness.*
70. For the story of Francisco Ferreira Gomes see Roquinaldo Ferreira, *Cross-Cultural Exchange in the Atlantic World: Angola and Brazil in the Era of the Slave Trade* (Cambridge: Cambridge University Press, 2012), chapter 6.
71. Ferreira, *Cross-Cultural Exchange,* 203.
72. Ferreira, *Cross-Cultural Exchange,* 204.
73. Ferreira, *Cross-Cultural Exchange,* 240.

Conclusion

1. See generally Mark Levene, *The Rise of the West and the Coming of Genocide* (New York: I. B. Taurus, 2005).
2. Reid, *Warfare in African History,* 107–46.
3. For a particularly important example see Merritt Roe Smith, *Harpers Ferry Armory and the New Technology: The Challenge of Change* (Ithaca, NY: Cornell University Press, 1980).
4. Aaron S. Fogleman, "From Slaves, Convicts, and Servants to Free Passengers: The Transformation of Immigration in the Era of the American Revolution," *Journal of American History* 85 (1998): 43–76.
5. For the scholarly debate over this divergence see Robert C. Allen, Tommy E. Murphy, and Eric B. Schneider, "The Colonial Origins of the Divergence in the Americas: A Labor Market Approach," *Journal of Economic History* 72 (2012): 863–94.
6. Fred Anderson and Andrew Clayton, *The Dominion of War: Empire and Liberty in North America* (New York: Viking, 2004), 247–73.
7. On the assimilationist project see Frederick E. Hoxie, *A Final Promise: The Campaign to Assimilate the Indians, 1880–1920* (Lincoln: University of Nebraska Press, 2001).
8. John Woolman, "The substance of some conversation with Paponahoal the Indian Chief at AB in presence of Jo. W-n AB Etc.," *Pemberton Papers,* 13:23, Historical Society of Pennsylvania. See Richard W. Pointer, "An Almost Friend: Papunhank, Quakers, and the Search for Security amid Pennsylvania's Wars, 1754–1765," *Pennsylvania Magazine of History and Biography* 138 (2014): 237–68.
9. Thomas Fowell Buxton, *The African Slave Trade and its Remedy* (New York, 1840), 268–69.
10. Andrew Porter, "Trusteeship, Anti-slavery, and Humanitarianism," in *The Oxford History of the British Empire, Volume IV: The Nineteenth Century,* ed. Andrew Porter and William Roger Lewis (Oxford: Oxford University Press, 1999), 198–221.

INDEX

For the benefit of digital users, indexed terms that span two pages (e.g., 52–53) may, on occasion, appear on only one of those pages.

322

INDEX